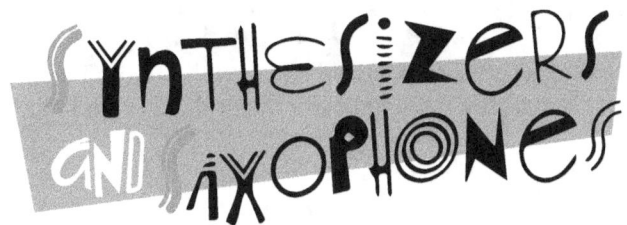

SYNTHESIZERS AND SAXOPHONES

THE STORY BEHIND GREAT MOVIE SONGS,
HIT SOUNDTRACK ALBUMS, AND
MUSICAL MOVIES OF THE 1980S

by **MICHAEL J. HEAGLE**

DEDICATIONS

Dedicated to my cousin David, who's been through a lot and never lost sight of the healing power of synths and bad movies...

SPECIAL THANKS TO

My perplexed but patient partner Tricia (thanks for affording me the opportunity to do this project),

sister Jennifer (brave explorer of new worlds and Queen of Cassettes, you had the best music first),

father Anson (for instilling a love of music both recorded and live, thanks again for taking us to the Clash – it's been a point of pride ever since) and mother Diana (for taking us to movies well above our age range, and I still have my skinny ties from Spencer Gifts),

and the bright young ladies of my life Mila and Kira (and now a puppy named "Rio") who love Michael Jackson too.

CONTENTS

LABYRINTH'S MAGIC DANCE — 235

LADIES AND GENTLEMEN, THE PUNKS — 241

ALEX COX: PUNK PROPHET — 253

THERE WAS DANCING. IT WAS DIRTY. — 269

MODERN EARTH GIRLS THAT DESPERATELY WANT TO HAVE FUN — 287

CRAZY FROM THE HEAT: THE DAVID LEE ROTH MOVIE — 311

DID MTV RUIN MOVIES? — 315

THE GREATEST 80S SOUNDTRACK SONGS — 321

PREFACE

The gloved hand of Ming the Merciless descends on a control panel marked "HOT HAIL." A thumping bass drum fills the theater, a lightning bolt strike of sound and picture working in concert would follow. I liked Star Wars, we all did, but Flash Gordon spoke to me in a different way. Was it the synthesizer pulse of Queen's "Football Fight" that sold me completely, or was it Ornela Muti in a satin jumpsuit? All. Both. Didn't matter. Long live Flash, Saviour of the Universe.

A cityscape, the likes of which had never been seen before, opens before us. A giant geisha made up of thousands of points of lights fills the side of a skyscraper, she smiles and a flying police car sails effortlessly through a wall of rain. On the soundtrack is a deep, full, analog synthesizer string section that sounds like making out feels. Later, a mournful, reverb-drenched saxophone reminds us of the film's noir roots, as if all the trench coats and fedoras didn't.

The simple combination of Devo's "Whip It" and shots from the Shaw Brother's 1970s Kung Fu movies formed the opening credit on our local UHF station, WVTV Channel 18 in Milwaukee, for their Saturday late night movie show "Black Belt Theater." Two great tastes that taste great together. My buddy Zeb and I would eat Totinos frozen pizzas (he added ketchup and mustard, three great tastes I admit I hadn't considered before) and watch it religiously and spend the next day speaking in broken dubbed English.

A bunch of British boys in high-fashion pastel suits are riding a yacht. Now one of them is trudging through a Sri Lankan landscape searching for a mysterious woman. They ride an elephant, they stand outside the ruins of a Buddhist temple, like a bunch of sexy Indiana Joneses.

The Terminator scans the crowd for the face of Sarah Connor as Kyle Reese glowers at the bar. Slow motion kicks in, the crowd dancing to Tahnee Cain and Tryanglz "Burnin' in the Third Degree." A guy with a skinny tie in the foreground, club lights and haze. The statuesque face of Arnold as he draws his enormous .45 long slide with laser sighting.

I remember learning the power of combining music and motion pictures through a few specific experiences from my childhood and adolescence. The fact that all of these are synthesizer-heavy cuts is telling. What was it about the sound of those machines that had been written off by "real musicians" as cold and clinical, that had been lurking around in the shadowy corners of music for decades, that provided such warmth to the pop and movies of the 1980s?

Add heavy rock guitar, and occasionally a sax solo, you end up with the sound of a generation raised on movies. A generation that could, at a moment's notice, pick up a small plastic box not much bigger than a paperback book – whether VHS or Beta – and relive those essential dreams again and again on their TV at home. To this home video generation, and the Madonna-wannabes and B-Boys and big-haired girls and boys, this book is dedicated.

WHAT'S INSIDE?

For the first volley into this subject, I have opted to limit myself to:

- **80s Movies that are musicals**
- **80s Movies where an aspect of the music business is shown**
- **80s Movies that feature performers known for their musical output first and as actors second**
- **Movies where 80s songs are used to good effect in montage**
- **Movies with great soundtrack albums of the period, or that produced chart hits on release in the 80s**

Also, I hereby surrender all attempts to be comprehensive in the first volume, and am intentionally cherry-picking things I want to sit through multiple times and write about at length. There will be omissions for which I may never be forgiven, and it was hard to leave out films that I love that do not meet the above specification.

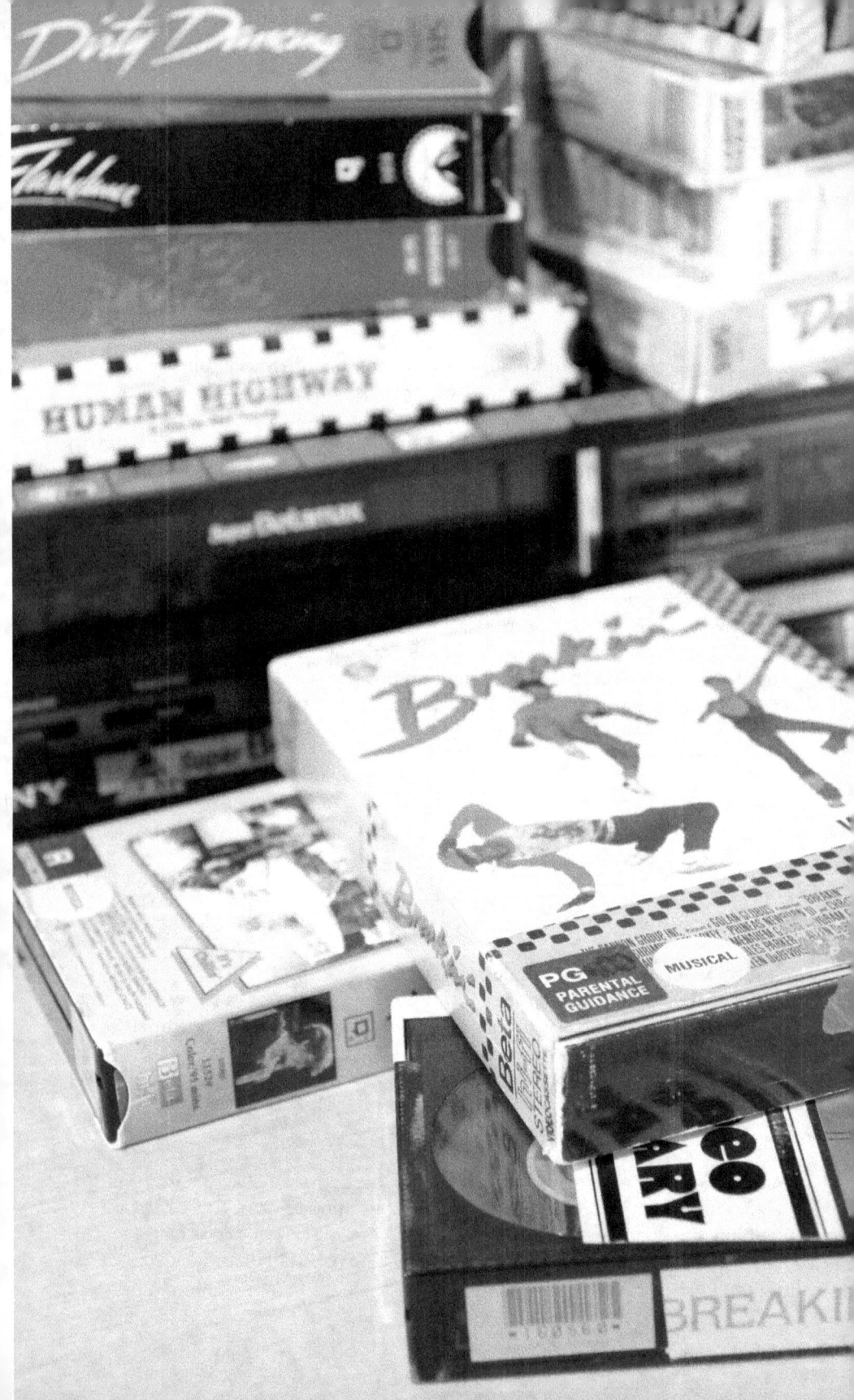

INTRODUCTION

For a while it seemed like the pop music and movies were inseparable. Radio sounded like MTV, MTV influenced TV and the movies, and the pop charts looked like the movie listings and vice versa. Now, current pop music is more likely to show up in a spendy commercial, or as part of a weekly montage that wraps up a police procedural on network TV. And if a pop song of the classic 80s variety is employed in a hit movie, there's as good a chance as any it's going to be used ironically. Why? Have we stopped being able to produce the magic ingredients of hook and instrumentation and just-shallow-enough lyrics that blend perfectly with a motion picture scene? Perhaps the classics are whipped out precisely for their baggage, or despite their baggage.

Unless you're under 30. For an entire generation, pop songs of the 80s have moved into an exclusively ironic punchline status. Training for something? Have some "Eye of the Tiger." Love at first sight? Have some Spandau Ballet "True." Where producers of the 80s may have been innovative or lucky in their juxtaposition, filmmakers and music supervisors of today are lazy, preferring the quick-in-and-out shorthand that a pop cliché affords them. And don't get me started on "Careless Whisper." No song deserves being dragged through the pop culture mud like that.

I came of age in the 70s and 80s, so I saw pop music go from album rock to disco to new wave to dance music. It was only ever temporarily pushed out by trends like alternative college radio or grunge, and then for a couple of years at a time. During my formative years, the period discussed in this book, movies and music shared a special relationship. Hits were big, and crossed all sorts of boundaries. I never thought it odd to be rollerskating at our small-town Wisconsin roller rink to music that originated in the cocaine-soaked gay clubs of NYC, nor was it odd when a couple of skinny white kids in my high school suddenly started breakdancing and dressing like they were from the Bronx. Music was the great equalizer, crossing race and class, region and religion, and did it faster than ever if you had basic cable or access to a VCR. And hit movies and MTV greased those wheels.

Not everything was pop sugar and fist-pumping anthems in the 1980s. As any disenfranchised youth from the era will tell you, choosing a genre of music that aligned with your level of social acceptance was a rite of passage for a lot of us. Growing up in a small town in Wisconsin, we were located squarely at the place where the wave broke, so to speak – we were the last to know about a trend, the last to get the new kind of clothes in the store. Still, a handful of us found outré labels to distance us from our football-playing and welding-shop classmates. To put not too fine a point on it, the stereotypes of *The Breakfast Club* were not far off.

Speaking for those of us in the Drama Department at MHS in the 1980s, you could divide the strange kids into a handful of camps. When Prince's *1999* arrived, there was a cadre of Minneapolis-sound kids who may or may not have put on a ruffled shirt at one point. There was a tiny but devoted group of UK-worshippers, my sister included, for whom Duran, The Cure, and Depeche Mode were litany. We had one breakdancer, and one speed metal and punk guy. And all were unified in a love of The Violent Femmes, who, heralding from Milwaukee, were considered "local." This music was for the most part way off the beaten track and not represented on radio. Cassettes were passed around and copied for the initiates. On home video, rare films that didn't make it to the local three-plex could let us peek into new musical worlds occasionally glimpsed in the wee hours of MTV (who was late in picking up on and playing to the subgenres with dedicated shows like *120 Minutes* and *Yo MTV Raps*). Movies like *Pretty in Pink* stood out from the pop pack, exploring areas of the music underground that appealed to the outsiders in all of us, and even managed to put what would have been outsider bands onto the charts.

Critics of the 1980s may label it a decade of emptiness and excess, but for those of us at the ground level it was a pinnacle of easy-going escapist entertainment that has proven hard to match. The generation that followed in the 1990s would consume it secondhand on cable and be equally entranced – a testament to the idea that "maybe you didn't have to be there," exactly, for it to have maintained its allure. And the fact that 21st century cinema seems stuck in a time loop, with Transformers and G.I. Joes and remakes of *Footloose* and reboots of *Ghostbusters* and more *Star Wars* movies, means that the decade may be here to stay.

Whether it was bubble gum pop, British new wave, the emerging urban and R&B sounds and proto-hip hop, or punk and metal, filmmakers of the 1980s managed to team songs with pictures in a way that has not been rivalled.

MONTAGE FROMAGE

I detest the use of the word "cheesy" when discussing B-movies. "Cheesy" should be reserved for advertising quick-serve macaroni product. (Mystery Science Theater 3000 gets a pass – you need it in the theme song because it's two syllables, and "low budget clunkers" doesn't fit.).

That being said, one of the founding tenets of the text is that there are certain sequences that use pictures and music in a way that only 80s films can, and these were undeniably influenced by the popularity of music videos. They can be goofy. Thus, we allow ourselves "Fromage," the French word for cheese, which adds a, shall we say, soupçon of class.

More importantly in a book about film, however, is Montage, the French term, to mount or to assemble. In some film lexicon, all editing is montage. Watch a Spanish or French film: the editor is credit reads Montage or Montaje. The very idea of moving rapidly between shifting points of view in space that is so natural to us now, must have been quite a shock to people first seeing it in silent films like *The Great Train Robbery*. The silent-era Soviets, namely Sergei Eisenstein, devoted a lot of attention to a type of montage that would elevate the meaning of shots through their placement, resulting in symbolic associations helpful in promoting Revolutionary ideas.

Montage sequence in American filmmaking, though, was about telling a lot of story in a little bit of time. That could mean condensing time, or parallel cutting between things happening simultaneously. In all cases, good filmmaking opts for a visual solution. Can you show how a character feels by cutting to what's in his head (*Footloose* "Never," p. 320)? Can you condense time to show someone getting better at a skill (*Footloose* "Let's Hear it for the Boy," p. 40)?

80s pop movies took that to a logical extension when combined with the economic motivation of selling a soundtrack album. Any opportunity to feature the music prominently was seized. If two valley girls who survived a mysterious comet-apocalypse happen upon an abandoned department store, then by god there's going to be some shopping, and pop music is the glue that holds good retail therapy together.

In this book, I try to single out some great montage moments and even try to rank them against each other. Not all 80s films succumbed to montage's delicious trap. But when they do, and when the feeling is right, you'll know it immediately. A lot of 80s films even warranted more than one montage (here's looking at you, *Karate Kid*)!

One historical note: In its defense, "cheesy" was first used as a slang term from 19th century Britain, meaning "showy and admirable." We hope you find the films within to be just that.

A WORD ABOUT SPOILERS

Nobody likes to have a plot spoiled, but by definition a book like this is going to address what happened in a movie. And hey, there's no statute of limitations on movie secrets. Plenty of people haven't seen *Howard the Duck* – and nobody's seen *Voyage of the Rock Aliens*! Will you get more out of a chapter if you've seen the film before? Maybe. In my experience as an adult with children who doesn't get to see first-run movies anymore, reading the first couple paragraphs of any review will let you know what you need to proceed and can be considered pretty safe. I'll admit I can't help but highlight some of the best laughs in a movie, so that can be risky because knowing about a gag in advance can hurt the experience. If a movie is well-known I'll spend less time synopsizing it. If a chapter is more about the music than the film, no synopsis may be necessary (knowing the specific plot points of *Caddyshack*, if they exist, does little to inform a discussion of Kenny Loggins' song).

As a filmmaker first, I generally hate film writing and criticism, and for this book I took a stance of "I love all movies, even the bad ones." And I do, making movies has taught me how hard it is to get your intention on the screen, so even the crappiest movies here are given the benefit of the doubt.

Writing this book was inspired by my total joy at discovering Michael Weldon's book The Psychotronic Encyclopedia of Film, a 1987 (totally pre-internet) compilation of mini reviews of, well, "Low Budget Clunkers" (see above). The capsule synopses of the films made me find as many of the films I could at my local video store and made me what I am today. (Rest in peace, **Intercontinental Video**, West Bank, Minneapolis, and **Discount Video**, Uptown, Minneapolis. Om and Bob, we all owe you! And thanks to Troy and the gang keeping up the good fight at **Video Universe** in Robbinsdale.) That is what I hope happens to you, seeking these films out and enjoying them as much as I did.

WE HOLD THESE TRUTHS
TO BE ALMOST EVIDENT

1. Most movies in the 80s had some kind of music.

2. Not all movies in the 80s were musicals, e.g. *Ghandi* or *Platoon*.

3. Some movies filmed in the 80s were musicals, but that doesn't mean that the music was "80s Music." 1980 is ripe with musicals that really should have occured a couple years previously, which makes more sense when you know that it typically takes two or more years to go from idea to marketplace (unless you're Menahem Golan of Cannon Films). How else do explain the 1980 releases of *Can't Stop The Music* (Village People plus Valerie Perrine) or *Xanadu* (er, ELO plus Gene Kelly)?

4. 80s music can be *distinctly* 80s (i.e., couldn't have occured in any other decade, vis a vis Madonna) or can have merely occured in the 80s (John Cougar Mellencamp would have done just as well in the 70s, for example).

5. Some of the **QUINTESSENTIAL 80S GENRES** discussed in this book have obvious roots in the decade before, especially:

   - **Punk** started and died in the 70s, but the punks lived on and produced increasingly 80s-type music. John Lydon of the Sex Pistols started a band that embraced synths, Billy Idol left Generation X and became an MTV star, The Clash got more reggae and more poppy until their demise, and so on. Also, the LA punk scene was late to launch and figures prominently in Hollywood movies.

   - **Electro R&B and Hip Hop** have their roots in disco and late 70s NYC. But no one will mistake *Breakin'* for a 70s movie.

   - **New Wave** hit the ground in 1978 or 1979 before it became mainstream in the 80s.

   - **Hair Metal** of the 1980s is a direct extension of what Black Sabbath and Led Zeppelin were doing a decade or more earlier.

6. Sometimes you can't imagine a movie without the added layer of an indelible soundtrack. The 80s were no exception.

WHAT IS THE BILLBOARD HOT 100?

Billboard magazine was founded in 1894, when people couldn't see movies yet so they stared at billboards for two hours. Okay, the second part isn't true, but the magazine has moved with the entertainment times, first covering circuses and fairs, the vaudeville circuit, and tent shows. As recorded music became a big business, Billboard was there. Founder William Donaldson even hired an African-American writer to cover black performers in 1920. The magazine rated popular music based on record sales and radio airtime, which splintered into increasingly specific markets. With the rise of rock and roll, the Hot 100 was introduced in 1955 and focused on tracking individual songs (while the Billboard 200 was focused on albums). For this book, I have identified songs as "hits" based on their Billboard stats. Many will be accompanied by the symbol below

MAXIMUM CHART POSITION REACHED

CHART

#1
1983

SIX WEEKS

POSITION

YEAR OF CHART

WEEKS ON THE BILLBOARD 100
IF IT REACHED #1, THIS MAY REFLECT ITS TIME ON TOP ONLY!

BELOW: THE SYNTHESIZER AND SAXOPHONES EPOCH, SEPTEMBER 7 1985, WHEN THE TOP THREE POSITIONS WERE HELD BY MOVIE SONGS

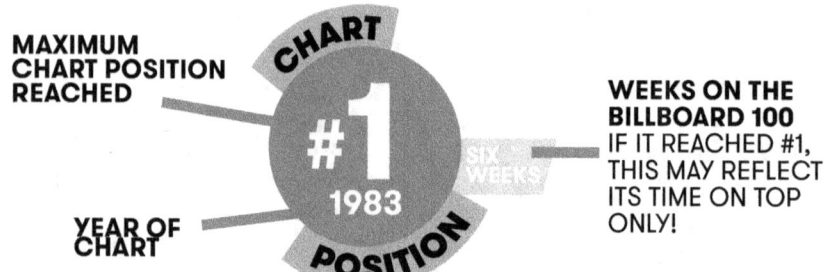

1

MUSICAL FANTASY

What is "diegetic music" and how did it become a source of income for the studios, setting off the trend for pop music as wallpaper in 1980s cinema?

When you hear music on the soundtrack of a film, it comes from one of two places – *reality* and *not reality*.

Reality: *Diegetic* film music emanates from an on-screen source. Somebody presses play on a boombox and the streets are filled with the sound of Din Daa Daa Din Doh Doh, loud enough for everyone to hear perfectly over the sound of LA traffic. Marty McFly's band The Pinheads auditions for the battle of the bands, and their song is heard by an uncomfortable teacher in a blazer who looks a lot like Huey Lewis in nerd glasses. We don't have to see that source for it to count – even non-discerning ears have been trained to know the difference between a song on a character's car radio and a song on the film soundtrack.

Not Reality: *Non-Diegetic* film music comes to our ears but not to the ears of the characters. Daniel LaRusso bikes to his new school to the strains of Bananarama's "Cruel Summer;" Tom Cruise and Rebecca De Mornay can feel it coming in the night so they hop a darker, emptier train to experience "Love on a Real Train" compliments of Tangerine Dream.

Is one technique more effective or memorable than the other? Ask someone to name a song from *Risky Business*, and chances are their pants will suddenly go missing, white socks will slide across floors, and before long they'll be demanding some of that "Old Time Rock and Roll." That does not diminish the fact that Tangerine Dream's more traditional cue on the score from the same film absolutely evokes the feeling of teenage sexual discovery and anguish!

Songs have been a part of film since before spoken dialog, when live accompaniment in the silent movie theater was a standard feature. The first "talkie" was a musical, and early sound films followed suit and did boffo business with song and dance pictures from *Gold Diggers of 1933* and *42nd Street* through *The Wizard of Oz*. But a series of unique and profitable uses of music in films of the 1970s made Hollywood stand up and take notice. Subsequent developments in the 1980s resulted in a synthesis of pop and movies, and it boils down to economic opportunity as much as aesthetic innovation.

WHAT CONDITIONS CONTRIBUTED TO THE MUSIC-FILM CONVERGENCE OF THE 80S?

The idea of movies made on quick turnaround to capitalize on a music act or trend was by no means new – producer Sam Katzman had written the rule book in the 1950s with movies like *Rock Around The Clock* or *Twist Around the Clock* – but the volume of music-related film product of the 1980s was a different breed, created by a convergence of consumer technology (from cable TV to the Walkman), commerce, and cultural concerns.

1.) Studios saw the money that could be made from an album tie-in.

Licensing a song affordably could pay dividends. Synchronization rights (paying for it's use on screen) and mechanical rights (paying to reproduce it and distribute it, as on a soundtrack album) being negotiated separately sometimes resulted in songs appearing in the film and not on the album. Sometimes songs would be licensed and omitted from the film, or purchased just to fill out the soundtrack album (as in "Music From and Inspired by The Film" -type compilations).

Music industry practice dictated that a band would put out a single (with B-side) prior to a new album release, and movie studios took a page from that playbook by releasing a potentially hit song from the soundtrack before the movie came out. Soundtrack success could fuel the film's success and vice versa. A prime example is chronicled in the June 21 1986 issue of *Billboard*: "On *Top Gun*, we're working with Paramount, who did *Footloose* with us," says Bob Wilcox, VP of marketing for the West Coast, Columbia Records. "The Kenny Loggins single ["Danger Zone"] came first, and then when the movie and its advertising start breaking, part of our job is to tie the two together with radio advertising, sniping [adding a sticker to an existing item to update information, as on the face of a record album], our POPs [point of purchase displays] in store. We establish the fact that the Kenny Loggins track is in the movie. And we do radio screenings in the major markets –so that radio jocks, personalities, and the press see the film."

2.) Albums and singles afforded cross promotional opportunity.

Having a chart topping song with the movie's title in it helped promote your picture for a fraction of the cost. Think about it, was it the film or the song that had kids across the world shouting a cheery call and response "Ghostbusters?"

(Below) A trade ad from 1980 illustrates the budding relationship between rock and movies.

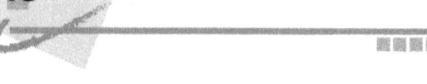

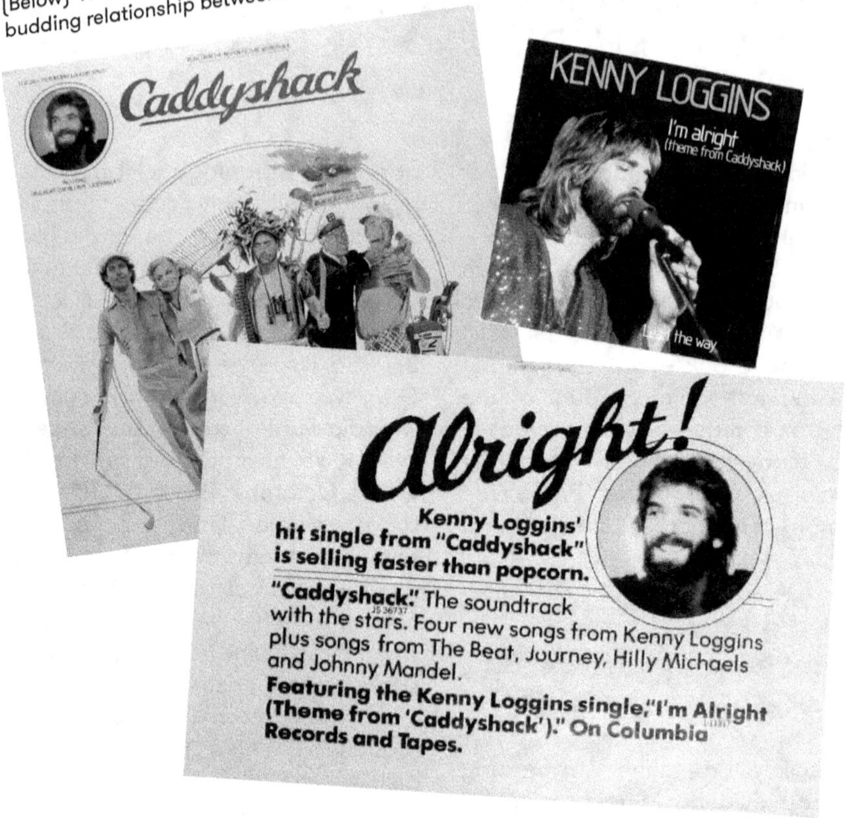

Marketing Director David Gales at Columbia Records in 1986 said: "we've been coordinating with Paramount's people on a day-to-day basis for nine months on [*Top Gun*]. From the get-go, you're coordinating your efforts and trying to create as many impressions as you can on both pieces of product. When Paramount advertises their movie, there's music on their TV and radio spots, and when we advertise our soundtrack we're obviuolsy talking about their movie. All you can do is expose, and hopefully you're doubling or tripling your impression base... What sets *Top Gun*, *Footloose* and *Purple Rain* apart from the old days of soundtracks is that their success came when film companies started taking soundtracks seriously ... rather than simply an ancillary product they would license off like T-shirts or caps. The real successes came when film companies started acknowledging the power of music and we forged this partnership with them."

3.) Film studios were purchased by non-filmmaking companies.

Is anything more typically 1980s, than Columbia's purchase by Coca-Cola in 1981? Cue the age of product placement. More importantly, studios were becoming parts of larger entertainment conglomerates whose assets included the apparatus to produce and distribute music. It is in this decade that the landscape of entertainment transforms into what it remains today, the almost exclusive domain of mega-corporations.

4.) The arrival of MTV signalled a cultural revolution of image and sound, for better or worse.

MTV made it okay to tell condensed stories without dialog, almost like the silent era's one-reelers. It's not a big leap to go from music video to big-screen montage. See the chapter "Did MTV Ruin Movies" for more on this touchy subject.

5.) The teenage demographic in the 80s was affluent.

Fashion and music were inexorably intertwined in the 1980s. Consider the "Madonna-Wannabe."

Madonna creates audio product, accompanied by strong and unique visual branding. The "Lucky Star" look of lace gloves and rubber bracelets became a mall staple, creating a cycle of consumerism with numerous beneficiaries. The brand is reinforced at every turn (album cover, music video, MTV Awards shows, *Desperately Seeking Susan*, repeat).

6.) Consumer technology changed the music/movie game.

Cable TV and the VCR are direct contributors to the success of films in the 80s. While both were perceived as the death knell of cinema, the opposite proved true, providing alternate streams of revenue as the audience took the cinema into their homes. Just as importantly, people could program their own content. Instead of relying on "what was on," folks could pick from a number of cable channels playing uninterrupted movies, or head to a local video store to take home a movie on tape. Couple that with the rise of the Walkman and you give the illusion of complete control over your media consumption that has only gotten more sophisticated in the streaming era.

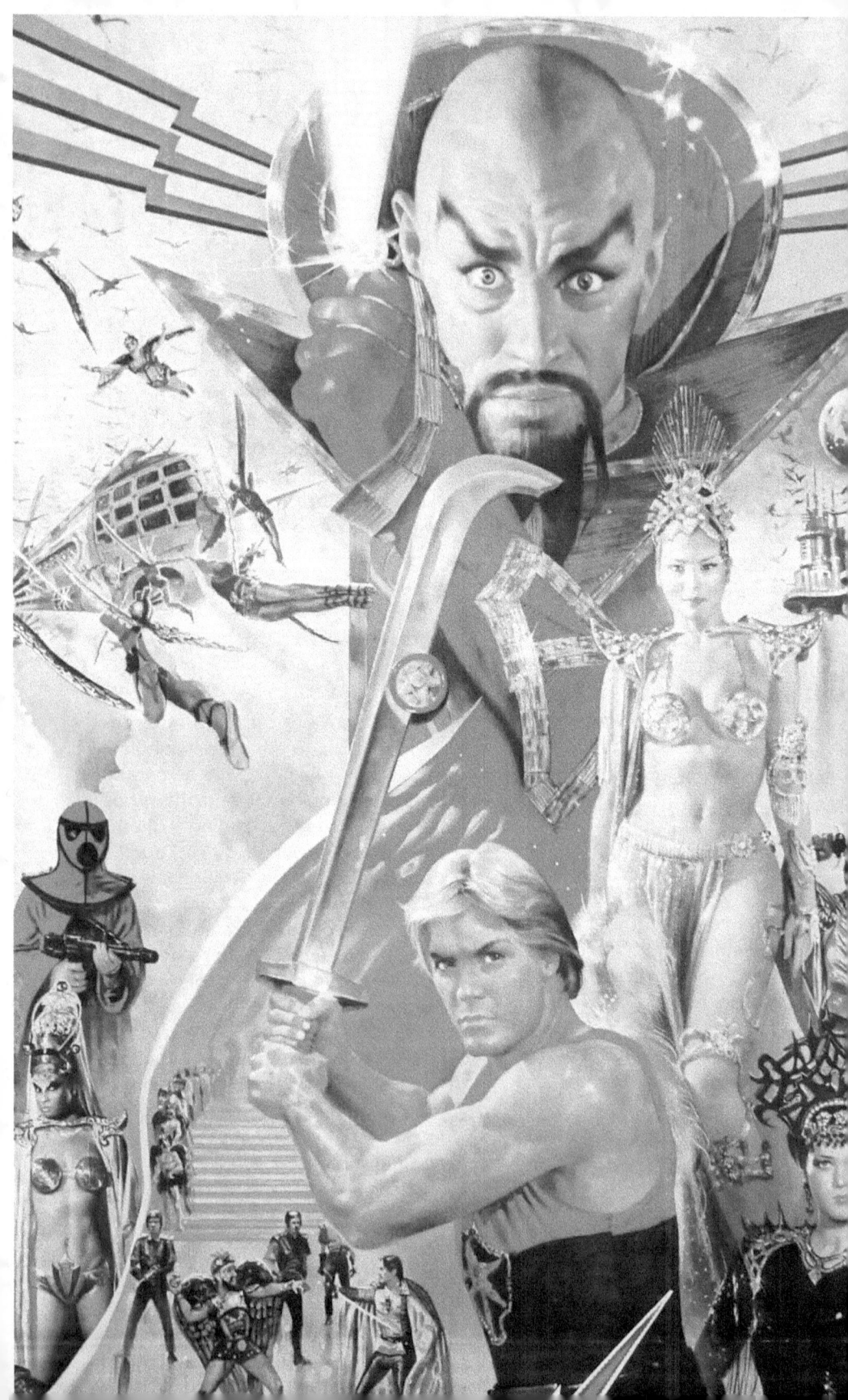

2

THEY WERE THE CHAMPIONS: THE ROCK SCORES OF QUEEN

When great rock bands are singled out to perform most or all of the score of the film, you end up integrating rock songs and scoring in a big way, and changing the feel of the finished film. English band Queen, purveyors of arena rock in the 1970s, found a special niche by translating their style of rock to the silver screen in the 1980s.

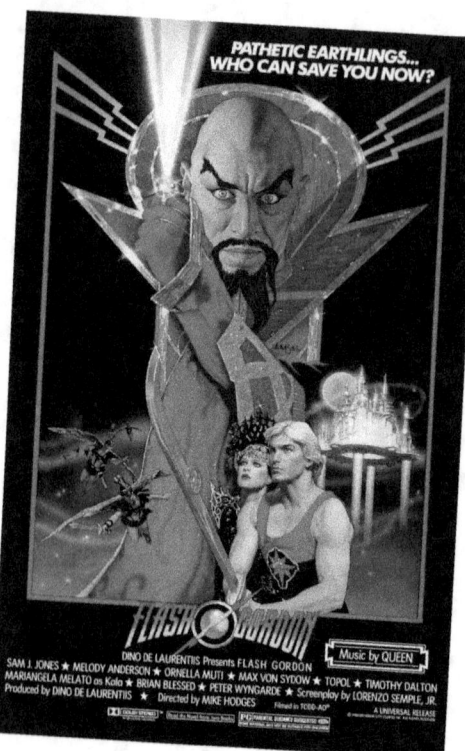

PATHETIC EARTHLINGS...
WHO CAN SAVE YOU NOW?

DINO DE LAURENTIIS Presents FLASH GORDON
Music by QUEEN
SAM J. JONES ★ MELODY ANDERSON ★ ORNELLA MUTI ★ MAX VON SYDOW ★ TOPOL ★ TIMOTHY DALTON
MARIANGELA MELATO as Kala ★ BRIAN BLESSED ★ PETER WYNGARDE ★ Screenplay by LORENZO SEMPLE, JR.
Produced by DINO DE LAURENTIIS ★ Directed by MIKE HODGES
A UNIVERSAL RELEASE

> "So you feel that you ain't nobody
> Always needed to be somebody
> Put your feet on the ground
> Put your hand on your heart
> Lift your head to the stars
> And the world's for your taking"

If one needed a reason to write a book such as this, it would be Queen, who prove the thesis – that rock music and 80s films are inseparable – with the one-two punch of *Flash Gordon* and *Highlander*. Both are rather modestly budgeted fantasy films, but with the epic sound of Queen raging down upon the soundtracks, seem larger than life and twice as expensive.

Back in the 70s, George Lucas had tried to wrestle the rights to Flash Gordon from Dino De Laurentiis. When Dino demurred, George grabbed a legal pad and cranked out something called *Star Wars*. Not to be outdone, Dino decided, that on the basis of that other space movie's success, it was time to get that Flash movie going. He lost a year to Nicholas Roeg's soon-to-be-discarded development of the property and started over with Lorenzo Semple Jr, known for his winking work on the 1966 "Batman" TV series. Dino soon thought he had a blueprint more in line with his image, but Semple thought that may have had more to do with his translator, who was rather lose with the details as she dictated the screenplay.

When it came time to choose a composer, director Mike Hodges put forth the idea of Pink Floyd. But Queen had caught wind of the project and their management arranged a meeting to express their interest. As Queen drummer Roger Taylor explains, "we've been offered quite a few films, but *Flash Gordon* was something which Brian and I were quite attracted to because of its sci-fi thirties connotations."

"We saw 20 minutes of the finished film and thought it very good and over the top."
–Brian May

"Over the top" proved an apt assessment of the film by May, who would compose most of the film's climactic battle music and ensure (with layers of monumental guitar) that the creative brief would be followed.

May said that "we wanted to do something that was a real soundtrack. It's a first in many ways, because a rock group has not done this type of thing before, or else it's been toned down and they've been asked to write mushy background music. Whereas we were given the license to do what we liked, as long as it complimented the picture."

"It was in our minds that we would be up for writing a soundtrack if the right one came along. We'd been offered a few, but most of them were where the film is written around music, and that's been done to death – it's the cliche of 'movie star appears in movie about movie stars,'" May stated

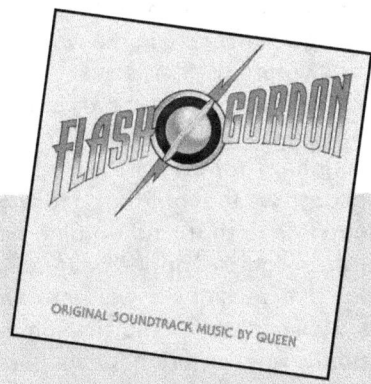

ORIGINAL SOUNDTRACK MUSIC BY QUEEN

SOUNDTRACK

- Flash's Theme
- In The Space Capsule (The Love Theme)
- Ming's Theme (In The Court Of Ming The Merciless)
- The Ring (Hypnotic Seduction Of Dale)
- Football Fight
- In The Death Cell (Love Theme Reprise)
- Execution Of Flash
- The Kiss (Aura Resurrects Flash)
- Arboria (Planet Of The Tree Men)
- Escape From The Swamp
- Flash To The Rescue
- Vultan's Theme (Attack Of The Hawk Men)
- Battle Theme
- The Wedding March
- Marriage Of Dale And Ming (And Flash Approaching)
- Crash Dive On Mingo City
- Flash's Theme Reprise (Victory Celebrations)
- The Hero

in a 1982 BBC interview. "We would be writing a film score in the way anyone else writes a film score, which is basically background music, but can obviously help the film if it's strong enough. That was the attraction, because we thought that a rock group hadn't done that kind of thing before, and it was an opportunity to write real film music. So we were writing to a discipline for the first time ever, and the only criterion for success was whether or not it worked with and helped the film, and we weren't our own bosses for a change." A quick look at Queen's body of work and you know that they are not ones to shy away from a bit of innovation or creative boundary pushing.

"I loved it. I really regard it as a challenge to put the score together and make it an organic part of the movie. Slightly tongue-in-cheek, but also with that spirit of adventure which I grew up with, because I used to go and see Flash Gordon at the Saturday morning movies when I was a kid," said May.

"We went in and saw some of the rushes of the film and loved it, and we all went away and made some demos separately, Roger, John, Freddie and me, and there came a day when we all got in the studio and played them back to Mike and to Dino and asked: 'This is what we've come up with. What do you think?'" May told the Independent. "There was a horrible moment when Mike jumped up and down saying, 'It's brilliant, it's brilliant', and Dino sat there with a face ashen and white as a sheet and obviously didn't enjoy it, and when it came to the theme I had written – you know, 'Flash' – well, Dino said, 'It's very good, but it is not for my movie.'"

Audiences weaned on science fiction films that took themselves a bit too seriously (*Star Wars*) or way too seriously (*Star Trek the Motion Picture*) were not prepared for a film that deviated this far from the mold. Played deadpan straight amidst the high camp proceedings and Italian-psychedelic design work, the film failed to find an audience.

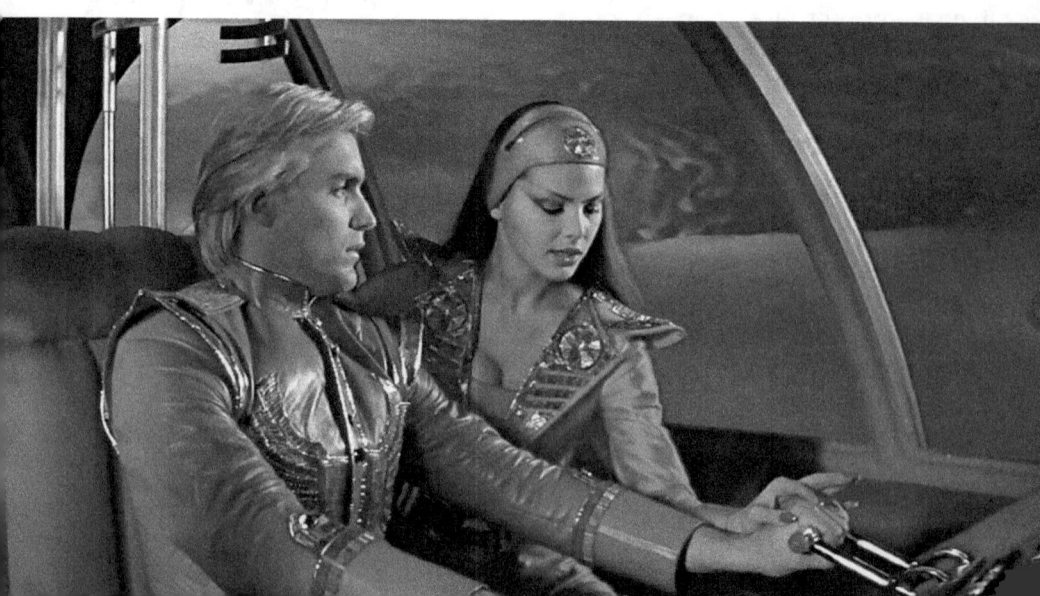

Only today has the film achieved the high cult status that it deserves. Meanwhile, Queen fans are split on the soundtrack -- with only two songs featuring a Freddie Mercury vocal, it is a departure from their usual work. Some may have issue with the amount of synthesizers, or that the album is chock full of sounds from the film.

Roger Taylor: "The album was totally under our control and it was our idea to put dialogue on the album. That wasn't the original idea. We thought we'd get little snippets to give some idea of what was happening in the film and some atmosphere of the story."

For kids of a certain age, owning the soundtrack was the only way to own a piece of the film or remain connected to the specifics of the story. I learned the dialog of *Young Frankenstein* from an LP record long before I saw the film, and I knew that the middle of *Star Wars* was the Millenium Falcon being sucked into the Death Star because that's where you had to flip over the record! So when the *Flash Gordon* soundtrack became the second cassette I purchased with my own money, the dialog and sound effects ensured that the film would be ingrained in my memory in a way most movies couldn't. Dialog like "strange object imaged in the Imperial Vortex" became like song lyrics (or, dare I say, Bible verse for we acolytes of the Saviour of the Universe). Sound effects like Ming's hypnotic ring became as relevant to me as the T.I.E. Fighter howl of *Star Wars*.

"Here we are, born to be kings – We're the princes of the universe"

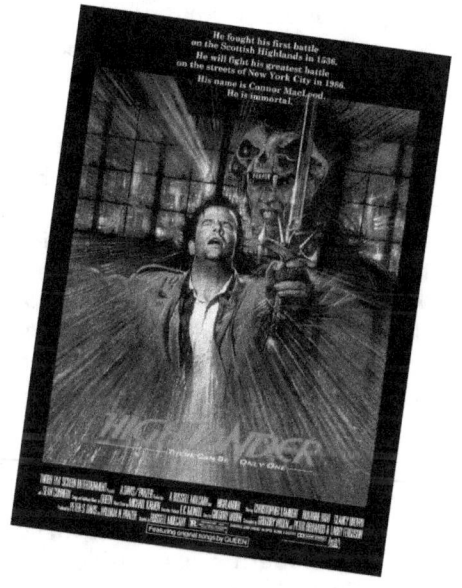

Highlander seems borne out of the success of 1984's *The Terminator*, with immortal warriors from another time waging war on the blue-lit night streets of a modern American metropolis. Here we swap NYC for LA, but the parallels abound. The hero is average and the villain is a behemoth. The hero wears tennis shoes and a trenchcoat, the villain wears punk trappings and hides out in a seedy hotel. Instead of the future it's the past, instead of sci-fi it's fantasy, instead of machine guns it's swords. Still, every swordfight is like a shootout, with swords that seem to explode on contact, and the similarly befuddled big city cops are equally mystified by their own pair of killers out of time. One is Connor MacCleod, an ancient immortal Scotsman with a samurai sword, the other is the Kurgan, a gruesome horror straight out of Conan.

The Queen bombast lands immediately with the glorious theme song "Princes of the Universe," as we open on a pro-wrestling bout at Madison Square Garden, with AWA stars Greg Gagne, Jim Brunzell, the Tonga Kid and the Fabulous Freebirds captured in action before a huge crowd (with some of the first wire-flying camera work by Steadiacm inventor Garrett Brown). Every time I watch this scene, I hope that one of the men in the ring is the Immortal that Connor is waiting for, but I'm always disappointed to find that it's a kind of kung fu Michael Caine character. Like *Terminator*, this must have been a fun movie if you knew nothing about it – dropped right into the action, here are two modern guys duking it out with swords in the quintessential 80s action location of a parking garage.

When one immortal kills another, the victor experiences The Quickening, a kind of supernatural orgasm as you absorb the other's strength and knowledge, and Connor's is complete with a fire hose erection and gushing oil pan (check it out again, it's there). The Quickening is apparently kind of like the Force in *Star Wars*, connecting you to all living things.

The film joyfully and seamlessly flips back and forth in time to tell its tale: how Connor found he was immortal, received training from mentor Sean Connery, fell in love with a bonny lass, and failed to grow old. As many people like to point out, the film is Accent Soup – with a Frenchman playing a Scot and a Scotsman playing an Egyptian/Spaniard, but it doesn't matter. Mulcahy defends it thus: "We didn't bother changing Sean's accent – this was Sean Connery! These guys had been around for centuries. They could have picked up accents from wherever." It's a fun movie, directed to the hilt (pun intended) by music video director Mulcahy (known for his groundbreakingly cinematic Duran Duran videos) with flying cameras and unapologetically canted cameras, wide angles and low angles and fun galore. Connery is nothing short of electric, proving again what a movie star looks and acts like, and his operatic fight-to-the-death scene is an homage to a dozen film classics.

This one almost starred a bunch of other people including Kurt Russell (who followed his gal Goldie Hawn's advice and took *Big Trouble in Little China* instead), but instead stars Christopher Lambert making his first English-speaking film. Sting, lead singer of The Police, was also considered as the lead (assumedly on the strength of his oddball turn in David Lynch's *Dune*) as well as considered for songwriting tasks along with additional music contenders David Bowie and Duran Duran.

While Queen's work for *Highlander* may be limited to six songs instead of the full cinematic score, the songs are among the band's best. Director Russell Mulcahy explains how it began: "Queen had done a great score for *Flash Gordon*, so we gave them a 20-minute reel of different scenes and they went: "Wow!" We'd only expected them to do one song, but they wanted to write one each."

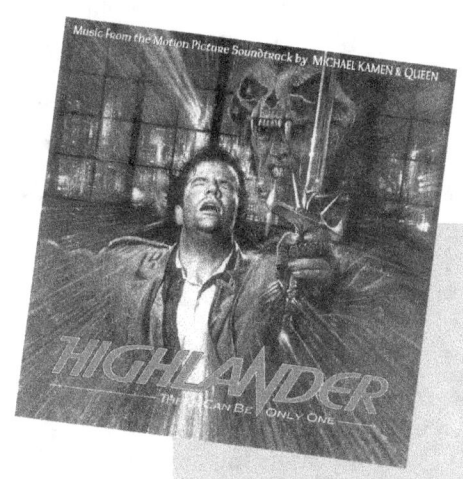

Freddie Mercury stated at the time "actually we get approached quite a lot to do soundtracks, and we're sort of very choosy. (*Highlander*) seemed to have that sort of bravado and a certain kind of magic."

Having just toured endlessly, Brian May remembered "we just wanted a rest, and then we saw about twenty minutes cut of this *Highlander* film, and we said 'great, that's us."

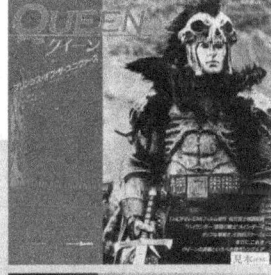

SOUNDTRACK

SCORE BY Michael Kamen

SONGS BY QUEEN:
Princes of the Universe
Gimme the Prize/Kurgan's Theme
One Year of Love
Hammer to Fall
Don't Lose Your Head
New York, New York
A Kind of Magic

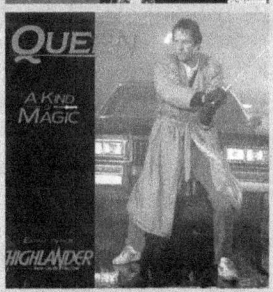

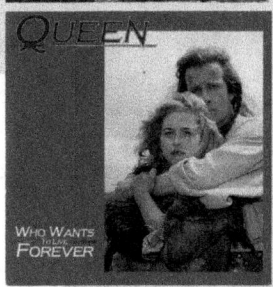

Luckily, the making of the film coincided with the production of Queen's twelfth studio album "A Kind of Magic." Taylor notes that selling an album as a complete soundtrack album could be a turn off for some people, who expect it to be "orchestral links and just background music, which it isn't at all. It's a fully fledged Queen album."

It's a Kind of Magic

Lyrics for this song and "One Vision" were originally one burst of writing by Taylor (later rewritten by Mercury when Taylor wasn't looking). A pop-version is featured on the album, a more rock-sounding one rounds out the movie's end credits. The name is inspired by a line of dialogue. "We all have our own ideas of how a song can be done," explained Freddie. With A Kind of Magic, "I felt that there was another, commercial streak, and I realized that (Roger Taylor) was going away to LA for about a week so I just got ahold of it and changed it completely. And he came back, I said 'well what do you think' and he said, 'oh, I like it.' It's a completely different song but, sometimes you can see something else in other people's songs, and I don't mind when they do that to my songs as well, we all help each other."

Brian describes the chemistry thus: "We're all still trying to use this beast which Queen is as a vehicle to get our own ideas across. And we all write very different kinds of songs, and it's quite a challenge to get them through this machinery and get them out... The challenge is to get something across in the right way which moves people."

Who Wants to Live Forever

Composed by May in the cab ride home from the 20-minute screening, and sung by May and Mercury on the album but Mercury on the movie, with orchestration by the film's composer Michael Kamen. Brian May: "What actually moved me is the subplot. The main plot is a kind of violent tale of immortals fighting each other to the death... The subplot is a tragic love story and it comes about because the hero can not die, but nevertheless he falls in love with people who can die... It came across to me very strongly, and I related it to my own life, and everybody's life. Love always does come to an end. And I had this song immediately in my head which is called 'Who Wants to Live Forever.'" Brian sings the song.

Gimme the Prize / Kurgan's Theme

A heavy rocker by May. Director Mulcahy, a self-avowed heavy-metal-hater, claims this as the least favorite of the contributions. Apparently Freddie Mercury and John Deacon hated it too.

Don't Lose Your Head

Referencing the story's frequent beheadings, this was composed by Taylor.

Princes of the Universe

This was released as the single

in the US, where the film debuted well in advance of its UK bow. British audiences were treated to "It's a Kind of Magic" as the single, as the film would not arrive on their shores until July. An operatic rocker by Mercury, which gets its name from the film's original title. This is the real barn-burner from the film. The music video stars Lambert and is directed by Mulcahy, and is shot on bits of the set from the film's climax. Lambert: "It was like having a private concert, with Queen on the stage, and I was just watching!" Roger Taylor remembers it thusly: "I find that most actors are frustrated rock and roll stars. I know Chris Lambert is! I imagine most rock and roll stars want to be actors!"

One Year of Love

"I ended up writing another slow ballad," says Deacon, "which is called 'One Year of Love' when he eventually decides to have another relationship with a woman again."

The tracks would be recorded for the film, turned in, and then tacked once again in terms of arrangement, length, and lyrics for the album release. "We rearranged a lot of the tracks, made them longer and wrote more lyrics, and tried to make them into fully fledged songs," recalled Deacon. "So they stand up in their own right; if you heard them on the radio they would sound like songs instead of incidental music."

For years, no official soundtrack to *Highlander* was released, but as the nine-song "Magic" contained the six songs heard in the film, it stood as a fine substitute. One song is heard on the radio in the film, "Hammer to Fall," from their previous studio album "The Works." Michael Kamen's score is period appropriate, favoring a majestic, epic arrangement for scenes in the past and a tighter, thriller format for the modern scenes.

Does the combination of screaming guitars and medieval Scotsmen work? Lambert thought this at the film's premiere: "when I saw the movie the first time, I was amazed at suddenly you've got some heavy rock music on some Scottish landscape, and it worked! It goes together, you don't ask yourself 'what is this music doing in this movie...' One pushes the other, and that's the power of good music if you have a potentially good movie."

In the end, maybe *Flash Gordon* works a little better on the whole because of the absurdly garish nature of that film, but that the songs for *Highlander* are able to stand alone as strong entries from one of the all-time great rock acts.

Shortly after the completion of Highlander, Freddie Mercury would test positive for AIDS, and the band's film output would come to a halt. The band continued to record until Mercury was unable to perform, but the glory days of bombastic film soundtracks were sadly behind them.

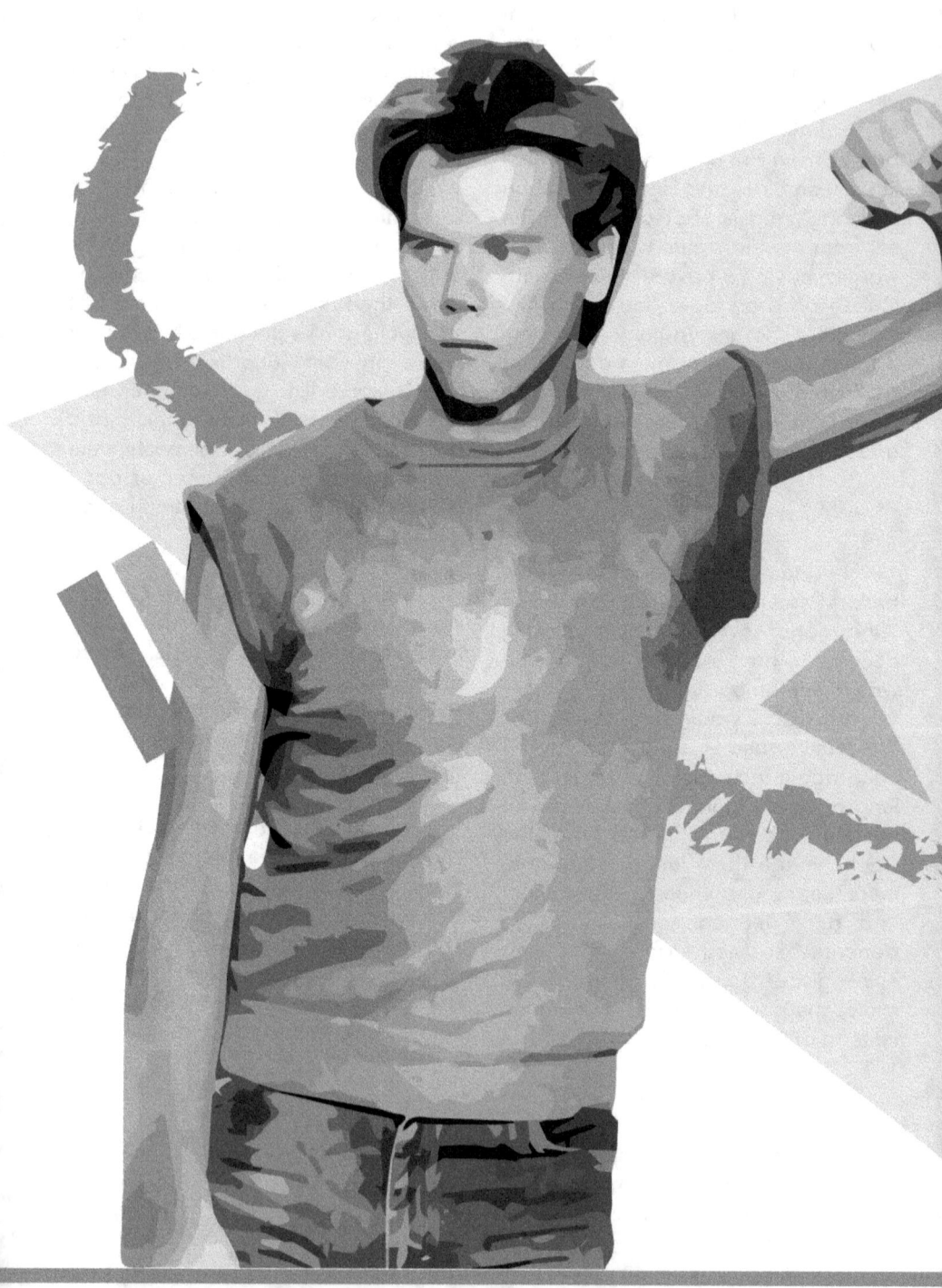

3

DANCING WITH MYSELF

Like the fight or the chase, dance is an art form that is enhanced through the power of cinema. Motion pictures bring a privileged point of view through clever camerawork, not to mention the magic of lighting and lenses and editing and the occasional dance double snuck in for good effect.

With Flashdance and Footloose you have a cinematic yin and yang of two young people who gotta dance, but unlike the classical musical, they stand alone, untethered from the romantic partner. Because sometimes, you just have to cut loose.

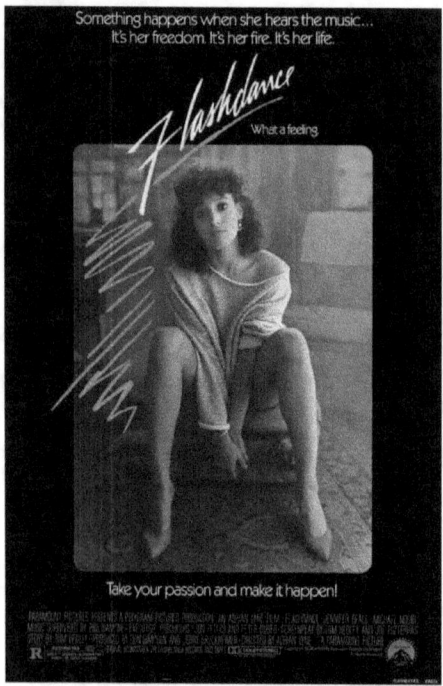

Something happens when she hears the music...
It's her freedom. It's her fire. It's her life.

Flashdance

What a feeling.

Take your passion and make it happen!

FLASHDANCE (1983)

Flashdance is a particularly 80s artifact – huge soundtrack, gorgeous glossy imagery, sexy objectification without redemption. You know, perfect Cinemax fodder. Some will argue it became the template for many films to follow, but few of those imitators succeeded visually or musically in the way that *Flashdance* did, rocketing it to the third biggest film of 1983. What it did prototype was the Simpson Bruckheimer era – this was producers Don Simpson and Jerry Bruckheimer's first outing together, and in it you can see the beginnings of the formula used to great effect through the 80s on collaborations like *Beverly Hills Cop* and *Top Gun*. While it lacks the explosions and car crashes of their

later efforts, *Flashdance* combines the highest of high end cinematography with top-of-the-line pop soundtracks. Because remember, if a film looks that good and sounds that good, it must be good.

Alas, that's about as deep as it goes and *Flashdance* is no exception, add that to the fact that it is directed by Adrian Lyne who made a career mostly out of controversial and sexy pics with questionable gender politics like *Fatal Attraction*. Even Lyne thought the film was dumb and recalls turning it down two or three times, he seized the $8 million budget and ran with it.

I suppose it shows that you should have an open mind, really. I think it's very dangerous waiting and waiting for the perfect movie to appear. –Adrian Lyne

Plot-wise, Alex (Jennifer Beals) is a welder by day and night club dancer by night, with the thought probably being this – if you can believe she can weld you can believe she can dance. She lives in an old warehouse and dresses like a spunky Soviet proletariat much of the time, and even attempts to sign up for a ballet audition in her steel-toed boots. A friend wants to be a figure skater, and upon failing takes up stripping, so the stakes are set for Alex to try a little harder. She gets a push from her boss Nick (Michael Nouri) who in addition to sleeping with her helps her get an audition.

The film revels almost exclusively in the surface, from the gritty textures of the sexy slums and industrial sites of Pittsburgh and the neon-red nightclub interiors to the sweat-soaked bodies and taut outfits of the dancers. The persistent rain and smoke and knockout locations may seem like the music videos of the period but have a big budget look that more closely resembles Jordan Cronenweth's imagery from *Blade Runner*. There was so much smoke in some of the dailies that Lyne was given a no-more-smoke edict, but soldiered on with as much haze as you see in the final film.

Lyne also knew he wanted to do a "wet" dance, something he thought would be new and naturally sexy, but when trying to show the studio executives his idea in a room without the advantage of his lighting and

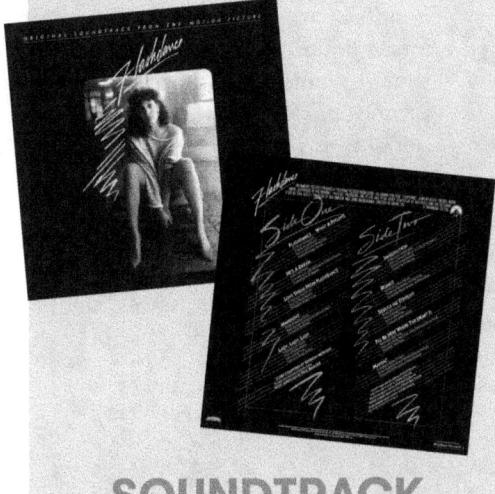

SOUNDTRACK

Flashdance... What a Feeling
Irene Cara / Giorgio Moroder

He's a Dream
Shandi

Love Theme From Flashdance
Giorgio Moroder

Manhunt
Karen Kamon

Lady, Lady, Lady
Joe Esposito

Imagination
Laura Branigan

Romeo
Donna Summer

Seduce Me Tonight
Cycle V

I'll Be Here Where the Heart Is
Kim Carnes

Maniac
Michael Sembello

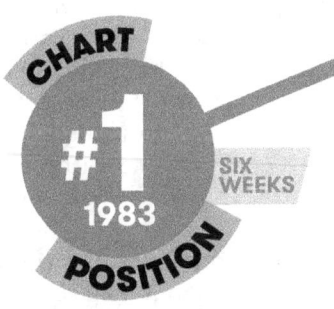

CHART #1 1983 POSITION SIX WEEKS

NOT ON THE ALBUM:
"Gloria" Laura Branigan AND "I Love Rock and Roll" Joan Jett and the Blackhearts

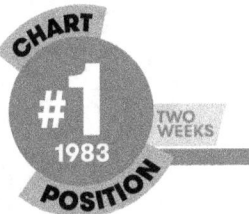

CHART #1 1983 POSITION TWO WEEKS

cinematography the idea fell horribly flat. The film was nigh but abandoned by the executives prior to its release, but the proof is in the pudding. And needless to say the wet dance that made it into the film became so iconic that it would appear on posters and promotion for the film, and go on to become an oft-parodied musical 80s moment

Chicago-born Beals recalls that although she needed to hit a certain emotional range for the film, the dancing department was covered. "They didn't have someone come in and double for me, they had four people come in... Because if I couldn't do something then I had one dance double. If she couldn't do it then you had another person. If that person couldn't do it, then there was a gymnast that came in. I mean there was a young boy who did some of the dancing. You know the poor thing had to shave his legs and put on a leotard."

Marine Jahan was the primary double, whose sharp athletic movement can be seen on display in Streets of Fire and tons of commercials and videos from the period. Jahan reportedly did almost all of Beals dancing, stating "it was way too complicated for Jennifer to know even how to begin." The film's extensive use of moody backlighting and quick cutting (and big hair wigs!) maintains the illusion perfectly, but Jahan was crestfallen to discover that her contract did not include screen credit. She was seated with choreographer Jeff Hornaday at a preview screening (and noting that they saw fit to credit the dog in the film), where he assured her "they were applauding for you," to which she replied "yes but they don't know it."

The audition scene at the film's conclusion is complemented by the leaps of gymnast Sharon Shapiro and the breakdancing of Richard "Crazy Legs" Colón of the Rock Steady

Crew. As the first major film to show breakdancing, it also served as the introduction of that art.

The film set off an international dance craze, further energized the aerobic exercise movement, and had a huge impact on the fashion of the time, when nary a single sweatshirt survived intact. There is some debate as to who originated the distressed, neckless sweatshirt look. Costume designer Michael Kaplan (*Blade Runner*) said he came up with the idea after seeing members of the Pennsylvania Ballet Company wearing them, but Beals claims that after she shrunk her favorite sweatshirt in the dryer she was forced to cut the neck open to fit her head through! "So the hole for my head was too small—I couldn't get my head through. So I cut around the hole. I wore it to one of the auditions and they liked it." Let's give Beals credit for at least one of the fashion moves, though – director Lyne saw her take her bra off without removing her shirt in a wardrobe fitting and liked the move enough to include it in the film.

Despite studio doubts, the film generated over $200 million worldwide, was the third highest-grossing film of 1983, and was nominated for three Academy Awards. Then there's the matter of that record-breaking soundtrack, which arguably set the trend for tie-in records and music videos featuring footage from the film. The LP sold six million copies and was notable as the first record to knock Michael Jackson's Thriller off the top spot, where the two jockeyed for position through 1983.

The name most associated with *Flashdance*'s music is Giorgio Moroder, the Italian songwriter responsible for more than his fair share of hits from the disco era and an innovator in the use of electronics in pop music (see sidebar). For *Flashdance*, he composed the score as well as the majority of the film's original songs, including "Flashdance... What A Feeling," "Love Theme From Flashdance," "Lady, Lady, Lady," "Romeo," and "Seduce Me Tonight."

The biggest of these songs was "Flashdance... What A Feeling," composed and produced by Moroder with lyrics by Keith Forsey and Irene Cara. Cara later expressed concern about taking on a collaboration with Moroder, fearing comparisons to his other disco muse Donna Summer. The song lived on the US Billboard charts for 25 weeks, including an insane six weeks at number one, and won Irene Cara the 1983 Grammy for Best Pop Vocal Performance, Female and the Oscar for Best Original Song.

Michael Sembello wrote two songs for the film, "Imagination" and "Maniac." The hit song Maniac was actually inspired by the William Lustig horror thriller Maniac, and temporarily featured some very different lyrics: "(Songwriting partner Dennis Matkosky) came up with the original kernel of inspiration and to me with the basic idea and groove and I believe the temporary lyrics for the chorus he had were: "He's a maniac, maniac that's for sure – He will kill your cat and nail him to the door..."

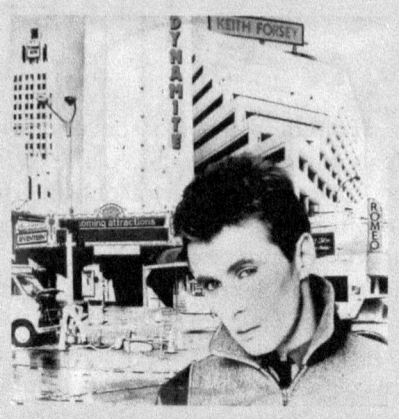

KEITH FORSEY

- Moroder's drummer, played on Donna Summer's records with Moroder
- Produced Nina Hagen, Psychedelic Furs, SImple Minds
- As producer of "Billy Idol" and "Rebel Yell" albums, largely credited with Billy Idol's mainstream success
- Co-wrote "The Heat is On" with Harold Faltermeyer for *Beverly Hills Cop* (1984)
- "The NeverEnding Story" (1984) Theme Song Lyrics
- Produced Mick Smiley's "Magic" for *Ghostbusters* soundtrack (1984)
- *The Breakfast Club* (1985) soundtrack – no, really, like nearly all of the songs were written and produced by Forsey
- "Don't You (Forget About Me)" written for Idol, hit #1 for Simple Minds

CAUTION: CONTAINS MAD HIT-MAKING!

"That direction obviously wasn't going to work at which point the genius of Phil Ramone, producer of the soundtrack who had the vision to see the potential of the song, asked us to change it to the present concept of a girl possessed with the passion of a gift for dance."

It was nominated for an Academy Award but disqualified as an original song, having been created in a different incarnation before the film version, much to Sembello's chagrin. The song makes great use of the then-new Linn Electronics LM-1 drum machine and Simmons electronic drums, in conjunction with the synthesizers it packs a potent 1983 punch. The song spent 22 weeks on the Billboard Hot 100 chart and stayed at #1 for two weeks!

Flashdance will not be remembered as a ground breaking film with an important message, but as a cultural mile marker in the growth of the soundtrack as commodity we have a great early contender.

they enter a town run by the tight morality of a fiery preacher, Reverend Shaw Moore (John Lithgow). Due to an unfortunate drinking and driving accident a few years prior, the town has railed against liquor, rock and roll, and dancing, the triumvirate they deem most directly responsible for the crash.

The Reverend's daughter Ariel (Lori SInger), on the other hand, is a sleeps-around firebrand who straddles speeding vehicles and – gulp – listens to a boombox. When her cassette of "Dancing in the Sheets" by Shalamar makes it into a boombox at the local drive-in, everyone within earshot begins bopping (and that is literally everyone, the sound apparently travels all the way back to the kitchen).

"Be careful with that – If your daddy hears you playing that he'll bust your butt."

–Chuck Cranston

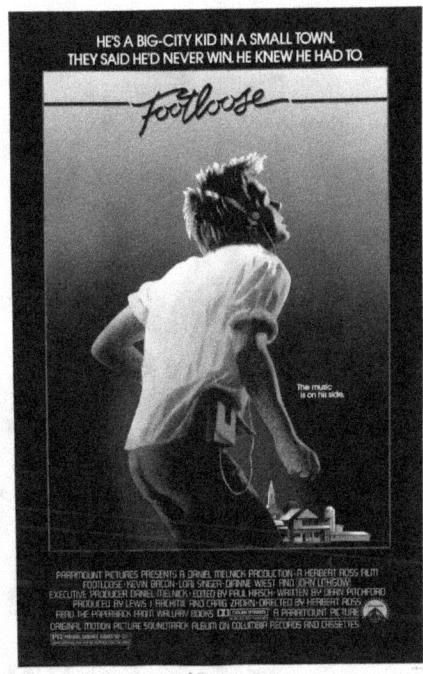

FOOTLOOSE (1984)

Based loosely on some real events in Oklahoma, Footloose is a film that reviewers hated but became a runaway hit, once again proving the usefulness of movie critics everywhere and launching star Kevin Bacon into the mainstream.

Ren McCormack (Bacon) is a slick big-city kid from Chicago Illinois with a penchant for skinny ties and banned books. When Ren and his mother move to the small, conservative Christian community of Bomont, Midwest, USA,

Before long, everyone in the town has it in for McCormack, whether trying to frame him with drugs, keeping him off the gymnastics team, or pulling him over for playing Quiet Riot on his car stereo. Sarah Jessica Parker plays Ariel's friend Rusty who keeps her up on Ren's activities, and Chris Penn is Ren's friend Willard who doesn't know how to dance. Penn genuinely didn't know how to dance, which inspired the subplot and scene in which Bacon teaches him.

When Ren tries to organize a Senior dance, the town is divided into

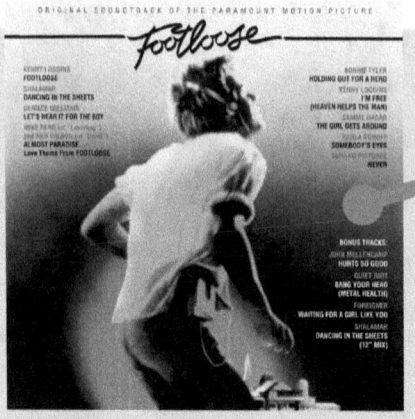

ORIGINAL SOUNDTRACK OF THE PARAMOUNT MOTION PICTURE

CHART #1 1984 POSITION

TEN WEEKS

THE ALBUM WAS TEN WEEKS AT #1, AND ON THE CHARTS FOR A WHOPPING 64 WEEKS

SOUNDTRACK

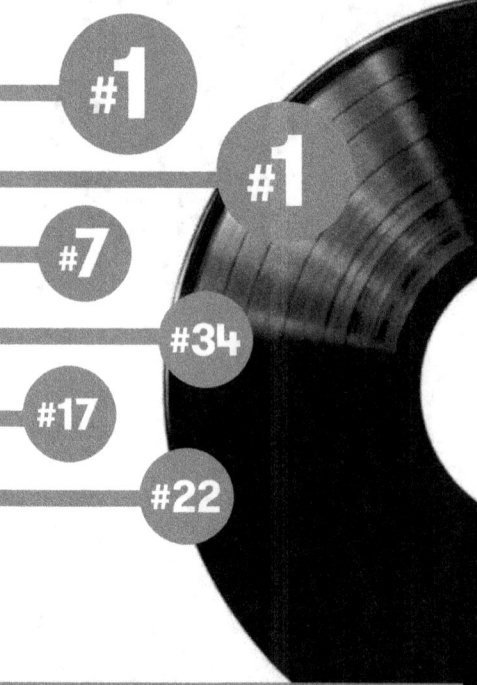

Footloose
Kenny Loggins
#1

Let's Hear It For The Boy
Deniece Williams
#1

Almost Paradise (Love Theme)
Mike Reno and Ann Wilson
#7

Holding Out For A Hero
Bonnie Tyler
#34

Dancing in the Sheets
Shalamar
#17

I'm Free (Heaven Helps the Man)
Kenny Loggins
#22

Somebody's Eyes
Karla Bonoff

The Girl Gets Around
Sammy Hagar

Never
Moving Pictures

NOT ON THE ALBUM:

Bang Your Head (Metal Health)
Quiet Riot

Waiting for a Girl Like You
Foreigner

Hurts So Good
John Mellencamp

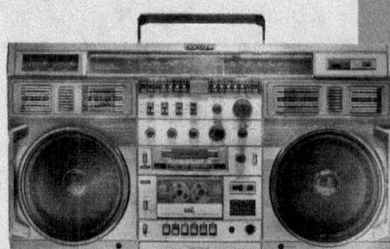

two camps: the kids and the stiffs. Rev Moore fears that "when kids dance together, they get sexually irresponsible," but doesn't realize that it's too late for his daughter, who's hip deep in sex drugs and rock and roll already. Unlike the corrupting influence of, say, Kenny Loggins, he favors classical music that "doesn't confuse people's minds and bodies." Seeking an inroad to the Reverend's heart, Ren attempts to use scripture to defend his choice in a city council meeting, but it isn't enough to sway the group. When at last he sets up a dance just past the city limits at the mill he works at, even the Reverend must admire his chutzpah.

This film generated one of the all-time blockbuster soundtrack albums, and nearly every song featured was rewarded with radio play when the film came out in 1984. The album reached number one on April 21 1984 and stayed there until June 30! The title track, used three times in the film, is arguably the perfect 80s movie song and is chronicled in greater depth later (p.90). So ubiquitous is the song "Footloose" that when attending weddings, actor Kevin Bacon is known to pay off DJs to NOT play it so that he can dodge the inherent responsibility to perform.

Footloose was one of the first movies to promote the film via the music videos, released in advance of the movie itself.

Bacon apparently based his character's look, and especially his haircut, on Sting of The Police who at the time of filming would have been one of the biggest acts around. The Police and Men At Work get a name check in an early scene in which the provincial Willard has never heard of either band, resulting in a "Who's on First" type riff.

Footloose may be considered the yin to Flashdance's yang, in a couple of ways. Certainly, Footloose is rural where Flashdance is urban, Bacon is the masculine and Beals is the feminine. Film critic Kathleen Carroll of the Daily News called Footloose "a sort of Boy Scout version of Flashdance," possibly because Footloose is so down-home and innocent compared to Flashdance's sexy, clubby

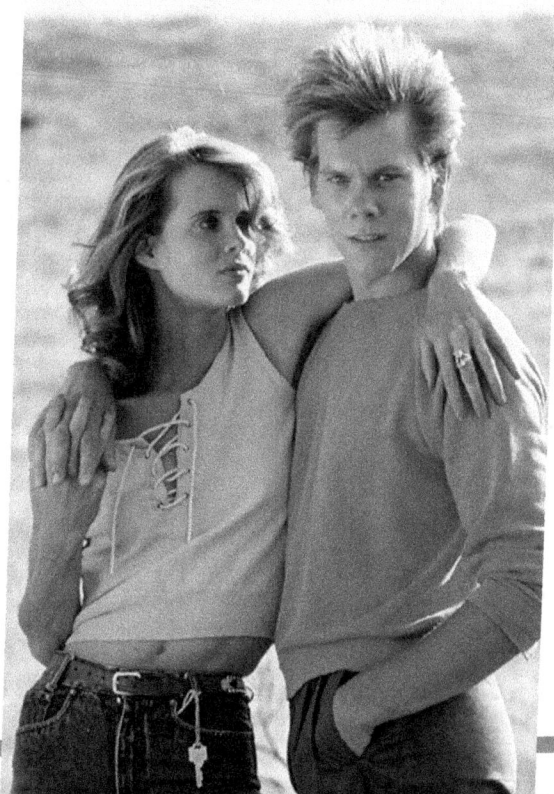

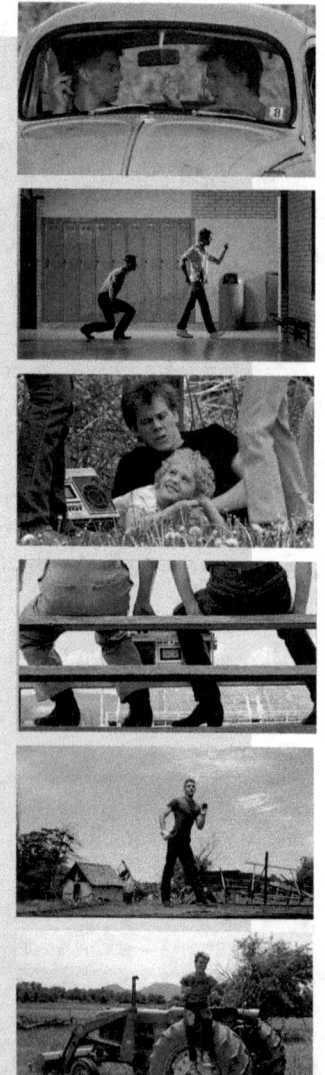

trashiness. For the dancing, there are parallels to *Flashdance* as well: in addition to having two gymnastic body doubles, Bacon's dance double was Peter Tramm (then the husband of *Flashdance* double Marine Jahan). Bacon was in his twenties by the time the film was made, only twelve years younger than his co-star John Lithgow.

The film's finale at the flour mill is a joyous dance number that is hard to hate, shot with such glimmering nostalgia that it is literally raining glitter. Yes, they dumped tons of glitter, swept it up, and did it again and again, warning the actors not to look up for fear of getting it in their eyes. That finale was originally shot in slow motion, but had to be reshot at standard speed because the resulting scene sucked the air out of the ending.

Lyrics for all of the soundtrack's songs were written by screenwriter Dean Pitchford, who said he "wanted the songs to be a subtext for the film. I didn't want tracks that had been left off old albums, 'trunk songs' that had been lying around." Music supervisor Becky Shargo thought it contributed to the soundtrack's success: "The reason soundtracks went through a lull in recent years is that they became mere compilations, like greatest hits packages. Kids got hip to it, and after a while it became passe."

MONTAGE FROMAGE
"Let's Hear It For The Boy"
Deniece Williams*
A crash course in the beat, and how to find it.

**RATING
8/10**

*Tom Snow, Dean Pitchford

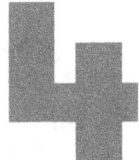

SONGS FOR A MUSCULAR ACTIVITY

If films of the 1970s were known for their realism and grit, the films of the 80s became known for a particular brand of testosterone-y action and cartooniness typified by the bulging biceps of Sylvester Stallone and Arnold Schwarzenegger. Today's critics write off the music of the period for the same reason they wrote off the films at the time: mindless aggression without a message. If there is a musical equivalent to a bodybuilder with a machine gun, the soundtracks from this chapter are it.

It's the eye of the tiger
It's the thrill of the fight
Rising up to the challenge of our rival
And the last known survivor
Stalks his prey in the night
And he's watching us all with the eye of the tiger

The combination of fist-pumping hard rock anthems and muscle-pumping action movies was kicked off by a film that marks the transition between decades, one foot firmly in the 70s and the other in the 1980s. *Rocky III*'s rousing anthem to face punching, "Eye of the Tiger," is another pillar of the temple of 80s movie music. And the song sits high among our "Greatest Song Countdown" for good reason. Its commercial success and picture-perfect placement in the film ensures it a lofty ranking, but also sets the tone for every future use of rock in 80s movies, especially among that subgenre of action films dominated by the Italian Stallion and the Austrian Oak.

Film actor and producer Tony Scotti had released Survivor's previous album, *Premonition*, on his label Scotti Brothers Records. Scotti played some of the tracks for Stallone and suggested their inclusion in the film, and Stallone was won over by the sound and style. Sly left phone messages for Jim Peterik and Frankie Sullivan, founding members of Survivor, to inquire. Guitarist Peterik recalls that "answering machines were still something of a novelty back then and to see that blinking light was a thrill. When I pressed the playback button I heard, "Hey, yo, Jim, that's a nice message you got there. This is Sylvester Stallone.' It was too thick to be really him, but it was him."

In the place where he anticipated the new song would go, Stallone was temporarily using a song he didn't have the rights to: Queen's "Another One Bites the Dust." As Peterik recalls "Frankie and I are watching this, the punches are being thrown, and we're going, 'Holy crap, this is working like a charm...' Frankie and I looked at each other and went, 'Man, this is going to be tough to beat.'" The guys from Survivor knew "we've got to try to top this."

Coming up with the song itself was a Balboa-esque combination of inspiration and perspiration. The opening came to Peterik while driving. A two hour jam session was recorded on cassette to capture any ideas. Back in the studio in Chicago, the song quickly coalesced. "I started doing that now-famous dead string guitar riff and started slashing those chords to the punches we saw on the screen, and the whole song took shape in the next three days." The version that made it into the film is the Chicago recording, but the album version that would go on to be a number one Billboard hit for six straight weeks in 1982 was labored over for a month in a subsequent session in Los Angeles. The band found it difficult to capture the energy of that original take.

"Right before the movie came out, I was driving down the freeway in Chicago, and I flipped my three favorite stations on and all three were playing "Eye of the Tiger" at the same time," recalled Frankie Sullivan. "But when it really hit me was when I went to see the movie in the theater and the whole place stood up and applauded when the song was over. And they didn't know who the hell we were, but then I thought, 'Maybe I had done a good job.'"

Peterik agrees, "it wasn't until I went to a Pizza Hut restaurant in some god-forsaken town in America. I was sitting there all alone, eating pizza when the song comes on the jukebox. This little 5-year-old girl jumps up from her seat, hits the dance floor and starts screaming, 'They're playing my song!, they're playing my song!,' and starts dancing to the song. I go, 'Now I know we have something.'" The song won a Grammy (for Best Rock Performance by a Duo or Group with Vocal) and Oscar nomination, a Golden Globe nomination, and won Best New Song by the People's Choice Award. Peterik is quick to credit Stallone for the song's power: "Stallone has a good ear for a hook. Just listen to his dialogue - he wrote those scripts. He came up with 'Eye

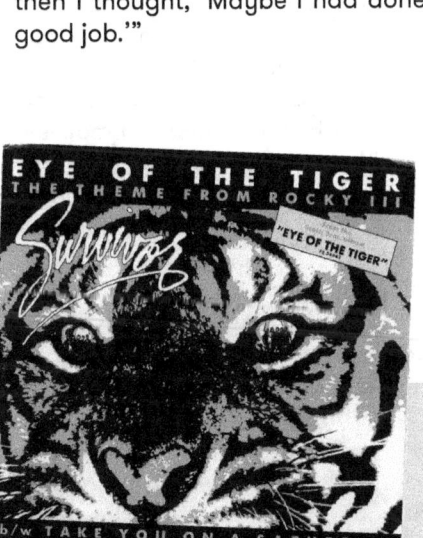

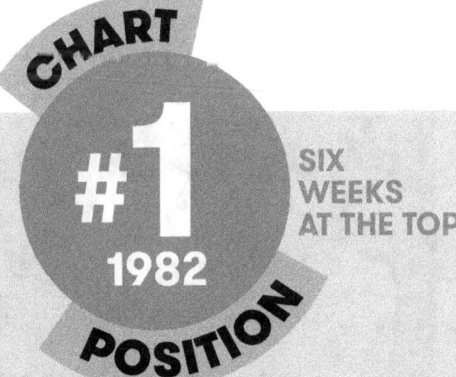

#1 1982 CHART POSITION — SIX WEEKS AT THE TOP

EYE OF THE TIGER

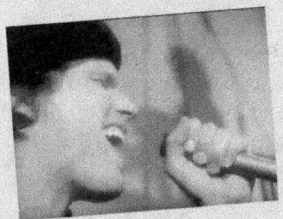

- Released May 29 1982
- Was going to appear in *The Karate Kid*, only to be replaced by Joe Esposito's "You're the Best"
- The band subsequently re-recorded the song for radio, which is the version most familiar to listeners
- Went platinum by August of 1982
- Oscar nominated, lost to "Up Where We Belong" from *An Officer and a Gentleman*

Of The Tiger' for that script and those hook phrases like 'I'm going to knock you into tomorrow.' All that stuff is Stallone, he's a genius with dialogue. Songs are nothing more than dialogue set to music as far as I'm concerned." Their future collaborations would also rely dialog selections from the film's screenplays for key lyrics.

At the same time, Stallone's chief competitor Arnold Schwarzenegger was making three sword and sorcery movies basically back to back, period type films where including a rocking 80s theme song might have not been considered the best idea (I heartily disagree on that, so I will remedy that by turning down the sound on my copy of *Conan* and cranking up some Dio). But 1984's *The Terminator* is set smack dab in the quintessential 80s Los Angeles, with neon nightclubs and car radios and a prominently placed Sony Walkman – all great places to explore some contemporary music.

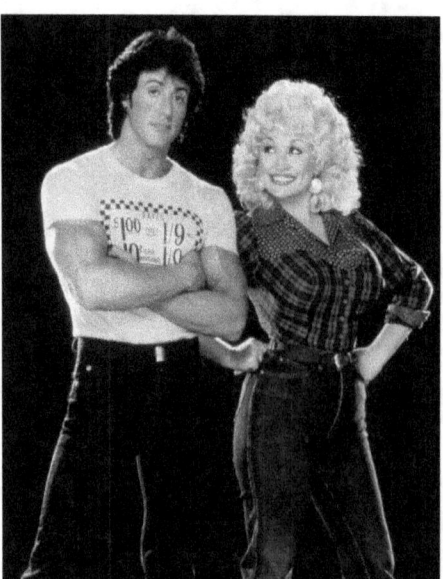

The songs skew towards synth pop with no less than three great songs by Tahnee Cain and Tryanglz. No hard rocking theme song plays out over the end credits (though hard cuts made it into the 1991 sequel, including the hit "You Could Be Mine" by Guns N' Roses).

Stallone's next films, *First Blood* (1982) *Rhinestone* (1984) and Rambo First Blood Part 2 (1985), would be a step back musically. *First Blood*'s soundtrack is limited to the sappy, seventies-sounding "It's a Long Road" by Dan Hill, and the sequel fares no better with the after-school-special morality of Frank Stallone's "Peace in Our Life." And then there's *Rhinestone*, a film in which Dolly Parton makes a bet with her manager that she can turn anyone into a country singer – including cabbie Nick Martinelli (Stallone). It's a sort of country music version of Pygmalion, but if Stallone had gotten his way it may have been much more interesting. Stallone later admitted "It was supposed to be shot in New York, down and dirty with Dolly and I with gutsy mannerisms performed like two antagonists brought together by fate. I wanted the music at that time to be written by people who would give it sort of a bizarre edge. Believe it or not, I contacted Whitesnake's management and they were ready to write some very interesting songs alongside Dolly's... [Instead], the film went in a direction that literally shattered my internal corn meter into smithereens. I would have done many things differently. I certainly would've steered clear of comedy unless it was dark, Belgian chocolate dark. Silly comedy didn't work for me. I mean, would anybody pay to see John Wayne in a whimsical farce? Not likely. I would stay more true to who I am and what the audience would prefer rather than trying to stretch out and waste a lot of time and people's patience." Still, Stallone sings in the film, a rarity.

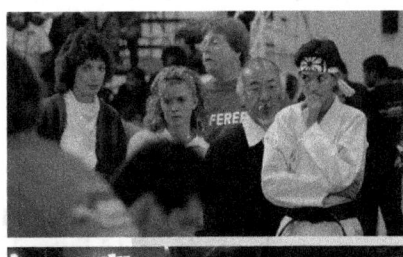

1984 gave us *The Karate Kid*, with perhaps smaller muscles but one of the finest heroic anthems of the period. If Bill Conti's score for the film never reaches the heights of *Rocky* (settling instead for a bit of Eastern mysticism with a decidedly un-Asian Gheorghe Zamfir on flute), his work as a songwriter for the film more than makes up for it. The key muscular track here is "You're the Best," written by Conti and performed by Joe Esposito. The film plays like a teenage *Rocky*, with the baby-Balboa transplanted from New Jersey to southern California. Young Daniel LaRusso (Ralph Macchio) runs afoul

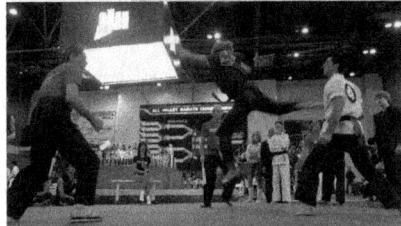

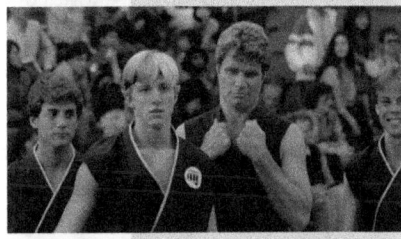

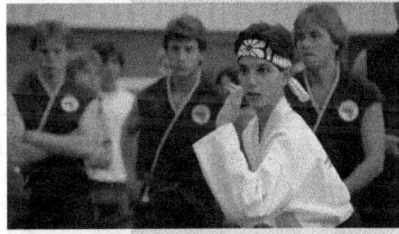

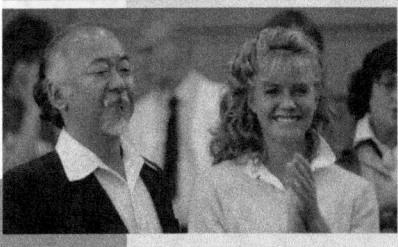

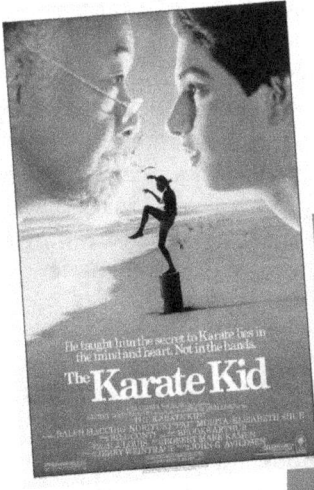

MONTAGE FROMAGE
"You're the Best" Joe Esposito*
This is what it's all about, powerful music and imagery working together

*written by Bill Conti

RATING 10/10

of the boys from Cobra Kai karate school, and must learn the art from quiet handyman Mr. Miyagi (Academy Award-nominated Pat Morita). While the movie hinges on Daniel learning karate for the first time, the song lyric clearly states "history repeats itself." Turns out this track was first intended for *Rocky III*, which would indeed be history repeating itself. Lyrics were by Allee Willis, who wrote songs for *Beverly Hills Cop* and *Howard the Duck*, before writing the hit theme song to the sitcom *Friends*. The 1986 sequel lacked any great rockers but fared even better on the charts, as Peter Cetera's "The Glory of Love (Theme from Karate Kid II)" spent two weeks at #1.

With *Commando* (1985) Schwarzenegger finally joins the ranks of muscular rock, albeit tentatively and

only in the safe slot of an end credits song. James Horner's tropical, *Miami-Vice*-ish synth score fills most of the available screen time, but "We Fight for Love" by Powerstation provides a supremely muscular conclusion to the over-the-top cartoon. Featuring replacement singer Michael Des Barres instead of original headliner Robert Palmer, this song comes hot on the heels of the wildly successful one-shot album by the band. Powerstation was made up of the guitar section of Duran Duran (Andy Taylor and John Taylor) and the drummer from Chic (Tony Thompson). Producer Bernard Edwards, another founding member of Chic, also produced Duran's James Bond entry "View to a Kill" that same year, along with Palmer's hit album *Riptide*.

Rocky IV takes the expectations from the third installment and cranks them to eleven, and the soundtrack is no exception. Once more to the rescue were Survivor's Sullivan and Peterik, this time working from a screenplay instead of an edit with temp tracks. "As soon as the delivery came, I remember taking my copy to the pool of our hotel and reading the whole thing in one sitting," recalls Peterik. "I soon realized that this battle was about more than just two fighters in a ring, but about the whole struggle between the ideologies of two rival nations. That became my focus as the lyric took shape."

"Stallone was there with a lot of suggestions. He knew what he didn't want, because 'Burning Heart' originally had the hook title of 'The Unmistakable Fire.' He goes, 'You can't call the song The Unmistakable Fire.' I think it was Frankie who said, 'At the beginning of the chorus, instead of 'In the human heart just about to burst,' let's say 'In the burning heart.'" I was avoiding that because there was already a song called 'Burning Heart' by Vandenberg and also, I always got a vision of heartburn. I decided I was thinking too much and we called the song 'Burning Heart.' Stallone was good with knowing what he liked and what he didn't like."

Like so many of these things, the song was written on the road while Survivor was on tour. "Over the next few days we would have the road crew set up our portable Wurlitzer electric piano, an amp and guitar in a separate hotel room so we could work during the day. As usual the music appeared simultaneously with the snippets of lyrics I was coming up with. A few cities down the road we had about 80 percent of the song done."

Also on the *Rocky IV* soundtrack is "No Easy Way Out" by Robert Tepper – it was on his upcoming Scotti Brothers Records album of the same name, Stallone heard it and snapped it up. "The Sweetest Victory" by Touch is close enough to a Survivor track to make you do a double take, and "Hearts of Fire" John Cafferty rounds out the rockers.

And yet the film's biggest hit was not from a power-rock band but the Godfather of Soul himself. James Brown's "Living in America" was written by Dan "I Can Dream About You" Hartman and Charles Midnight. Brown had not been on the Billboard charts for ten years, but came back with a vengeance with the track, landing at #4 amidst an impressive 19 weeks on the chart. It would be Brown's second biggest song – his song "I Got You (I Feel Good)" reached #3 twenty years previously – and contained the distinctive vocal exclamations that would be sampled on every dance and hip hop track from that moment on. The horns were supplied by The Uptown Horns, a New York section that backed the J. Geils Band on their Freeze Frame album and played on "Love Shack" by The B-52s.

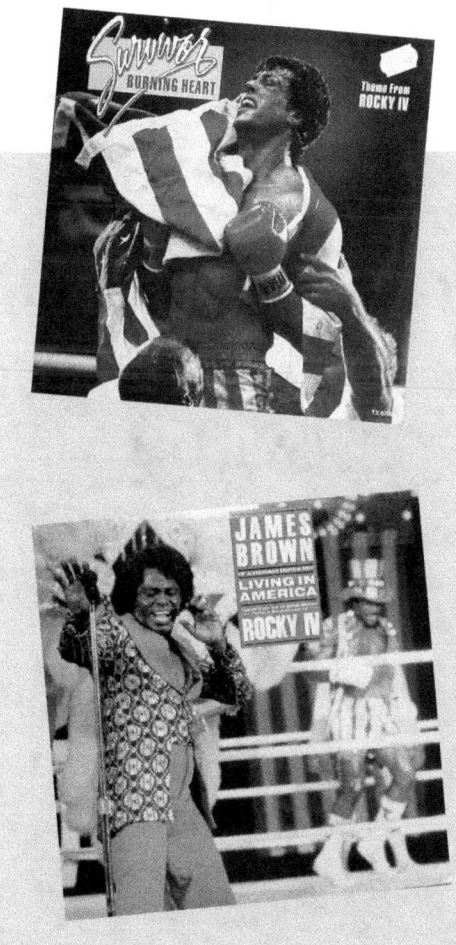

Stallone returned to the Scotti Brothers stable for the outrageous cop thriller *Cobra* (1986), once again employing Robert Tepper ("Angel of the City") and John Cafferty. ("Voice of America's Sons"). The standout on the soundtrack, though, is "Feel the Heat" by Jean Beauvoir, the mohawked former Plasmatics bassist and session musician. The film's love theme, "Loving on Borrowed Time," is a duet by Gladys Knight and Bill Medley. Medley would be involved with one of the decade's biggest movie duets the following year for *Dirty Dancing*.

Schwarzenegger misses another musical opportunity with the contemporary action film *Raw Deal* (1986), and *Predator* (1987) is set in a jungle where the opportunities for motivated songs are scarce, but the soldiers do crank a Little Richard song on the way to the DZ. Sometimes, after all the muscle-bound mayhem, what's called for is a little relief, rather than more testosterone. Cue Harold Faltermeyer's song "(Restless Heart) Running Away With You", sung by John Parr. If you find the romantic subplot of *The Running Man* (1987) feasible, then a song like this will hit home. This is one of those tunes where if you play it for someone and ask them to name the film, a hyper violent actioner like *Running Man* is the last thing they'll think.

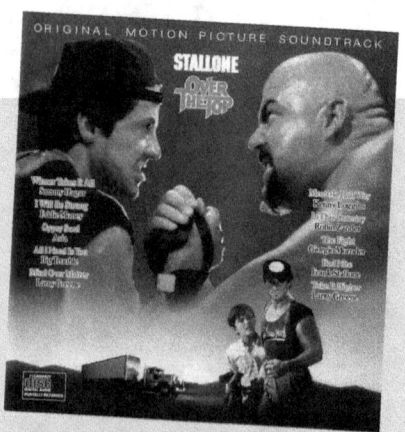

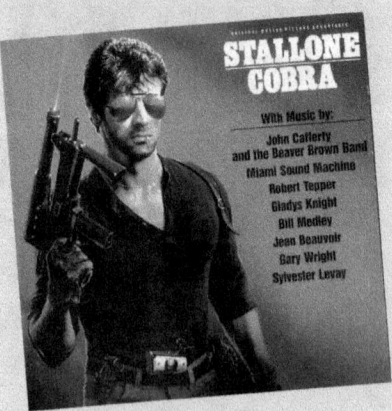

The best truck-driving and arm-wrestling film around, *Over The Top* sports a picture perfect soundtrack that belies the film's modest budget. Maestro Giorgio Moroder empties his notebook of whatever was left over from his exhaustive *Top Gun* output, and the results make for not only the best Cannon Group soundtrack, but one of the best of its kind.

"In This Country" – Robin Zander
"Gypsy Soul" – Asia
"All I Need is You" Big Trouble
"I Will Be Strong" – Eddie Money
"Meet Me Halfway" – Kenny Loggins
"Mind Over Matter" – Larry Greene
"Winner Takes it All" – Sammy Hagar (with bandmate Eddie Van Halen providing that slippery bass solo)
"Take it Higher" – Larry Greene

All of these are written by Moroder, who shows once again his mastery of songwriting, producing (all tracks sound like they belong in the mouths of the original artists), and deep understanding of what a film needs. All employ the pulsing electronic foundations and rough-but-radio-friendly guitar work that made the *Top Gun* tracks so successful, in addition to his inimitable ear for melodic hooks. Many of them could easily be tracks from *Top Gun* ("In This Country" has the anthemic *Top Gun* signature, "All I Need is You" is a just breath away from "Take My Breath Away").

Stallone's soundtrack output never again reaches the quality and quantity of the *Over the Top* soundtrack. The film *Lock Up* uses Survivor's "Ever Since the World Began" and Jim Peterik's other band Ides of March doing his song "Vehicle." 1989's *Tango and Cash* employs some radio rockers to fill out the soundtrack though no accompanying album was released.

Final Assessment: When it came to the soundtrack, Stallone rocked and Schwarzenegger did not. While Sly often included some painfully sappy ballads in his films, the amount of pure testosterone makes up for any shortcomings.

HONORABLE MENTIONS

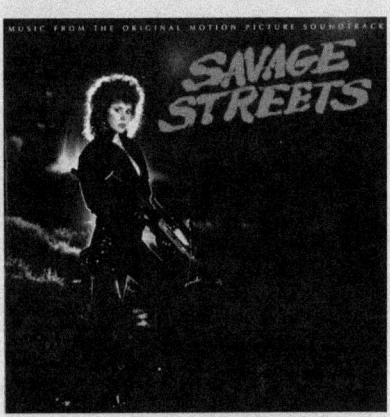

This hard-to-find album will have you out seeking revenge in no time. With angry rockers from John Farnham ("Justice for One," "Innocent Hearts," "Nothing's Going to Stand in Our Way") and Michael Bradley ("In the Night," "Killer")

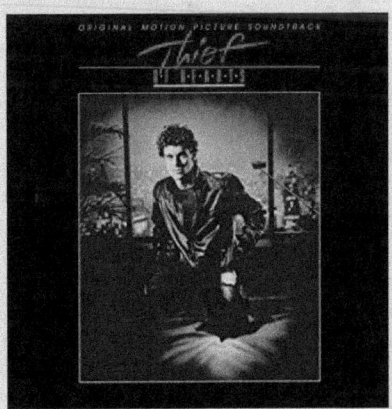

Loads of poppy snyths complements of 1984-era Harold Faltermeyer, with Melissa Manchester and E.G. Daily handling the vocal chores.

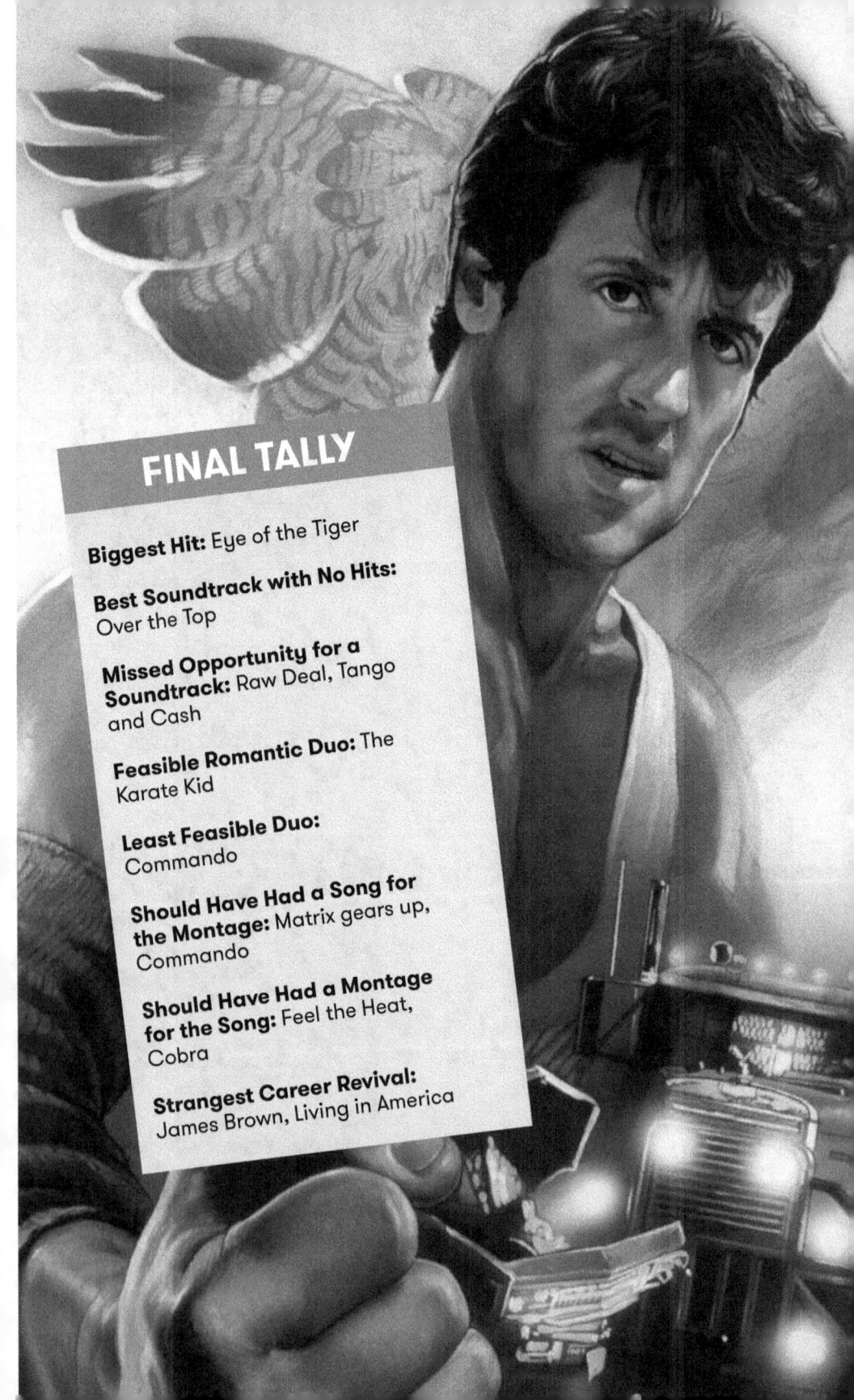

FINAL TALLY

Biggest Hit: Eye of the Tiger

Best Soundtrack with No Hits: Over the Top

Missed Opportunity for a Soundtrack: Raw Deal, Tango and Cash

Feasible Romantic Duo: The Karate Kid

Least Feasible Duo: Commando

Should Have Had a Song for the Montage: Matrix gears up, Commando

Should Have Had a Montage for the Song: Feel the Heat, Cobra

Strangest Career Revival: James Brown, Living in America

5

MUNICH MACHINE: GIORGIO MORODER

When the world was through with disco, one of its most talented songwriters and producers translated his love of electronic music to one of the most successful 80s soundtrack composers – and in turn, pop songwriters. Comparing himself to the decade's other blockbuster composer, Giorgio Moroder says "if you consider more classical composers like John Williams, who I think is the best – he doesn't write songs. But I write songs and the scores. So that's a little bit of an advantage for me."

Influential and prolific, Giorgio Moroder survived the "disco sucks" backlash and the fall of 80s synth pop to be revered as a DJ and dance music pioneer in the 21st century. Born in a German-speaking province of Italy in 1940, he played guitar and bass in several bands before settling down in Munich, Germany. He founded the recording studio Musicland there, which would host some of the greatest bands of the 20th century from Queen to Led Zeppelin to the Rolling Stones. Like many in the industry, his introduction to synthesizers came via the pioneering work of some of the masters.

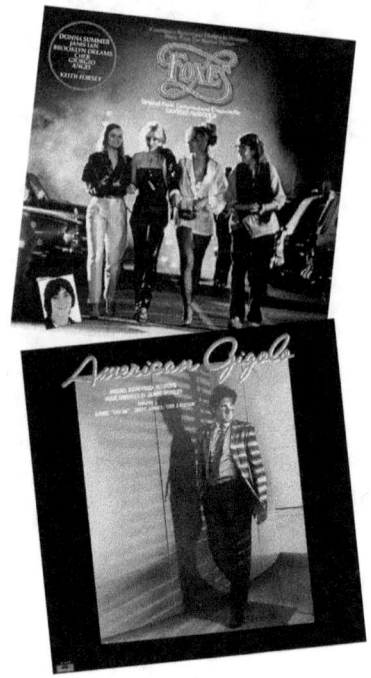

"I was listening to Walter Carlos, when he played the album *Switched-On Bach*," Moroder says. "I thought, 'This is the instrument which I would love to use.' And then I found this guy in Germany who had one. It changed, a little bit, my life." Moroder also had his eye on other German-based synth bands. "I liked Kraftwerk. I liked a lot of Tangerine Dream—they had a lot of really good songs. They may have not influenced me but I was listening definitely to them."

But it was disco songs, like his infamous Donna Summer collaboration on "I Feel Love," catapulted Moroder to stardom. Brian Eno told David Bowie that the song was "going to change the sound of club music for the next 15 years." He was right, but underestimated its longevity by a power of three! Bowie himself was in the habit of playing people the 12" version of the song and proclaiming it "the sound of the future." He was at least partially right – Moroder had been so inspired by the cantina scene in *Star Wars* (which he felt did NOT sound like the future) that he wrote the electronic heavy Donna Summer track in response.

His post-disco output was marked by an association with hit *film music – his 1979 synth score for Midnight Express* won an Academy Award, further legitimizing its use as an instrument for film and opening the doors for hundreds of similar low-budget scores in the decade that followed. Moroder recounted the project's beginnings in a 2014 interview with Jordan Cronk for Mubi. com.

"Casablanca Records one day just asked me if I wanted to do a score for a movie. And that was a big surprise because I had never done anything like that. So then I spoke with [director] Alan Parker, who wanted me to do the music for *Midnight Express*, and wanted a synthesized score.

Basically, he liked the music I had done for "I Feel Love." And there's one scene in the movie where a guy escapes and he said, "Give me something in the style of 'I Feel Love'" – something like a bass line that gives the feel of him escaping, to get some suspense. And he liked the piece I did. And the rest was very easy."

Any ideas Moroder had were quick to translate to the screen. "It was great because I basically was able to do most of it by myself with no director or producer sitting next to me... Then when we mixed it down that was a day or two in Munich and it was a great day to finally see it properly in front of the director and making some little changes. That was definitely my favorite one."

With Oscar statue in hand, the next decade would prove to be a lucrative and creative one, with two projects immediately underway for a 1980 release.

FOXES (1980)

The coming-of-age drama *Foxes* focuses on a handful of late 70's California girls, among them Jodie Foster and Cherie Currie, the lead singer of The Runaways. A fair amount of the action revolves around the rock scene, but the music is pure disco, including the Moroder/Summer "On the Radio," which reached #5 on Billboard's Hot 100.

AMERICAN GIGOLO (1980)

"For *American Gigolo*, Jerry Bruckheimer and Paul Schrader told me "We need a song for the beginning. We need a song for when they go into the discotheque. Then we need a love song here..." So the song was absolutely part of the movie, but at the same time it was part of the soundtrack."

"Call Me" – With a monumental six weeks at number one – surely a record for a song written from the point of view of a male prostitute – Debbie Harry and Blondie explode onto the international scene complements of Moroder, whose original instrumental track was first offered to Stevie Nicks.

"Love and Passion" – with lyric contributions by director Paul Schrader, Love and Passion boasts some of the dance floor scope of the Moroder/Diana Ross collaborations

"Night Drive" – an instrumental piece poised on the border between disco and synthwave, using the basic melody of "Call Me"

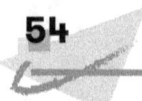

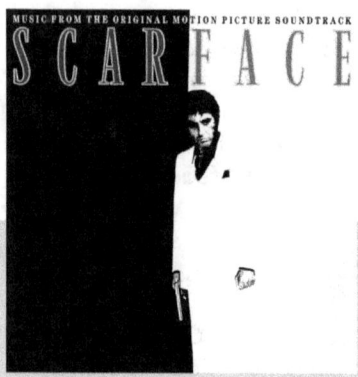

SOUNDTRACK

Scarface (Push it to the Limit)
Paul Engemann

Rush, Rush
Debbie Harry

Turn Out the Night
Amy Holland

Vamos a Bailar
Maria Conchita

Tony's Theme
Giorgio Moroder

She's on Fire
Amy Holland

Shake it Up
Elizabeth Daily

Dance Dance Dance
Beth Anderson

I'm Hot Tonight
Elizabeth Daily

Gina and Elvira's Theme
Helen St. John

CAT PEOPLE (1982)

A sumptuous remake of the 1942 film that traffics in eroticism and horror, Moroder was hired for the score and theme song. A collaboration with David Bowie ensued: "I started probably two months before I had to deliver the final score. And I had this song and Paul and I decided that there's only one guy whose image is perfect [for a film like this]. So I gave him the song and he wrote the lyrics and then we recorded it quickly in Switzerland." Bowie re-recorded the song for hit album *Let's Dance* in 1982, brightening up the original version which ran very dark for a pop album.

FLASHDANCE (1983)

Moroder's song "Flashdance... What a Feeling" is one of only thirteen 1980s songs to make it onto the American Film Institute's 100 Years, 100 Songs list. It sat atop the Bilboard Top 100 for six weeks. (see p 32)

SUPERMAN III (1983)

Used only minimally in the film (and often only in an instrumental capacity), Moroder produced four pop songs and a synth cover of the main title march.

"Rock On" / Marshall Crenshaw
"No See, No Cry" / Chaka Khan
"They Won't Get Me"/ Roger Miller
"Love Theme" / Helen St. John

SCARFACE (1983)

The *Scarface* soundtrack is a Giorgio Moroder album from start to finish. Despite the film's huge acceptance later in life with a gangster-rap audience, director Brian De Palma fought off the studio's inclination to re-release the film with a hip-hop soundtrack, and has been quoted as declaring the Moroder work "perfect."

DC CAB (1983)

Moroder provided the score and some of the songs (co-written with frequent collaborator Pete Bellotte)

"The Dream" / Irene Cara
"Knock Me On My Feet" / Champagne
"Single Heart" / DeBarge
"Party Me Tonight" / Stephanie Mills

METROPOLIS (1984)

Moroder personally oversaw a complicated, two-year restoration with what source materials were then available, ensuring the best transfer possible but still working towards an edit that was more palatable to modern audiences. Moroder worked at home to create an edit, selecting the best elements from a variety of international sources.

He was inspired by a recent screening of Abel Gance's silent masterpiece *Napoleon*, in which Carmine Coppola had done a new score. "I liked the fact that he performed it live with a big orchestra, but that was one time at the big cinema in New York. But I wanted [*Metropolis*] to be released as a movie."

THE NEVERENDING STORY (1984)

Former Kajagoogoo lead singer Limahl hit #6 US (and #1 on the more fanciful pop charts of Norway and Sweden) with this Moroder composition. Sporting lyrics by Keith Forsey, the song fades out like most pop songs – but it also fades in, making it a "Neverending" song.

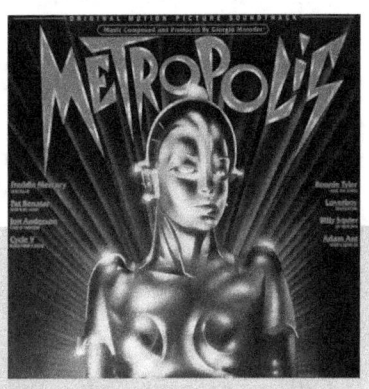

SOUNDTRACK

Love Kills
Freddie Mercury

Here's My Heart
Pat Benatar

Cage of Freedom
Jon Anderson

Blood From a Stone
Cycle V

The Legend of Babel
Giorgio Moroder

Here She Comes
Bonnie Tyler

Destruction
Loverboy

On Your Own
Billy Squier

What's Going On
Adam Ant

Machines
Giorgio Moroder

ELECTRIC DREAMS (1984)

In addition to the percolating poppy score, Moroder drums up a UK hit with Human League lead singer Philip Oakey providing the vocal. The film was directed by prolific music video maestro Steve Barron, who had made "Billie Jean" for Michael Jackson, "Burning Up" for Madonna, and "Africa" for Toto.

TOP GUN (1986)

Moroder's infamous "Danger Zone" collaboration with Kenny Loggins is chronicled elsewhere in the book, but that still leaves one of Moroder's biggest hits – "Take My Breath Away." He was already working with the band Berlin on the song "No More Words," and offered them the song. Though band members balked at the idea of another writer's work, finally the label told them they had to do it. Berlin had no hits at that point – "No More Words" had not yet hit shelves – but they took it on to great success.

It was a #1 hit, won an Oscar and a Golden Globe. Berlin's manager had been so confident that they wouldn't crack the top ten with the song, he offered to have his hair cut into a mohawk if they proved him wrong. Not only did he get that haircut, MTV filmed the process.

In September of 1986, Moroder opened The MusicTeam, aiming to provide a turnkey solution for producers looking to fashion a hit soundtrack. "So many soundtracks and even albums these days have multiple producers," he said in Billboard Magazine, "the logistics can be nightmarish. Why not have a team to do some projects together? The basic idea will be to provide film companies with complete soundtracks. At the same time, we'll be sensitive to the needs of movie producers about the type of music they are looking for in their projects." Among those composers included on the talent roster were the biggest names in soundtrack: Harold Faltermeyer, Keith Forsey, and others. Working out of his three-room Oasis Studios in North Hollywood, Cannon films Over The Top would be the first project under the MusicTeam banner.

As the 1980s wound down, Moroder took a step back: "I thought, 'OK, I did it, I've had six or seven No 1s, I've got my gold records, financially I'm OK, now I'll do whatever I want.'" He dropped out of music for a period in the 1990s and took on other creative ventures worthy of the king of disco – he co-designed an Italian sportscar (the Cizeta-Moroder V16T), his own brand of cognac, and a futuristic pyramidal building meant for Dubai. Following a collaboration with Daft Punk and a resurgence in his work, he has embarked on a world tour that has put him in front of crowds of 30,000 people.

6

STARS WITH GUITARS

With the rise of MTV, the idea of starting a band or becoming a rock star saw a resurgence, the likes of which probably hadn't been seen since the British Invasion. If music videos were popular and sold records, couldn't movies about the process of music-making also do well?

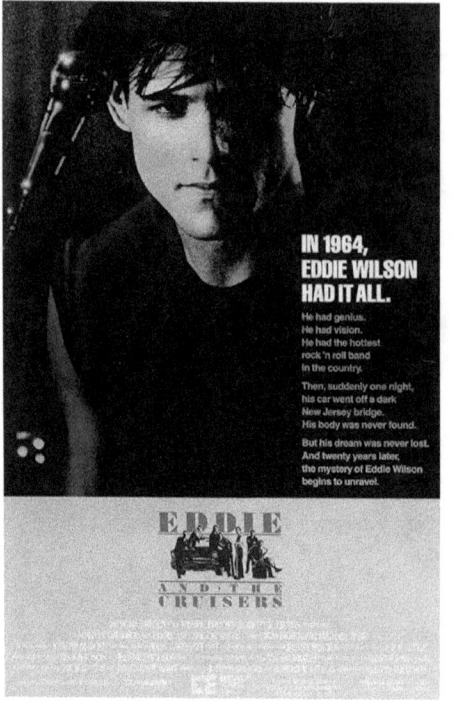

IN 1964,
EDDIE WILSON
HAD IT ALL.

He had genius.
He had vision.
He had the hottest
rock 'n roll band
in the country.

Then, suddenly one night,
his car went off a dark
New Jersey bridge.
His body was never found.

But his dream was never lost.
And twenty years later,
the mystery of Eddie Wilson
begins to unravel.

EDDIE
AND THE
CRUISERS

EDDIE AND THE CRUISERS (1983)

Eddie and the Cruisers is an effective drama that takes the world of roots rock and combines it with a *Citizen Kane*-like mystery and structure, packed with some great actors giving performances. While audiences didn't embrace it upon its original release, it gained new lease on life when the film was played in heavy rotation on HBO (some 26 times in July of 1984 alone). Between its ubiquity on cable and the videos circulating on MTV, the late exposure of the film propelled the album into Billboard's top 10, and continued to sell for years (by 1989, it had sold three million copies).

It's twenty years after the mysterious disappearance of rock and roll singer Eddie Wilson (Michael Paré). A Springsteen-ish singer with John Cougar-ish looks, Eddie apparently drove his '57 Chevy off a bridge following the completion of his bleak, and unreleased, second album. The story is framed by the investigation of a journalist (Ellen Barkin), and the recollections of the surviving band members, depicted in period flashbacks to 1963. Questions abound: Did Eddie fake his death? Did the tapes from the "Season in Hell" sessions survive? And who is the mystery man haunting the band members?

Eddie's former band members are going with their lives in different ways. Lyricist Frank (Tom Berenger) plies poetry as a high school English teacher. Manager "Doc" (Joe Pantoliano) is a disc jockey with aspirations to find a frontman and put the band back together, or at least act as a technical consultant on a proposed Eddie Wilson bio-movie. Bassist Sal (Matthew Laurance) is milking the old act at the Holiday Inn circuit. Each of them has had their living quarters turned over by break-ins, as if somebody is looking for something. Singer and Eddie's ex-girl Joann (Helen Schneider) has received mysterious phone calls and signals that suggest Eddie is on the other line.

Flashbacks illustrate the rise of the band, the personal challenges, and the eventual fall of the act when Frank's darker Rimbaud-inspired lyrical takes result in an album too far ahead of its time. After a heated

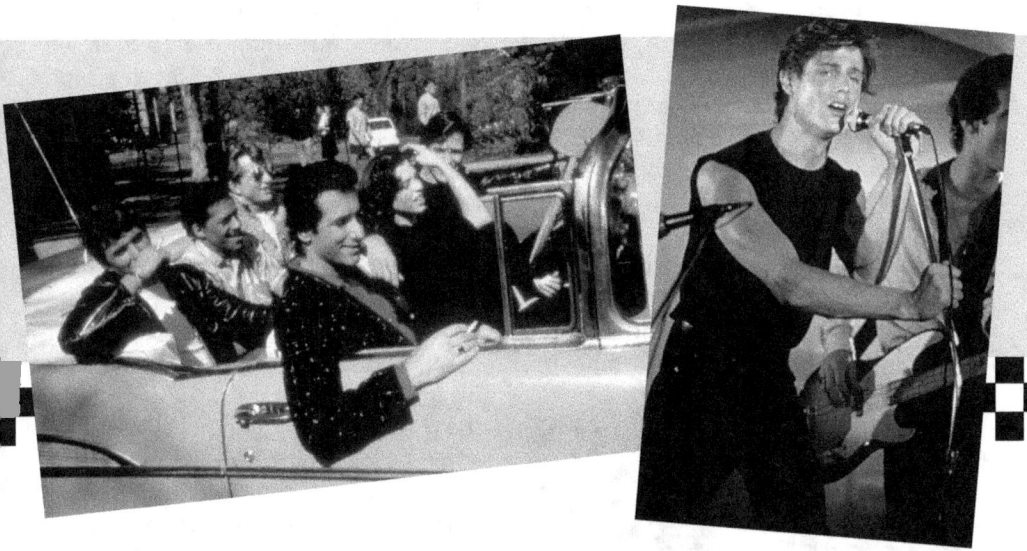

argument with record executive Lew (played by the film's real music supervisor Kenny Vance), Eddie flees the studio with Joann and escapes to a cathedral made out of car parts. He drives off into the sunrise and is never heard from again.

Back in 1983, someone is following Joann around in a 57 Chevy, making phone calls and ringing her with Eddie's old signal. You have to watch it to find out who's behind the mystery.

The film traffics in a kind of rock music wish fulfillment with the nagging questions: what if our favorite artists had one more hit album waiting in the vaults, or what if that rockstar who died too early survived in hiding? Director Martin Davidson was no stranger to period drama (*Lords of Flatbush*), and though there's not a lot of visual distinction between the period bits and the modern day scenes, the whole thing moves at a clip. The screen story is based on a novel by P.F. Kluge that has been rightly classified as a thriller – in the book the remaining band members are hunted down and killed (sounds like re-make time)! While the book is set in the doo-wop era, Davidson imagined an archetypal rocker in the mold of Dion, Jim Morrison and Bruce Springsteen. As Kluge reportedly said at the time of sale, "If a butcher buys a cow, is he gonna make changes?"

Rick Springfield lobbied for the part but producers feared he would be too recognizable a name in both music and acting to really inhabit the role. As Davidson argued, "I don't want the Rick Springfield story. It should be an unknown. People want to believe it really existed. It can't be Rick

Springfield and the Cruisers." George Thorogood and the J. Geils Band were also discussed before Michael Paré was discovered working as a chef in a New York kitchen.

Paré claimed to be able to sing and play guitar, but did neither. Paré's convincing work here was enough to snag him future roles, but Davison sometimes struggled to get a strong enough performance. In a key scene where he reacts to the loss of a friend, he had "to break down. We had 500 extras standing around, and Michael was having a hard time finding it,"

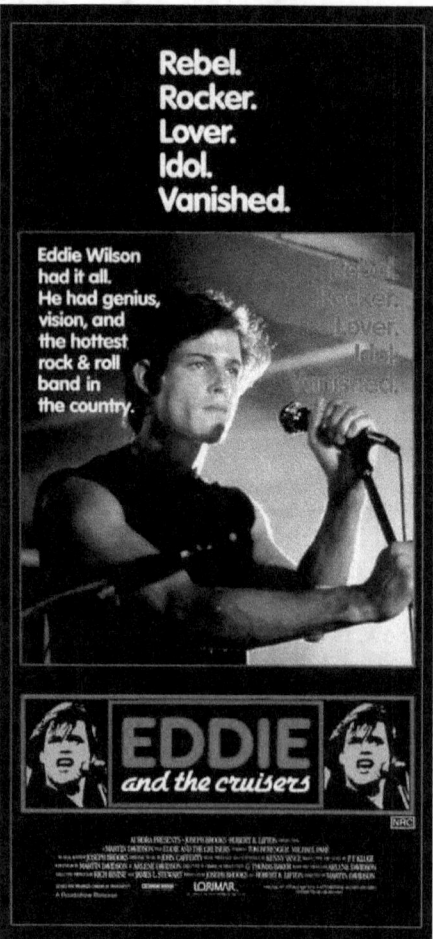

Davison recalls. "I used the situation to bring him to tears. I battered him to the point I've never battered an actor in my life. To the point it was almost too unkind. But when it was over, we hugged, and I knew I had a scene which would work in the movie."

The site of Eddie's junkyard hideout is based on a real New Jersey location. The famous "Palace of Depression" was a strange labor of love project built by a former businessman who had lost his fortune in the stock market crash and believed he was instructed by angels to build the structure out of the garbage that remained on the site when he bought it for $7. The original palace burnt down, but this unlikely movie-style recreation is a production design dream that helps underscore the scene. Eddie's quote: "He actually believed you could build a castle out of a bunch of junk. What a crock."

The Springsteen-esque Jersey sound was achieved by Jersey natives John Cafferty and the Beaver Brown Band. Early in their careers, they received advice from The Boss himself, whose advice helped them discover their songwriting chop. Cafferty likened it to "getting batting tips from Mickey Mantle."

Kenny Vance, the film's music supervisor, who had performed a similar role on *American Hot Wax* and *Animal House*, had remembered a musical act he had seen about a year before. As Vance says, "I wind up finding these guys and go up to Pawtucket, Rhode Island, where they're were about a day away from getting day jobs. They're sort of staring at me, 'Oh, another bull--- - story. I say, 'No, this is for real.' " The director's association with Stallone (having directed him in Flatbush) got him access to Scotti Bros Records to distribute the highly-successful album. Vance also sang the vocals for Sal in the Holiday Inn scenes.

The film's soundtrack is peppered with a vintage hits, and packed with traditional rock songs that worked on 80s pop radio as contemporary tunes thanks to the then-current rootsy revival of Springsteen and Cougar. The score is a neat blend of synth and guitar work. While most of the music would pass for roots rock music, the one song from the fated "Season in Hell" album is a haunting, dramatic, dirge-like cue that raises goosebumps.

The 1989 sequel, aptly titled *Eddie and the Cruisers II: Eddie Lives*, sees Michael Pare return in the title role.

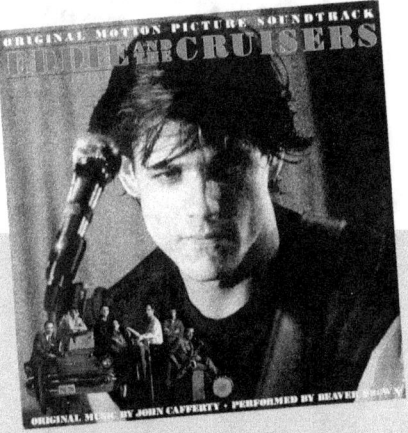

On The Dark Side

Tender Years

Runaround Sue

Down On My Knees

Hang Up My Rock And Roll Shoes

Wild Summer Nights

Boardwalk Angel

Betty Lou's Got A New Pair Of Shoes

Those Oldies But Goodies (Remind Me Of You)

Season In Hell (Fire Suite)

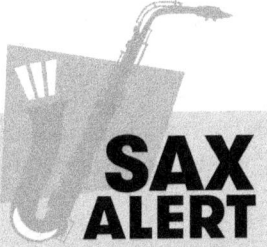

SAX ALERT

Michael "Tunes" Antunes plays Wendell Newton, the Cruiser's doomed sax player. He was the only real musician in the group and actually played for John Cafferty. The character appears to be modeled in part on Springsteen's saxist Clarence Clemmons.

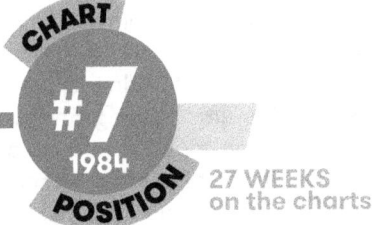

CHART

#7

1984

POSITION

27 WEEKS on the charts

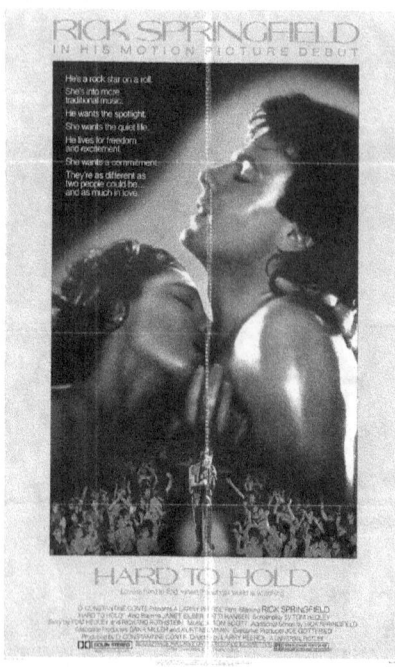

HARD TO HOLD (1984)

Rick Springfield is an Australian singer who was making chart hits there in the early 70s, and was briefly repositioned as a teen idol who even starred in his own Saturday morning cartoon on ABC by Filmation called *Mission: Magic!* For most Americans, however, his career started when he was cast in daytime drama *General Hospital* in 1981. This coincided with the release of his album *Working Class Dog*, which succeeded in a way even his management didn't expect, and he split his time touring and working on the soap opera. He's appeared in more than his share of sci-fi and fantasy roles, including the pilot for *Battlestar Galactica*, the 1998 sci-fi film *Legion*, a show based on a DC comic (*Human Target*), a vampire film (*Nick Knight*), the shows *Supernatural* and *American Horror Story*. "Bing Crosby said the important thing was to become multimedia," Springfield said in a 1984 interview. "I don't know if all this was part of a game plan for me, it was just by chance that I got into acting, but now it feels like it's some kind of design."

Hard to Hold is a romantic comedy lacking any chemistry or sexiness and is unimaginative even by romcom standards, but is a lovely tour of San Francisco with some exemplary concert footage that looks authentic because it is. The film opens with a funny update on *Hard Day's Night* – a post-concert Springfield locks himself out of his dressing room and escapes the crowd wearing only a too-small towel. Borrowing a pair of pants and a car from fat roadie Casserole (Peter Van Norden), he accidentally crashes into pretty child psychologist Diana (Janet Eilber) and falls immediately in love despite her lack of interest. Meanwhile the band struggles to record another album because without records there's no concerts, and the whole thing is complicated by his former lover and songwriter Nicky Nides (Keith Richards' wife Patti Hansen). The film co-stars Springfield's buttocks, which steal every scene they're in.

What qualifies the film for discussion is the music, and there's a good dose but not enough to elevate it to a great rock movie. His onscreen band is made of legitimate musicians and lends an air of credibility lacking from some films of the type: with drums by Mike Baird (Hall and Oates, Eddie Money, Billy Idol), Tony Fox Sales on guitar (Iggy Pop, David Bowie's Tin Machine), Robert Popwell on bass (The Young Rascals, Aretha Franklin) and Bill Mumy (yes, *Lost in Space* Billy Mumy who is a multi-instrumentalist) on keyboards. Springfield noted that concert takes were done about eighteen times: "It's been a real different experience compared to all the TV I've done which is a real 'first take' [thing]."

Springfield's character Jamie Roberts stays in the penthouse suite at the Fairmont Hotel, used to better effect as Sean Connery's room in Michael Bay's *The Rock*. His song, "Love Somebody," was written while shooting at the hotel, which is also known as the first place Tony Bennett sang "I Left My Heart in San Francisco."

Of the film, Springfield would like to personally offer his apologies to all. "That was one point in my life where [my ego] got the better of me. I remember the first time I read the script, I threw it across the room and said, 'This is garbage.' And then they said, 'Well, we're going to give you this much money.' And I said, 'Oh, I can make this work!'"

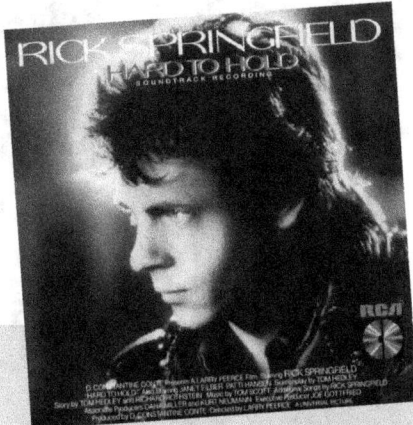

CHART #5 1984 POSITION

#26
Love Somebody
Don't Walk Away
Bop 'Til You Drop #47
Rick Springfield

Taxi Dancing
Randy Crawford

SAX ALERT

S.F.O.
Stand Up
Rick Springfield

When The Lights Go Down
Graham Parker

The Great Lost Art of Conversation
Rick Springfield

Heart of a Woman
Nona Hendryx

I Go Swimming
Peter Gabriel

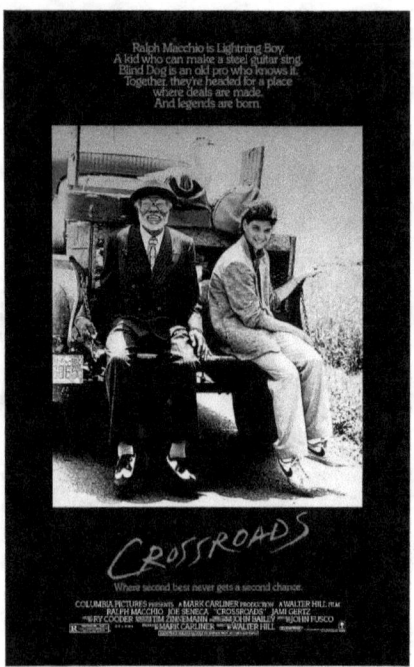

CROSSROADS (1986)

Crossroads answers the question, "did bluesman Robert Johnson really sell his soul to the devil at the crossroads to achieve his legendary musical status?" And, did he really have one song that he didn't record that could rocket teenage blues guitarist Eugene Martone (Ralph Macchio) to stardom?

At first blush the film looks like an attempt to cash in on a *Karate Kid* scenario – a teenager from New York falls under the tutelage of a master many years his senior – but Walter Hill's film is a less suburban and much darker tale, with a pretty thrilling and oft-copied conclusion. A prologue

shows Johnson making his infamous deal with an emissary of the devil in 1930's Mississippi, and then recording the songs that would make him infamous. A clever transition catapults us forward in time with technological specificity; as the 1930s acetate master of his song dissolves to a 1980s cassette going into a boombox. Eugene Martone, a student of classical guitar at Julliard, is obsessed with the Delta Blues and believes he's tracked down one of Johnson's contemporaries, harmonica player Willie Brown (Joe Seneca). Brown has been doing time for murder, at a "state pen, a prison ward, and an old folks cage." Martone gets a job as a janitor at the minimum security hospital where the elderly Brown resides, and drills him with questions about his past. Brown sees his way out of the facility: he promises to teach the kid the missing song, if the kid will break him out and get him home to Mississippi.

They get out of New York, head south, and when they run out of money Brown gives the kid the full bluesman experience as they "hobo" their way deeper and deeper into the south. Martone trades in his watch for a Fender Telecaster, a Pignose amp, and a used fedora hat, calling himself Lightning Boy Martone. On the road they run into Frances (Jami Gertz), a teenage runaway trying to get to California. Willie Brown knows they'll get more rides with her legs than they will with Martone's thumb, and so they team up.

And here's where it goes darker than *Karate Kid* ever could. The deeper they travel into the south, the less storybook it gets. Frances has no qualms about prostituting herself to a man three times her age get where she's going. The racism becomes more and more overt. Even the local black cops have it in for the trio. Lightning Boy falls for Frances, and when she leaves them the kid has finally fallen low enough to really channel the blues.

When they find the crossroads, Brown has the kid play a bit to lure out old you-know-who. Now the devil's emissary (Joe Morton) is a yuppie in a nice car, but the stakes are the same. And the slick, smiling Scratch himself (Robert Judd) appears to make the deal. If Brown wants out of the contract, the kid has to play his latest protege in a guitar contest. Lightning Boy cockily agrees, and they are transported to a dark, church-like interior where a sinister congregation awaits the battle. The devil's guitarist is a patently-80s Steve Vai, whose satanic antics are more heavy metal than blues. The end battle music is formulated around a classical piece by Niccolo Paganini – recall that Paganini allegedly sold his soul, as well – and with the help of Willie Brown's mojo the kid rides to success.

The script by John Fusco was written while he was a student at NYU, he sold it to Columbia Pictures after winning first place with it at the national FOCUS awards. His experience as a traveling blues musician fueled the screenplay and lends credence to the story, and director Walter Hill continues his collaboration with Ry Cooder on the soundtrack. Guitarist Arlen Roth was hired as a musical consultant; over the course of two months, for four days a week, Roth brought Macchio up to snuff on the instrument and did a stellar job of it. Cooder was originally intended to play the devil's guitar man Jack Butler, which would support the blues-vs-blues ending of the original screenplay. But this was the 1980s, as Roth laments. "I tried to fight tooth and nail against that last scene having the '80s heavy metal vibe, but Tim Zinnemann, the producer, would always say, 'But Arlen, this is 1984' — to which I would always reply, 'Yes, and you'll be permanently dating it as such, rather than keeping it timeless!'"

"For several of the guitar scenes, especially the ones down in Mississippi, Walter Hill would let me sit in the director's chair, since he knew nothing about what was really going on," recalls Roth. "That was a great thrill. Also, many of the parts were done right on the spot, because he'd say, 'Ralph should be playing here!' So I would record a new piece at that moment, live, and then teach it to Ralph in his trailer. I always created pieces that I knew were within the parameters of what Ralph could look believable doing, since I had created that language for him on the guitar." Macchio's classical guitar parts were recorded by Bill Kanengiser, and as such the final battle is really a blend of the work of four people, not including Macchio.

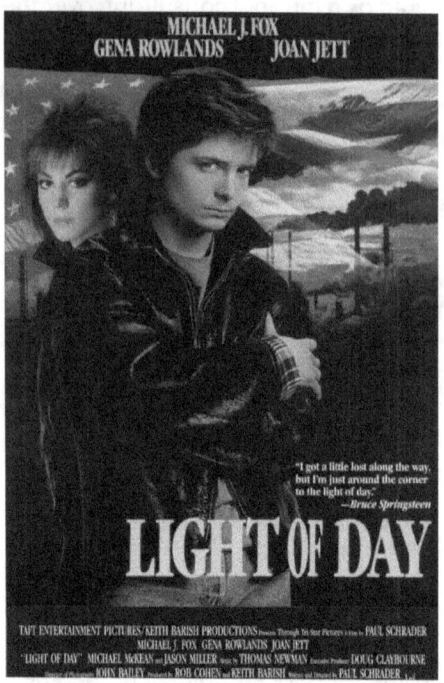

MICHAEL J. FOX
GENA ROWLANDS   JOAN JETT

"I got a little lost along the way, but I'm just around the corner to the light of day."
—*Bruce Springsteen*

LIGHT OF DAY

TAFT ENTERTAINMENT PICTURES/KEITH BARISH PRODUCTIONS Presents Through Tri-Star Pictures a film by PAUL SCHRADER
MICHAEL J. FOX GENA ROWLANDS JOAN JETT
'LIGHT OF DAY' MICHAEL McKEAN and JASON MILLER Music by THOMAS NEWMAN Executive Producer DOUG CLAYBOURNE
Director of Photography JOHN BAILEY Produced by ROB COHEN and KEITH BARISH Written and Directed by PAUL SCHRADER

LIGHT OF DAY (1987)

This one almost ended up being titled *Born in the USA* and was to star Bruce Springsteen. For a while, The Boss had entertained a foray into acting, but (perhaps wisely) changed his mind. Director Paul Schrader had requested a song from Springsteen to use in the film, and Bruce delivered "Born in the USA," itself inspired by certain phrases in the script. Springsteen ended up liking the song enough to take it back and feature it on an album that would soar to insane heights of success, and offered up a replacement that became the film's title: *Light of Day*.

The Barbusters are a working class Cleveland band led by siblings Patty (Joan Jett) and Joe Rasnick (Michael J. Fox). Bu (*Spinal Tap*'s Michael McKean) plays bass and works in the same factory as Joe. There's a drummer, a roadie, and they do their shows for weekend chump change. Patty, a single mother with a five-year old son named Benji, is willing to rob houses to get better gear. Joe shares the parenting duties with young Benji and pays off his sister's debts when she gets caught stealing.

Patty and Joe's mother (Gena Rowlands, *The Notebook*) is a pious Christian fundamentally at odds with her daughter's lifestyle, and their father (Jason Miller, *The Exorcist*) is a quiet man whose life revolves around his wife. Patty is prone to flying off the handle at mentions of God and religion, and often leaves Joe holding the kid when she runs away from her mother's overbearing influence.

A seasonal layoff at the plant (that makes commemorative Charles and Diana Royal Wedding Trays) gives the band the excuse to pool resources and hit the road, through a series of snowy midwestern dives and shows that barely break even after expenses. Joe catches Patty using young Benji to steal steaks for the band, and he makes off for home with the kid. When their mother finds out that they've been leaving the child at the motel alone while they do their gigs, she's reached her limit.

Bu says he's going back to work to catch up on the bills that got away from them while they were on tour, and is going to play with another band – a dreaded top 40 cover band

– to make ends meet. Patty auditions for a metal band called the Hunzz, and joins the group, leaving Benji with Joe. His efforts to lure her home to see her child fall on deaf ears. Only when their mother goes into the hospital for a cancer operation does Patty return. The family's long-time spiritual advisor Reverend Ansley is there for support in the hospital, and Patty recoils from him – soon we find out that he's the father of Benji, and only after an emotional and private conversation do Patty and her mother reach reconciliation. After her funeral, Patty and Joe take to the stage together for the title track.

This is one of the films from this period intended to allow Fox to stretch dramatically, and in it we see him swearing (a bit), smoking (a little) and reading *Penthouse* (not graphically). Although Fox was a smoker in real life, he had made efforts to avoid being photographed with cigarettes so as to not encourage the habit with young fans. Fox learned guitar and along with Jett and a backing group played live in front of an audience to net him that intangible experience of doing it for real. *Back to the Future* fans should note Fox using his real singing voice here, a perfectly adequate rock music voice. The two are convincing as siblings, and Jett handles her dramatic work admirably. Jett comes across as little older than a teenager here, though she was almost 30 at the time of filming.

The picture was shot mostly in Illinois, including various Chicagoland music venues and industrial landscapes. Michael Rooker is in the

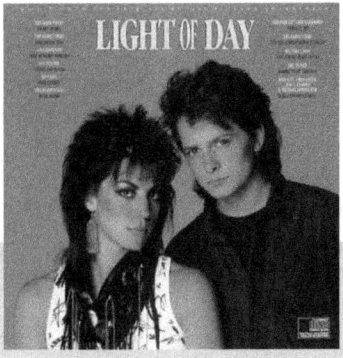

SOUNDTRACK

Light of Day
The Barbusters

This Means War
The Barbusters

Twist It Off
The Fabulous Thunderbirds

Cleveland Rock
Ian Hunter

Stay With Me Tonight
Dave Edmunds

It's All Coming Down Tonight
The Barbusters

Rude Mood
The Barbusters

Only Lonely
Bon Jovi

Rabbit's Got The Gun
Joan Jett & The Hunzz

You Got No Place To Go
Michael J. Fix

Elegy
Thomas Newman

film for a half a second, and music fans should keep their eyes peeled for an impossibly young Trent Reznor behind the keyboards as a member of The Problem (formerly known as The Sins). The enormous man who haggles with the brother and sister about the terms of their contract was Jolly Roger, a staple of the Chicago industrial music scene. The Fabulous Thunderbirds perform live in concert.

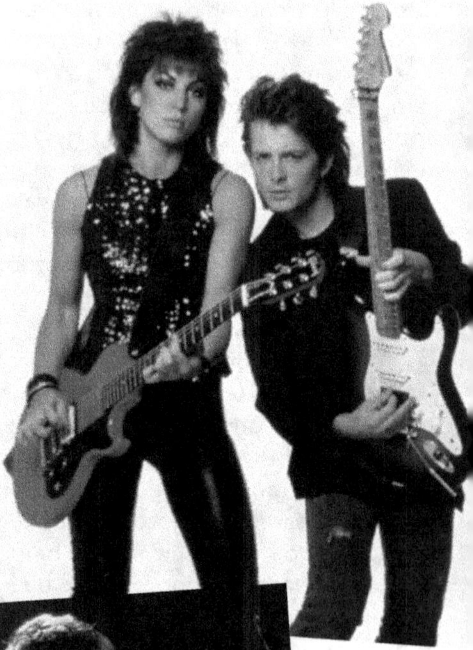

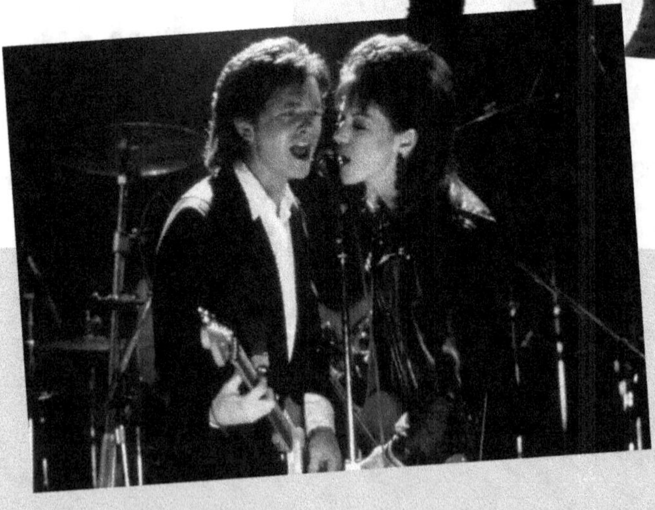

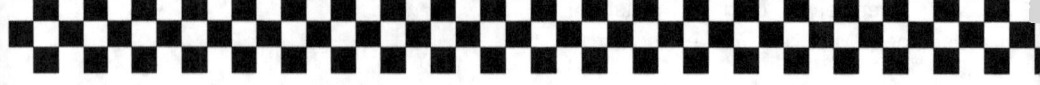

7

HARD ROCK, SOFT CELS

Once upon a time, the power of adult fantasy, album rockers, and the Canadian animation industry converged to produce a pair of unique films. For a brief moment, it looked like western animation had finally grown up. But whether it was the costly nature of animation or limited audience appeal that didn't exactly generate a Star-Wars-sized response, it didn't matter – the trend quickly burnt out. But it did leave us two midnight movie gems.

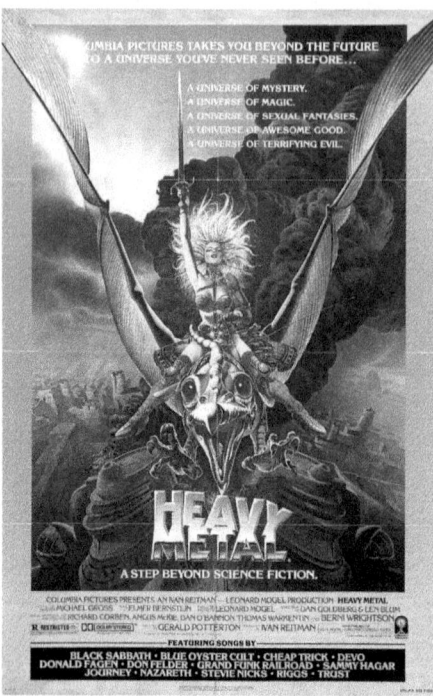

HEAVY METAL (1981)

Heavy Metal was poised for greatness: it featured some of the biggest comedians in Canada (SCTV actors Harold Ramis, John Candy, Joe Flaherty, Eugene Levy), one of the biggest movie producers of the time (Ivan Reitman, who had produced *National Lampoon's Animal House* and directed *Meatballs* and *Stripes*), a big Hollywood writer (*Alien's* Dan O'Bannon) some of the biggest names in comics (Richard Corben, Bernie Wrightson), and some of the heaviest hitters in pop and rock music.

If you're already a fan of the source material (a long-running comic magazine with an emphasis on adult European sequential art), you might see the casting as flippant, or the music as pedestrian. So what if the bands on the soundtrack were almost completely American and skewed AOR (Ex-Eagles! Ex-Fleetwood Macs! Ex-Steely Dan!) or were getting a little long in the tooth by 1981 (Nazareth, Black Sabbath, Blue Oyster Cult)? There's enough great tunes to go around, and some even match the visual material to a "T."

That the film is juvenile and irresponsible is exactly the point – it jettisons any of the deeper thinking behind the smarter comic sources and settles for lurid titillation, at which it mostly succeeds. Given Reitman's track record, the filmmakers undoubtedly saw this outing as a close kin to the *National Lampoon* brand (like *Heavy Metal*, a counterculture magazine embraced by college-age boys, full of sex, drugs, and rock and roll – and owned by the same parent company). Given the nature of the material and the marketing, it is likely that the film was only ever meant to be consumed at midnight movie screenings, with an ample buzz from the hallucinogen or inebriant of choice.

SOFT LANDING

In a sequence originally conceived by *Alien* screenwriter Dan O'Bannon for the magazine, a Corvette convertible is jettisoned from a Space Shuttle and is piloted to Earth by a man in a space suit. The guitar-driven song "Radar Rider" by Riggs gets the party off on the right foot; the car was accomplished by extensive rotoscoping.

GRIMALDI

The man from the opening sequence has brought a mysterious green object to Earth; he dissolves when he touches it. His daughter is threatened by the green orb, known as the Loc-Nar – the self described "sum of all evil." It's the glue that aims to hold the scattered narratives of the film together.

HARRY CANYON

Based in part on Moebius' story "The Long Tomorrow," Harry Canyon is a cab driver in a grungy futuristic New York city, complete with robots and illegal aliens – the kind from space. Fans of *The Fifth Element* will likely recognize some of the themes and incidents that were lifted from this story and its source material.

- "Veteran of the Psychic Wars" (Blue Öyster Cult) – fitting the tone of the film nicely, the lyrics are written by BOC's Eric Bloom and British fantasy author Michael Moorcock.
- "True Companion" (Donald Fagen)
- "Heartbeat" (Riggs) – accompanies a spirited car and hover-bike chase through the streets of NYC
- "Blue Lamp" (Stevie Nicks)
- "Open Arms" (Journey) – a #2 Hit from their 1981 album Escape, and undoubtedly the highest

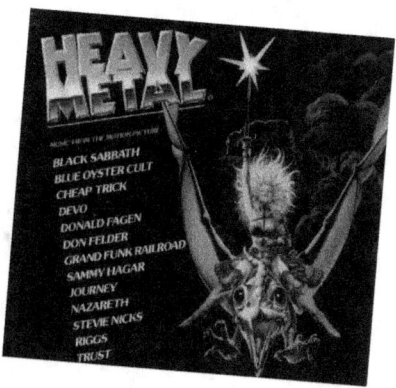

profile pop song in the film. Used as recommended, as a sexy love song for Harry and his busty female fare.

DEN

Based on the Richard Corben comic story, Den is a classic fantasy piece with a muscular hero, an evil queen, and the threat of human sacrifice to the evil god Uhluhtc (yep, that's Cthulhu backwards). John Candy's humorous voice over provides witty observations that keep this piece from getting too serious, and the striking purple and orange artwork makes a good effort at replicating Corben's style. No rock tunes in this one, just Elmer Bernstein's traditional score (similar in flavor to his score for Reitman's other big 80s hit, *Ghostbusters*)

CAPTAIN STERNN

Square-jawed space Captain Sternn has been an epically naughty boy – he's on trial for 12 counts of murder, 14 counts of armed theft, 22 counts of piracy, 18 counts of fraud, 37 counts of rape, and one moving violation. But as he tells his lawyer Charlie, he's "got an angle."

"Reach Out" by Cheap Trick is used to good effect as Sternn's star witness turns against him, enraged and hulking out to gargantuan proportions complements of the Loc-Nar.

B-17

A nightmare worthy of EC Comics, written by Dan O'Bannon. The Loc-Nar turns a bullet riddled B-17 into a haunted house, awakening the dead crew and prompting a crash landing. Don Felder's "Taking a Ride" makes an eerie match to the atmospheric, gory visuals.

SO BEAUTIFUL AND SO DANGEROUS

Based on a stunningly illustrated Angus McKie story featured in the pages of the magazine, this one goes for broke on the 70's-style counterculture concerns – blind politicians, the military industrial complex, heaps and heaps of drugs (good Nyborg, man), and free love with a robot.

"Earth women who experience sexual ecstasy with mechanical assistance always tend to feel guilty!"

This episode also jams in the most music:

- "I Must Be Dreamin'" Cheap Trick
- "Queen Bee" Grand Funk Railroad
- "Crazy? (A Suitable Case for Treatment)" Nazareth
- "All of You" Don Felder
- "Heavy Metal" Sammy Hagar
- "Prefabricated" Trust

TAARNA

Taarna takes the basic image – a silent warrior who rides a strange winged creature – from the Moebius stories Arzach, but expands it into something between John Carter of Mars and a spaghetti western.

"The Mob Rules" and "E5150" Black Sabbath
"Through Being Cool" and "Working in the Coal Mine" Devo
"Vengeance (The Pact)" Blue Öyster Cult

The soundtrack album peaked at number 12 on the Billboard 200 chart, and nicely encapsulates the clash of music cultures at work in the late 70s and early 80s. Just as the music of Heavy Metal is caught between hard rock and new wave worlds, the album feels like what might be on the radio if your 1979 Chevy Van could pick up the signal as it travelled between the distant galaxies depicted in the movie. The film's visuals are the work of 1000 artists in 17 countries, working quickly (11 weeks) to produce the project.

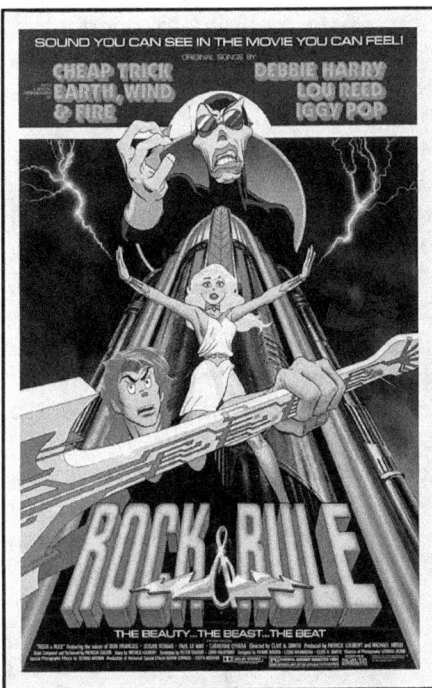

ROCK & RULE (1983)

A wonderful window opened following the success of *Heavy Metal*, with the opportunity for quirky adult-oriented films to find an audience and lead a long healthy life on the midnight movie circuit. If animation was easier to do, we might have seen more films like *Heavy Metal*, but the complexity of production versus the size of the audience was such that no one really tried to capitalize on its success. Ralph Bakshi had been down this road before with adult-oriented animation, and even apocalyptic ones like *Wizards* (1977), but 1983's *Rock & Rule* should taken the prize. Just how did audiences miss out

on an animated film about mutant anthropomorphized street animals in a rock band, with drug use and cursing and Lou Reed, from the people who brought us the Care Bears?

Omar, Angel, Izzy, and Stretch are bandmates (the band is called "The Drats," which is not mentioned in the American cut of the film but was the working title of the movie) in the post apocalyptic city of Ohmtown, populated by mutant street animals. It's got vaguely Middle Eastern architecture, boasts the biggest remaining power plant, and is the home of superrocker Mok. Mok is a sorcerer/rock star bent on world domination, coming across like a wild-eyed, tripped-out mutant Mick Jagger. When a recent concert proves to be a couple seats short of being completely sold out, the vengeful Mok decides to lay ruin to the already ruined Earth. To do so, he must find the Armageddon Key, and the special vocal frequency needed to unleash a powerful demon from another dimension. And who should have that "one voice" but local singer Angel?

Mok invites the band up to his vast mountain retreat, where his rollerskating dog-goons The Schlepper Brothers (Toad, Sleazy, and Zip) welcome them. Mok drugs the boys and kidnaps the girl, whisking her away in a massive airship to his residence in Nuke York, a Blade Runner-esque tower situated atop Radio City Music Hall. Omar and the boys snap out of it, steal a cop car, and drive across the wasteland to Nuke York but are waylaid by the authorities.

Angel escapes briefly with the plump, plush Schlepper sister Cindy as she makes her nightly rounds to a disco called Club 666, touted as "the hottest antigravity club in the city." Earth Wind and Fire provides "Dance Dance Dance," consumed by a crowd of tattooed, cross-dressing, and scantily dressed mutants. Omar and the band track down Angel but are captured and tortured by Mok, forcing Angel to cooperate with his plans to sing for him. The boys are brainwashed and sent back to Ohmtown, but Mok's "Carnage Hall" (yes that's spelled right and it's pronounced Car-NAY-gee) concert proves a failure. The interdimensional demon destroys the venue before failing to fully materialize, with the offscreen destruction delivered by surviving fans in a series of news reports). Mok requires more power for the spell, and the only place to get it is Ohmtown.

Angel is drugged and wired directly to Mok's machines, where her singing is controlled by Mok's theremin-like hand gestures. The boys snap out of their stupor in the nick of time, and rush to her aid. The demon materializes looking like pulsing, backlit raw hamburger (which it appears to be, based on the behind-the-scenes footage). Omar arrives pissed off and ready to fight, and joins Angel in her song. A duet turns out to be the antidote, fulfilling the prophecy that "no ONE" can send back the demon but a duet between Debbie Harry and Robin Zander of Cheap Trick can. It's "one voice, one heart, one song," that sends the demon back and Mok plummeting

to his doom, as the power plant is illuminated by the same backlit glow that would be used to good effect in the Care Bears magic in years to come.

Rock & Rule actually went into production concurrently with *Heavy Metal* starting in 1979, requiring Nelvana to skip out of providing animation work for that film. Employing 300 animators over the course of four years is not cheap, and the film cost a whopping $8 million – quite nearly putting Nelvana out of business. I think it's a fair price to pay, for the movie is fully, lovingly animated with almost no cheats, peppered with special effects, airbrush animation,

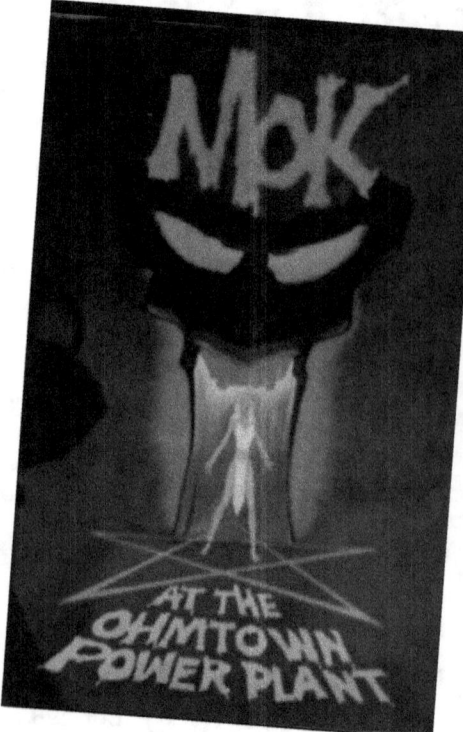

and nascent computer graphics. The evocative apocalyptic design work should get any *Heavy Metal* fan salivating, whether you were introduced to *HM* via the magazine or the movie.

The original script for R&R is an expansion of their short film "The Devil and Daniel Mouse," and explains some of the family-oriented roots of the story. As work progressed, the story got darker and more adult. The character of Omar, voiced originally by Greg Salata, was deemed dour and unpleasant. MGM/UA was set to distribute it but demanded changes upon seeing the final cut, resulting in the recasting of Omar and some expensive story changes. Omar was revoiced by Paul Le Mat (*American Graffiti*) and softened a little bit. The version with Salata was aired on Canadian TV, and sports a better sound mix and some missing material.

Perhaps the music of the film fares better, though no soundtrack album was released the individual works ended up in most of the artist's recorded catalog somewhere. Debbie Harry was instructed by the directors not to perform as an animated character but with the full faculties of her rock persona to give the characters presence and weight, and her appearances in Angel's songs are among the best in the movie. Mok is mostly voiced in song by Lou Reed, which doesn't seem like a great match to his more animated speaking performance, and then by Iggy Pop which seems more convincing to me. Reed's "My Name is Mok" works the best of Reed's songs, according

to Reed "I could identify with (Mok) up to a point, and become that way with him, have him breathe as a real person." When the film shows Mok throwing off powerful bursts of magic as he struts for the camera, Reed says he was happy to see something on screen that was as good as his song (suggesting that maybe he is a little more Mok like than I thought)! Iggy Pop's brief was to "inflict," so he pondered what to inflict on the audience and came up with "Pain and Suffering, a pretty dark tune with lines like:

A cow floats Upside down in a river of mud
The skull of a ghost makes love to you, You're my doll
A cat, black with green eyes And blood everywhere

The final song "Send Love Through" is a complicated technological collaboration between the film's electronic music composer Patricia Cullen (whose minimalistic score provides some great analog soundscapes for the movie), Chris Stein and Debbie Harry from Blondie, and Cheap Trick's Robin Zander. Multitrack tape masters were shipped back and forth from Canada and the cities where the bands were working, and required several machines working synchronously to thread up the tracks that results in a dense collaboration between all three parties.

The film's failed initial release in the US netted a paltry $30K, thanks in part

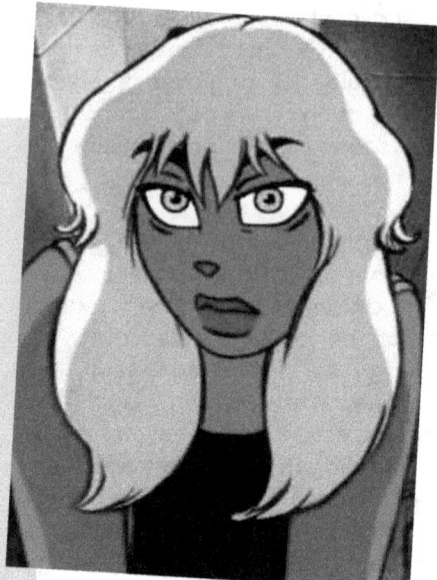

ON THE SOUNDTRACK

- **Deborah Harry** – Angel's Song (rewritten and released as May Be For Sure on the 1989 album Def, Dumb and Blonde)
- **Deborah Harry** – Invocation Song
- **Cheap Trick** – Born to Raise Hell
- **Cheap Trick** – I'm The Man
- **Cheap Trick** – Ohm Sweet Ohm (all three Cheap Trick songs were included on their 1996 boxset, Sex America: Cheap Trick)
- **Lou Reed** – My Name Is Mok
- **Lou Reed** – Triumph
- **Earth Wind & Fire** – Dance Dance Dance
- **Melleny Brown** – Hot Dogs and Sushi
- **Iggy Pop** – Pain & Suffering (released as an extra track on the 2003 re-release of his Zombie Birdhouse album)
- **Deborah Harry and Robin Zander** – Send Love Through

to a regime change at distributor MGM, but found its footing in the HBO-Showtime late night airings that followed in subsequent years. I think that it's oversight is criminal, and this is a gem that's superior to most of *Heavy Metal*. The presence of some drug use, some boobs, and some swearing are all that keeps it from being an all-audiences film, unless you parent like I do and it goes right into circulation with the Disney pics.

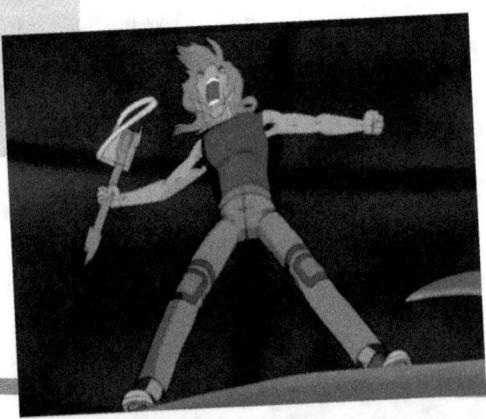

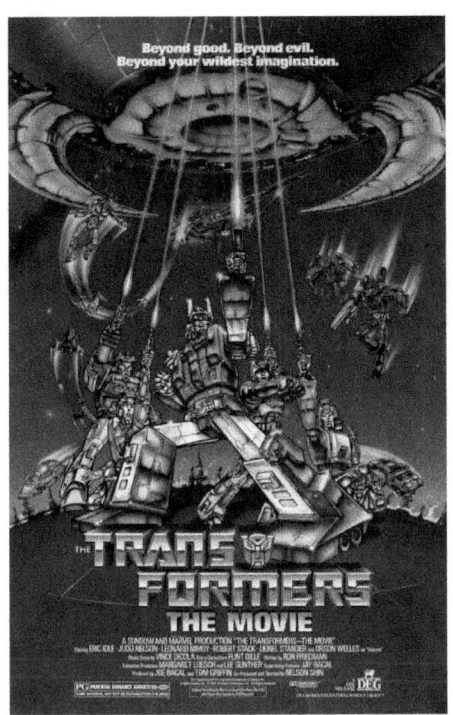

THE TRANSFORMERS: THE MOVIE (1986)

Certainly the movie with the most "the's" in the title, The Transformers: The Movie may be the first feature length animated film based on a tv-show based on a toy (but it won't be the last).

In the far-flung year of 2005, two warring races of mechanized aliens fight each other and a planet-sized robot voiced by Orson Welles. Welles died five days after recording the tracks for the film, telling his biographer before he passed away "you know what I did this morning? I played the voice of a toy." This is strictly for people who were already

into it – either the toys or the cartoon or both – but is energetic, epic, and exhausting.

The high-end Japanese production was budgeted at six times the normal cost of the episodic animation and it shows, with loads of hand-animated destruction hurtling through every frame. It really is the genetic material of a dozen similar big budget films decades later, with very little to follow and too much to look at. The Autobots and kin inhabit a world where specifically 80s technology – cassette players, Mack Trucks, and fighter jets – has learned to speak in a combination of violent threats and jokey one-liners. Coupled with the soundtrack it is a distinctly 80s document.

That soundtrack is wall to wall rock music, and when it's not all-out songs it's a heavy-guitar and synth score by Vince DiCola that adds a lot of apparent production value in that 80s sort of way. The picture and sound are appropriately married, there's nary a moment of silence to go with the exhausting visuals. Amazingly, the music is way heavier metal than was featured in the movie Heavy Metal. The album was another Scotti Brothers record, a name often associated with big soundtrack records of the period.

Stan Bush was a singer songwriter mostly known for soundtrack contributions around this time, although he had released one self-titled album in 1983. He submitted songs for the 2007 live action Transformers film but they were not used, including a remake of "The

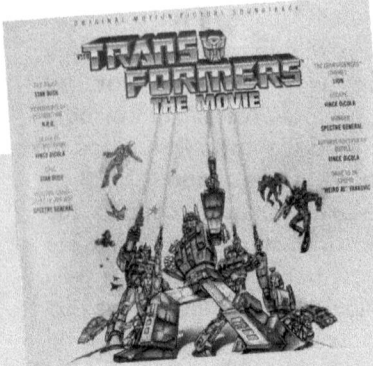

SOUNDTRACK

The Touch
Stan Bush

Instruments of Destruction
N.R.G.

The Death of Optimus Prime
Vince DiCola

Dare
Stan Bush

Nothin's Gonna Stand in Our Way
Spectre General

The Transformers (Theme)
Lion

Escape
Vince DiCola

Hunger
Spectre General

Autobot/Decepticon Battle
Vince DiCola

Dare To Be Stupid
"Weird Al" Yankovic

Touch." Additionally, that song was co-opted by Paul Thomas Anderson for a memorable scene from *Boogie Nights* (1997).

Spectre General is the screen name of Canadian heavy metal band Kick Axe, who changed their name for legal reasons on the soundtrack. "Nothing's Gonna Stand in Our Way" is a cover of a song from the film *Savage Streets* (1984). The band broke up a few years later.

Yankovic's "Dare To Be Stupid" sounds like it should be out of place if you're a fan (and spot on if you're not), but works great in the film. The tune is an elaborate on-the-nose recreation of a Devo song, produced by Rick Derringer so accurately to the Devo sound that Mark Mothersbaugh himself was flabbergasted: "I was in shock," said Mothersbaugh. "It was the most beautiful thing I had ever heard. He sort of re-sculpted that song into something else and... I hate him for it, basically."

8

HUMAN HIGHWAY

What is Human Highway? Surreal prototype for 1980s independent film movement? Extended Devo music video? Drunken Neil Young concert pseudo-documentary? To answer that we must look at the roots of both artists and figure out how they converged and collided with an all star cast in 1982 for a meandering but wholly unique feature film.

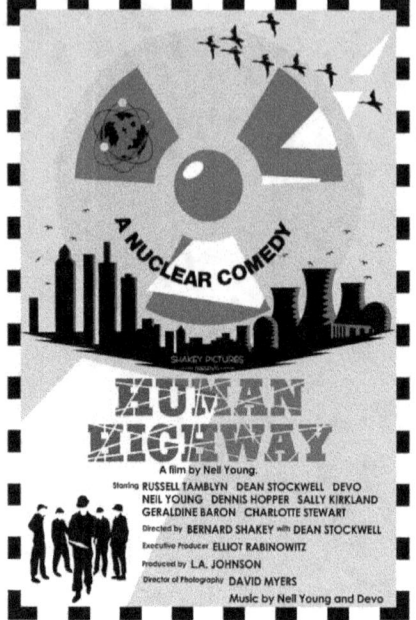

one equally rich with experimentation. Some of *Young's songs that appear in Human Highway* are featured on his 1982 album *Trans*, one that seems equally inspired by Devo and the work of German pioneers Kraftwerk.

Young's son Ben had been born with cerebral palsy, and could not speak or communicate; Young and his wife Pegi were spending 15-hour days at therapy programs. Having recently purchased a Sennheiser Vocoder VSM201 and Synclavier, he observed a remarkable reaction from his son Ben when he spoke to him through the heavy distortion of the vocoder. In many ways, *Trans*, which features several songs in which the vocals are vocoder-effected, is meant for his sons and about his sons' condition.

Trans has been out of print in the US for years and was the subject of a lawsuit with Geffen Records, who demanded $3 million in lost sales over Trans and the rockabilly tinged follow up *Everybody's Rockin'*. They argued that they signed him to do Neil Young records not uncommercial experiments, making him the first artist to get sued for not sounding like himself. Since Geffen had given Young full creative freedom on the records, they lost in court.

Devo formed at Ohio at Kent State University following the infamous National Guard shootings; founder Gerald Casale was himself a witness to the shootings. "Until then," Casale has recalled, "I was a hippie. I thought, the world is essentially good." The idea that man was regressing, de-evolving, took root from the incident.

Neil Young may be a name you don't immediately associate with filmmaking, yet he has been using film as an extension of his enormous creative output since 1974, when he took the reins of his concert film *Journey Through the Past*. His 1979 film *Rust Never Sleeps* (whose title was inspired by one of Devo's pre-fame day jobs as graphic designers for Rustoleum) must have given him quite the taste for increasingly weird cinematic hijinks, capturing a wild stage performance that included robed Jawas from *Star Wars* crawling around oversized amplifiers.

Anyone who can tell the difference between a flowerpot hat and plastic hair knows what kind of imagery and sounds to expect from Devo at this point in their history, but for Neil Young the period of 1978-1982 was

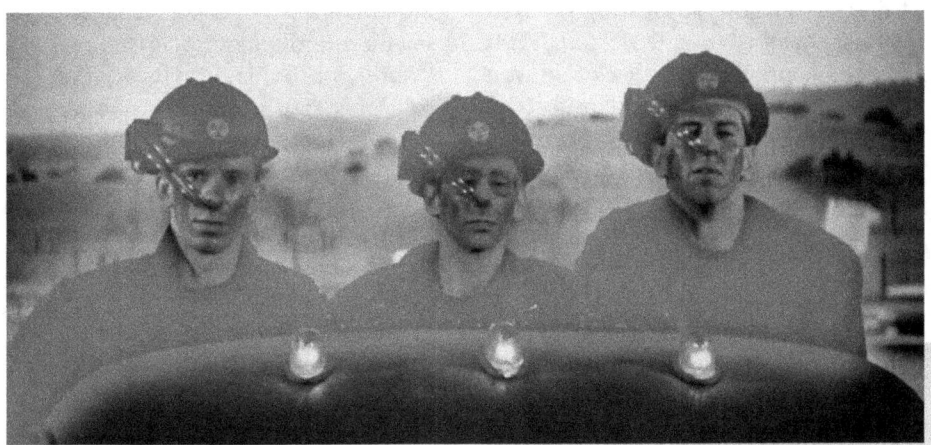

It's easy to argue that Devo's entire stance is one of anti-corporation, arriving when they did (as the counterculture was being crushed by the corporate culture) and arriving as they did, lampooning establishment songs like the Rolling Stones' "Satisfaction." Their adoption of a mechanized, synth-dominated sound long before it was fashionable made them stand apart from the crowd, and when the rest of the world caught up to that sound it made them seem a quirky novelty act with one notable hit.

Devo started making promotional films with Minneapolis-based filmmaker Chuck Statler, long in advance of MTV. Statler met Devo's Mothersbaugh and Casale at Kent State and recorded their first filmed performance in 1971. Devo had seemingly run its course, and having tried the usual routes to musical success they were about to hang it up.

DEVO
- Come Back Jonee
- Worried Man
- Hey Hey, My My

NEIL YOUNG
- Mr Soul
- Computer Age
- Transformer Man
- We R In Control / CCTB = Chemical Computer Thinking Battery
- Sample and Hold
- Computer Cowboy

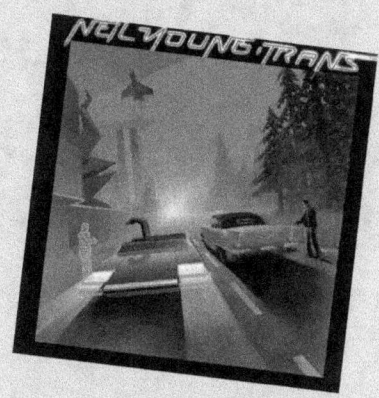

At a late-night diner meeting between Statler and Casale, Statler pitched the idea of making a Devo film. That film, *The Truth About De-Evolution* won a prize at the Ann Arbor Film Festival in 1976 and attracted the attention of David Bowie, who helped get them signed at Warner.

Neil Young first saw Devo when they played the Starwood Club in West Hollywood in 1977 and knew immediately he wanted to work with them. At first, this consisted of the initial filmed segment that would be later incorporated into the film as a dream sequence. The unrehearsed Devo-Young duet on Neil's "Hey Hey My My," was shot in 1978, and cut down from a much longer section to ten minutes.

It may come as no surprise that *Human Highway* had no script. One of the film's producers was Jeanne Field, who also crewed on *Eraserhead* and *The Last Waltz* – and doesn't *Human Highway* seem like the mutant child of both of those in retrospect? Field reportedly presented Neil with a treatment that proposed a sort of Rock and Roll *Wizard of Oz*. It would feature Neil as a dorky mechanic, which as a tinkerer, mechanic, and lover of model trains he very much was. According to actor Russ Tamblyn, shooting days would begin with the question "What's the plan today, Neil?" to which he always replied "The plan today is no plan!" Scenes would be shot, and someone would transcribe what was spoken into script form afterwards, a method that Young claims was inspired by Charlie Chaplin's process.

Additional scenes were filmed on a tour bus and in Taos, New Mexico, before the bulk of shooting began at Raleigh Studios in Los Angeles in 1981. The company shot for two months in the self-contained world of the diner and its environs, with a young Kevin Costner uncredited on the crew as one of the stage managers.

Casale reports that Devo started out merely providing the opening scenes but started being integrated more and more as the shoot progressed. Mothersbaugh

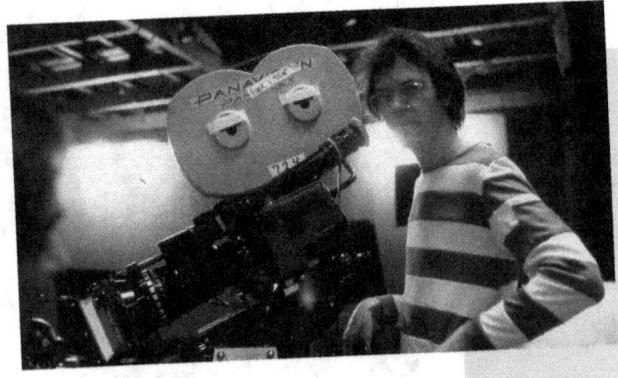

A BOY NAMED LIONEL

Neil Young plays Lionel, a name inspired by his love of toy trains. In true "I loved it so much I bought the company" style, Young was part owner of the Lionel train company, is listed as co-inventor on several of their patents, and remains on its board of directors today.

was turned off by the atmosphere on set that oscillated between rock-star worship and drug-soaked party. "We were kind of repulsed by the whole experience. I thought Dennis Hopper was retarded when we met. He couldn't say his lines. He couldn't speak a sentence. He just ignored every direction he got. He was a short-order cook in the movie and he was playing with a knife and he ended up cutting Sally Kirkland really bad. She ended up suing Neil Young."

If the story is about anything, it is about the last day on earth before a nuclear holocaust, and the goings on between some less-than-normal people at a diner and gas station in rural America. Dean Stockwell is the diner's new owner, a man so bitter he puts salt in his coffee. He plans to torch the place to collect the insurance, which might be a good idea as the neighborhood nuclear reactor seems doomed to blow at a moment's notice.

Young's character is Lionel, an innocent dummy who appears to be wearing Mark Mothersbaugh's glasses. The rest of the cast labels him a "dork." He comes across like a cast member of *Revenge of the Nerds*, but seems rooted in classic comedic characters that date back to the silent era. Russ Tamblyn as his partner Fred is a great slapstick foil, and the two have some Laurel and Hardy-like banter. They're clearly having fun, and it's up to the audience to join them, but the film's lack of traditional structure is enough to put off anybody who isn't up to the task. Young also plays his own idol, a loungey-looking singer named Frankie Fontaine who appears briefly in the back seat of a limousine.

Young is not the only one doing double duty in the film. Dean Stockwell appears in a photograph as the father of his other character. Dennis Hopper is a short order cook as well as a businessman on his way to Megapolitan City, that arrives at the diner to declare:

"I don't feel, I'm an executive."

It's all bizarre from there. Lots of live animals appear on set, including an owl, a crow that bites Neil on the nose, and a raccoon that gets fed by Dennis Hopper out the back window of the kitchen. Lionel plays a song by striking his wrenches with a hammer. He narrates his mechanical procedures like an astronaut reporting an operation back to mission control. When he is knocked out by a tool to the head (Fred thinks he may have gotten a "conclusion"), he dreams himself a music celebrity and watches a totally country-westerned Devo perform "Come Back Jonnee" to a punkish crowd. A group of Native Americans build a pyre out of cigar store Indian statues.

When the air raid sirens go off and missile launches suddenly from the nearby silo, Devo mascot-character Booji Boy arrives in a truck and hands out radiation-symbol-adorned shovels for folks to dig their own graves.

"You got any last minute shopping to do, you better get it done now, 'cause this planet's got the shits and it's about to blow. There ain't nobody getting out of this one. So dig that hole and dance!"

The remaining cast joins in an exuberant, joyous production number of "Takes a Worried Man" using their shovels as props before the bombs drop.

In his biography *Shakey*, Young seems to cite Godzilla films as an influence on the movie's use of miniatures and sets "Cheap Japanese horror-movie kind of things? I like that vibe. I like something that's so unreal that you could believe it..." He also claimed, "I wanted it to look like a storybook so people could realize that there was nothing real about it."

Young saw filmmaking as a way to keep music from becoming boring, a chance to play and to experiment with acting. That sense of play is evident in *HH* and maybe puts it in the same category as *Magical Mystery Tour* – directed by a rock star who didn't know any better. "I really like the art of filmmaking," Young said. "It has to be something that sparks me to do it — to have a thought and an idea. That's probably why I haven't made that many films."

Could *HH* have had an impact on David Lynch, fresh off of *Eraserhead* and *Elephant Man*? There are undeniable parallels between *HH* and *Blue Velvet*, with the obvious casting of Dean Stockwell and Dennis Hopper, the oddball Americana angle and artificiality that would be used to good effect in Twin Peaks. It predates Alex Cox's weirdness (complete with *Repo Man's* Fox Harris as a sheik, or Dennis Hopper as a businessman per *Straight to Hell*) and perhaps predicts *Pee Wee's Playhouse* completely artificial and retro world.

I was introduced to this film on VHS in the 1990s, but the film has since been re-edited and restored, with an additional eight minutes of footage and now sports a soundtrack remastered directly from the on-set dialog tracks. "It's kind of grown on me with time," said Mothersbaugh. "At the time, we discounted it, but 10 years ago, I went to some arts cinema and saw it again. I liked it more in retrospect. Devo actually has some of the best parts of the movie. It's a truly weird piece of history."

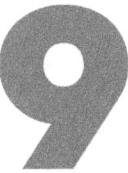

DANGER ZONE: THE IMPORTANCE OF BEING KENNY

Wherein we unironically explore the impact of one Kenneth Clark Loggins on the phenomenon of popular music in 80s films. Yes, we're doing this. A chapter on Loggins. It deserves a whole book.

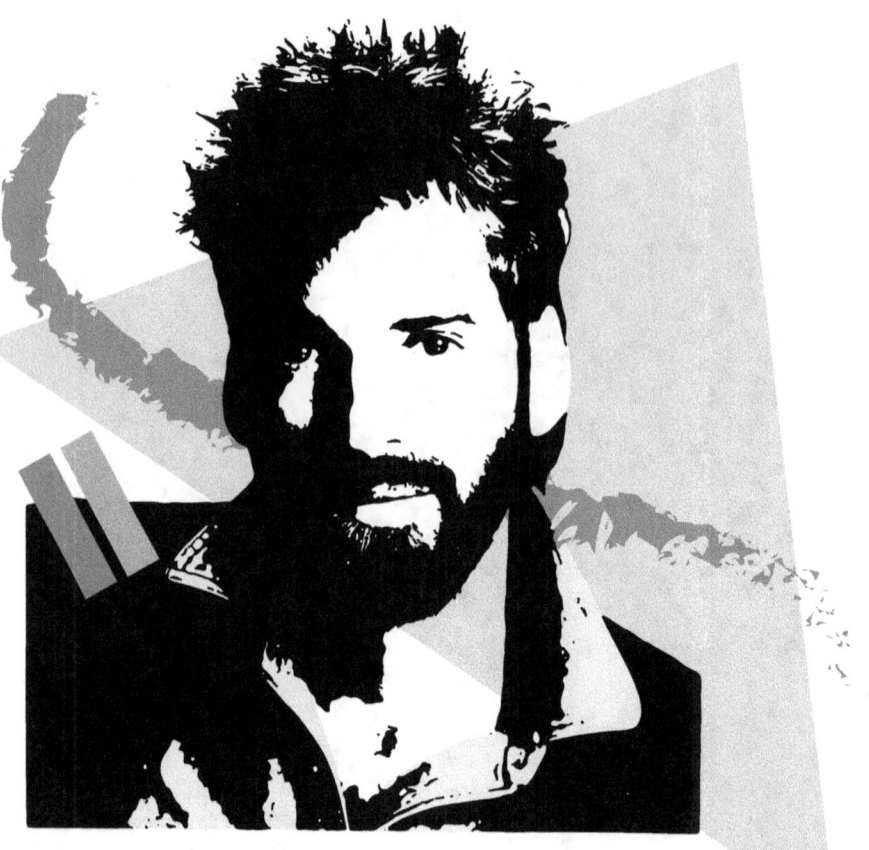

Kenny Loggins cites seeing the Jimmy Cagney film *Yankee Doodle Dandy* at age 8 as the inspiration to take up songwriting. That he should then be forever linked to movie songs is appropriate enough. The unofficial King of the Movie Soundtracks has since come to terms with the responsibility: "It doesn't hurt to have a title like that, I suppose," he says modestly. "But I actually think Celine Dion did more than I did. That's my guess, I remember she had a string of them for a while." Fair assessment, but in the 80s it was Loggins who held court, and he found himself at the forefront of an industry shift that would prove to be very lucrative for songwriters who understood the craft of storytelling. And being rockstar cool helped everybody involved. "The hipper the music, the hipper the movie," Loggins says. "Hollywood jumped on it." With the synergy between movie and soundtrack so closely aligned in the 80s, it begs the question: with movies like *Footloose*, were the songs successful because of the movie or the other way around? Loggins responds with trademark modesty. "I think that's debatable, but I think it was the movie — and the songs didn't hurt... I'm fortunate in that I was associated with movies that have become such cult classics."

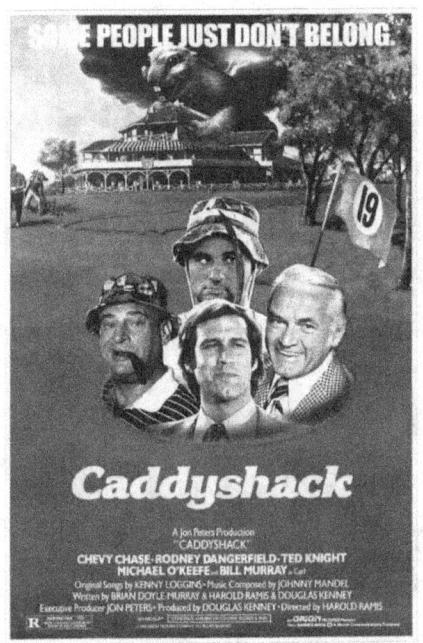

CADDYSHACK (1980)

Is *Caddyshack* the first 80s comedy? While spawned from the same petri-dish that produced *National Lampoon's Animal House*, it sets the stage for the type of comedy that would become the trademark of the 80s. One can argue that *Animal House* and *Blues Brothers* are 70s films – with a 70s sensibility that stems from that no-holds barred (and drug fueled?) *Saturday Night Live* culture, and steeped in nostalgia for a time that had passed – both musically and culturally. But *Caddyshack* is a contemporary film with contemporary songs, and sets the tone immediately with a fantasy element that must have seemed radical at the time. Is it that much of a reach between the super-intelligent gopher of *Caddyshack* and the ghosts of *Ghostbusters*? In fact *Caddyshack* might be the more fantastic of the two films, as even fewer of the characters in *Caddyshack* are grounded in any kind of reality. Director Harold Ramis admits that the opening with the gopher excused nearly all kinds of behavior to follow, and let all the actors off the hook no matter how outrageous their take on the material. "And it didn't hurt having a really good Kenny Loggins song at the beginning," said Ramis.

Loggins was offered a shot at making songs for the film thanks to his relationship with the film's producer Jon Peters, who would go on to redefine the role of the producer with the 1989 megahit *Batman*. Peters had joined his parent's hairstyling business and happened to create a wig for Barbra Streisand in a 1974 comedy called *For Pete's Sake*. Peters and Streisand struck up a relationship that would see him dating her, producing her albums, and then producing her film *A Star is Born*. Nice career trajectory, Jon! Loggins had written the song "I Believe in Love" for that film, and as such was an early choice for *Caddyshack*.

Loggins recalls: "When I did "I'm Alright," most pop music was not in movies. It was a brand-new thought. We wondered if pop music would even work in movies. Jon Peters left Barbra Streisand and went solo, and the first movie that he produced was *Caddyshack*, and he knew that it had to be a rock and roll soundtrack. He was young enough to get that idea."

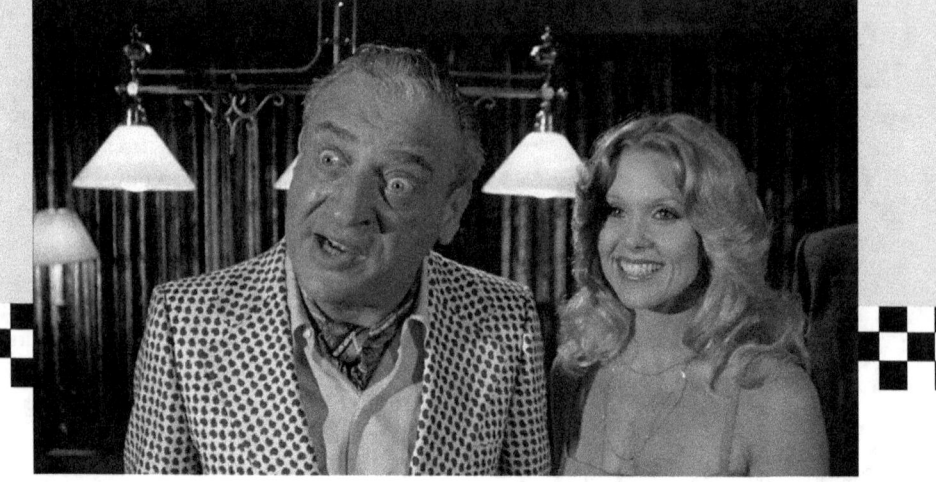

I'm alright
Nobody worry 'bout me
Why you got to gimme a fight?
Can't you just let it be?

"I'm Alright" (Billboard #7) was inspired by what is ostensibly the film's lead character, Danny Noonan. "The character was trying to figure out where he fit. But at the same time he wanted people to leave him alone and let him find his own way. So I wanted to grab him and summarize that character, and that's what 'I'm Alright' is doing."

Eddie Money was recording in a nearby studio, and Loggins convinced him to sing on this song. Money can be heard singing certain lines, including "You make me feel good!" Money was unhappy that he never got credit for his contribution. "I'm not a fan of Kenny Loggins to tell you the truth," he told a radio show host in 2014.

Any of Loggins trepidations about his rock reputation after providing a soundtrack for a dancing gopher have since vanished. "The gopher's my best friend now, we sell 'em at concerts." The song peaked at #7 on the US Billboard Hot 100, and stayed on the charts for 22 weeks in 1980.

Also in the film are "Mr. Night and "Lead the Way." "Mr. Night" was another upbeat, classic rock-type track with pounding pianos and saxophones over a slap bass foundation, originally found on his 1979 album "Keep the Fire." "Lead the Way" is a straightforward ballad that's so heartfelt it seems out of place in the film, but remember that the movie was conceived as a coming-of-age story for the young caddies. It was only in the editing room that the original story would be overshadowed

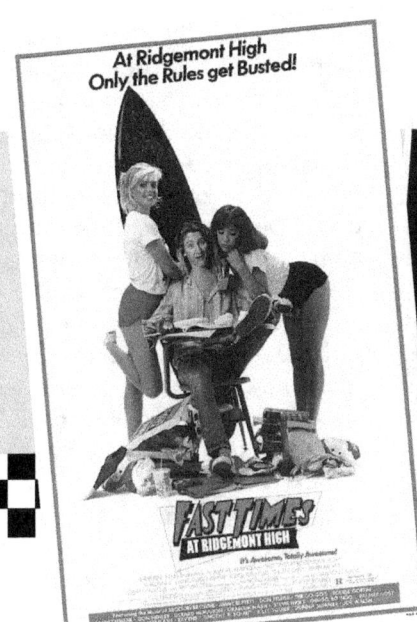

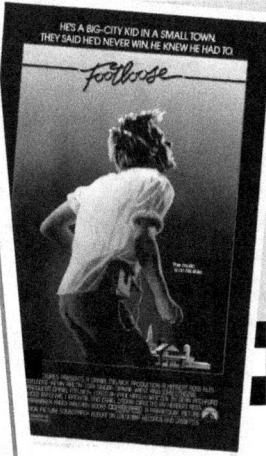

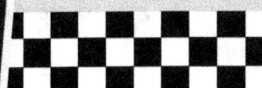

by the raucous slobs-versus-the-snobs subplot, and the film soon focused on the comedy legends that starred, not the young talent.

PERSONAL BEST (1982)

The Robert Towne-directed sports film uses two older Loggins songs, including the sad song "You Don't Know Me," from 1976's *Celebrate Me Home* album, and "What a Fool Believes" with Michael McDonald. That song is most well known for its recording by the Doobie Brothers in 1979 but represents the first collaboration with McDonald. "I'd like to say we were writing together before we met," Loggins said. "We had both been hunting each other down to do some writing. As I pulled up to his house I was getting the guitar out of the trunk and the door to his house

was open and I heard him in his room practicing song ideas. He had this one idea. He didn't have any words yet but he did that mumble thing and my imagination grabbed me. As I started knocking on the door, he stops and my imagination kept going and I heard dee dah dah doo doo doo. So I knock on the door and say 'Mike, hey, I think I know how that next part goes.' So I went in and we kept writing right on that same song." The pair won a Best Song Grammy - Loggins' first - for the tune in 1979.

FAST TIMES AT RIDGEMONT HIGH (1982)

It's hard when you want somebody
And it feels like anybody will do

"Never Surrender" is a collaboration, co-written with the Eagle's guitarist Don Felder. It's a rousing rocker with a synthy base and prominent guitar work, and a great duet between the two. Strict Eagles fans would point to this song as the start of the slide away for Felder, from the Eagle's trademark folk sound to the poppier (read "electronic") 80s material that would characterize his 80s catalog (culminating in "The Heat is On" from *Beverly Hills Cop*).

FOOTLOOSE (1984)

**Been working so hard
I'm punching my card
Eight hours for what?
Oh, tell me what I got**

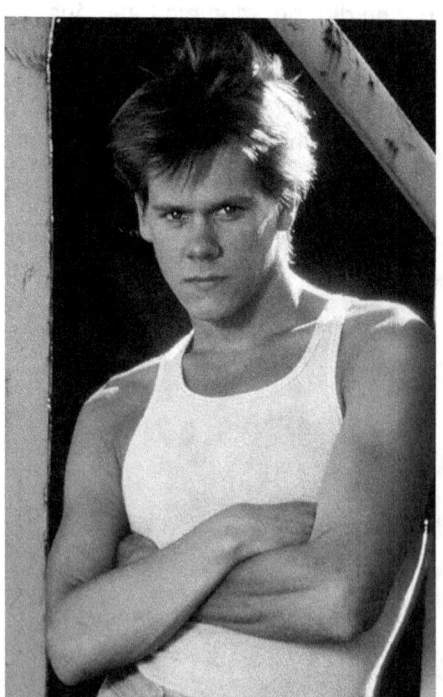

With the title song that would perhaps define Loggins career, he found himself collaborating with an unusual partner: the film's screenwriter. "I had been collaborating with Dean Pitchford as a songwriter, and Dean and I would write lyrics together." Among those collaborations was "Don't Fight It," which was a hit he shared with Steve Perry in 1982. "One day (Dean) came to me and said, 'you know, I wrote a screenplay and I'd love for you to check it out.' And I thought, oh that's cool, sure, I'll give it a look. And you have to remember in those days, even the cab driver that dropped you off had a screenplay. It wasn't extraordinary that a friend of mine had a screenplay... He says 'I'd like for you to write some songs with me for this screenplay, so that I can show up not only as the writer of this screenplay but also as a songwriter."

This would also be the only time that Loggins would write for a film that had been neither shot nor at least partially edited. "It hadn't been filmed yet, as opposed to what we normally do you go to see a screening of something.. Like with *Caddyshack* I saw a screening of an unfinished movie, then I plugged in songs into scenes that I thought would be cool. But with this there was nothing to see."

Bassist Nathan East, who missed out playing on Michael Jackson's *Thriller* the day he left to tour with Kenny Loggins, recalls the song was constructed gradually over the course of the tour, such that everyone was pretty sick of it when it came time to do it – but at that point it was so well practiced that they did the whole thing in one or two takes. Loggins confirms: "I built it out at soundchecks. As I was working the tune up, I would have the band play different parts and gradually the song developed."

Loggins happily admits to finding inspiration for the song from a variety of places: the drum beat is a variation on David Bowie's hit "Modern Love," and the original groove is derived from the intro to Mitch Ryder's "Devil With a Blue Dress." The ahhs are the build and release are from "Do You Love Me," and "Twist and Shout" – "It's a classic rock move," he admits, and the sum of these influences helps create a sense of rock timelessness. "I've always admired rock and roll songs that can build on the simplicity of the basic idea. And I think the power of 'Footloose' is it's got just one real kernel idea, that chorus... It doesn't do a lot of left turns."

Loggins injected a modern 80s sensibility with synths and a very hot drum sound. "The drum break came about because the Simmons Drums were new then. It was the beginning of actual electronic drum pads. I had Tris Emboden, who was the drummer on that track, work out a drum part based on the Simmons sounds and built the whole bridge out of that."

While the song was intended only for the final senior dance in the film, it would find a home at both the beginning and end credits. Actor Kevin Bacon recalls hearing the song go from demo to completion, and turning into a quintessential 80s film hit: "The first time I heard 'Footloose...' it was just Kenny on guitar... All the production stuff, from the demo to what the record actually became is such a giant leap. That record, from start to finish, and I mean this in the best way, is just ear candy." And that candy stayed at the number one spot on the Billboard chart for three weeks straight, making it Loggins' biggest hit.

Was Loggins surprised by the success of *Footloose*? "How can you predict that a movie is going to jump out of the box the way it did? Kevin Bacon really stole the show that year. He made that movie what it was. It was a matter of timing. I had had a top 10 hit with 'I'm Alright' from Caddyshack, so my career was ready to jump open. Rock 'n' roll in the movies was a (relatively) new idea back then. And MTV had just come in. We caught the front edge of that movement."

Loggins says he's grateful for having "Footloose" as part of his repertoire. And so are his fans. "It always gets people up and dancing and gives me a climax to my show," he says.

Heaven helps the man who
fights his fear
Love's the only thing that
keeps me here
You're the reason that I'm
hanging on
My heart's staying where
my heart belongs
I'm Free

The team of Pitchford and Loggins also wrote "I'm Free (Heaven Helps the Man)" for the film. It's just as good as the title track but didn't receive the

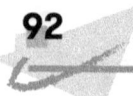

same level of airplay – how could it? Still, it peaked at a formidable #22 on US Billboard and spent 14 weeks on the chart.

ROCKY IV (1985)

Given the bombastic nature of Rocky movies, "Double or Nothing" is a surprisingly middle-of-the-road love theme/duet Kenny Loggins performs with Gladys Knight. In a soundtrack that boasted two new Survivor songs, not to mention an amazing return to the charts for James Brown (via Dan Hartman's "Living in America"), this was a weak runner up. Harmless, but no hit.

TOP GUN (1986)

Top Gun is an exercise in flash that has been called "a live action recruiting poster" (NY Times), and a homoerotic celebration of war, but it produced the Best Song (Academy Awards), the best selling soundtrack of that year (and ninth of all time), and was the top grossing movie of 1986. Made with the cooperation of the Department of Defense, the Navy saw a 20% increase in recruiting after the film. To be fair, a similar increase was seen after *An Officer*

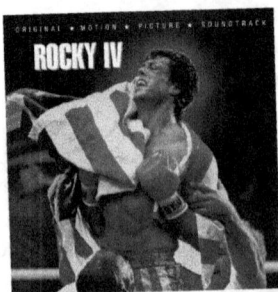

and a Gentleman, so it's hardly a new phenomenon, but *Top Gun* made a lasting impact – one that some say has contributed to a decline in "smart" summer movies. Historians love to single out *Jaws* and *Star Wars* as two blockbuster films that ushered in the culture of mindless entertainment, but as author Mark Harris aptly asks, "Who would you rather have in charge—someone whose definition of a classic is Jaws or someone whose definition of a classic is Top Gun?" ("The Day the Movies Died," GQ, 2/10/11)

In it, hot-shot Naval aviators learn the value of teamwork, fight a nameless but vaguely Soviet enemy (whose black planes and faceless pilots may as well have been Darth Vader), and have sexy romance. Like a high school football player on cocaine, it's muscular, juvenile and exhausting. That Kenny Loggins contributed two songs, including a career-defining one, almost didn't happen – the numbers were not in his favor.

Loggins called the soundtrack a "cattle call. Every top writer, musician, or performing artist was invited to a multiple of screenings." Giorgio Moroder recalls it may have been between 300 and 400 people, mostly composers, all interested in doing some score or some songs. By this time in 1985, the success of *Flashdance* and *Footloose* were firmly on the financial books, and dollar signs were in the eyes of every aspiring songwriter. The film's music editor Bob Bedami related how they were tasked with trudging through one hundred cassettes in a typical sitting. If anyone shouted "pass," sometimes within five seconds of starting the song, the tape was torn from the machine and the next would be played. Someone else in the room could make a case to continue, but it was a case of first impressions and only the strong survive.

Bodies working overtime
It's man against man

Loggins thinks he was in the third or fourth packed screening of *Top Gun's* rough cut. He took one look around the room, knew he was up against stiff competition, and decided to take "the path of least resistance." He targeted a scene he knew no one else would touch, the infamous volleyball scene that showcases the male stars, shirtless and baby-oiled to a shine. His solution was to "just write a rock tune with a good, positive, powerful groove, and let the

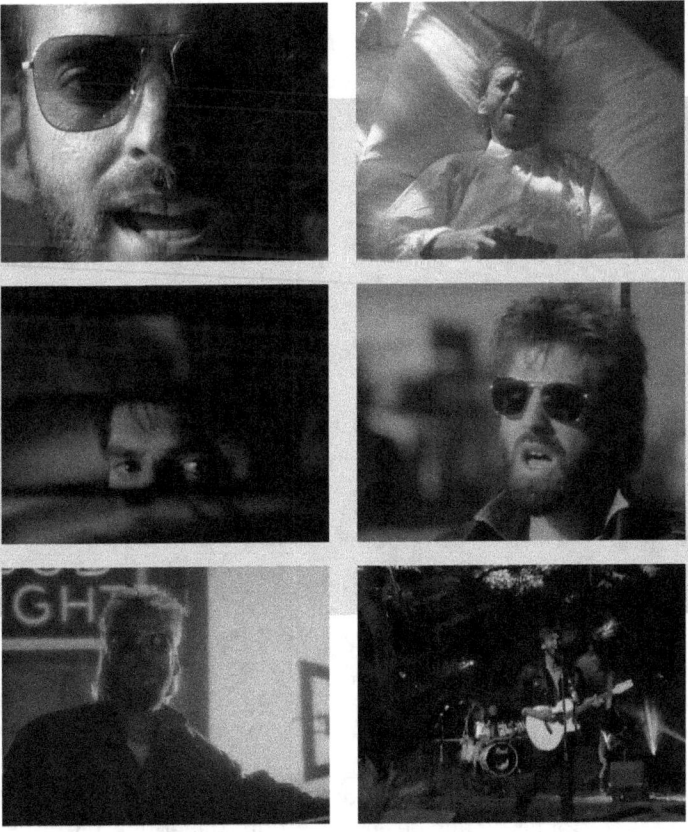

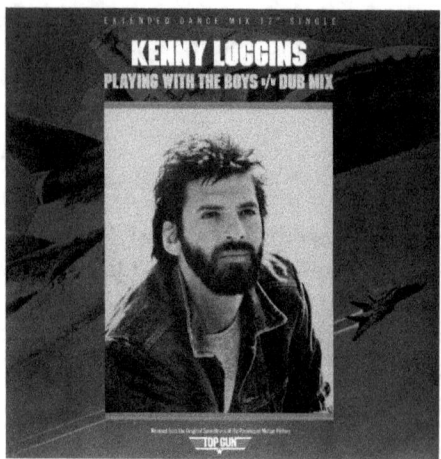

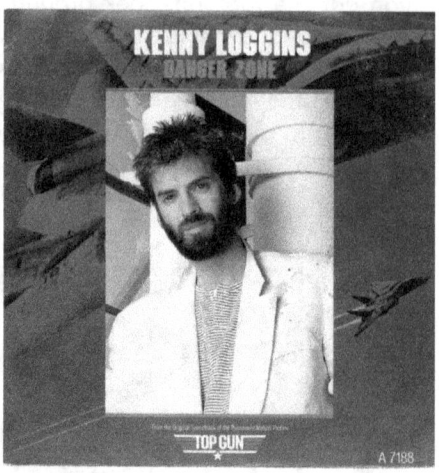

Gun Anthem" based on Bruckheimer's script and stories: "he told me about the young pilots, who sit there waiting for takeoff, listening to Billy Idol. It was a rock and roll situation to me," Faltermeyer says. A driving guitar sound would be required to compete with the film's white noise, as only rock guitar accents could cut through the fighter planes, and he used Billy Idol's guitarist Steve Stevens to bring it all around to the beginning.

editing do the rest. To capture the spirit of that playful moment, a release from the tension of the rest of the movie. So we made a straight ahead rock and roll piece of that era." The tune certainly transcends the (in retrospect, blatantly) homoerotic content, and spent 12 weeks on the charts as a result of that soundtrack's immense popularity, peaking at 60 on the Hot 100.

> Revvin' up your engine
> Listen to her howlin' roar
> Metal under tension
> Beggin' you to touch and go

Already on the list of composers was Harold Faltermeyer. Producer Jerry Bruckheimer had noted Faltermeyer's enthusiasm and creativity when he was Moroder's arranger and engineer on music for *Cat People* and *Flashdance* (also Bruckheimer films) and had recently recruited Faltermeyer to create a theme and songs for his hit film *Beverly Hills Cop*. Faltermeyer wrote the "Top

Meanwhile, Giorgio Moroder had determined from screening the film that he needed to produce two songs: a rocker and a ballad. He composed two that the producers didn't like, then returned with two they did. The first was "Danger Zone." The lyrics came from Tom Whitlock, an aspiring lyricist and, appropriately, a car mechanic who specialized in Ferraris and Lamborghinis. Several bands were considered, Starship was offered the tune, but given their history as a protest band they were worried about alienating old fans, due to the pro-war position of the movie and the lyrics. When Toto dropped out at the eleventh hour, Moroder needed someone to sing.

Loggins recalls, "I was already in the studio when (they asked) 'can you get Kenny Loggins in here, because I need a singer yesterday!' They were already dropping music into the movie and they didn't have a voice for that." Loggins asked "it it uptempo? Yes? I'll do it. I'd been writing nothing but ballads and I needed a rocker for my show." He cites Tina Turner's recent rock and soul vocal style from the album *Private Dancer* as a big influence on the approach. "I brought that in as my model of where I wanted to take my vocal. And I think that's why I ended up singing 'day-unger zo-unn!' I was doing Tina Turner."

"In those days, if the movie didn't hit, no one would ever hear it anyway," Loggins notes. "But if it did hit, then you had a hit record. It made sense to me to just go for it. But I committed to it having never heard the song."

This would be his only song made with Giorgio Moroder. On the subject of his collaboration, Loggins has said

this: "(Moroder) liked to work fast, and didn't really delve into inventing new sounds or new ways of doing things. He would get an engineer who was smart and quick and would say 'Make it sound good.' There was a Yamaha keyboard called the DX7 – it was new at the time and is now one of the classic keyboards — and he was the only one I knew who used all the stock sounds, and never tried to create anything new out of it. And he had huge hits, with all the stock sounds. We sat and messed with the chord substitutions, but it was pretty much what Giorgio wrote."

"Danger Zone" would prove to be Loggins' second biggest hit, reaching the #2 position with 21 weeks charting. While it has become somewhat of a punchline musical cliché, the impact it had at the time can not be ignored. One wonders: how many speeding tickets must have been issued in 1986 as a result of this stratospheric cinematic theme song?

OVER THE TOP (1987)

In a lifetime made of memories
I believe in destiny
Every moment returns again in time
When I've got the future on my mind
Know that you'll be the only one

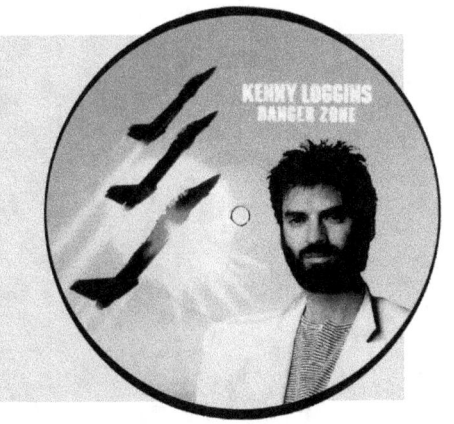

Loggins provides a radio-ready tune for the Golan-Globus Stallone film. called "Meet Me Halfway." The accompanying music video cashes in heavily on his "Danger Zone" persona, complete with leather jacket and aviator shades. This one topped

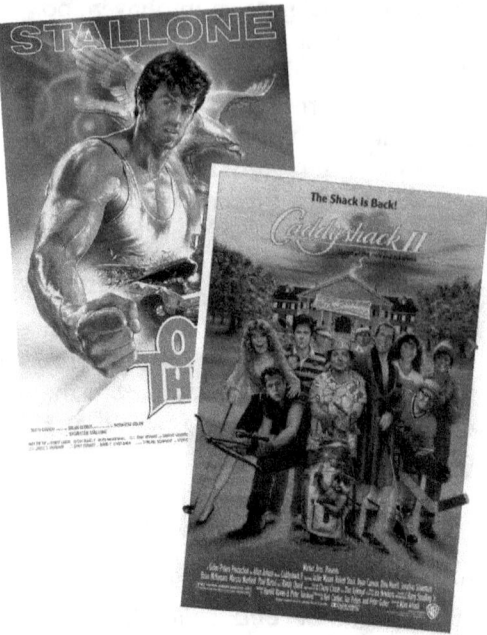

Chevy Chase clone is played by Chevy Chase. The song fared better, his fifth highest charter at #8 in 1988 (America was suffering from Loggins withdrawal).

Today, Loggins acknowledges that the craft of pop-songs-for-films has changed. When selecting an existing song is seen as an easier path than creating a new song, the song's purpose as direct support for the story can be lost. Placing songs with little care for their emotional impact, and with an emphasis simply on album sales, can hurt a film. "There's a craft to it," Loggins says. "You have to get ahold of the emotional content that is being conveyed, and they don't do much of that anymore." The change in purchasing habits of music fans may be to blame as well. When a movie does not inspire new songs, and there is a smaller audience for buying albums of any kind (let alone the somewhat more marginalized genre of movie soundtrack), both the business and the art can be hurt.

out at #11 US Billboard with a total of 25 weeks on the chart. The song likely evolved into a DJ favorite at proms and high school dances, its association with a movie about arm wrestling long forgotten.

CADDYSHACK II (1988)

I'm going all the way
Sooner or later, gotta love somebody
I don't care how long it takes

With "Nobody's Fool" Loggins delivers a fine, anthemic power-rocker for an ill-conceived return to the *Caddyshack* well. *Caddyshack II* stars Jackie Mason as a Rodney Dangerfield replacement, Dan Aykroyd as a Bill Murray replacement, and Robert Stack as a Ted Knight replacement. The disappointing

10

TRUE STORIES

The 80s was a time when artsy postmodernism snuck into the mainstream. TV shows like Pee Wee's Playhouse or Twin Peaks subverted expectations and pushed the possibilities of the medium, only to be pushed back into obscurity to make room for more sitcoms in the 90s. In True Stories, Talking Heads frontman David Byrne combines the format of a documentary with the rules of a musical and the atmosphere of a David Lynch film – or at least a Coen Brothers movie.

"What time is it? No time to look back....."

David Byrne has called his directing debut "*60 Minutes* on acid," which makes it sound a lot darker than it actually is. In fact, tonally the film is a move away from Byrne's early-80s jerky paranoia to an acceptance of America's rural oddness, represented here by the soon-to-be-150-year old (fictional) town of Virgil, Texas. Perhaps appropriately, one of the film's producers is Karen Murphy, fresh off of *This is Spinal Tap*.

During cross-country tours with the Talking Heads, Byrne was known to collect tabloid papers and save the more outrageous clippings. He then made drawings of characters and scenarios that filled his wall at home. *Stop Making Sense* director Jonathan Demme suggested Byrne use the writing duo of Beth Henley and Stephen Tobolowsky (known to most as the perpetually sunny insurance salesman Ned Ryerson in *Groundhog Day*) to put the stories to paper, with the concept being "what if all these stories were true?" They delivered a draft, but by the time they heard back from Byrne he had retooled it completely. Byrne then asked their permission to use Henley and Tobolowsky's names in the credits as the writers, so as to make the film appear less of a vanity project.

Byrne spent time in the Dallas-Fort Worth area researching and trying to capture the tone and voice of that unique state, as well as picking possible locations. Byrne would handle directing, his band providing the music, and Byrne would appear as a sort of observer named simply "The Narrator" in the end credits. And herein is one of the things that makes True Stories truly special. If you consider David Byrne's persona – the strange, awkward, boxy-suited stage character – he is kind of an alien. That's how he plays it in *True Stories*, someone who seems to be observing this type of lifeform for the first time and trying to make sense of it. He comes across as a kind of large-headed Mister Rogers in a cowboy hat, an android confounded by middle America but ready and willing to come to pleasant terms with it. He addresses the audience directly, but can interact with the denizens of the town who do not see the camera. The Narrator is often seated behind the wheel of his red convertible; no effort is made to present the obvious rear-projected backdrop as anything but artifice, there's even a joke made out of an absurdly wobbly steering wheel. His car radio plays the film's underscore so clearly, that he remarks what good reception the radio has.

At the same time, it's a deeply personal observation of everything mundane. "I really enjoy forgetting," the Narrator says. "When I first come to a place, I notice all the little details. I notice the way the sky looks. The color of white paper. The way people walk. Doorknobs. Everything. Then I get used to the place and I don't notice those things anymore. So only by forgetting can I see the place again as it really is." In doing this we are invited to look much more closely at the film's formal compositions and stylized set design, and to pick up on the bit characters and their numerous quirks. And like the Narrator, we forgive these people – and the film welcomes all kinds, the ugly people, obese people, elderly people, ethnically diverse people, and numerous children. Among the cast are fifty sets of twins. It's an amazingly positive world view that perhaps only a stranger could have. Sometimes the narration sounds like it could be lyrics from a Talking Heads song, such as when he admires the cookie-cutter subdivision homes: "Look at this. Who can say it isn't beautiful? Sky, bricks. Who do you think lives there? Four-car garage. Hope, fear, excitement, satisfaction."

The other great part of *True Stories* is John Goodman, and he's the film's genuine heart. If there is anything akin to a straightforward narrative in the movie, it's mostly centered around Goodman's character, the reluctantly available bachelor Louis Fyne, who is quick to admit "I'm 6'3" and maintain a very consistent panda bear shape." The only thing he wants is matrimony, and he's tried just about everything. In addition to working at the town's computer manufacturing plant (based loosely on Texas Instruments, then a huge force in computing), he is an aspiring songwriter and singer. He is set to perform a song at the town's sesquicentennial celebration, "A Celebration of Specialness," but is completely focused on finding a mate. He even makes a TV commercial

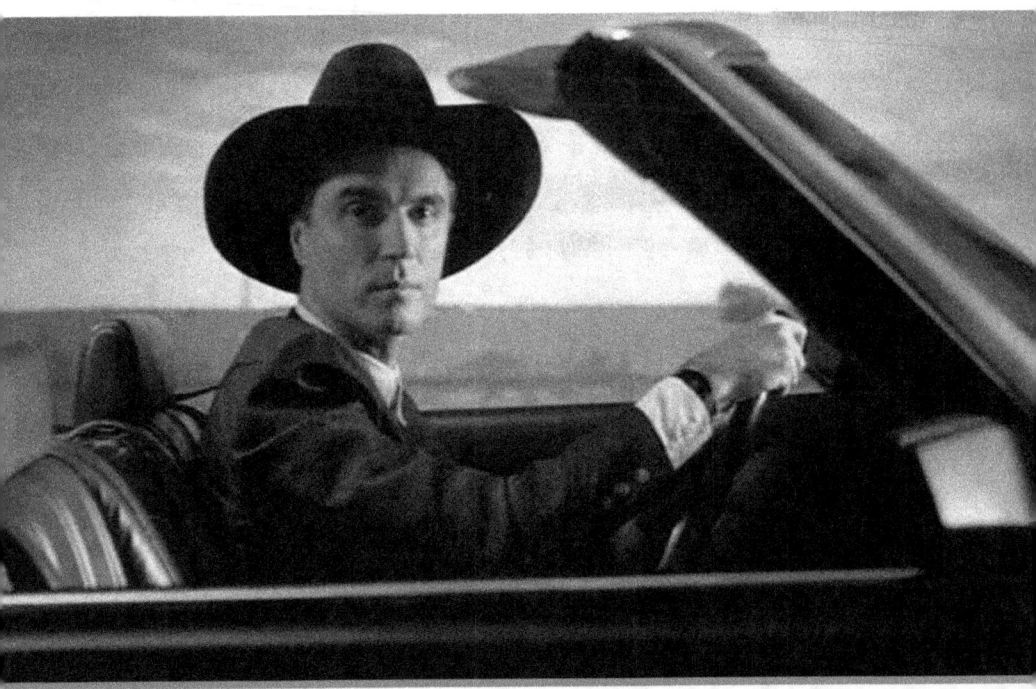

for himself with a phone-in hotline.

The town is full of entirely singular characters. The role of "The Preacher" is based in part on the Texas-based pseudo religion The Church of the Subgenius. In a sermon rich in conspiracy lore and imagery, the song "Puzzlin' Evidence" pays homage to the alleged assassin of The Subgenius' fictional "founder" J.R. "Bob" Dobbs. Spalding Gray plays the head of the computer company, a man who speaks to his wife only through the intermediaries of his children, and waxes spiritual about the new economic model of technology. There's some wonderfully tall tales related by "The Lying Woman" (Jo Harvey Allen), who is connected to everyone and has something to say about everything. There's also "The Lazy Woman," a woman who is in bed for the entire film, and has a machine for turning the pages of her magazine. Roebuck "Pops" Staples of the Staple Singers is the Lazy Woman's Vodun-practicing butler (that's voodoo for the uninitiated), and also provides Fyne with a love charm. One gets the impression that this town is just down the road from *Pee Wee's Playhouse*, or in a Coen-Brothers Texas that's less *Blood Simple* and more *Raising Arizona*.

There are about thirty pieces of music in the movie either written by Byrne or produced by him, but he takes a wonderful risk when he has the featured songs sung by the oddball cast. This puts *True Stories* in league with the other risky music film from 1986, *Under the Cherry Moon*, in which another big 80s wunderkind

hitmaker opted to put the acting before the singing. And if I'm not mistaken, these songs are also sung live on camera instead of lip synced. The accompanying album played it safe, though, and substituted Byrne's trademark vocal for the quirkier musical takes from the film. *True Stories* would be one of the Talking Heads least successful albums, despite the hit "Wild Life" that gained a respectable #25 on the Billboard chart. Byrne's songs here are not only up to the standard of some of the Talking Heads best output, but they point the way to the maturity Byrne would achieve as he struck out on his own, with quintessential lyrics addressing consumer culture, loneliness, the dead end jobs so common in small towns, and the need to be loved.

In the film, "Wild Life" plays out like a massive karaoke session, with all manner of people running on stage to fill in a line. Kids, fat folks, Louis Fyne, and a Billy Idol and Prince impersonator are among the participants. The song "Dream Operator" sees Miss Rollings (Swoosie Kurtz) presiding over a surreal fashion show in a mall.

One of the film's great segments is the song "Love for Sale." It's a straight-up music video with the Heads featured prominently, while a wealthy woman lying in bed watches it on TV and comments throughout (in a stream of consciousness attack that might have set the groundwork for Beavis and Butthead). The video itself employs shots from mid-80s television commercials and then posits the band as product, covering them in chocolate and wrapping them in foil. The recreations of glossy adverts from the period are creepily accurate.

The song "Radio Head" is about a man (Tito Larriva, of the Plugz and Cruzados) who can pick up signals about people with his head. "People Like Us" is performed by John Goodman. If you love Goodman (this is one of his great roles) and have committed fully to the movie by this point, the song makes for a great, moving climax.

True Stories represents an interesting developmental stage for one of the 20th century's more provocative artists. Where he could have kept going down a path of art-house New York sophistication, here he takes a moment to come to terms with rural America as a only an alien can (he was born in Scotland and moved to the US at age 8). "I guess a lot of people here seem to be kind of proud of what they are," Byrne told the Chicago Tribune in 1985. "They are what they are, and that's okay; they're not gonna try and hide it. What's nice is they're more tolerant of other people's individuality." And the film was upbeat enough to raise questions from interviewers at the time, and elicit answers such as this in an interview for English television: "Yeah, it's pretty cheery. In an odd way it kind of endorses all those things. And says that they're all okay, and this is a viable alternative... I guess I have my moments of optimism and my moments of extreme pessimism (he laughs) but it seemed to work better for a film for it to be more upbeat. It's

an easier way to draw people in, and then you can kind of slip the downbeat things in underneath, as I guess what they call subtext or something like that," he grins impishly, and you're convinced he knows exactly what he's doing.

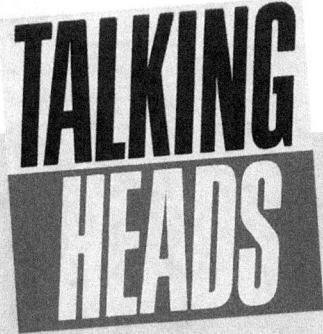

TALKING HEADS

Love For Sale
Puzzlin' Evidence
Hey Now
Papa Legba
Wild Wild Life
Radio Head
Dream Operator
People Like Us
City of Dreams

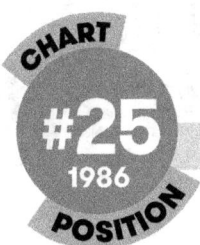

CHART **#25** 1986 POSITION

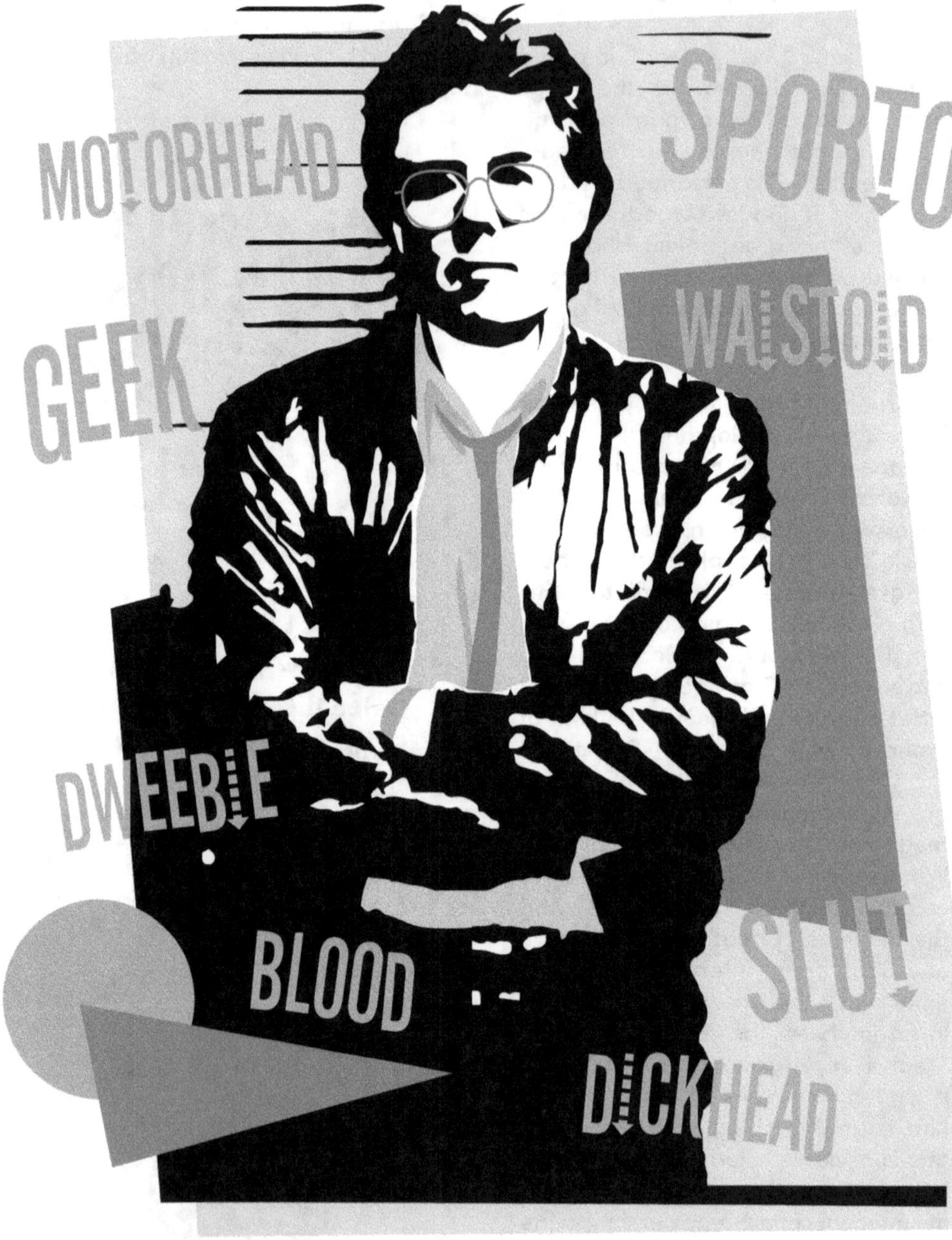
MOTORHEAD
SPORTO
GEEK
WASTOID
DWEEBIE
BLOOD
SLUT
DICKHEAD

11

IN HIS OWN CLASS: JOHN HUGHES

In the 1980s, few directors (and NO writer-directors) made as consistent a body of work as John Hughes, whose very name is synonymous with 80s cinema. Much has already been written about the Brat Pack films, with their formula of character-driven anti-plots and fourth-wall breaking comedy. What Hughes did with music, especially with bands that wouldn't be considered pop acts, was even more interesting.

John Hughes grew up in Michigan before moving outside of Chicago to the town of Northbrook Illinois, ending up at a big school called Glenbrook North High. It's obvious to imagine that Hughes' vivid memories of being the new kid at school were a rich bank from which to draw for his screenplays, but he credits the arrival of The Beatles and Bob Dylan with really igniting his creativity.

He became a gag writer for Rodney Dangerfield and Joan Rivers, and later contributed stories to *National Lampoon* magazine (where his short story "Vacation '58" would inspire the screenplay to *National Lampoon's Vacation*). His midwestern, outsider approach was different enough from his LA contemporaries to make a mark, and with the success of *Vacation* he was allowed to direct his debut film, *Sixteen Candles*. Where other 80s teen films like *Porky's* and *Last American Virgin* depicted an over-sexed primitive, Hughes' teens sounded like and acted like actual people.

Hughes' adoration for rock music is evident throughout his career (one wonders what he could have done with an all-out musical), and as such begs inclusion into a book about 80s music and movies. And if his integration of music and film was better than most, it's because he held this belief: "We put the song in there because it was part of the movie. You couldn't take that song out of the movie, couldn't take that movie out of the song." Here are 5 tricks Hughes liked to employ in his scripts and films, along with specific instances in his best teen films for those keeping score.

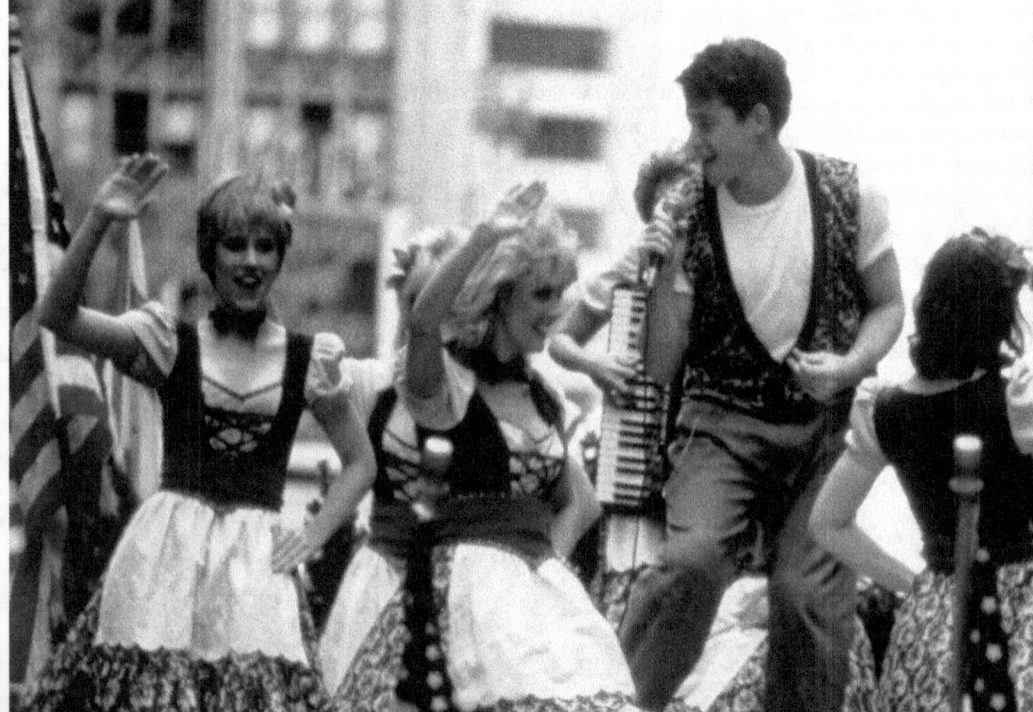

1: NAME THAT TUNE

Hughes (and/or his editors, or his music supervisors) loved to use classic soundtrack cues as a comic counterpoint. He calls them out in his screenplays: "A little spook music" to describe some skulking teens in *Sixteen Candles* becomes Henry Mancini's theme from *Peter Gunn*. He was definitely not the first one to do this – how many of us Saturday-morning-cartoon-weaned-kids learned about Wagner, Turkey in the Straw, and Frank Sinatra watching Bugs Bunny? Hughes approach to comic cues was much like the Warner Brothers cartoon composers, setting the tone comically and instantly with something recognizable, often from his own childhood TV consumption.

2: ALTERNATIVE RADIO GOLD

It's hard to imagine the jock from *Breakfast Club* listening willingly to, say, New Order. But as otherwise outre bands like Simple Minds and OMD invaded the top 40, even he couldn't avoid hearing them. Association with Hughes' films elevated singles from great, lesser-known bands to blazing, if temporary, stardom. His ear for new, underrated, often British acts that perfectly captured the teen angst depicted on screen was legendary, and an entire generation of fellow outsiders came of age to the songs featured on his soundtracks.

Many of us went a step further and sought out the full-length albums from those artists, becoming devotees long after the pictures faded. The 80s may have seemed like an era of one hit wonders if you simply stood at a distance and watched the charts, because 80s radio made short work of Euro bands with a much bigger and deeper catalog. Thanks to great placement in a popular film or a high profile music video, these acts were sometimes given just an iota of the attention they deserved. Bands like Simple Minds didn't cruise along for years, get lucky on one song, and vanish into the night – their catalog is filled with albums that have as much depth and sonic variety as more critically lauded discs (Nirvana's *Nevermind* is one that comes to mind, since it is credited with putting a stake through the heart of 80s pop records).

Hughes appears to have chosen specific songs to include in the films quite early in production, early enough to even influence costume choices, according to Oscar-nominated designer Marilyn Vance. "He'd say, 'Okay, this scene, I'm going to drop this music into there,' and he'd play it, and it was incredible. It just danced in your head: wow, this means that and it just came together – for the actors as well."

Hughes himself said in a 1986 interview for MTV, "To have a song work for the movie, it can't just be written apart and shoved in," Hughes said. "It's got to come out of the action. It's got to talk about the characters, not the story, it has to augment that action."

3: THE WALLPAPER OF THEIR LIVES

Alternative music invaded the films from the ground up, influencing their costumes and production design. Punk rock's embrace of the thrift store is in evidence as a way to indicate a character's socio-economic class, and MTV's cultural, multi-genre blender is clearly referenced in outfits like Ducky's from *Pretty in Pink*. Like all good motion picture costumes, the actors wear their characters on the outside, but with Hughes special brand of outliers, the trappings are a potent mix of antique store discoveries and contemporary finds, a walking collection of cool that undoubtedly influenced like-minded teens throughout the decade.

And 80s contemporary pop music is literally the wallpaper in these films, as Hughes provides further insight to their character by which band's posters they have on their bedroom walls.

4: THE JOHNNY HUGHES SING-ALONG SHOW

Perhaps influenced by Tom Cruise's *Risky Business* solo act, Hughes loved to put in a "realistic" musical number – performing to music that is realistically emanating from an onscreen source rather than emerging out of the ether. MTV kids were too hip to really break into song with out-of-nowhere musical accompaniment, but were not above air guitar or singing in the shower –or singing to a Beatles hit coming out of a parade float's PA system.

The device serves a number of purposes. It gets a song in, lets an actor rip it up, it encourages playfulness and appreciation of music of all genres. Here Hughes is like the cool uncle, sharing that mixtape with bands like Echo & The Bunnymen and New Order, then slipping in some Otis Redding on the side to further your education.

Likewise, his characters often express themselves with snippets of songs, acapella.

5: THE BIG HIT

Some of the films elevated tracks that would have barely made an impact to actual hits, but Hughes never saw the music as a crass money grab or a way to fill seats. "I don't look at the album as a marketing tool, because I think if you do that then you're going to fail. It's really betraying the music," he said.

"It's arguable whether a hit song is gonna add to the business a film does. There are plenty of films that didn't do any business and sold a million albums... When I approach a band, I want to respect them and be respectful of their music. I'm not gonna say, 'Look, you guys are real hot so we'll stick you in the movie and we'll get it in all these stores and all these stations.' That isn't right."

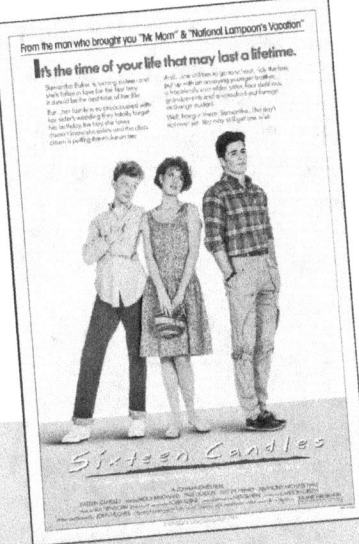

SIXTEEN CANDLES (1984)

Molly Ringwald turned sixteen but her parents forgot her birthday. She wants bigger boobs. The Geek (Anthony Michael Hall) hits on her, but she wants the cute senior boy (Michael Schoeffling). Distracting adventures involve a foreign exchange student (Geddy Watanabe) and the geek's efforts to live up to his reputation as a ladykiller.

It's quite funny and outrageous, with a few situations that didn't age very well (some cringeworthy racial & sexual things that betray the movie's age), and lots of neat bit parts with John and Joan Cusack, Brian Doyle Murray, and Jami Gertz. Hughes wrote the film over a single Fourth of July weekend with Ringwald's headshot pinned to the wall for inspiration.

NAME THAT TUNE

Hughes and company employ numerous musical jokes – some as simple as a gong accompanying the recitation of Long Duk Dong's name (which gets into that racial muck I was speaking of earlier – Watanabe, a Japanese American actor with no accent, is doing a vocal impersonation of his Korean friend, while playing a Chinese teenager that sometimes wears a kimono) or the oft-licensed "Turning Japanese" by The Vapors. In terms of old soundtrack chestnuts, The *Dragnet* and *Peter Gunn* themes are employed to rapidly suggest intrigue, and Nino Rota's "Speak Softly Love" from The Godfather is used to give dinner with the Rizchecks an appropriately "organized crime" air.

ALTERNATIVE RADIO GOLD

Hughes turned to Ringwald for help in finding songs for the film; among the songs she introduced him to was The Psychedelic Furs "Pretty in Pink" which would surface later. Not on the album but featured in the film were: "Love of the Common

People" (Paul Young), "Kajagoogoo" (Kajagoogoo), "Happy Birthday" (Altered Images), "Rumours in the Air" (Night Ranger), "Wild Sex in the Working Class" (Oingo Boingo), "Little Bitch" (The Specials), "Growing Pains" (Tim Finn), "When It Started to Begin" and "Whistle Down the Wind" (Nick Heyward), "Ring Me Up" (Divinyls), "Rev-Up" (The Rezillos), "Young Americans" (David Bowie), and "Young Guns" (Wham!).

THE WALLPAPER OF THEIR LIVES

Ringwald's room (a set that was built in the same gymnasium where they filmed the dance scene) has a Stray Cats poster on the all. Jake's room sports a poster for The Police's album Synchronicity.

THE BIG HIT

The brilliant music was supervised by Jimmy Iovine, who engineered a number of seminal 70s albums before producing discs like Tom Petty's *Damn the Torpedoes*. His 21st century accomplishments – signing Tupac Shakur, creating a headphone brand with Dr. Dre, or creating a huge streaming music empire with Apple – sound like they're taking place on another planet if you've been reading this book for very long.

And atypical of the entries in this book, the only soundtrack album that was released is merely a five song EP. Any hit thing that was featured in the film earned that title on its own album, like Billy Idol's "Rebel Yell"

(Billboard #46) and Spandau Ballet's "True" (Billboard #4). The song most associated with the film is "If You Were Here" by Thompson Twins thanks to its prominent climactic placement.

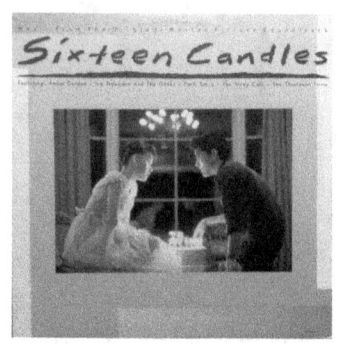

SOUNDTRACK

16 Candles
Stray Cats

Hang Up The Phone
Annie Golden

Geek Boogie
Ira and The Geeks

Gloria
Patti Smith

If You Were Here
Thompson Twins

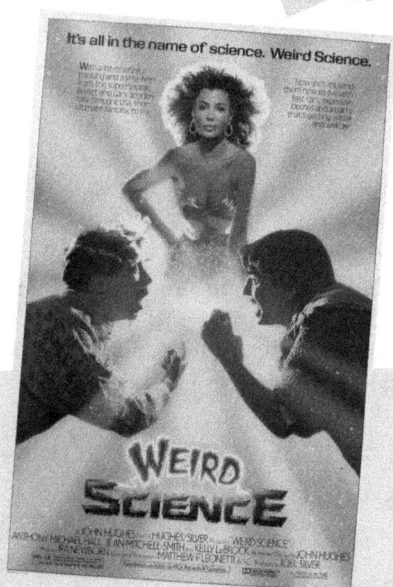

WEIRD SCIENCE (1985)

Wyatt (Ilan Mitchell-Smith) and Gary (Anthony Michael Hall) connect a home computer to a government mainframe and generate a horny boy's dream girl out of pictures of naked women, Einstein, Houdini, and David Lee Roth. The result is Kelly LeBrock.

Based very loosely on a 1950s EC Comic of the same name (I'm guessing the "dropping an Icee on the boys at the mall" might be a new addition to the tale), this one throws maturity to the wind with an absurd central premise and heaps of embarrassing juvenile sexual fantasy. This film illustrates how essential Anthony Michael Hall was to Hughes' output at the time; Hall's acting in this and other Hughes films set a new comic standard – call it casual realism. Certainly this one has its share of bad choices (getting drunk in a Chicago blues bar results in Hall morphing into a kind of Eddie Murphy) but I believe that Hall's natural vocal and comic style was copied by many actors, including Robert Downey Jr in some of his later roles. The two had plenty of time to study together as co-stars on one season of Saturday Night Live, along with fellow Hughes-alumni Randy Quaid and Joan Cusack, further cementing Hughes' influence on comedy of the period. Big points for using Road Warrior Vernon Wells reprising his role as Wez, but points revoked for making his sex slave a woman (Jennifer "Repo Man" Balgobin). Bill Paxton delivers the ultimate big brother with the worst haircut and savage burns ("You two donkey-dicks couldn't get laid in a morgue.")

NAME THAT TUNE

There's something like a Dragnet cue underneath the boys' private Joe Friday-inspired rapidfire conversation in the bathroom ("Okay, but whatever happens, we've gotta give Lisa a shot. I don't wanna hurt her feelings. Any girl's lookin' for a long lean bone job from me.") Composer Ira Newborn produces a suitably Mad Max cue for the mutant bikers. "Gonna Fly Now," the theme from Rocky gets a moment at the film's conclusion.

ALTERNATIVE RADIO GOLD

The soundtrack is just as weird as the movie but it all seems to work, with cuts from many genres of music. Sadly missing from the album is "Tenderness" by General Public. The band listed as Ira and the Geeks is the film's composer Ira Newborn, Hughes go-to collaborator.

THE WALLPAPER OF THEIR LIVES

General Public, Talking Heads, Depeche Mode, and Human League posters adorn Wyatt's room.

THE BIG HIT

Oingo Boingo's title track is as big as it got in the US, with a #45 placement on Billboard Hot 100. Danny Elfman says writing the song was as fast as the phone call requesting it. "I got a call from John Hughes talking about the movie, and wouldn't it be fun, and I literally wrote it [in my head] while I was talking to him... I ran down to my studio and recorded it and sent it out... I managed to not lose it or turn on the radio and have it erased long enough to get down to my studio and record it." As with *Sixteen Candles* a couple of songs that weren't on the album were bigger in their own right, including Van Halen's "Oh Pretty Woman" (#12 in 1982!) and "Wanted Man" by Ratt (#38 in 1984).

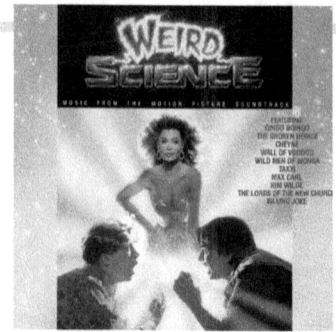

SOUNDTRACK

Weird Science
Oingo Boingo

Private Joy
Cheyne

The Circle
Max Carl

Turn It On
Kim Wilde

Deep in the Jungle
Wall of Voodoo

Do Not Disturb (Knock, Knock)
The Broken Homes

Forever
Taxxi

Why Don't Pretty Girls (Look At Me)
The Wild Men of Wonga

Method to My Madness
Lords of the New Church

Eighties
Killing Joke

Weird Romance
Ira and the Geeks

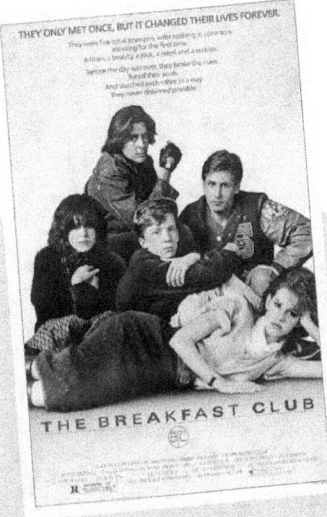

THE BREAKFAST CLUB (1985)

accent) did not fit in the film. Had the film been shot in 1983, Hughes would have cast John Cusack as Bender and sister Joan as Allison. The library is a set that was built in the gymnasium of the school location in Illinois; the whole thing cost $1 million and made $51.5 million.

Saturday March 24th, 1984. A "brain, an athlete, a basket case, a princess and a criminal" are in detention at Shermer High School in Shermer Illinois. As they are dropped off by their parents, we see from their interactions a hint of why they might have ended up here. Assistant Principal Richard Vernon (Paul Gleason) is a strict disciplinarian who assigns them an essay conveniently centered on the theme of the film: each must write a thousand words explaining "who you think you are."

The film is more dramatic and realistic than most of the Hughes films, and benefits from the three week rehearsal schedule and shot-in-continuity production method that was used. This was originally supposed to go into production before *Sixteen Candles* and be Hughes first film, thus the small scale (one location, taking place on one day, small cast). In fact, he shot *Ferris Bueller* scenes at the same time as *Breakfast Club* to save money. Rick Moranis was filmed as the janitor, but the studio decided that his outsized character (with a Russian

NAME THAT TUNE

Lots of air guitar occurs in the film, but only one is accompanied by a vocal: Bender mouths the opening chords to 1967's "Sunshine of Your Love."

THE WALLPAPER OF THEIR LIVES

Allison (Ally Sheedy) is seen with a LP of Prince's 1999. In a scene cut from the film, she uses Bender's switchblade (remember she took it?) to break into a teacher's locker. The discovery of the album there gives her some insight into the faculty: "You know what this means? They're human."

JOHNNY HUGHES SING-ALONG SHOW

Bender gets the whole gang whistling the World War One-era song "Colonel Bogey March." The song was revised in WWII as an anti-Hitler song, and is immortalized in pop culture through its use in 1957's *The Bridge on the River Kwai*.

All dance in their own particular way to Karla DeVito's song "We Are Not Alone."

THE BIG HIT

Drummer/Producer Keith Forsey was brought in to supervise the film's music, hot off of Billy Idol's huge success with *Rebel Yell*. Forsey had written "Don't You (Forget About Me)" for the film, co-written by former Nina Hagen guitarist Steve Schiff, and originally intended for Bryan Ferry. A scheduling conflict prevented him from participating, and the song was reportedly offered to Annie Lennox and Cy Curnin of The Fixx before Forsey went to Simple Minds.

"Don't You (Forget About Me)" got them their American audience and proved to be a #1 hit, if only for a week, and hung around the charts for 22 weeks in 1985. Their next album would benefit from the exposure in the US, sending "Alive and Kicking" into the top ten. The ever-practical Hughes saw it this way: "Simple Minds worked for *The Breakfast Club* in the context of the film, [even] if you never bought the record. We didn't put the song on there to sell records. We put the song in there because it was part of the movie. You couldn't take that song out of the movie, couldn't take that movie out of the song. That's what I try to do."

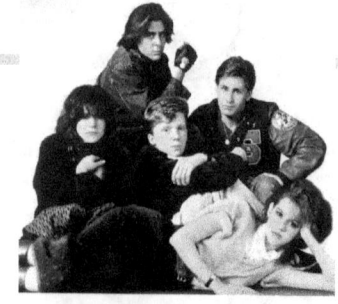

THE BREAKFAST CLUB

SOUNDTRACK

Don't You (Forget About Me)
Simple Minds

Waiting
Elizabeth Daily

Fire in the Twilight
Wang Chung

I'm The Dude
Keith Forsey

Heart Too Hot to Hold
Stephanie Spruill

Dream Montage
Gary Chang

We Are Not Alone
Karla DeVito

The Reggae
Keith Forsey

Didn't I Tell You
Joyce Kennedy

Love Theme
Keith Forsey

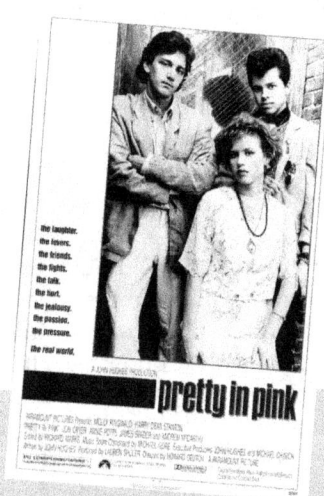

PRETTY IN PINK (1986)

Molly Ringwald is from the wrong side of the tracks and dresses like a grandma; she attends an upscale high school where she is perpetually derided by mean girls. When a rich boy (Andrew McCarthy) shows interest, her best friend Duckie (Jon Cryer) is crushed.

Directed by Howard Deutch, this one has the hallmarks expected from a Hughes screenplay, but lacks the more blatant comic touch of the Hughes-directed equivalents. James Spader continues to perfect his elitist jerk persona, and both Ringwald and Cryer puts their hearts into it. For Hughes, the screenplay was therapy: "I wrote Pretty In Pink the week after we finished Sixteen Candles. I so desperately hate to end these movies that the first thing I do when I'm done is write another one, then I don't feel sad about having to leave and everybody going away."

The script originally called for Ringwald to end up with Duckie, whose role almost went to Michael J. Fox and Robert Downey, Jr. A test screening of the film in which Cryer and Ringwald end up together was received poorly by teen girls and the studio backpedaled. Ringwald agreed that the chemistry between Andie and Duckie is a friendship one rather than a romantic one: "he always seemed like the gay best friend — the gay best friend who doesn't know he's gay yet." Cryer, on the other hand, says "I want to stand up for all the slightly effeminate dorks that are actually heterosexual. Just 'cause the gaydar is going off, doesn't mean your instruments aren't faulty. I've had to live with that, and that's okay."

ALTERNATIVE RADIO GOLD

This soundtrack is a catalog of great music genres for the high school outsider – how many films can boast three New Order tunes, plus some Echo & the Bunnymen, PLUS some Smiths?

The Psychedelic Furs 1981 art-rock track "Pretty in Pink" was brought to

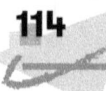

John Hughes attention by Ringwald herself, and lyrically is much darker than the film. Singer Richard Butler points out "The song was about a girl who kinda sleeps around, and thinks it's really cool and thinks everybody really likes her, but they really don't. She's just being used. It's quite scathing." Butler says that Hughes "totally got the whole thing wrong. (The film) was nothing like the spirit of the song at all. It's really hard to say whether it was damaging for us. I suppose we got tied in with the story of the film, and if that's what people thought the story was about, and didn't look much further than that, they were getting a very false impression." The version in the film (and the one that that became famous) is the 1986-re-recorded version, which charted at #41 and 18 in the UK.

THE WALLPAPER OF THEIR LIVES

Music is the lingua franca of many of Pretty in Pink's characters. Andie works at Trax, a record store run by the cool Iona (Annie Potts). Iona's outfits are contemporary and punky (is that latex, Miss Potts?). But we find she was a beehive-bedecked 60s chick in high school, and has a Sid Vicious shrine at her Chinese-restaurant apartment. Her store has decor that positions it as a cool place to find edgier music, and you can spot a lot of posters and album flats from performers who are on the soundtrack like Jesse Johnson and Suzanne Vega. Dweezil Zappa, who acts in the film as pal Simon, also boasts an album poster in the store. A poster of The Smiths, however,

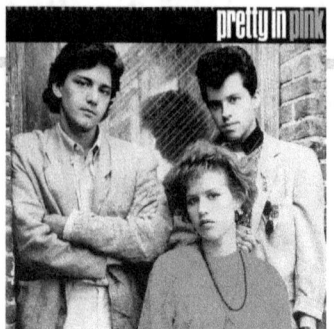

SOUNDTRACK

If You Leave
Orchestral Manoeuvres in the Dark

Left of Center
Suzanne Vega

Get to Know Ya
Jesse Johnson

Do Wot You Do
INXS

Pretty in Pink
The Psychedelic Furs

Shell Shock
New Order

Round, Round
Belouis Some

Wouldn't It Be Good
Danny Hutton Hitters

Bring on The Dancing Horses
Echo & The Bunnymen

Please Please Please Let Me Get What I Want
The Smiths

warrants its own loving close up at the end of a scene – now there's a bit of product placement we can get behind.

The group spends a lot of time at a music club where The Rave-Ups perform "Rave Up/Shut Up" and "Positively Lost Me." Ringwald was a fan of the LA-club-based group (their name is written on the cover of her school notebook in Sixteen Candles). Their lead singer was dating Molly's sister.

JOHNNY HUGHES SING-ALONG SHOW

Duckie lets it rip with a no-holds-barred lip-sync cover of Otis Redding's 1966 version of a song that dates back to 1932, "Try A Little Tenderness." Selected by director Deutch, "it needed to be a heartbreaking song that would express just how Duckie felt," he recalls, "how hurt he is and how much he's in love with this woman. And we fall in love with him because we all related to that." As a crooning plea from Duckie to Andie, it's spot on, and typical of the kind of 60s nostalgia tune popping up with great frequency in the 80s as the Baby Boomers ran the studios. The dance choreography was carefully planned (the night before) by choreographer Kenny Ortega. It was intense enough to wear a hole in Cryer's infamous shoes, which were from an LA punk store and one of a kind.

THE BIG HIT

Orchestral Manoeuvres in the Dark had provided the song "Goddess of Love" from their album The Pacific Age, but when the ending was reshot, a new song was required. "We had 2 days to write a new track at Larabee Studios in L.A. We worked until 4 a.m. writing a rough version and sent a motorbike to Paramount," said OMD co-founder Andy McCluskey. "John heard it, liked it, and our manager phoned us at 8 a.m. and told us to go back in and mix it."

If it looks like the prom kids can't dance, don't blame the band. "The song had to be 120 BPM 'cuz that's the tempo of 'Don't You (Forget About Me),' which is the track they actually shot the prom scene to," McCluskey said. "Unfortunately, the editor obviously had no sense of rhythm because they are all dancing out of time in the final film."

Having a massive American hit is a double-edged sword for singer/bassist McCluskey. "To many Americans, we are a one hit wonder, even though we had several other hits. Nothing as big as 'If You Leave.' It's a blessing... but a shame that it overshadows so many other good songs for the US audience. We have many European fans who hate the song."

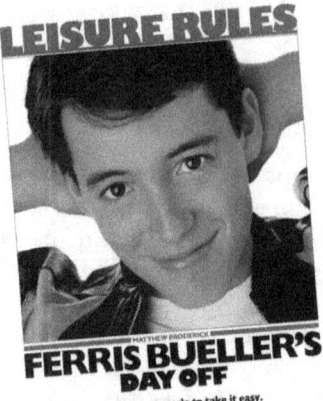

LEISURE RULES

MATTHEW BRODERICK
FERRIS BUELLER'S DAY OFF

One man's struggle to take it easy.

A JOHN HUGHES FILM
PARAMOUNT PICTURES PRESENTS FERRIS BUELLER'S DAY OFF
MIA SARA ALAN RUCK and MIA NEWBORN Music by PAUL HIRSCH Casting MICHAEL CHINICH
Produced by JOHN HUGHES and TOM JACOBSON Written and Directed by JOHN HUGHES
A PARAMOUNT PICTURE

FERRIS BUELLER'S DAY OFF (1986)

Impish Ferris (Matthew Broderick), who can't "possibly be expected to handle school on a day like this," devises an increasingly complicated scheme to skip school a few weeks before graduation. He drags along hypochondriac Cameron (Alan Ruck) and girlfriend Sloane (Mia Sara) to a host of Chicago landmarks, evading Dean of Students Ed Rooney (Jeffrey Jones) and his angry sister (Jennifer Grey) along the way.

The film, Hughes most outright love letter to Chicago, was written in a week, and offers a bigger scope than most Hughes films through extensive location work and expensive production numbers like the Von Steuben Day Parade. The film was shot from a first draft and originally clocked in at two hours and 45 minutes, meaning that the "shortening of the script had to come in the cutting room," as editor Paul Hirsch (*Star Wars*, *Footloose*) noted. The amount of trivia collected about this film, and the amount of love heaped on it from fans and critics, suggests that it may be the most popular of Hughes' teen comedies.

NAME THAT TUNE

John Williams' theme from *Star Wars* is used for a laugh when the parking garage attendants take flight in Cameron's father's Ferrari.

ALTERNATIVE RADIO GOLD

The mid-80s saw a kind of psychedelic resurgence, and English band The Dream Academy was one of the purveyors of this 60s look and sound. Fresh off their 1985 hit "Life in a Northern Town," Dream Academy gets some mileage on the *Ferris* soundtrack, including an instrumental cover of The Smiths' "Please, Please, Please, Let Me Get What I Want" which features in the museum scene. Singer Nick Laird-Clowes: "You remember how in films there'd always be the psychedelic sequence where everybody looked at flowers for awhile and everything went super-colorful? Well, it was definitely the equivalent for a teen movie when they bugger off school and go to look at the (Georges-Pierre) Seurat exhibition, and you get lots of close-up on the pixilation, and it was wonderful." That scene went from being the least loved scene in

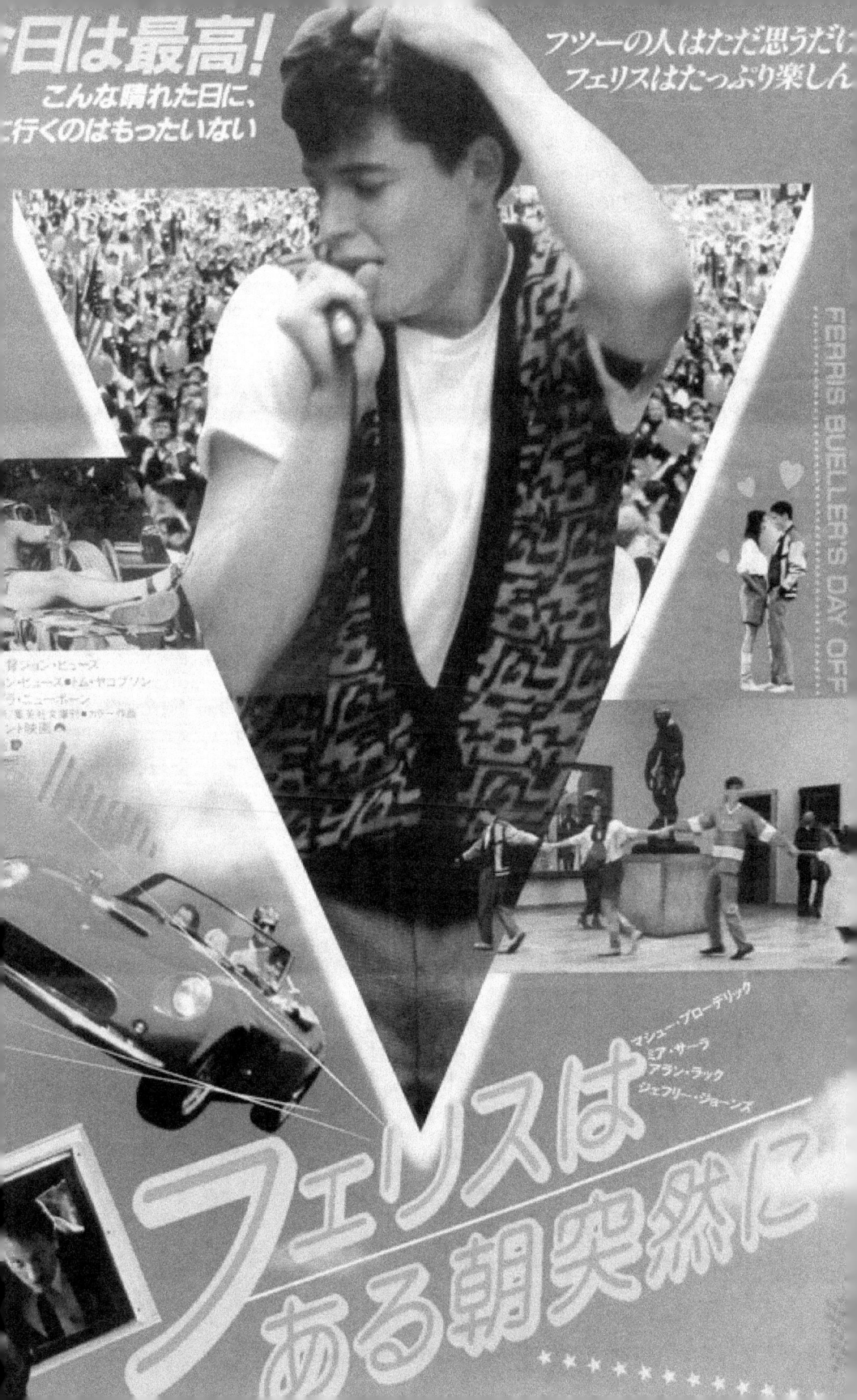

previews (when it was accompanied by a classical guitar piece and occurred after the parade) to being a poignant counterpoint to the rest of the breakneck wackiness. Their song "The Edge of Forever" also hits home in the film's conclusion. A couple of edgier UK acts, Mick Jones and Don Letts' project Big Audio Dynamite and concept band Sigue Sigue Sputnik, also appear.

THE WALLPAPER OF THEIR LIVES

Ferris' bedroom sports more posters per square inch than can be easily chronicled, but we have confirmed sightings of Cabaret Voltaire, Killing Joke, Flesh For Lulu, and The Damned. He sleeps beneath an oversized Bryan Ferry poster.

JOHNNY HUGHES SING-ALONG SHOW

Ferris features what is likely the most important lipsync scene in cinema, and it's hard not to get swept away with crowd of 10,000 extras, even if Ferris is singing to two songs from 1963.

Danke Schoen: Hughes hated the song with a passion, calling it the "most awful song of my youth. Every time it came on, I just wanted to scream, claw my face. I was taking German in high school – which meant that we listened to it in school. I couldn't get away from it." And you won't be able to get away from it either, as it pops up two other times

in the film. Dance choreography for the number was worked up by Kenny Ortega.

Twist and Shout: The film renewed interest in the song, putting it back in the chart 23 years later at, coincidentally, #23. Awareness of the song with record-buying youths was also bolstered by Rodney Dangerfield's cover for Back to School the same year. Ortega's choreography was ditched by Hughes on set, who wanted it to look more spontaneous.

THE BIG HIT

If there's an official sound to Ferris, it's "chka-chk-aaah," which makes Swiss band Yello's oddball electronic song "Oh Yeah" the hit of the film. Through association with the film it somewhat miraculously charted at 51 on Billboard Hot 100 (and even higher on the Dance charts) in 1986.

At the time, an official soundtrack was not released for the film – but 100,000 7" singles were sent out to members of his fan club. "A&M [Records] was very angry with me over that," Hughes said. "They begged me to put one out, but I thought 'who'd want all of these songs?' I mean, would kids want "Danke Schoen" and "Oh Yeah" on the same record?" 20 years later, La-La Land Records did put out a CD with both songs on it.

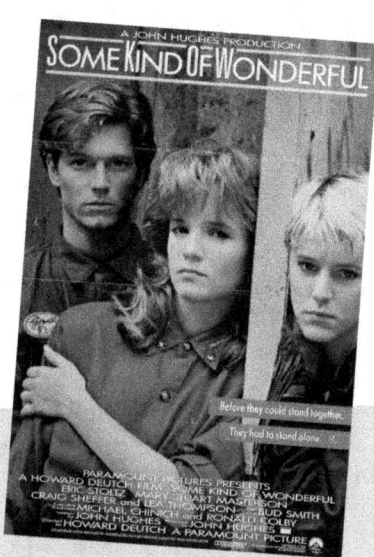

SOME KIND OF WONDERFUL (1987)

Didn't like how *Pretty in Pink* ended? Want the plucky sidekick to win? *Some Kind of Wonderful* makes amends (viva Duckie!) in a gorgeous and engrossing, if downplayed way.

Artist Keith (Eric Stoltz) has a crush on popular girl Amanda Jones (Lea Thompson), thus ignoring the natural chemistry he has with his long-time female friend, the spunky, boyish Watts (Mary Stuart Masterson). Against all logic, Keith trades in his college fund for one ultimate date night – an almost pathological attempt to render all future date ideas null and void, with an antique car (chauffeured by Watts in a uniform, no less), expensive meal, private museum tour that reveals a stunning painting he made for his date, and a private conversation on the stage of the Hollywood Bowl.

As with *Pretty in Pink*, Hughes offered roles to Molly Ringwald and Andrew McCarthy, who very rightfully feared they were making the same movie over again. With a new cast, however, the dynamic changes dramatically – recall as you watch that

Stoltz and Thompson were almost the duo of Marty and Lorraine in *Back to the Future*, and you can see what that would have done to the energy of that film here. It was Stoltz who helped the production approach Thompson, who added a layer of vulnerability when she felt the character was written as little more than physically attractive. Craig Sheffer is uncomfortably icky as popular boy Hardy Jenns, and Elias Koteas makes an interesting punk called simply "Skinhead."

While Hughes was writing the script with director Deutsch, he stayed up late one night blasting music, and walked in at 5:30 in the morning with what was supposed to be a rewrite. "We needed five pages, and it was 50 pages." Deutsch recalls. "I said, 'What did you do?! What is this?' and he said, 'Oh, I didn't do that. I did something else. Tell me what you think?' And it was *Ferris Bueller's Day Off*. He wrote the first half of the movie in, like, eight hours, and then finished it a couple days later." Deutsch was so smitten with Thompson that he commissioned ten paintings until he found one that he liked, and he subsequently married her.

Martha (Valley Girl) Coolidge was originally set to direct, and envisioned a darker, less-verbal approach to the film. Hughes didn't buy it and had her fired along with some of the cast she had already set up. Filming had begun, with Stoltz in the lead and Kyle MacLachlan as Hardy; Stoltz' more rebellious shoulder length hair was then cut and his character cleaned up to fit the new vision.

Roger Ebert ended his review at the time this way: "*Some Kind of Wonderful* is yet another film in which Hughes and his team show a special ability to make an entertaining movie about teenagers, which is also about life, about insecurity, about rejection, about learning to grow. I sometimes have the peculiar feeling that the kids in Hughes's movies are more grown up than the adults in most of the other ones."

NAME THAT TUNE

Watts is named after Rolling Stones drummer Charlie Watts, and Amanda Jones is named after the Stones song of the same name, which makes for some rather distracting use on the soundtrack

ALTERNATIVE RADIO GOLD

"I Go Crazy" by Flesh for Lulu was a college radio staple, but only one of

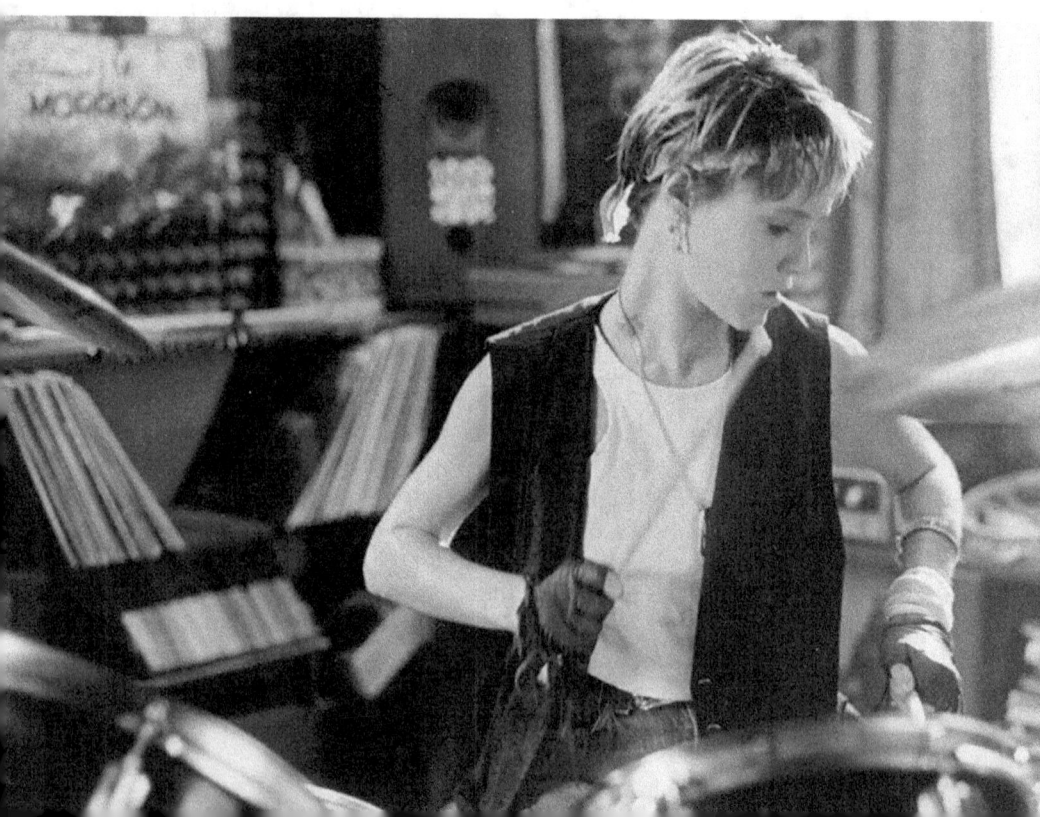

the band's songs ever penetrated the charts ("Postcards from Paradise"). It gets about four plays in the film.

THE WALLPAPER OF THEIR LIVES

Watts' rehearsal room sports posters of the bands General Public, Sex Pistols, Go-Go's, Depeche Mode, and The Ups.

THE JOHNNY HUGHES SING-ALONG SHOW

The Rolling Stones version of "Miss Amanda Jones" backs a getting-ready montage, and Keith sings soapily along in the shower for a moment.

"You can't judge a book by its cover."

"No. But you can tell how much it's going to cost you."

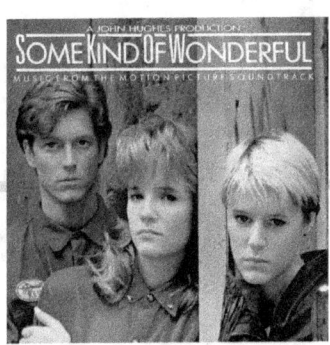

SOUNDTRACK

Do Anything
Pete Shelley

Brilliant Mind
Furniture

Cry Like This
Blue Room

I Go Crazy
Flesh for Lulu

She Loves Me
Stephen Duffy

The Hardest Walk
The Jesus and Mary Chain

The Shyest Time
The Apartments

Miss Amanda Jones
The March Violets

Can't Help Falling in Love
Lick The Tins

Turn to the Sky
The March Violets

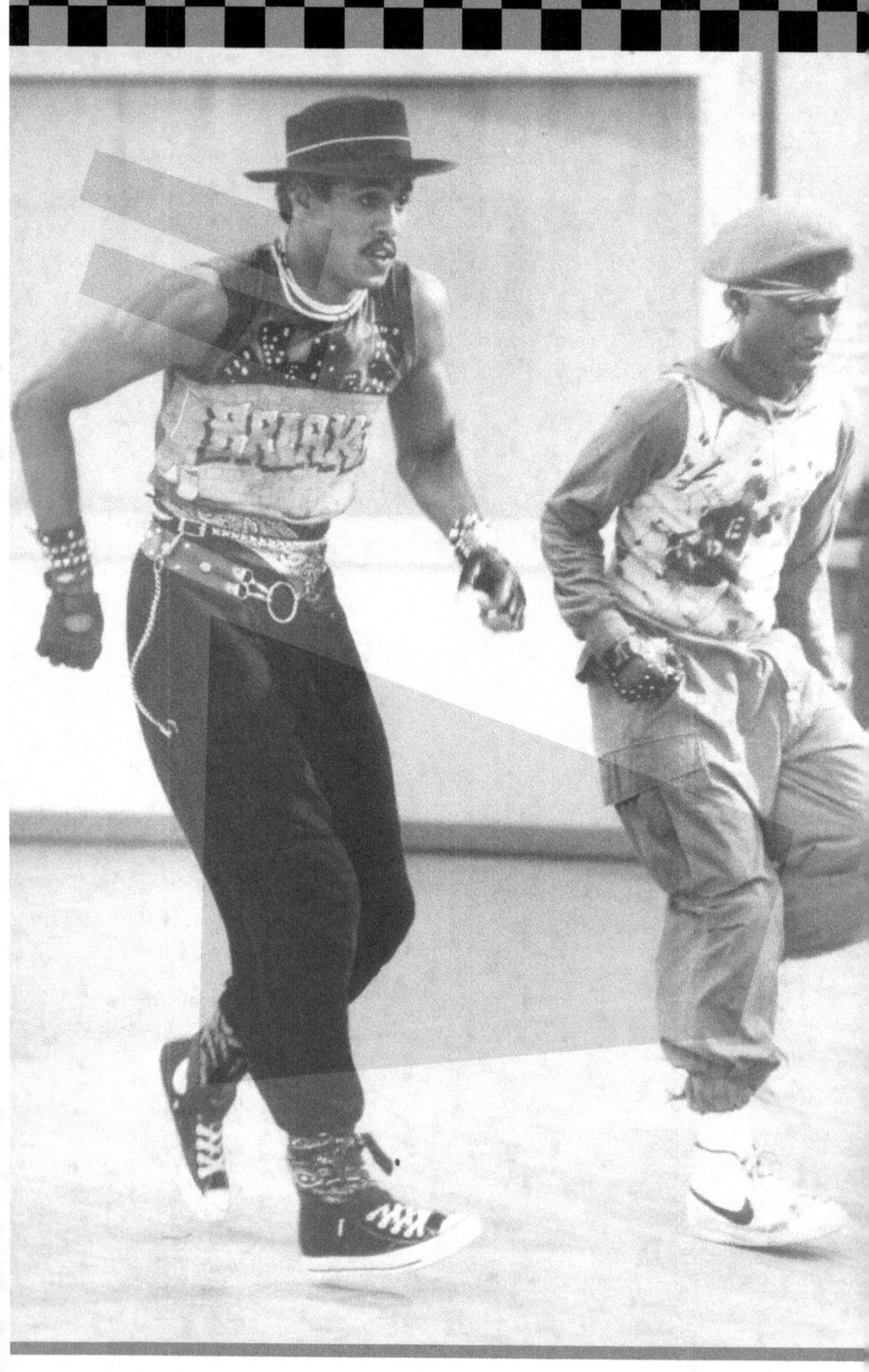

12

RAPPERS & BOMBERS, BREAKERS & LOCKERS

While breakdancing movies may have been a passing fad, the lasting influence on urban dance can not be understated. Between movies and MTV, the hip-hop wave spread into middle America and forever shifted the dynamics of popular music around the world.

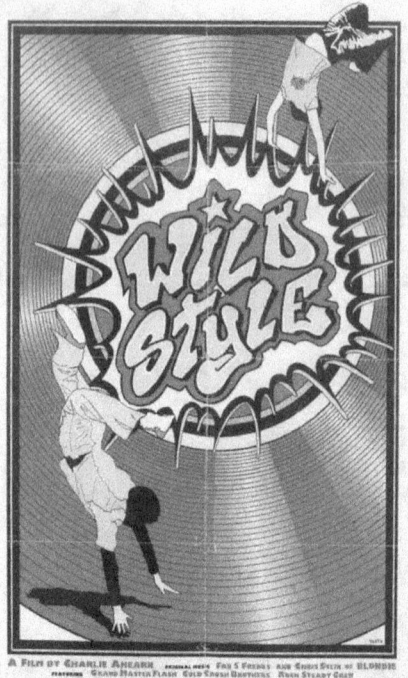

A FILM BY CHARLIE AHEARN ... FAB 5 FREDDY AND CHRIS STEIN OF BLONDIE
... GRAND MASTER FLASH COLD CRUSH BROTHERS ROCK STEADY CREW

WILD STYLE (1983)

Wild Style is about as independent and off-Hollywood as you can get: stark, cheap, and straightforward. It's raw authenticity stems from the fact that it was improvised by non-actors on real locations, long before the movie studios were aware of the immense cultural movement that was awakening in the the boroughs of New York City. You have to like it raw (and stiff, flat-lit, and rudimentary) to get through this movie, but when viewed as a time capsule it presents a snapshot of ground zero of the hip hop revolution.

Zoro and Rose are famous graffiti artists, portrayed here by famous graffiti artists "Lee" George Quiniones and Lady Pink. Zoro works his spray magic on subway cars, and is tempted by the prospect of an interview that could bring attention to his work, but fears that it would lead to police raids and worse. The reporter, Virginia (Patti Astor), is from an entirely different art world; white, uptown, establishment. She sports a bleached white punk haircut and listens to Blondie in her car; when the car dies en route to her interview with Zoro the neighborhood kids push it the rest of the way. Virginia spirits Zoro away to an upper class art party, where there are sexual advances on the young artist, and talk of a TV-special. Eventually Zoro helps repaint a bandshell for a climactic rap showcase, which he observes from high above the stage in a rapturous state.

Though centered around the graffiti culture, there's dance footage and MC footage galore to make up time in the loosely plotted film, including dance outfits like the Rock Steady Crew, and MCs like Fab Five Freddy, Cold Crush Brothers, Busy Bee Starski and Grandmaster Flash. If the producers had been able to compensate the artists, much more of the final concert would have been featured (as it was performances by Furious Five, Treacherous Three and Grandmaster Flash are cut from the film but restored in DVD versions). The end concert was filmed multiple times due to technical problems, but what remains in the film is shot nicely and has great sound. There is no lipsyncing in the film, which makes it one of the only of its type in this 80s Hip Hop Movie list.

Wild Style has no real conflict and no real conclusion, but is the first boots on the ground in what would be a brief but profitable movement of 80s hip-hop movies. Little more than a student film in quality, Wild Style would spawn immediate copies like *Beat Street* and become the defacto research document for later entries like Netflix's *The Get Down*.

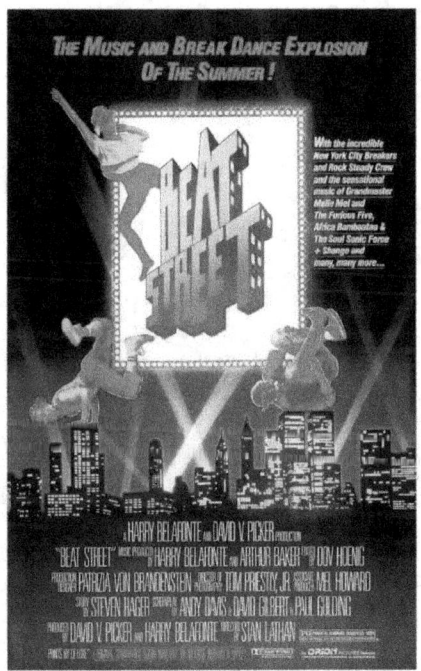

BEAT STREET (1984)

A relatively gritty look at the South Bronx music and graffiti scenes, through a slightly Hollywood narrative lens, *Beat Street* was shot in the real deal locations in the winter of 1983 and looks it. Real train tunnels, real subway stations and streets astride hollowed-out tenements give the rather thinly-written proceedings a jolt of authenticity. But where *Beat Street* rises above some of the other films of this genre is in the extended musical numbers, with on-screen performances by Grandmaster Melle Mel & the Furious Five, Doug E. Fresh, Afrika Bambaataa & Soulsonic Force and the Treacherous Three (featuring Kool Mo Dee). Unfortunately, the energy and skill of the real performers tends to overshadow the film's hero, an MC played by Guy Davis, and you can't really believe that legendary DJ Kool Herc (in a cameo appearance) sees the next big thing in Davis.

Beat Street is like the 1950s musical films like *Rock Around the Clock*, where a thin bit of plot allowed the producers to string together a series of musical performances. As a film genre, you don't get much cheaper than that, and producers are guaranteed a decent return – not for the film's story elements but the chance to see big screen performances by musical acts both important and marginal. *Beat Street* delivers on those performances, almost outnumbering the dramatic scenes and certainly going on for longer uninterrupted stretches. There are some jaw droppers. An elaborately costumed number with Afrika Bambaataa and the Soul Sonic Force (+ Shango) is a great eyeful. A talent show audition gives us the excuse to jam loads of acts into a few short minutes, at which point something called Andy B. Bad performs a song that is a hilarious anti-New Wave highlight (which swiftly receives a "next" from the judges but then goes on for another few horribly great bars).

But if you're like me, what you came here for is the dancing. I audibly shouted in amazement at gravity-defying dance sequences with Rock Steady Crew, New York City Breakers and Magnificent Force, which have some of the best floor stunts put on film (especially those taking place at NY club The Roxy). Unlike the sister film from 1984, *Breakin'*, only one secondary character in the film does any dancing, so there's a bit of a disconnect in the sequences and their relevance to the story.

On record, this was the first movie to inspire two soundtrack album releases (and a planned but ditched third attempt). Given the track listing on the film, it seems necessary! And since movies are distributed internationally (unlike, say broadcast entities like MTV), this film is credited with bringing visibility to the hip hop movement throughout Europe and especially Germany (where the film's distinctive mix of rap, Latin freestyle dance sounds and train "bombing" created a version of hip hop culture where those elements were inexorably intertwined).

Beat Street was reportedly based on a five-page treatment by Village Voice journalist Steve Hager, who wrote articles on hip-hop culture. Local rival dance groups, the Rock Steady Crew and the New York City Breakers, who appear in the film as the Beat City Breakers and the Bronx Rockers, respectively, remained on opposite sides of the set during filming to preserve their tension.

In the end, it can be a long slog to get to those performances and perhaps it's only as authentic as a Hollywood movie can be. For example, the graffiti that is featured in the film was made by the art department, and the characters wear Kangol hats and Puma sneakers (Puma was a sponsor and had its logo featured prominently on the album) despite the dancers' insistence that it wasn't authentic. And you can see why the Kangol hats were more of a rapper's thing, as in one scene where a body-popping dancer nearly loses his during some frenetic activity.

The lead character's attempts at innovations in the art (recording drips of water, experimenting with a Synclavier computer) don't lead to anything but a rote curtain call performance that incorporates many of the musical acts under the guise of a gospel-saturated memorial to their fallen friend. Still, great clothes, evocative locations, Rae Dawn Chong's smile, and some historical hip hop figures make it worth the effort. Is it as good as the genre ever got? Possibly.

BELAFONTE'S BEAT STREET

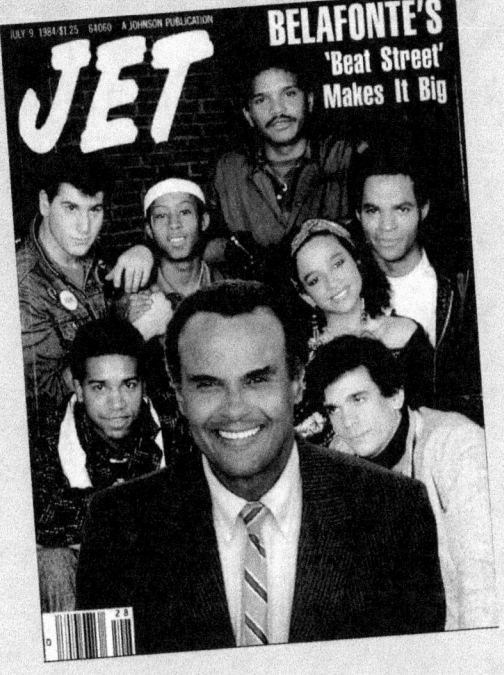

Harry Belafonte is a singer, songwriter, and activist, whose album *Calypso* became the first LP to sell more than a million copies in the U.S. within a year. Belafonte won a Tony award and was the first African American to win an Emmy in 1959. Harry Belafonte produced *Beat Street* and oversaw much of the accompanying album with partner Arthur Baker.

Actor Jon Chardiet (Ramon) says that Belafonte believed "hip-hop was an urban art form that hadn't been co-opted by white people. And before it got co-opted by the world and would appear on McDonald's commercials, he wanted to show it in all of its purity. He felt the movement, the hip-hop movement, was about all of this angst after the '70s, when you could murder somebody on the street and get away with it."

Belafonte stated in Jet magazine (July 9, 1984) "What appealed to me was being witness to the creation of a real folk art that developed under its own steam. The entertainment industry didn't create this. It was born on its own and it will go at its own pace to its own conclusion." Fending off comparisons to the competition *Breakin*, Belafonte said "the qualitative difference is that I think our film deals in a very honest way with the hopes and aspirations of the people of the community. We don't just exploit the break dancing."

VINCENT CANBY on BEAT STREET

"The film's melodrama adequately supports the nearly nonstop music and dancing, but the film itself is best understood as a trailer for the soundtrack album, the music for which was produced by Mr. Belafonte and Arthur Baker. If the album catches the intensity and wit of the film's big finale, it should be a smash."

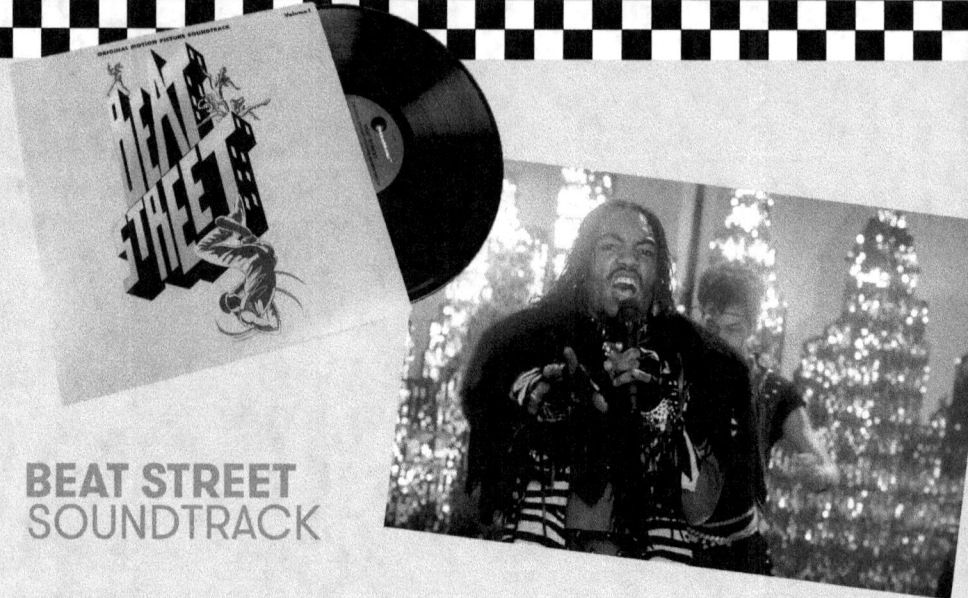

BEAT STREET
SOUNDTRACK

VOLUME 1

Beat Street Breakdown
Melle Mel

Baptize the Beat
The System

Strangers in a Strange World
Jenny Burton and Patrick Jude

Frantic Situation
Shango

Beat Street Strut
Juicy

Us Girls
Debbie D

This Could Be the Night
Cindy Mizelle

Breaker's Revenge
Afrika Bambaataa & Soul Sonic
Force

Tu Cariño (Carmen's Theme)
Rubén Blades

VOLUME 2

Son of Beat Street
DJ Jazzy Jay

Give Me All
Juicy

Nothin's Gonna Come Easy
Tina B.

Santa's Rap
The Treacherous Three featuring
Doug E. Fresh

It's All Right by Me
Jenny Burton

Battle Cry
Rockers Revenge

Phony Four MC's - Wappin'
Ralph Rolle

Into the Night
La La

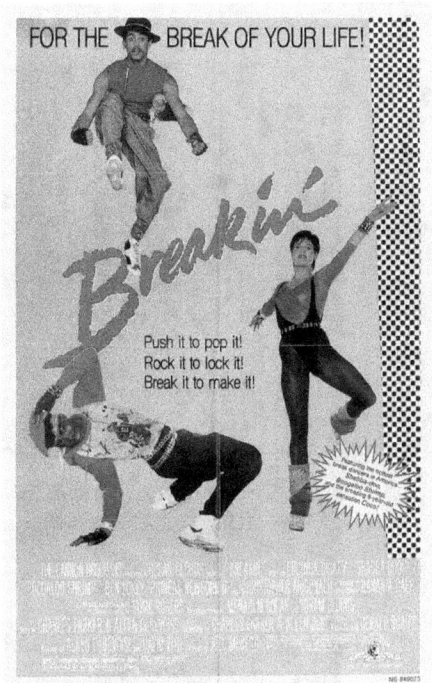

FOR THE BREAK OF YOUR LIFE!

Breakin'

Push it to pop it!
Rock it to lock it!
Break it to make it!

BREAKIN' (1984)

The Cannon Group, Inc., was not known for movies that were representative of real life. Their studio brought the world *Death Wish*, *Delta Force*, and more *Ninja* movies than you could shake a sai at. They were Hollywood's flashy Israeli cousin, exaggeration piled upon cheap excess. Perhaps that's why *Breakin'* and it's hastily assembled sequel (released May and December of 1984 respectively) are such a great entry into this discussion.

The *Breakin'* films are patently West Coast, to Beat Street's Old School East Coast, sunny and colorful where Beat Street is gritty and real. Lit like a musical and as much a *Flashdance* clone as anything, *Breakin'* shows us a world of Venice Beach and gym freaks and slick professional dancers with scarcely a tip of its hat to the "ghetto" through dialog. In classic Los Angeles fashion, lead Kelly (Lucinda Williams) is a waitress who dreams of being a dancer. And there are heaps upon heaps of spectacular dancing from choreographer Jaime Rogers. If it sometimes comes across as a hip hop *West Side Story*, it should, as Rogers starred in *West Side Story* in 1961 and continued to choreograph for TV and film throughout the 70s and 80s. The transitions into dance numbers come fast and furious and are much more organic than most films, flowing freely from dialog and situation like the best movie musicals.

Despite the urban trimmings this is indeed a classical movie musical: what would you expect from a breakdancing movie that name drops Fred Astaire before having a street corner dance solo with a broomstick? The Hollywoodisms continue throughout, culminating in a great bit where top hat and tails get ripped down and converted to street wear for a contentious audition.

Is there any street cred to be found in *Breakin'*? West Coast rapper Ice-T makes his screen debut and has an extended opportunity to provide his looser, So-Cal style rhymes to a dance sequence. But that's about it. Only the pretty bits of Los Angeles are trotted before the cameras, the "ghetto" is shown as a sunny neighborhood with happy families and backyard garage studios. The heroes have nice convertibles and great clothes. *Breakin'* exists in a world that's miles and miles from the cold, snow-flocked ruins of the Bronx in *Beat Street*. The film's antagonists are a slightly threatening dance teacher (Ben Lokey), and a very unthreatening but equally skilled rival dance gang called Electro Rock.

Watch out for Jean Claude Van Damme in the crowd at Venice Beach early on, jump starting his career cleverly by dancing front and center in a revealing shirt (but you will never unsee how short he really is). Menahem Golan reportedly made the film after his daughter saw some breakdancers on Venice Beach, and within three weeks it was shooting. Aware of the competition, he declared "We must beat *Beat Street*," and launched a race to get his breakdance film into theaters first.

Breakin' is so optimistic it's hard to hate it, thanks solely to the the film's upbeat music and central characters, the TKO Crew. Lucinda Dickey is a spectacular dancer but plays it down to earth and "aw shucks-y;" she was a

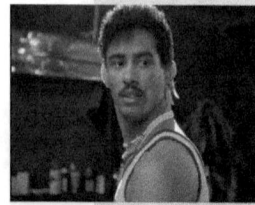
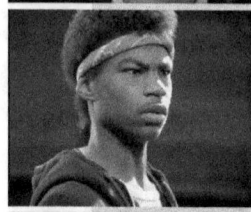
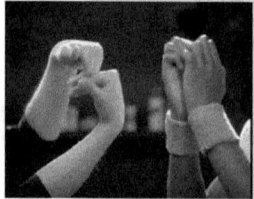
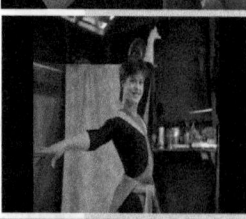
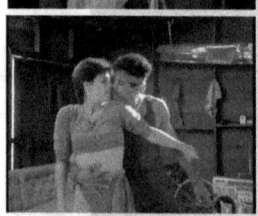

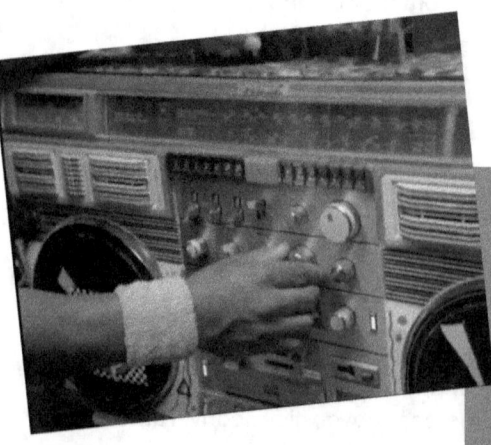

MONTAGE FROMAGE
"Ain't Nobody" Chaka Khan

Ozone and Turbo reluctantly teach Kelly to dance "street." Fantastic song, pure montage joy...

RATING
9/10

gymnast and jazz-trained dancer that Golan thought could be a big star in a post-*Flashdance* film landcape.

Adolfo "Shabba Doo" Quiñones and Michael "Boogaloo Shrimp" Chambers are charismatic and cool buddies, despite being 12 years apart in age; Quiñones likens their on-screen relationship to Dean Martin and Jerry Lewis. Quiñones was 29 at the time of filming, and was on tour with Lionel Richie, for whom he had done choreography for the video for "All Night Long." Fellow Richie tour dancers Chambers and Bruno "Pop'N'Taco" Falcon also left the tour to do the film. Chambers called it "the *Enter the Dragon* of hip hop, 'cause he had the best of the best. There were no stuntmen, and we weren't actors, we were all green. They just said 'put 'em on camera!'" Tension between Quiñones and Dickey was real, as he reportedly resented anyone lacking in the proper street credentials. This

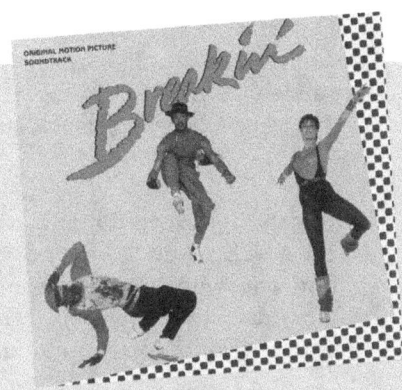

SOUNDTRACK

Breakin'... There's No Stopping Us
Ollie & Jerry

Freakshow on the Dance Floor
Bar-Kays

Body Work
Hot Streak

99 ½
Carol Lynn Townes

Showdown
Ollie & Jerry

Heart of the Beat
3V

"Street People
Fire Fox – Music by (Ollie & Jerry)

"Cut It
Re-Flex

Ain't Nobody
Rufus and Chaka Khan

Reckless
Chris "The Glove" Taylor & David Storrs - Rap by Ice-T

NOT ON THE ALBUM:
"Tour de France" by Kraftwerk... A great song for broom dancing!

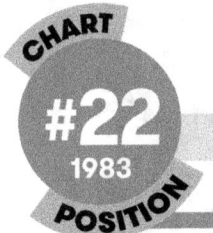

CHART

#22

1983

POSITION

Also #1 on R&B Charts
US Hot Black Singles

extended to co-star Chambers, as well.

On the film's lasting impact, Quiñones feels that if *Breakin'* hadn't succeeded at the level that it did, "we wouldn't know hip-hop as we know it today."

Roger Ebert gave it half a pass at the time, dubbing it "sweet and high-spirited and with three dancers who are so good they deserve a better screenplay," and correctly lauding it for "dance sequences of astonishing grace and power." It became one of Cannon's highest grossing films, with a worldwide gross of over $57 million on just over a one-million-dollar investment. And with a return like that, Menahem couldn't resist a second trip to the breakdancing bank.

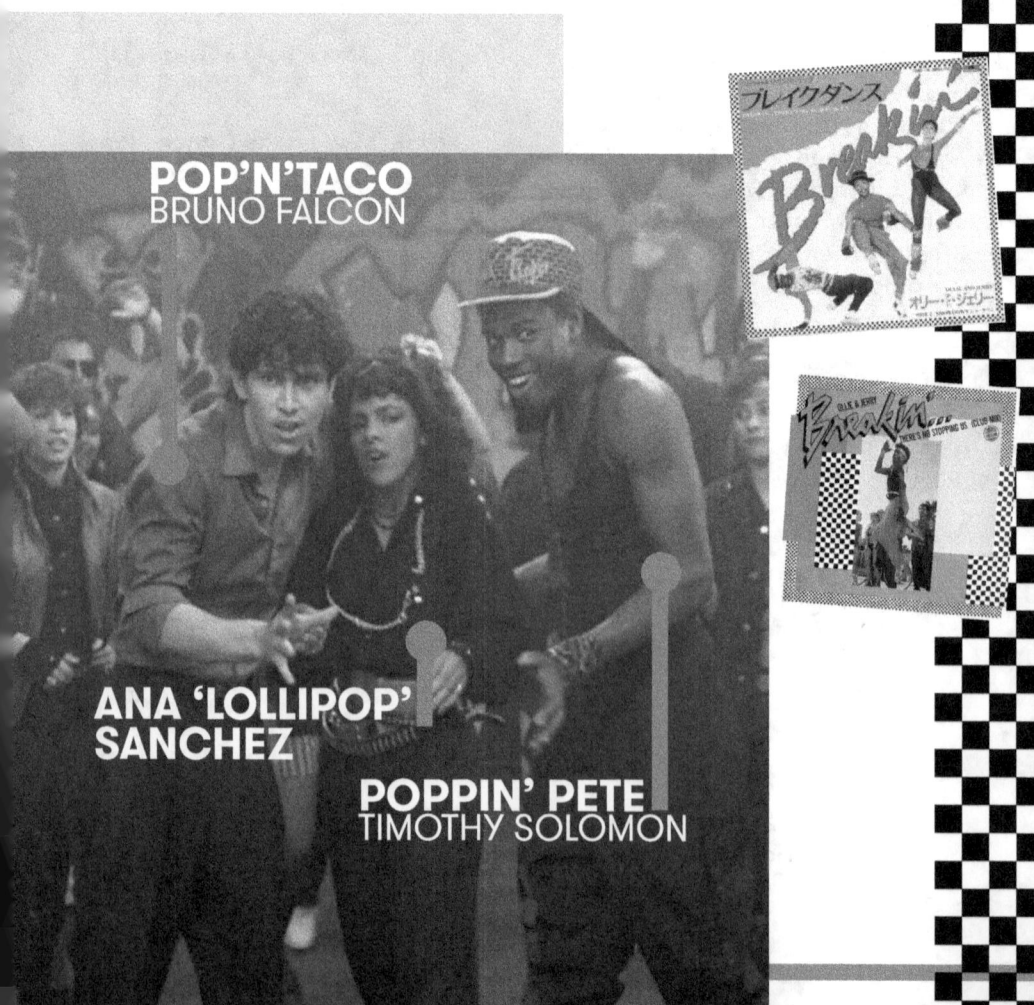

POP'N'TACO
BRUNO FALCON

ANA 'LOLLIPOP' SANCHEZ

POPPIN' PETE
TIMOTHY SOLOMON

OZONE
SHABBA DOO

- Adolfo Quiñones
- Founding member of The Original Lockers with Don "Campbelllock" Campbell, Fred "Rerun" Berry and Toni Basil
- Choreography for Madonna and onstage for Who's That Girl Tour 1987
- In Chaka Khan's "I Feel For You" video

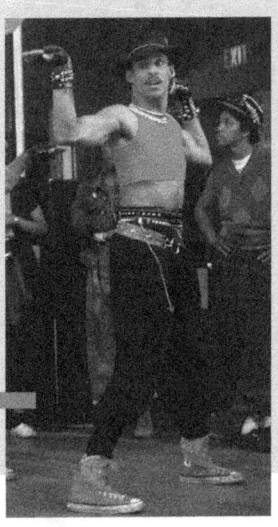

KELLY
LUCINDA DICKEY

- Featured dancer in Grease 2
- Did Ninja 3: The Domination before the Breakin films, though it was released after
- Also stars in *Cheerleader Camp*

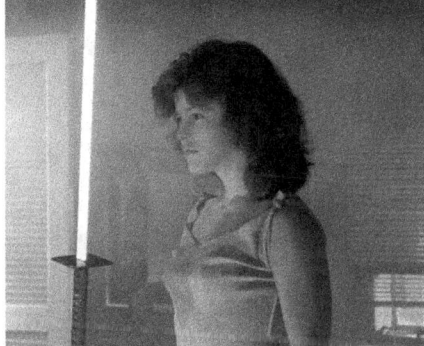

TURBO
BOOGALOO SHRIMP

- Michael Chambers
- Was in Lionel Richie video for "All Night Long," and inspired the song "Dancing on the Ceiling"
- Says he based his moves on sci fi films like *Clash of the Titans* terming the movement "liquid animation"
- Played "Urkel Bot" on TV's *Family Matters*
- *Reportedly* introduced the backslide aka moonwalk to Michael Jackson (and became a defacto poppin' trainer for Michael)

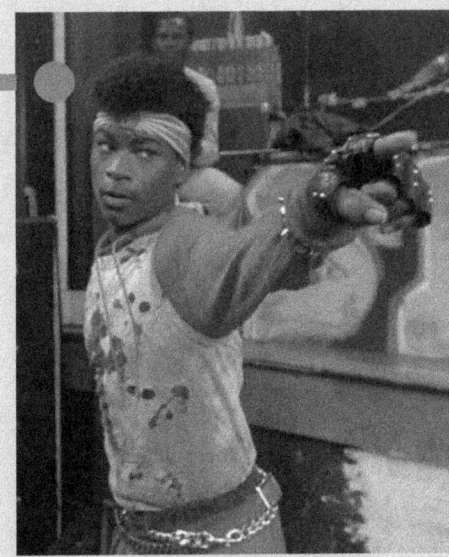

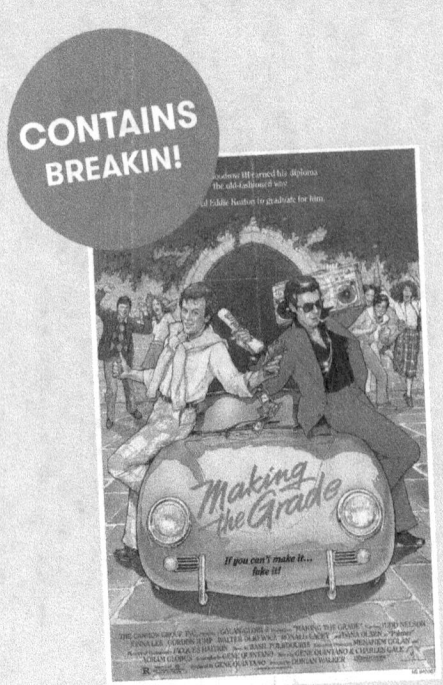

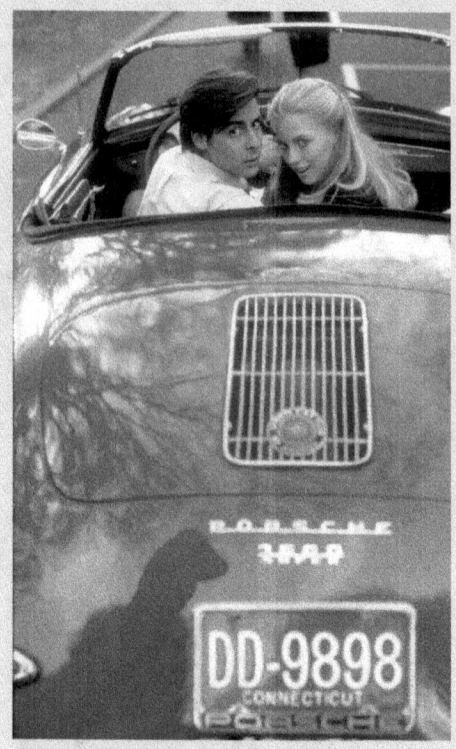

MAKING THE GRADE (1984)

While not a breakdancing movie, this Judd Nelson vehicle employs a dance scene to move the plot forward and is weird enough to mention here, mainly because of how well it defies credulity. Judd Nelson (who comes across as a prototype to pal Robert Downey Jr.'s 80s-era persona) plays Eddie Keaton, a largely unlikable con-man living out of his car, whose financial predicament with a volatile bookie (played by an early Andrew Dice Clay) forces him to go on the run. A chance meeting with spoiled rich kid Palmer Woodrow (Dana Olsen) gives him his way out: pose as Palmer at his prep school while he's out shirking responsibility on the slopes. If he can finish the school year and graduate, he gets $10,000.

Most of the jokes that follow poke fun at the nascent "preppy" culture of the 80s, with much ado about pink shirts, IZOD shirts, layering shirts, wearing a sweater around your neck with a shirt, and being snobby. But when it comes time to impress the heart-stopping debutante Tracey Hoover (Jonna Lee), Eddie breaks out his latent breakdancing skills to "Something About You" by Re-Flex. An obvious double does the hard work, and Nelson "robots" weakly in the closeups. She is instantly won over and the romance blossoms from there, once again demonstrating the power of a good floor routine. The rest of the film is a toothless *Animal House* and is mostly harmless, with a B-grade soundtrack of new wave material.

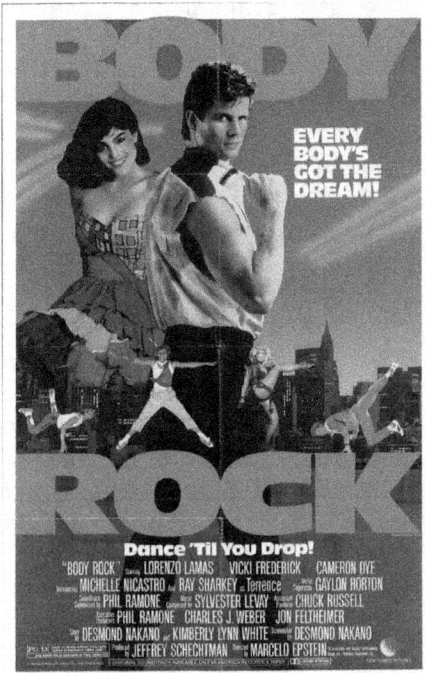

BODY ROCK (1984)

Leave it to New World Pictures to give us the barely-about-dancing dance movie. Chilly D (Lorenzo Lamas) comes out of the NYC street scene, where it seems like everybody but him is good at graffiti art and break dancing and rapping. After a $1 lessons from a kid who is the best dancer in the movie, Chilly somehow talks his way into a position at a new nightclub where he emerges inexplicably as a giant star.

Fans of films like Paul Verhoven's *Showgirls* will recognize the embarassing pleasures that await. Part of the contract with any audience is the successful suspension of disbelief. The unlikely fantasy of *Body Rock* is that anyone would identify Lorenzo Lamas as a great street talent, or that they would elevate him to a headliner at an upscale neon-drenched nightclub.

The film kicks in right away with dancing and spray painting to set up Chilly's roots, where there's a few nicely shot breakdancing routines using slow motion. Chilly thinks his painting is going to break him in to the big money, but seizes upon an opportunity at a new nightclub.

When Chilly and the Body Rock Crew perform their rap audition/introduction, there seems to be no relationship between them and the music (possibly recorded without the aid of a guide track on set), and the results is that they appear to be the worst rappers on film. There's even an eyepopping black-lite dance sequence that lets Chilly avoid any actual performance work; smoke machines and nunchaku add to the proceedings.

Chilly mentors wealthy female fan Claire (Vicki Frederick) which escalates into a physical relationship devoid of any on-screen chemistry but successful in removing Lamas' shirt (though most of his wardrobe is sleeveless anyway). In his defense, Lamas is huge and traditionally good looking, and the camera likes him. He's a TV-decent actor but strains credibility as a dancer or singer. Did I mention he sings?

"Smooth Talking" is the imaginary hit in the film, staged here with a

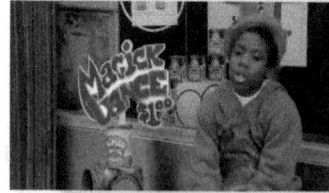

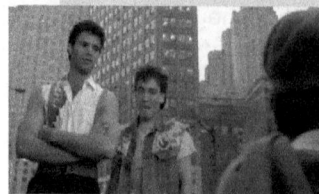

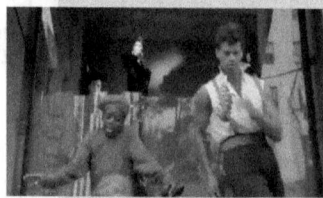

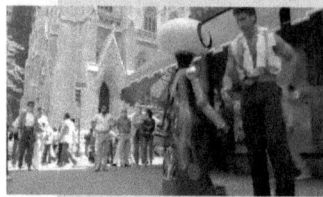

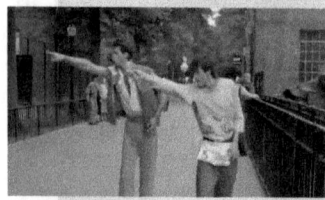

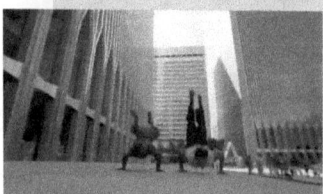

muscular geisha, a gal in chains, and a dancer in some kind of sewer or drainage pipe. Lyrics include:

"I'm going to stalk you like an animal, and eat you like a cannibal and make your body pay"

It's songs of that caliber that make the investment in watching the film pay off. There's what turns out to be a very silly scene where the now-successful Chilly returns to his own neighborhood and says hello to the locals, including speaking directly to the camera when there's no one else on the street. He doesn't break the fourth wall so much as give it a good bending, but it does break any sense of disbelief the film might have earned to that point.

Chilly gets banned from the club after he punches the club's (older male) business partner who kissed him, and has to negotiate his way back inside. With Chilly the headliner gone, there's a dance number in front of a cool 30 foot wide ghetto blaster, and when the cassette door opens up in a burst of fog juice to eject Chilly's protege/sex toy singing his song "Smooth Talker" the stakes are raised. Chilly bursts onto the stage and takes over the show, bringing his old crew up despite the management's

MONTAGE FROMAGE
"Teamwork" David Lasley

Chilly learns street dancing from Magick (La Ron A. Smith). Contains zoo animals, subway travel, and dancing outside the WTC and other NY landmarks!

RATING
5/10

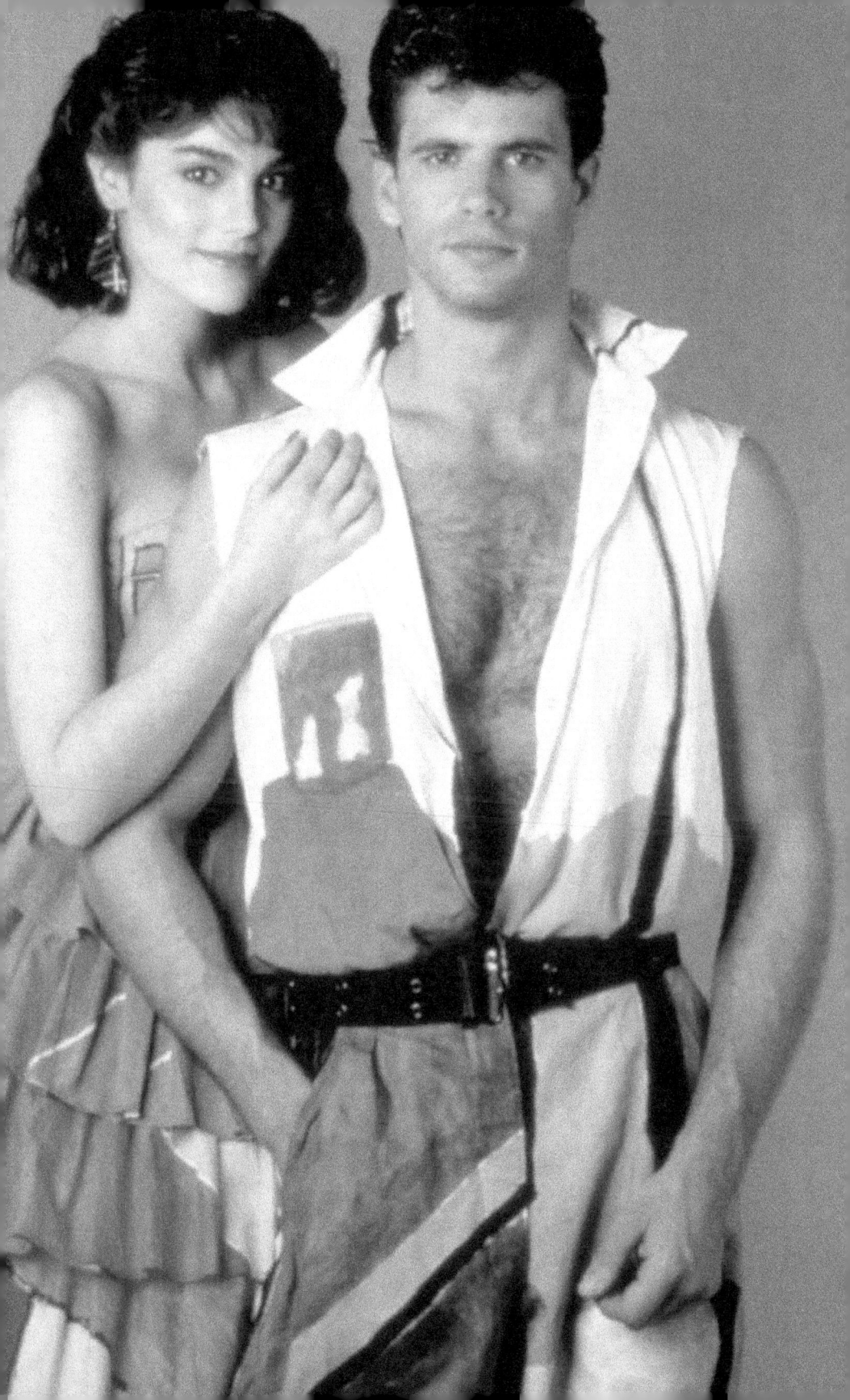

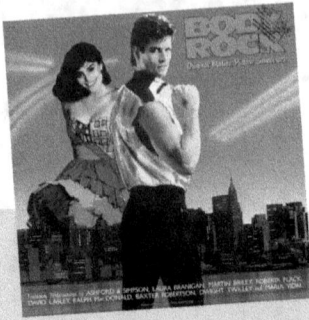

SOUNDTRACK

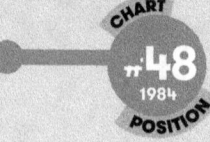

CHART #48 1984 POSITION

Body Rock
Maria Vidal

Teamwork
David Lasley

Why You Wanna Break My Heart
Dwight Twilley

One Thing Leads to Another
Roberta Flack

Let Your Body Rock (Don't Stop)
Ralph McDonald

Vanishing Point
Baxter Robertson

Sharpshooter
Laura Branigan

The Jungle
Ashford & Simpson

Deliver
Martin Briley

The Closest to Love
Ashford & Simpson

protests. The crowd rebels, the club owners relent and a Broadway-meets-Breakdancing number ensues.

Don't come for the dancing because there's not quite enough good numbers to salvage it, but there is enough second-rate 80s music to go around, and many an embarrassing laugh to be had. The Razzies ranked it as one of the Top 100 Enjoyably Bad Movies, if you go for that sort of thing. Maria Vidal's theme song broke into the Billboard top 100 at #48 but #8 on US Dance chart and #11 in UK. Soundtrack album on EMI America.

Great New York locations and cinematography by indie-film-master Robby Muller make up for plenty of dead spots in a pretty barren plot landscape. His final shot is kind of an amazing magic hour postcard-perfect triumph that belongs in a better movie.

NOT ON THE ALBUM:
"Fools Like Me," sung by Lorenzo Lamas, which topped at #85 in 1985, making it Mr. Lamas' only hit...

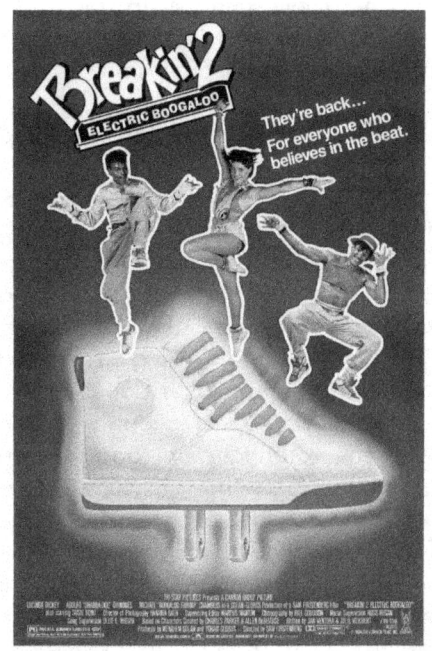

BREAKIN' 2: ELECTRIC BOOGALOO (1984)

Breakin' 1 ends with a quick summary of itself, and a plug for a part two – an *Electric Boogaloo* – right in the end credits, like some kind of "James Bond Will Return" promise. And if the Hollywood musical overtones were evident in part one, they let their Rodgers and Hammerstein flag fly completely for *Breakin' 2 Electric Boogaloo.*

Breakin 2 is Judy Garland and Mickey Rooney with boomboxes, the put-on-a-show plot device is aimed at raising $200,000 to save the Miracles Community Center from evil corporate development (in true 80s fashion, it's a mall). We find out that Kelly is a rich girl going against her parent's wishes. Since *B1*, she's gone back to doing more traditional dance but has grown tired of the chorus line routine. Now she must decide between Paris, Princeton, or saving the neighborhood.

Breakin' 2 is, to put it mildly, bonkers. When a musical number kicks in, it is so infectious the entire neighborhood is engulfed, with police officers and mail carriers flipping around as a mob joins in the cheery festivities. Kelly is given a tour of the community center by a mime. Nunchucks are used in a dance number. The boys have a sex-ed lesson with a stuffed dummy. Turbo dances on the ceiling. Ozone dances on the roof. Ice-T appears to be backed up by extras from *Road Warrior*. A massive dance routine erupts in the hall of a hospital, engulfing everyone present. *Breakin' 1* comes across like a documentary in comparison to the delirious PG charms of *Breakin' 2* – and PG they are, with no bad language, no drug use, no overt sexuality or violence. Star Shabba-Doo Quiñones readily admits "*Breakin' 2* was more of a cartoon."

The conflict in *B2* is paper thin, and any commitment we have to the characters is merely residual from *B1*. As in the first, the relationship between Kelly and Ozone is hard to define and unresolved, with subplot friction from Ozone's apparently-ex-girlfriend and Kelly's wait-a-minute-you're-engaged?- WASPy fiance. At times, one gets the feeling of walking in on a soap opera mid-season and being expected to pick up the details or go with the flow. The conflict over the Community Center is resolved in a series of deus-ex-machinae that are over before you can pop and lock, with all the antagonists giving up in rapid succession during a blinding neon conclusion. It's a bubblegum Beat Street riot of sherbet-colored outfits, pure 1984.

If *B1* was produced quick and cheap, that's nothing compared to *B2*. To get it done between the box office success of *B1* and a December release, Cannon employed three shooting units and seven editors to get it all done. Quiñones recalls that the schedule consisted of four days of dramatic scenes, then a dance number, alternating those scenes so they could prep different departments and keep up with the nine week workload. Some production shortcuts work in favor of the film – lots of wide shots succeed in showing off the dance numbers – but the laughably bad script does not help the rushed production.

The movie makes up for story shortcomings with some outrageous production numbers. Inspired by a Fred Astaire number from the film *Royal Wedding*, Golan wanted Boogaloo Shrimp to dance on the ceiling of their little garage studio. They borrowed the rotating set rig used in the production of *Nightmare on Elm Street*, and according to Shrimp the scene inspired the 1986 song "Dancing on the Ceiling" recorded by his former employer Lionel Richie. Combining the breakdance style with the rotating room gag is very effective, and the inclusion of a skylight provides a great surface for some of the spinning moves. Less effective is the very strange hospital number, which was based on a sketch called "Doctor Boogie" that Quiñones had done for the NBC variety show on which he was a choreographer and featured dancer, called *The Big Show*. The "vibrating" doctor in that scene is dancer Dane "Robot" Parker, who does the same full-body shiver as a featured dancer in Michael Jackson's "Beat It." Quiñones also recommended

THE FASHION OF BOOGALOO

Unlike the practical NY hip-hop style, with its slippery nylon track suits chosen for their light weight and floor-defying properties, the LA style shown in the *Breakin'* films is inspired by punk and heavy metal. The leather and studs look was popular with music groups looking to create a tough image, and an important early adopter was Michael Jackson. While a jacket full of zippers or studs may have been impractical to roll around in, it did create an image that worked great on film. Shabba-Doo's selection of a foxtail as ornament was influential, in the DVD commentary for *Breakin' 2* he states that he picked up his tail at a punk store in the Harajuku neighborhood of Tokyo.

Steve "Sugarfoot" Notario to play the role of the villain and new leader of the rival Electro Rockers, because he didn't like him for copying his troupe The Lockers and thought that negative energy would work here.

It was released to 1600 theaters, an insane amount for a low budget film, but earned only $15 million, perhaps suggesting that the fad had passed (or that December 21 is not a great time to sell a summer dance movie).

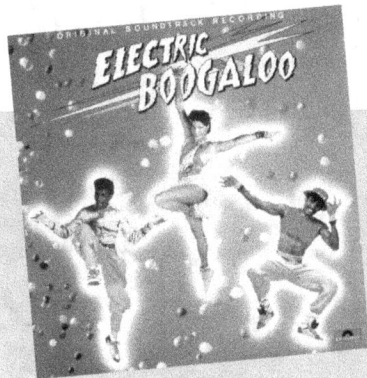

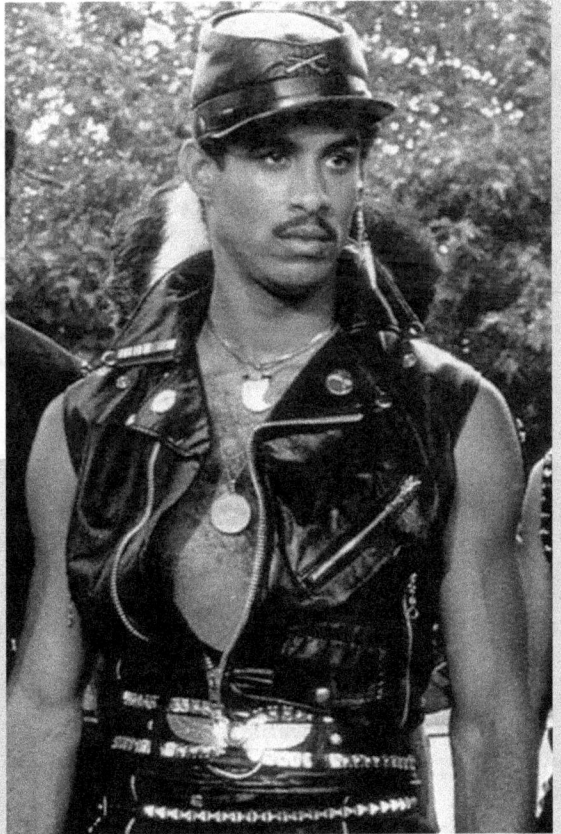

SOUNDTRACK

Electric Boogaloo
Ollie & Jerry

Radiotron
Firefox

Din Daa Daa
George Kranz

When I.C.U.
Ollie & Jerry

Gotta Have the Money
Steve Donn

Believe in the Beat
Carol Lynn Townes

Set It Out
Midway (Bruce Nazarian)

I Don't Wanna Come Down
Mark Scott

Stylin', Profilin'
Firefox

Oye Mamacita
Rags & Riches

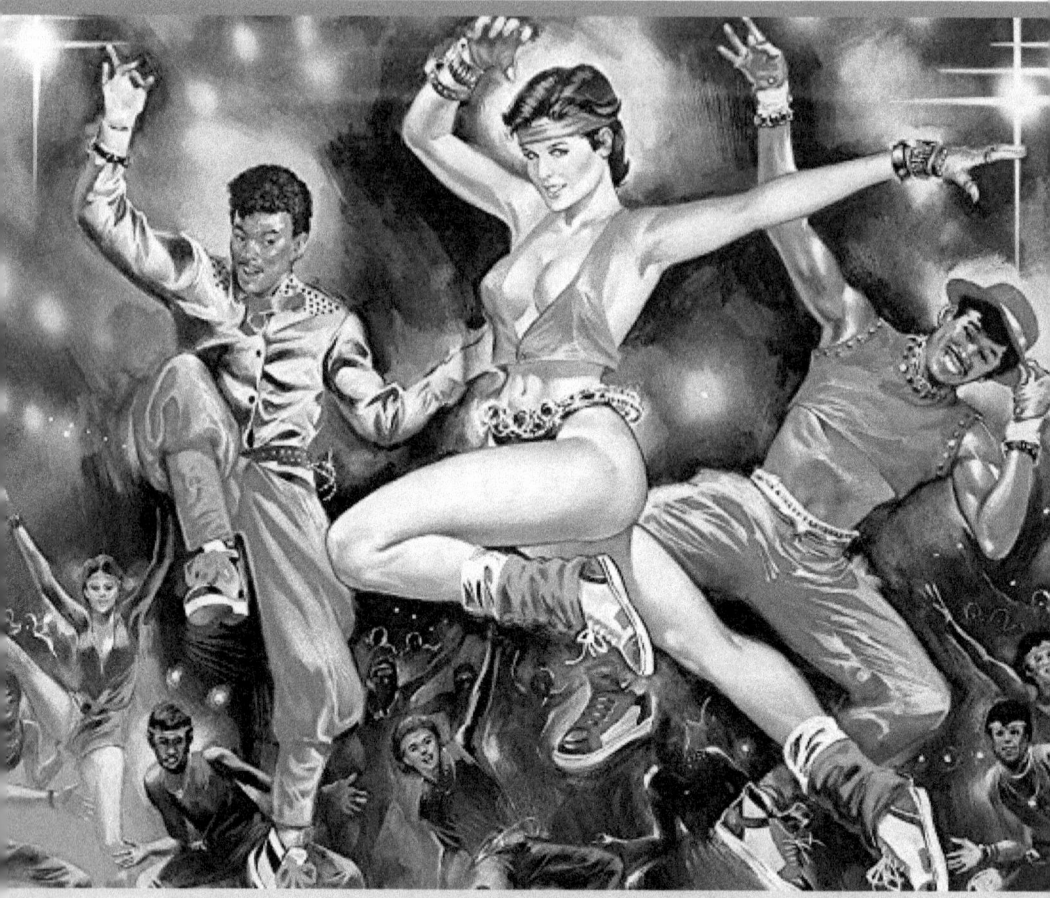

ROGER EBERT ON BOOGALOO

"a movie that wants nothing more than to allow some high-spirited kids to sing and dance their way through a silly plot just long enough to make us grin...

"Electric Boogaloo" is not a great movie, but it's inexhaustible, entertaining, and may turn out to be influential. It could inspire a boomlet of low-priced movie musicals -- movies not saddled with multimillion dollar budgets, Broadway connections, and stars who are not necessarily able to sing and dance. And at a time when movie musicals (as opposed to movie sound tracks) are seriously out of touch with the music that is really being played and listened to by teenagers, that could be a revolutionary development."

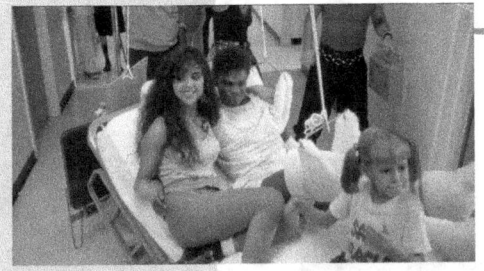

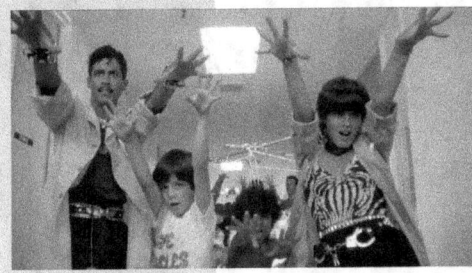

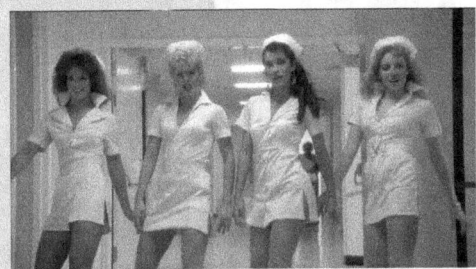

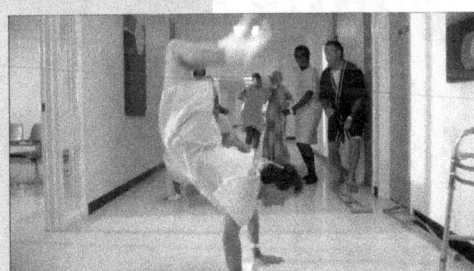

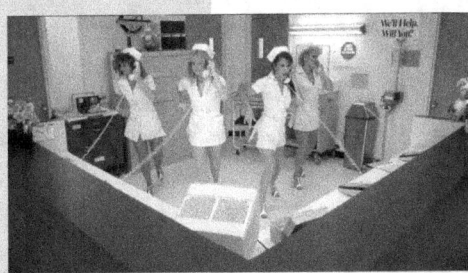

MONTAGE FROMAGE
"When I.C.U" by Ollie & Jerry

RATING 7/10

Mind altering breakin' goodness ensues when madness erupts in the intensive care unit.

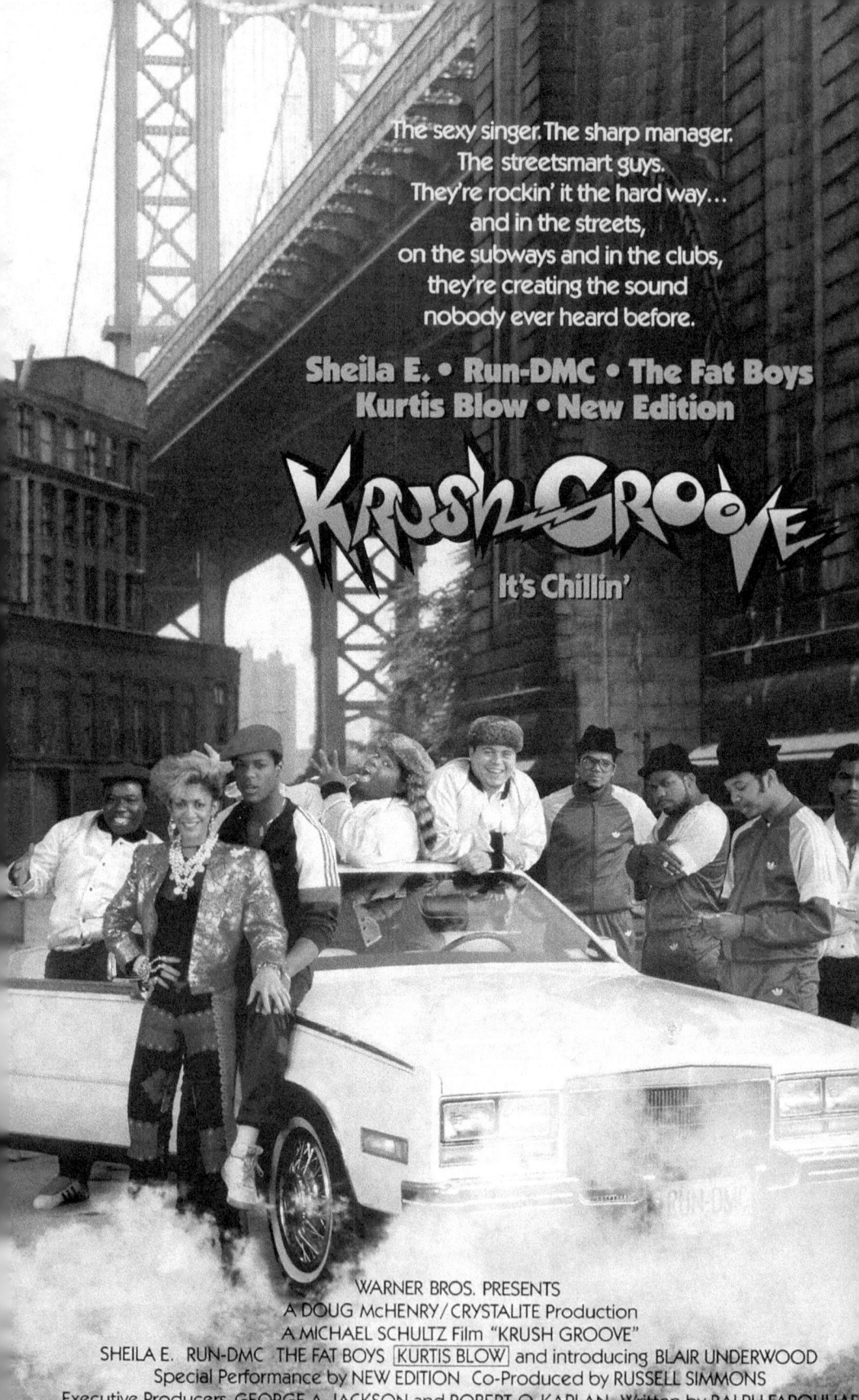

KRUSH GROOVE (1985)

The incredibly true story of how the Fat Boys got their name, and how Sheila E almost slept with Run from Run DMC, and – okay, it's not a totally true story. But the parallels are there.

Russell, but not the real Russell, is running a music label out of his dormitory (which really happened with Def Jam Records) with Rick Rubin, the real Rick Rubin. Real rappers and musicians come and go, and get some actual screen time with varying degrees of acting chops exhibited. When it comes to the drama, everybody gives it a go. Even Kurtis Blow has a scene with the film's star and holds his own. Joseph "Run" Simmons has to carry a lot of the movie, as does Sheila E, even if it's only a pretty loose story and series of episodic conflicts broken up with some good on-stage performances. The thin plot makes you realize how tight and straightforward some of the other films of this category are by comparison (while not innovative, *Breakin'* maintains its forward movement and has logical cause and effect relationships). This one is also a hard R for some persistent foul-mouthed trash talk of a type that's absent from some of the genre's other films.

Krush Groove is shot on great locations with the often-beautiful red-drenched cinematography of Ernest Dickerson (who would go on to work for Spike Lee). Dickerson is allowed enough poetic license to make this one of the intermittently best looking of the Old School movies. It's essentially a musical version of one of the AIP blaxploitation movies of the 1970s, but unlike those the movie fails to elevate any of the conflicts or bad guys to truly epic drive-in status. There's a smidge of a plot here, when dorm-room music mogul Russell passes up an offer and his acts all leave the label, he ends up in hock to a tough hustler and tries to save the label (and his ass) by signing Sheila E. In the end though, we didn't come for the plot, and this one fills the need to see your cult music heroes in action on stage and off, and was a good cheap way to introduce this music scene to middle America via the multiplex.

Sheila E rocks the Minneapolis look (this period's frock coats and ruffle shirts are a direct influence from the 1984 film *Amadeus*) and sound and performs her hit "Love Bizarre." Co-written and performed with Prince, it is one of the many songs by the Purple One that were gifted to other artists and became hits in their own right, but appears for the first time in this film. It's a duet, and Prince's vocal is featured, so when it comes time in the movie to acknowledge his part of the song, a band member steps forward and tries to fill Prince's (tall and tiny) shoes. The unfortunate guy who gets that task does what he can to make it look right and more or less pulls it off, but in comparison the music video from the same footage cuts out of those moments to dramatic scenes from the film. You might be able to fool 'em on the big screen, but you can't lie to 'em on MTV.

Early rap stage outfits, as shown in films like this, can be insane, showy,

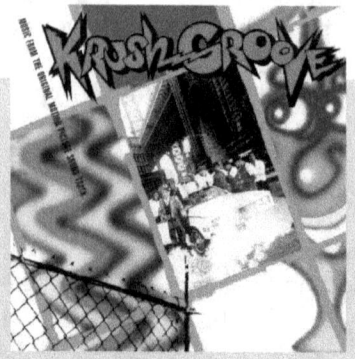

SOUNDTRACK

(Krush Groove) Can't Stop the Street
Chaka Khan

I Can't Live Without My Radio
LL Cool J

If I Ruled the World
Kurtis Blow

All You Can Eat
Fat Boys

Feel the Spin
Debbie Harry

Holly Rock
Sheila E

She's On It
Beastie Boys

Love Triangle
The Gap Band

Tender Love
Force M.D.'s

Krush Groovin'
Fat Boys, Run DMC, Sheila E, Kurtis Blow

and Funkadelic. Kurtis Blow goes with a jaw-dropping black leather long-tails tuxedo, white athletic shirt, and matching top hat. This glam look fits in well with the P-Funk-sized outrageousness that we see in *Beat Street* and *Breakin'*, but *Krush Groove* sets the new standard for the old school look in all the other scenes. Run DMC appear in their trademark uniforms, Adidas track suits or black leather suits (with Adidas underneath), with their fedoras always in tow. It's as iconic a look as you get. The baby faced Beastie Boys appear for a too-short moment, performing "She's On It," and look amazingly timeless in gear that's probably appearing right now at a college campus near you.

When the performances kick in, you quickly understand why they produced the film in the first place, and why Run DMC will always be one of the best. The strength and clarity of their voices and rock-tinged arrangements made them the inevitable break-out act that brought hip hop to the rest of

CLOSE DANCE SENIOR PROM TAKEAWAY HIT:

"Tender Love" by Force M.D.'s
Absolutely representative of that 1984-85 love song sound. Featured in the film's love scene between Sheila and Russell, which is about four beautiful Ernest Dickerson shots long but suddenly looks and sounds like we're in a much bigger movie.

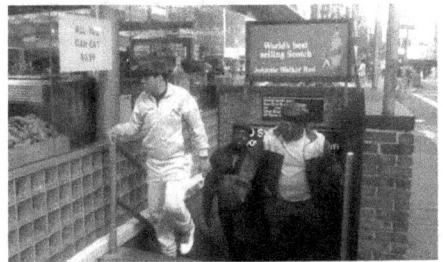
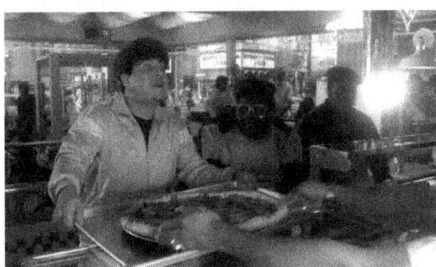
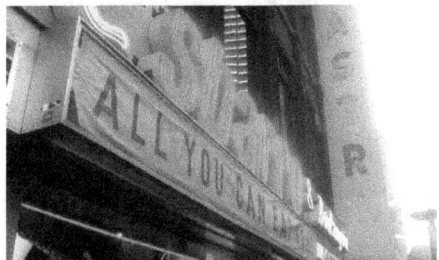
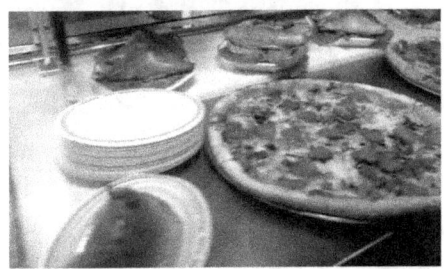
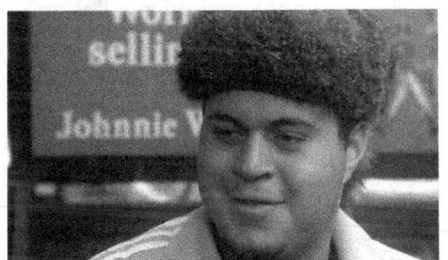
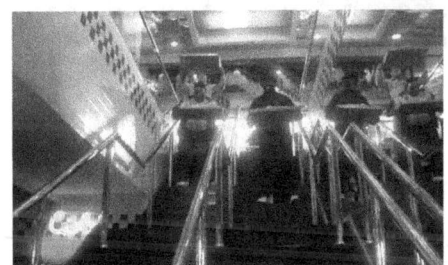
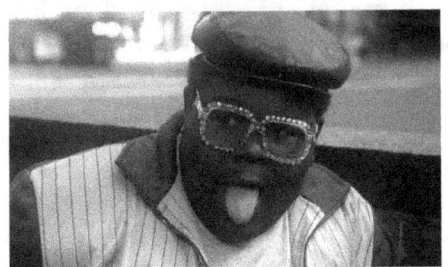
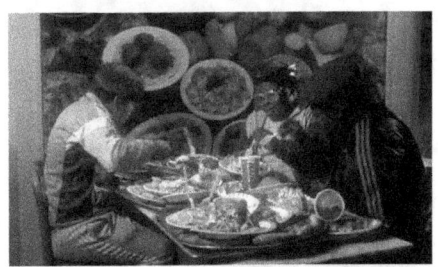

MONTAGE FROMAGE
"All You Can Eat" Fat Boys

The Boys, fresh off a disappointing audition, emerge from the subway, sobbing. A Sbarro restaurant beckons, with a sign proclaiming "$3.99 ALL YOU CAN EAT."

**RATING
8/10**

the country. Kurtis Blow, in addition to being the Music Supervisor of the film and writing the music on the Fat Boys songs, brings that silky, original New York MC voice to the proceedings. But this is a film that jams as many other players in as it can. Some acts sneak in under the rather dubious auspices of "auditions" or "talent shows" like the Tin Pan Apple Talent Contest (and though it sounds like a plot device from a Little Rascals short, it was a real radio contest that propelled Fat Boys to fame).

LL Cool J appears for the first time, bringing the plot to a halt in an impromptu audition despite the protests of the main characters. He manages to show everybody up in less a minute.

> **"Yo what's up? I said no more auditions, man!"**
> –Jason Mizell/Jam Master Jay

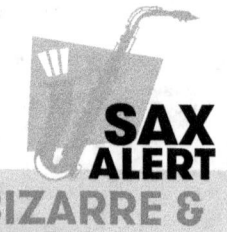

SAX ALERT
LOVE BIZARRE & HOLLY ROCK

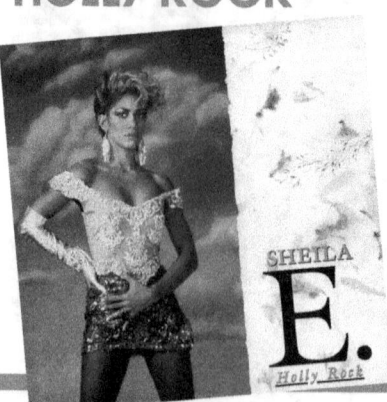

That brings us to the other story that's going on in Krush Groove – the one starring The Fat Boys. One reason it seems to be another film is that it follows a different set of musical rules. Where the Run DMC story plays out with "diegetic" motivations for each musical number, The Fat Boys are allowed full reign to break into song in the classical musical theater sense. Kicked out of class (apparently they're in high school? "You all get "F" for fetal pig!") they break into "Don't You Dog Me" in the halls. But the film's eye-bulging jaw dropping highlight is "All You Can Eat."

At the talent show, the Fat Boys stop being the "Disco Three," embrace their size and become an inexplicable instant sensation, winning first place and a recording contract (but getting upset when they don't get the 2nd place prize of a stereo). The drama comes to a head when Russell is beat up by some of the bad guy's enforcers, and Run comes to his aid. Everything gets wrapped up in one very hasty package, and everybody's sorry in one long shot in the dormitory hallway, and we're on to the curtain call. Deals are made with the literal "suits" and it's time for one more ensemble song, with Fat Boys, Run DMC, Sheila E, and Kurtis providing musical closure.

RUN DMC

MUSIC EXPOSÉ

- Founded Hollis, Queens, 1981
- First hip-hop group to achieve gold, platinum, and multi-platinum status
- First nominated for a Grammy Award
- Simmons originally DJ-ed for Kurtis Blow
- Hard rock sound and street-clothes aesthetic changed direction of hip hop

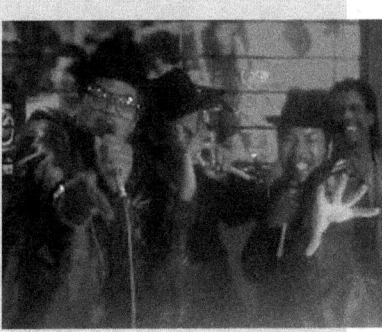

FAT BOYS

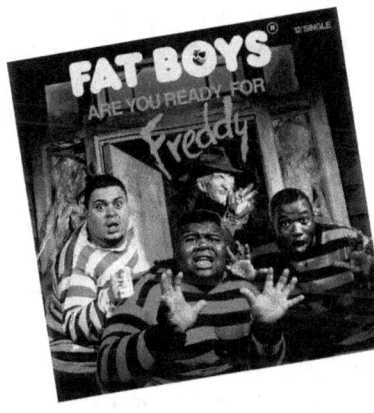

- Their manager was Swiss and set them up advertising for Swatch watches.
- Darren "Buff Love" Robinson was among the first to beatbox on record
- Recorded "Are You Ready for Freddy?" for Nightmare on Elm Street 4
- Buff died of a heart attack in 1995 at age 28

SHEILA E

- Sheila Escovedo is of Creole & Mexican descent
- Grew up lipsyncing to the records of her idol, Sammy Davis Jr
- Prince had been arguing with his bassist Andre Cymone about "which one of us was going to marry you," soon Prince would ask Sheila to marry him
- Some of the East Coast rappers from the film resented her attempting to rap in "Holly Rock"
- Prince was shooting Cherry Moon at the same time and told her not to do the love scene and briefly quit the film over the mounting pressure. Kurtis Blow told her "You just keep being you."

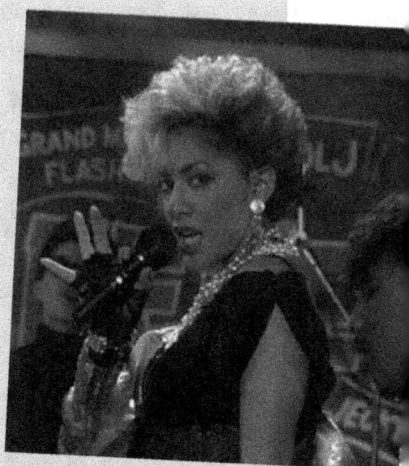

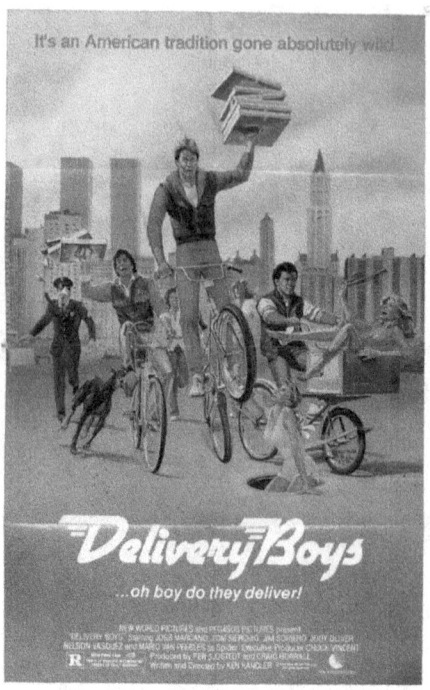

It's an American tradition gone absolutely wild

Delivery Boys

...oh boy do they deliver!

DELIVERY BOYS (1985)

It's *Porky's* meets *Beat Street* in this NY cheapie, released in 1985 but with an aesthetic and sense of humor that feels five years out of date. The marketing campaign emphasized the comedy aspect but you wouldn't know it from the film's opening, which gets us right into the break dancing in a Brooklyn church, with some terrific floor work and insane moves – we've seen someone spinning on their head, but never spinning on someone else's head. As we are introduced to the cast, we get a real sense of an authentic, pan-ethnic boroughs crew, with Puerto Ricans, Italians, and a Jew. It's slim on the African American

representation if you don't count the film's antagonists, led by Mario Van Peebles as an over the top Jamaican bad guy "Mister Spider," sporting metal teeth and a theatrical fashion sense. He and his equally flamboyant bodyguards arrive at Ben's Pizza, the central headquarters of the dance crew known as Delivery Boys. Most of them are employed in that capacity at the pizzeria, and Spider is there to deliver a message to the restaurant's spunky young dispatch Angelina: make sure the Boys don't compete in the upcoming Brooklyn Bridge Break Dance Off (with winnings valued at $10,000). He reminds Angelina what happened to the last crew that beat his team Devil Dogs, and it involves some serious voodoo witch doctor shit – which she later reports "spider said he was going to shrink your head and... Other parts." Spider presents the results of his last head (and other bits) shrinking right there in the restaurant, to prove his point.

This film is more vocal about race and ethnicity than the other early hip-hop films, with bits like "don't be prejudiced because he's blond," and "you're dancing white, you gotta dance like a Latino." Some of the exchanges and loose acting make it feel homemade or documentary, but the story is so outrageous it can only be constructed. There's some great offbeat moments and cartoony sound effects – a couple of the boys are sparring, the punches interspersed with loving comments of "you're the best," "no you're the best" until it ends in a chirping birds knock out worthy of a Warner Brothers cartoon. Angelina sends the Delivery Boys on fool's errands, traps designed to keep them out of the competition. Max ends up in a sex-slave situation uptown, Joey gets turned into a piece of modern art, and Conrad gets experimented on in a top secret government laboratory that appears to be working on erectile dysfunction medicine. To tell you the results of these hijinks would be to spoil the film's loopy fun, but it's the subtle details that keep you watching in wonder. One dancer stands before the church altar in a crop top shirt and shorts, begging the Lord for help to win the dance. A character must escape across town, in drag, complete with heels. Art patrons drink urine from champagne glasses. A stranger loans out a pair of shorts as one might bum a cigarette.

Eventually we must return to some dancing at the Brooklyn Bridge Dance Off, sponsored by WKTU FM 92 and a horribly unhip local women's panty magnate (there's a lot to unpack there but you'll get it when you see it). The final dance-off devolves into an outright rumble but the Delivery Boys come out on top, and the film ends with a campfire acoustic ballad sung by the film's de facto hero Max. The whole thing is bonkers, and somehow strangely compelling thanks its plucky low budget authenticity.

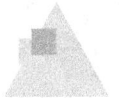

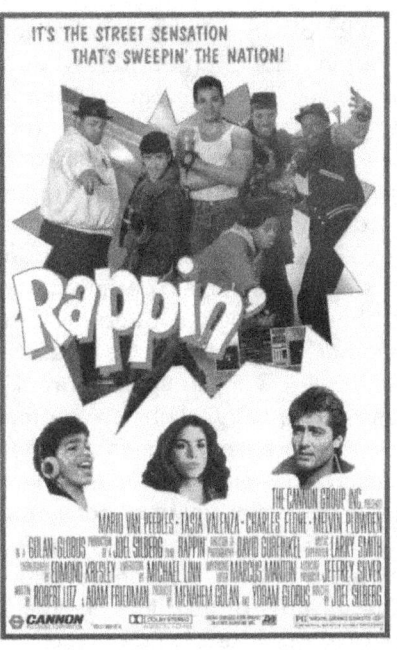

RAPPIN' (1985)

Breakin' director Joel Silberg gets right back to business with another Cannon quickie that could have been a cute urban retelling of the Robin Hood myth but ends up a meandering mess. It's a musical that never commits to being a musical, and a movie about rapping that has no good rappers in it. Like the Breakin' films, the plot is a mess; unlike the Breakin' films the main cast has not been hired for their musical skill and so if you came for the music you're out of luck. The film probably seemed out of touch at the time, and now seems way off the mark with its flavorless rap and ballet-tinged choreography. Street cred is low on this one, despite a diverse cast and the grisly old world urban locations of Pittsburgh.

Mario Van Peebles is John Hood, "Rappin' Hood" (get it?) who has just been released from an 18-month jail term to find his neighborhood threatened by an old nemesis and a new real estate developer. He rhymes a lot, at inappropriate times, and about very unhip subjects such as the color yellow. Van Peebles performance is dubbed by original Sugarhill Gang member Guy "Master Gee" O'Brien. Sugarhill Gang's groundbreaking song "Rapper's Delight" was among the first breakout hits in the genre when released in 1979, and established a lot of the old school conventions that would permeate the business for years to come. O'Brien is also the older brother of the film's co-star, *The Last Dragon's* Leo O'Brien who plays Hood's little brother Allan, and shows the same charm and screen presence as he did in Dragon, rescuing just about all the scenes he's in.

Awkward tunes are shoehorned in throughout the film, but there's never enough music in quantity or quality to save it. Once or twice there are outright musical numbers where the characters break into song and are accompanied by a score, notably in "Snack Attack," a prolonged number that occurs in a grocery store warehouse. Fresh produce is fondled and gamey rhymes are made, and one is not sure why there's a raw chicken or a whole cake sitting out in the warehouse but it's only a movie and a Cannon film at that.

The film provides the usual excuse

LEO O'BRIEN

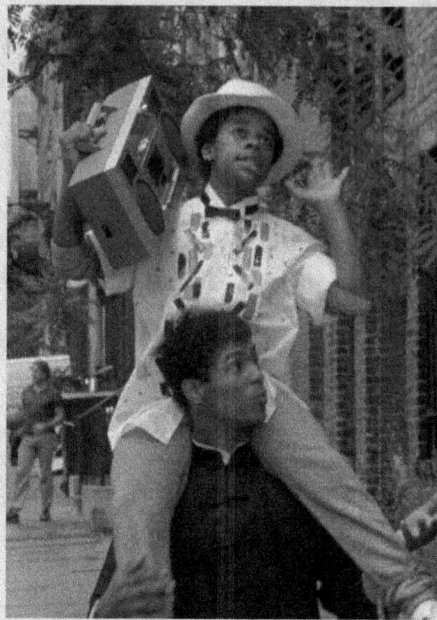

Leo O'Brien in THE LAST DRAGON (1985)

Leo appeared in some television shows and three films including New Jack City (1991). In 2011 an argument with a friend over a chair resulted in an altercation, he was shot three times. He lived for a year before succumbing to complications and died in 2012 at the age of 41.

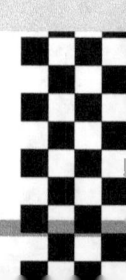

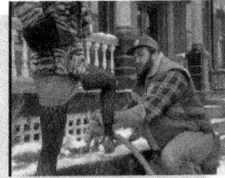
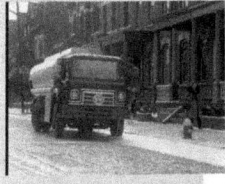
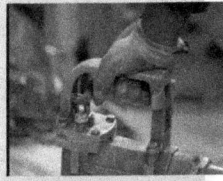
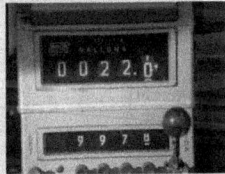
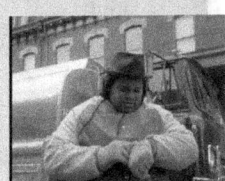
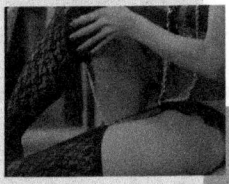

for performance shenanigans by making the love interest (a darn-cute Tasia Valencia as Dixie) an employee at Powerplus Records, a recording studio-slash-record label involved in Pittsburgh's burgeoning business of ballad production. Bits of Van Peebles' G-rated raps may have been co-written by Ice-T, who makes an appearance auditioning for the record producer. Despite the fact that Ice is toting an Uzi during the audition, the producer gives him a hard pass and opts to pick up Hood for a one-day recording session after he breaks up a fight in the bar by rapping a public service announcement about the dangers of alcohol.

"Did you ever think about going pro with your rap?"
                                        –Dixie

The primary, if flimsy, conflict in the film comes from gang member Duane, who has a long-time beef with Hood and just really wants to fight him (he cites it as reason "number one" in the film in a three part plan). He is an absurdly bad bad guy, and lovers of melodramatic movies will likely make it through this one just to get a dose of Duane's daytime drama looks and acting chops (not strictly an insult, as actor Charles Grant was in *The Edge of Night, Dallas, Santa Barbara,* and *The Bold and the Beautiful*)

MONTAGE FROMAGE
"Call Me" D. Terrell

Not a rap number, this peppy rocking number lets Hood live up to his promise to "help the needy instead of make money for the greedy"

RATING
4/10

DIRECTOR JOEL SILBERG WORKS THE TRENDS

Breakin (1984) Breakdancing
Rappin' (1985) Rapping
Bad Guys (1986) Pro Wrestling
Lambada (1990) Lambada-ing

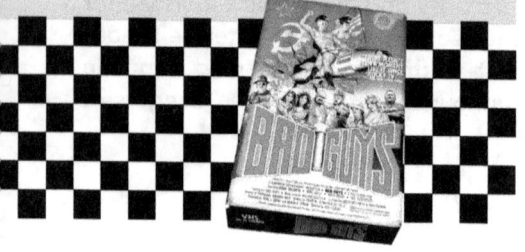

"I'm gonna fix your ass, Rappin' Hood."   –Duane

The music occasionally comments on the action directly and literally, as when Hood raps in the studio a direct voice-over narration to a scene that is occurring in a totally different location. Hood has to round up some cash to save his brother Allan from the "Slime of Crime" (don't be fooled by the name, it's not as cool as it sounds). Once in a while it gets as weird as you wanted, such as The Force M.D.'s "Itchin' for a Scratch." Basically it's one of their signature R&B-tinged tunes with scratching, and a couple of fun vocal impersonations when members of the band do a Michael Jackson and James Brown-inspired bar or two.

When a neighborhood kid is hospitalized with hypothermia, Hood and company live up to their Robin Hood promise for a moment and steal a fuel truck, bringing heat to the diverse and downbeat neighborhood. Finally the real-estate guys unleash the full hired muscle of Duane's gang of reprobates on the neighborhood, who vandalize homes and businesses. After disarming Duane, Hood appears in court to defend the neighborhood. While movies set in some kind of normal world would have the hero plead his case with sincerity, this film surrenders to it's absurdity and Hood raps his complaint, only to be joined by the whole community. I can't imagine this was considered a cool ending in 1985, but by this point is wholly cringeworthy and maybe you enjoy that sort of thing. It always hurts to see what could have been a good movie go bad; that the film succumbs to full-on musical theater rules a couple of times derails any attempt at genuine drama, and any emotional collateral that is built up (I managed to genuinely care about little brother Allan for example) gets thrown out the door with a cringeworthy song.

If you're not laughing in disbelief yet, the credits song will do it, as the whole neighborhood (from the old Jewish baker lady to the Greek gyro peddler to the guy with the Italian shop and the Chinese green grocer) all get a couple of bars of rap to enforce their ethnic stereotype. Let's call this one a missed opportunity, and it delivers just a little bit under what we've come to expect from Cannon.

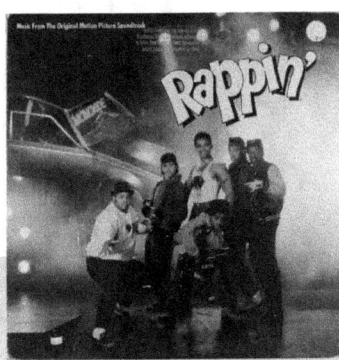

SOUNDTRACK

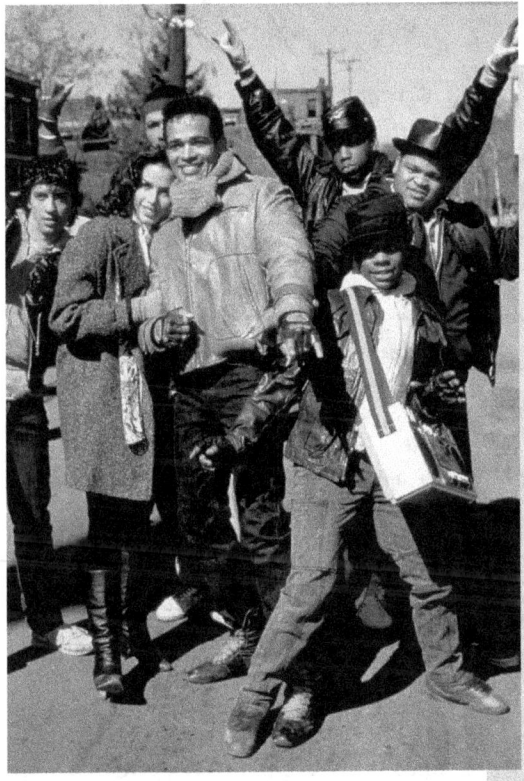

Rappin'
Lovebug Starski

Snack Attack
Mario Van Peebles, Eriq La Salle

The Fight Rap
Lovebug Starski

Neighborhood Walk
Mario Van Peebles

Itchin' for a Scratch
Force M.D.s

Flame in the Fire
Warren Mills

Call Me
D. Terrell

If You Want To (FU12)
Lajuan Carter

Golly Gee
Tuff Inc.

First Love Never Dies
Eugene Wilde, Joanna Gardner

NOT ON THE ALBUM:
"Killer" by Ice-T.

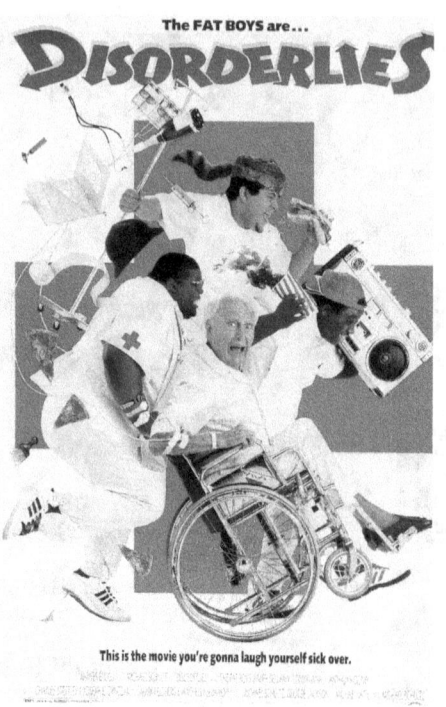

The FAT BOYS are...

DISORDERLIES

This is the movie you're gonna laugh yourself sick over.

DISORDERLIES (1987)

Rich gambler Winslow (Anthony Geary, "Luke" from *General Hospital*) is in debt to some *Miami-Vice*-ish latino gangsters. He will inherit his ailing uncle's fortune if only the old man would just get it over with and die already. To speed the process, he hires "the worst orderlies in the history of nursing care." Enter The Fat Boys, Mark Morales (a.k.a. "Prince Markie Dee"), Damon Wimbley ("Kool Rock-Ski"), and Darren Robinson ("The Human Beat Box"). Poorly staged slapstick gags, cartoon sound effects (a "boinggg" is funny, right?), and a modicum of beatboxing ensue.

On paper it's so promising – a hip-hop Three Stooges set in the world of *Scarface* – but could not be taken to that delicious level. Even the inclusion of overqualified Ralph Bellamy (*Trading Places, Coming to America*) doesn't elevate the material, though at times it seems like the template for 1989's *Weekend At Bernie's* (hauling around an unconscious guy to nightclubs and such). The whole thing is surprisingly free of hip hoppery – the boys listen to Bon Jovi in the car – but there is a musical number crowbarred in at the 50-minute mark, in the form of a rap cover of The Beatles "Baby You're a Rich Man" that shares the chorus and a Paul McCartney name drop but that's about it. We never return to that electric, "anything can happen" feeling that was present any time The Fat Boys were around in *Krush Groove*.

In addition to squandering most comic opportunities, the film wastes cameos from musical artists Helen Reddy, Ray Parker Jr, and even The Beach Boys (who were probably just a pick-up shot left over from a day of shooting the video for their shared version of "Wipe Out" from the same year). Even the best of these cameos, with Rick Nielsen of Cheap Trick getting his car swiped by the Boys, is an ill-conceived throwaway that wouldn't matter to a hip-hop audience. Comic underscore is done by J.J. Jeczalik, a founding member of Art of Noise, which incorporates some of the sample-based noises you'd expect from that act. An oddly diverse soundtrack album was released, but with only one Fat Boys track probably didn't win over any fans.

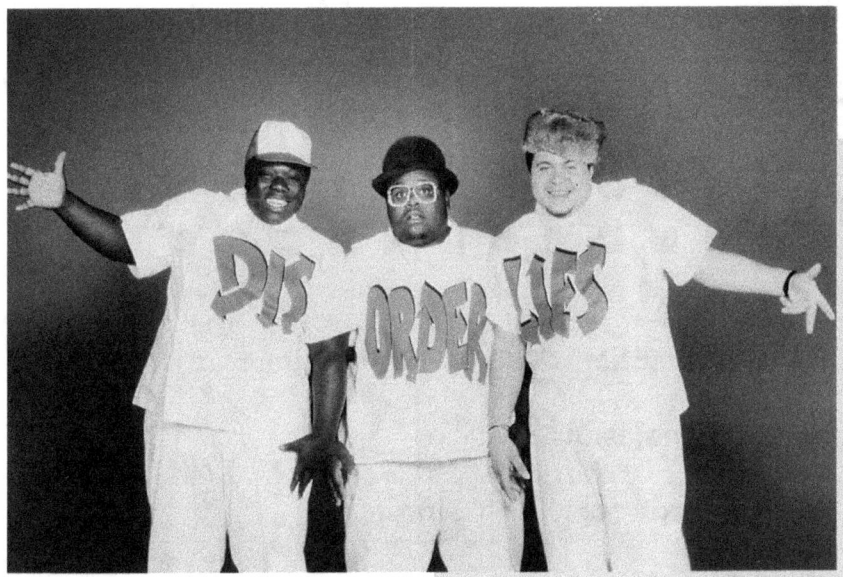

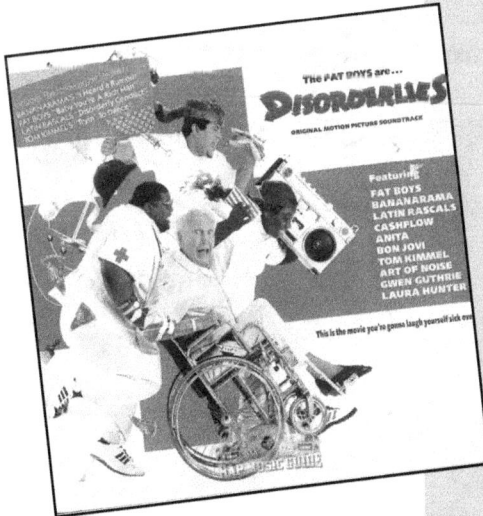

SOUNDTRACK

Baby You're a Rich Man
Fat Boys

I Heard a Rumour
Bananarama

Disorderly Conduct
The Latin Rascals

Big Money
Ca$hflow

Don't Treat Me Like This
Anita

Edge of a Broken Heart
Bon Jovi

Trying to Dance
Tom Kimmel

Roller One
The Art of Noise

Fat Off My Back
Gwen Guthrie

Work Me Down
Laura Hunter

FINAL TALLY:

Most Authentic: Wild Style, Delivery Boys

Best Drama: Beat Street

Best Soundtrack: Krush Groove

Best Cinematography: Krush Groove

Best Costumes: Breakin' 1 & 2

Best Choreography: Breakin'

Most Authentic Breakdancing: Beat Street

Worst Script, and That's Saying Something: Rappin'

Best Intentional Comedy: Delivery Boys

Best Unintentional Comedy to Watch Under the Influence: Body Rock

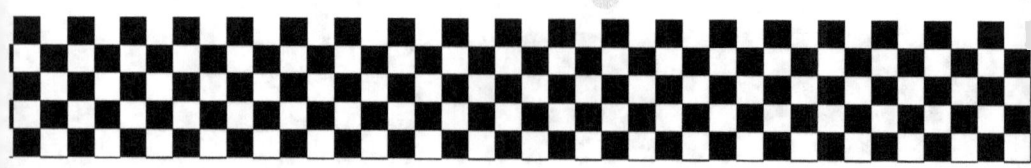

13

STREETS OF FIRE

"Streets of Fire is, by design, comic book in orientation, mock-epic in structure, movie-heroic in acting style, operatic in visual style, and cowboy-cliché in dialogue. In short: a rock'n'roll adventure where the Leader of the Pack steals the Queen of the Hop and Soldier Boy comes home to do something about it."

STREETS OF FIRE PRESS KIT

Hot off the mega hit *48 Hours*, director Walter Hill and producer Larry Gross (along with Joel Silver) were in the enviable position of having several studios willing to greenlight almost anything they could muster quickly. Hill, who created the mythic *The Warriors*, was interested in tackling another "comic book" movie. This was no comic book movie in the modern sense, attempting to contemporize an old 60s comic book property with young stars and special effects, but a film whose distance from reality could be measured by the broad archetypes and rapid-fire pacing of that genre of storytelling. A child of the 50's, Hill wanted to make a paean to teenage thrills filled with things like:

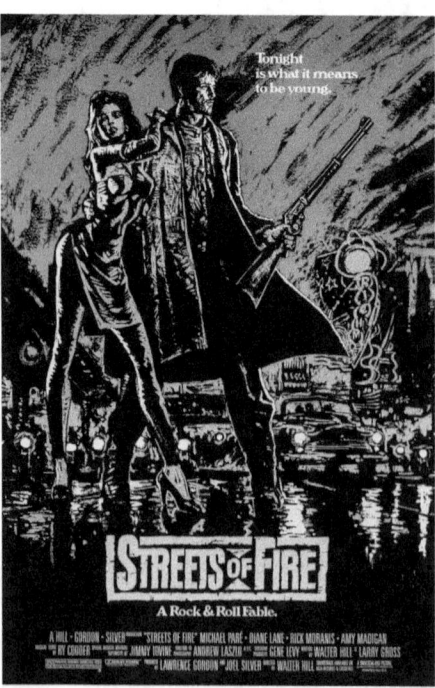

"custom cars, kissing in the rain, neon, trains in the night, high-speed pursuit, rumbles, rock stars, motorcycles, jokes in tough situations, leather jackets and questions of honor."

Hill was out to make thinly veiled westerns with white knuckle tension. In 1983, post *Warriors* and post *Blade Runner*, and in the era of a rising force called MTV, he settled on a half musical, half action film, taking place in a retro-40s-50s "other world, a far off places where genres collide." The results would be so unique as to drive away all but the most adventurous filmgoer, but so utterly odd as to develop a strong cult following in the years to come.

Teenage movies were in the air. John Hughes was starting his run of successful movies. Francis Ford Coppola had done two movies with young casts, *The Outsiders* and *Rumble Fish*. This was going to be a universe without people over 30. Likewise, Coppola and others and done a series of films where the artifice was celebrated, and though this was a kind of mythic tale like *The Warriors* had been, *Warriors* had the benefit of real places and even real gang members to fill its ranks.

Like Sergio Leone's westerns taking place in a West that never quite existed, Hill's nameless city of districts (The Richmond, The Battery) is almost completely artifice, cobbled together from Universal's backlot city streets and select locations like Chicago's elevated trains and subterranean

Wacker Drive. It is dripping with decay and almost always night, the street traffic is almost all faded behemoths from the 40s and 50s. The diners and bars are wrapped evocatively in a distressed patina of peeling paint and grease stains, and the wet-streets-and-neon environs rival *Blade Runner*.

Ellen Aim is the lead singer of The Attackers, and the biggest thing to come out of the Richmond district. In the middle of a big concert in her home neighborhood, she is kidnapped by The Bombers, a gang from the nearby Battery district. Tom Cody, a tough-talking merc who is Ellen's ex-boyfriend, is summoned to rescue her. While classically simple and mythic in plot, the film's real appeal is the heaps of atmosphere and wall-to-wall music.

Hill wanted to use original 50s music but the studio wanted original songs, and recruited songwriter Jim Steinman and producer Jimmy Iovine to accomplish the task. Steinman is most known for his operatic style on albums like Meat Loaf's "Bat Out of Hell," and having cut his teeth in musical theater it is no surprise. The songs he creates for *Streets of Fire* suffer from a 1970s bombast that keeps this from being a great new wave movie (which is surely what it looks like), but does contribute to the sense of a film "out of time." In the opening concert we are convinced it is not strictly a period piece, with a rapid-fire MTV cutting style that contrasts with the 1950s-outfitted Attackers wardrobe (and the unmistakable Simmons electronic drum sounds emanating from the acoustic kit on stage). Steinman's

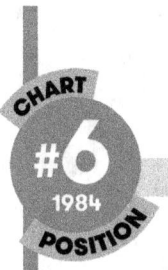

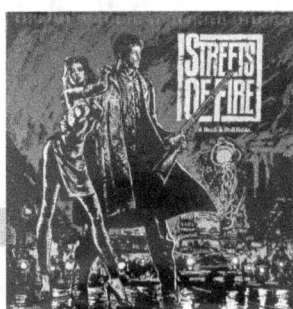

SOUNDTRACK

Nowhere Fast
Fire Inc.

Sorcerer
Marilyn Martin

Deeper and Deeper
The Fixx

Countdown to Love
Greg Phillinganes

One Bad Stud
The Blasters

Tonight Is What It Means to Be Young
Fire Inc.

Never Be You
Maria McKee

I Can Dream About You
Dan Hartman

Hold That Snake
Ry Cooder

Blue Shadows
The Blasters

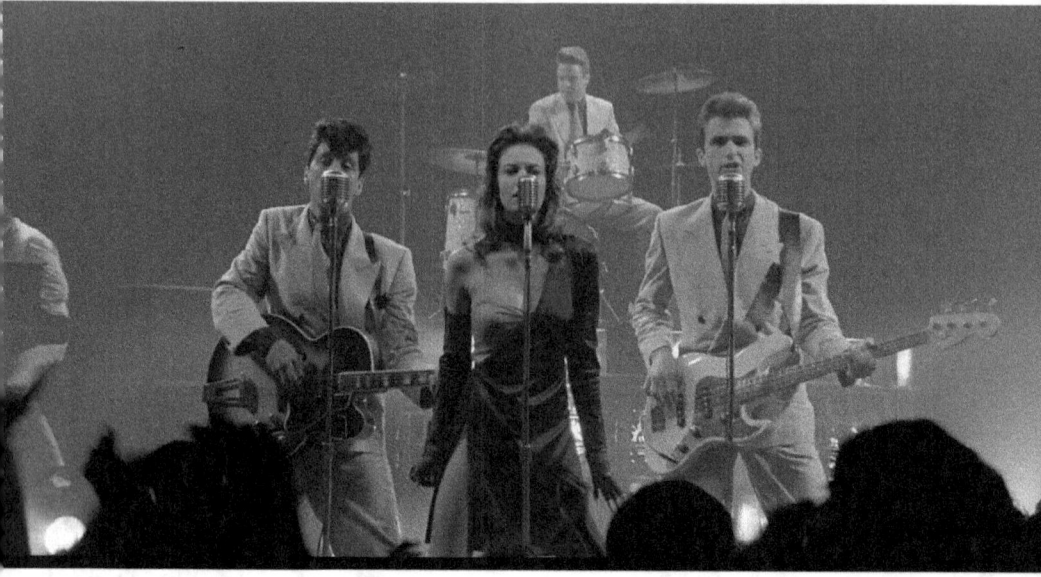

signature choir backup would be put to similarly melodramatic use on Bonnie Tyler's "Holding Out for a Hero" from *Footloose*. To give Ellen Aim her voice, the producers edited the performances of singers Laurie Sargent and Holly Sherwood into one consistent and credible performance, credited as "Fire Incorporated." Aim herself, played by the not-yet-eighteen Diane Lane (who got her last high school report card delivered to the set), does an admirable job lipsyncing to the songs, aided in rock authenticity by choreographer Jeffrey Hornaday.

Elsewhere, the film manages a more outright 50s and 60s musical tone. While James Horner was hired to create a traditional score, his work was abandoned and replaced with the persistent and retro work of Ry Cooder, who employs a hard-edged boogie throughout the film with slide guitar and harmonica.

The city seems to be teeming with musicians. At the Bomber's hangout, the rowdy dive bar Torchies, LA-based rockabilly punk outfit The Blasters provide on-stage entertainment, including an effective cover of the Leiber and Stoller song "One Bad Stud." Of special note here is the club's powerhouse of a stage dancer, an absurdly athletic Marine Jahan (hot off her gig as Jennifer Beals' dancing double in *Flashdance*). Cody's ragtag group hitches a tour bus ride with a black doo-wop group called the Sorels. In the city's red light district, aspiring singer Baby Doll (the diminutive E.G. Daily, the only one of the gang who looks like they live in 1984) joins the gang. One half expects the film's bad guys to really be after a record deal, not so strange when you consider that Shattuck's lieutenant is front man Lee Ving from the LA-punk band Fear (and, as usual, is all-too convincing as a crazy biker).

The film's cast is a dream for 80s film fans (though it would have been nigh unstoppable with the once-in-consideration cast of Tom Cruise, Daryl Hannah, and Edward James Olmos). For those keeping score we have Rick Rossovich (*Terminator, Top Gun*), Bill Paxton (*Terminator, Aliens*), Rick Moranis (right off *Strange Brew* and a breath away from *Ghostbusters*), and the incomparable and electric Willem Dafoe as Shattuck. Amy Madigan's character McCoy is perhaps the most interesting, since she suggested she take the role of the male, Mexican sidekick to Cody. As Walter Hill was the person who had suggested Ridley Scott gender flip the role of Ripley in Alien, he was quick to agree, and the results are interesting and ahead of the curve.

The film was originally going to end with Ellen Aim performing the Bruce Springsteen song "Streets of Fire," and they went as far as filming the sequence as part of the big concert at the Wiltern Theater. When Springsteen pulled the rights, director Hill was perfectly satisfied with the film ending after the Sorels perform their song, he breakout hit for the movie, Dan Hartman's "I Can Dream About You." Hill felt that ending on that song gave the film a nice emotional uptick, but the producers insisted on another Steinman song that frankly spoils the strong ending with yet more Meat-loaf-iness. It was written in two days, the accompanying reshoot was marred by an overly expensive rebuild of the theater and Diane Lane in a less-convincing wig to replace her recently shorn hair. Perhaps obviously, ending with a Springsteen song would have been the best of these options, but on the upside it's hard to imagine a Steinman/Iovine arrangement of that song that wouldn't have left a sour note. *Streets of Fire*, like its contemporary *Blade Runner*, also had a jettisoned voice over, in this case done by Tom Cody's sister played by Deborah Van Valkenberg, and perhaps its inclusion might have changed the overall impressions of the film.

Streets of Fire was deemed dead on arrival in 1984, failing to make back its cost at the time and irrevocably altering Michael Paré's career trajectory. I'm not saying Steinman's work is to blame for the film's reception, it's too oddball to have been accepted at the time. But speaking from a synthesizers and saxophones standpoint, one wonders what the film would have done in a different set of contemporary musical hands.

As convincing evidence that under different musical hands the film might have been a hit, one need only look at the music-video within-the-movie, "Sorcerer." This song was written by Stevie Nicks (already better), in 1972 (interesting) during her time with Buckingham Nicks, a brief collaboration prior to their joining Fleetwood Mac (you were saying?). It's a knockout song, here sung by Marilyn Martin with Nicks and others providing background vocals. Between that song, the Dan Hartman hit, the great rockabilly songs and score, it all might have been a much neater musical package.

And, with such accompaniment, might we have been able to see the proposed pair of sequels, The Far City (purported to take place in a snowy city) and Cody's Return (set in the desert)? Paré should have had a greater success considering the mini-hit *Eddie and the Cruisers*, but never quite gained the kind of wide audience acceptance of his similarly-skilled peers. And the 80s was not without its share of movie stars for whom acting was a secondary concern.

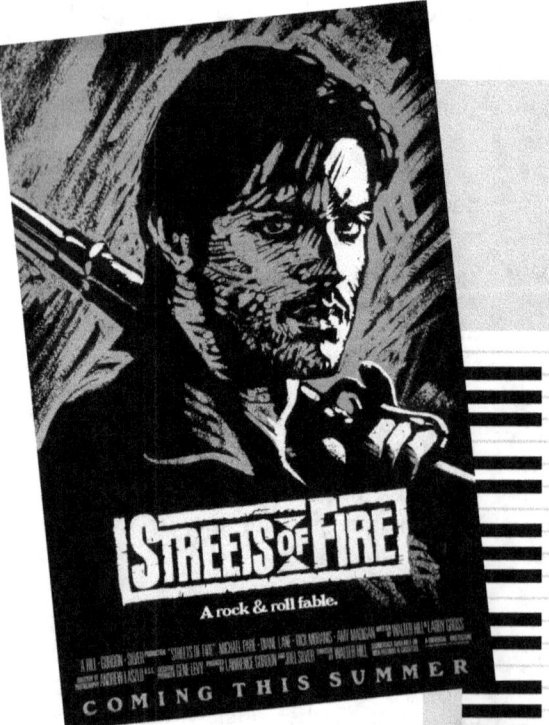

"I CAN DREAM ABOUT YOU"

- Film Version sung by Winston Ford
- Film version lipsynced by Stoney Jackson
- Dan Hartman's recording would be the one on the charts, peaking at #6 US
- On the Billboard chart for 25 weeks

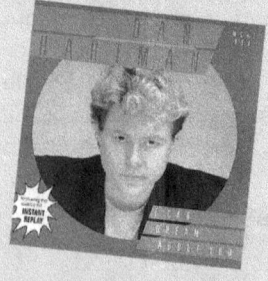

14

PRINCE AND REPEAT

You might call Prince a control freak. Besides playing all of his own instruments, The Purple Polymath from Minneapolis had already been directing his music videos by the time he starred in Purple Rain. Rumor has it the hired video director for "When Doves Cry" was given some magazines and asked to wait in the hall. It would only be a matter of time before Prince took the director's chair on a feature.

PRINCE
IN HIS FIRST MOTION PICTURE.

STAGE DOOR

Purple Rain

PRINCE
PURPLE RAIN
A CAVALLO, RUFFALO and FARGNOLI Production
APOLLONIA KOTERO · MORRIS DAY · OLGA KARLATOS and CLARENCE W

**"Baby, I'm a star
Might not know it
now
Baby, but I are,
I'm a star –
I don't want to
stop, till I reach
the top"**

It's big, it's sparkly, it's smokey, and it's purple. Regardless of what critics may say, *Purple Rain* is the most luscious looking musical movie of this period, and its songs are among the most successful and timeless of the entire decade. But it's the one-two punch of the album and the film itself that launched Prince into mainstream success – it's hard to believe that prior to the movie, he only had one crossover album, *1999*, and had never cracked the top five on the pop charts.

Pressure was on to get Prince to re-sign to Warner Brothers after the success of the album *1999*, and he put up an ultimatum: "He'll only sign with us if he gets a major motion picture," Prince's manager and producer Bob Cavallo told *Spin Magazine*. "It has to be with a studio—not with some drug dealer or jeweler financing. And his name has to be above the title. He wasn't a giant star yet. I mean, that demand was a little over the top."

As members of Prince's band The Revolution attest, for months Prince had been toting around a notebook – a purple one, no less – writing down ideas for a movie that would feature himself and the band in a kind of mythic expose of the Minneapolis funk music scene. He knew a motion picture would be the next logical step in his rise to greatness.

Those around him knew that Prince saw that superstardom as his destiny. "Growing up, like anyone would practice their instrument, he practiced his face; he practiced what you look like on camera," said keyboardist Lisa Coleman. "He would videotape himself in his bedroom at night, just talking or doing things, and he'd watch himself to see what he looked like. He really worked on it as if he was a dancer or something, training himself for being a big star."

"I don't know how you describe his obsession," said tour manager Alan Leeds. "It was beyond confidence. It wasn't even arrogant. It was destiny, and either you're on board or you're going to miss out." So Cavallo pitched it to directors and producers, and Prince invested half a million dollars himself, an investment that was soon matched by his managers.

Part of the film's success lies in the inherent mystery of the man himself: starting with the release of *1999*, he stopped talking to the press. Even so, much of what he fed the press to that point was riddled with contradictions; audiences still were unsure of his sexual preference or ethnic background. And if *Purple Rain* is semi-autobiographical, it just as much raises the details of his tale to mythic proportions.

The film's director was Albert Magnoli, a recent USC film school graduate, who helped take an early script, push the music elements, and ensure that it served as an "emotional biography" of the artist. A key part of this was tapping into a side of Prince that he might not have wanted to show. "I was able to discern a tremendous amount of vulnerability in him, which the material I'd studied hadn't given me," Magnoli said. "When Prince is performing, he's extremely assured. But what I saw walking across the lobby (when I first met him) was a very vulnerable kid." Were it not for the vulnerability he shows in the film, Prince's character, known only as The Kid, would be nearly unredeemable.

In some ways, the timing of the film could not have been better, with 1984 in the midst of a box office boom, music videos at the height of their visibility, and black artists becoming

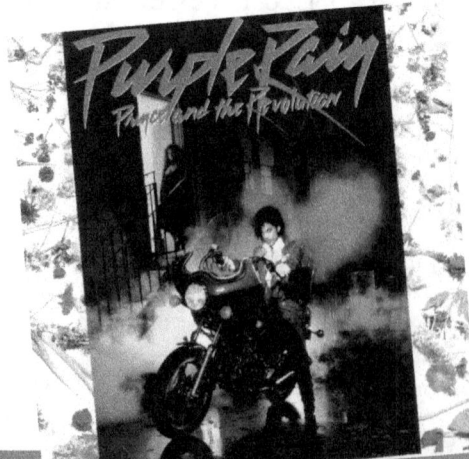

mainstays in the mainstream music world. But it's a miracle the film got made: here is a $7 million dollar film, not quite a cheapie at that time, directed by a first-time director, and starring an artist who was not yet a household name. The rest of the cast are simply the actual band members, playing themselves. One can begin to understand how the studio might balk.

To put some perspective on how Warner Brothers perceived the property, the studio heads wanted John Travolta for the lead. The producers held their ground, but this was the kind of thinking they were up against. How else could they convince audiences (beyond the initial rush of music fans on opening weekend) to come to the theater and watch a movie about a relative unknown from a totally unknown music scene in the middle of nowhere? The studio would hedge their bets throughout the process, but the fact remains that the film that should have been made actually survived the Hollywood pipeline and made it out the other side.

The lead female role was meant for Vanity, but sources differ as to why she did not stay in the role. One theory was she balked at the salary and was in the process of breaking out of the Prince offshoot band Vanity 6 anyway; some say it was a relationship blowout with Prince that prompted the walkout. Magnoli said that Martin Scorsese wanted her to play Mary Magdalene in *Last Temptation of Christ* so she traded up (that film got delayed and she would subsequently miss out on it).

Jennifer Beals was offered the part but turned it down. Gina Gershon auditioned. After seeing hundreds of Vanity clones in leather and lace, the director and casting agents were surprised by the authenticity of a woman who arrived in sweatpants. Actress/model Patricia Kotero was hired, and rebranded "Apollonia" by Prince – after Michael Corleone's first wife in the film *The Godfather*. Alas, her work in front of the camera fell short of expectations and resulted in scenes being truncated or reshot (reportedly a third of the work is reshoots). While there was speculation at the time that Apollonia was another one of Prince's girlfriends, she says was dating David Lee Roth at the time.

Everyone in the cast of newcomers trained in acting classes, and some in dance, at the Minnesota Dance Theatre. Co-star Morris Day was kicked out of those classes for fooling around, but it was that energy that he would translate to the screen to good effect. He would reportedly miss shoot days due to drug use, however, resulting in his on-screen partner Jerome Benton carrying some of those scenes.

Day had always been a source of needed comic relief in Prince's real life, and their relationship was apparently not as strained as the film makes it out to be (Day would even wash Prince's car for a couple of bucks now and then, according to Melvoin). Anything like competition between the acts was just a case of serious one-upmanship. The Time became such a formidable live band that they would

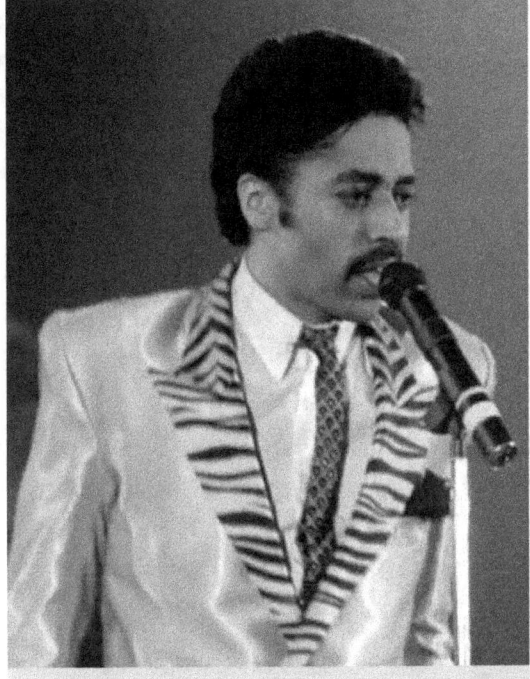

THE FURTHER ADVENTURES OF THE TIME:
PURPLE RAIN 2 ?

BOB CAVALLO: "Warner Bros. had no rights for a sequel. I had this idea: *Purple Rain 2: The Further Adventures of the Time*. It would start with Prince in some big arena, playing one of his incredible concerts. The Time are there, about to go to Las Vegas because they won a contest to play a lounge in a big hotel. And the basic story would be the Mob were the people who booked them, so they eventually get into trouble, and the only friends that they have are the showgirls. Well, for some reason, Morris thought that character took away his manhood."

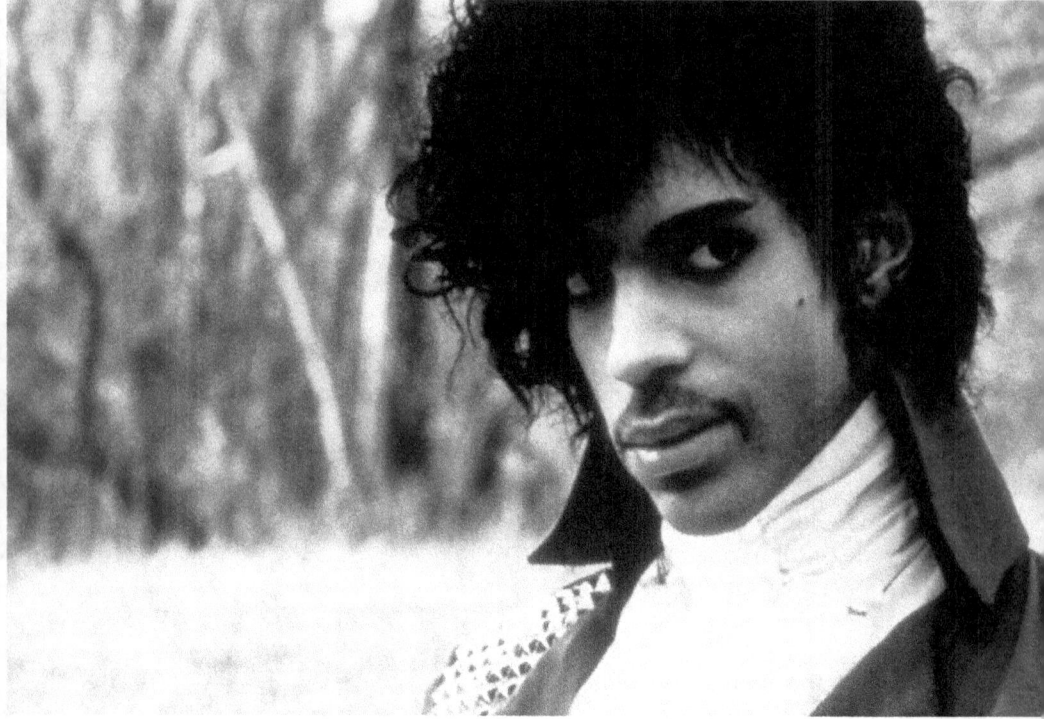

raise the stakes every night, and each band was forced to keep up with the other. Still, any glance at the two bands' stage set-up in their shared rehearsal space – the epic equipment of The Revolution on one side of the warehouse, and the diminutive stage of The Time on the other – left little doubt whose act ruled.

Morris bodyguard and valet in the film, Jerome, is played Jerome Benton, the real-life brother of The Time bassist Terry Lewis. As legend has it during a live performance by The Time, Day flippantly asked for someone to bring him a mirror. Benton responded by ripping a mirror out of the club's restroom and bringing it on stage for Day to comb his hair. From that moment on, Benton would become a part of the stage act. Prince

seized upon the chemistry and built their roles to fit.

The film courted controversy from the get-go, with the most common complaint being about the film's streak of misogyny, with some scenes culminating in violence against women. A point of contention was a scene in which Morris has a nagging girlfriend thrown into a dumpster. The studio was prepared to cut the scene, but the filmmakers asked to test it with an audience. Possibly the only way to react to that scene is to laugh in disbelief, and test audiences did just that. It ended up staying in. More sticky were scenes in which the Kid strikes out at Apollonia, but the argument was made that the story sets up the behavior in scenes with the Kid's father. Interestingly, for a movie about a rock and roll club, drinking and drugs are largely absent, and a racy sex scene was shot for multiple ratings (it was the "R" rated one that stuck)

The film was shot in Minneapolis until they couldn't contend with the November snow drifts and perpetual 20-degree temps, at which point Los Angeles stands in fairly convincingly. Watch for the First Avenue facade to change to an obvious art deco impostor at one point in the film as Prince drives by on his motorcycle.

The film looks great throughout, but it's the stunning stage sequences that make the film a lasting document of a music revolution. As producer Cavallo remembers, "We were a few weeks behind, and we had four weeks set to shoot the music. So I said to Prince, 'You know, Albert is gonna want to do 20 takes, he's gonna want different angles.' And Prince, he almost changed color. 'I'll give him one take for each song.' I said, "'No, that's extreme. What if we just did a couple of takes with a bunch of cameras?' We got a bunch of cameramen, and Prince, who's unbelievable, always hit his mark. If he did three takes, there was no change. Within a week, we had done the four weeks' work." The band had rehearsed all numbers extensively, and the camera operators were all at the top of their game. The musical performances had in some cases been recorded in front of a live audience previously, and consummate performer Prince proved a master of lip sync.

The club was dressed in additional neon and stage lighting, and was filled with glamorous-looking extras, some made up in new-wave face paint. As Magnoli recalls, "We had over 900 extras who came to the set every day, excited. They gave the whole scene a tremendous amount of realism. And we didn't know it at the time, but those images had a tremendous amount of influence on the direction that MTV took." He cites the simple inclusion of audience hands in the foreground shots of the performances as one element that was quickly incorporated into the music video vernacular.

THE SONGS:

The songs of Purple Rain are not only a mix of greatest hits and supporting tracks, but they also function at a higher narrative level, commenting on the action in a way that is absent from most urban musicals. Director Albert Magnoli claims that Prince brought no less than 100 original songs as contenders for the soundtrack. Even with that wealth of material, "When Doves Cry" and "Take Me With You" were not yet written at the time of filming. On several occasions, Magnoli provided Prince with specific direction for songs and lyrics that would act as a counterpoint to the onscreen action.

The accompanying album is not a soundtrack, per se, as it omits songs by The Time ("Jungle Love," "The Bird"), Dez Dickerson ("Modernaire") and Apollonia 6 ("Sex Shooter"). It is simply a Prince album, quite probably the best one in a storied career, with the sequencing of tracks tastefully ordered for the LP format.

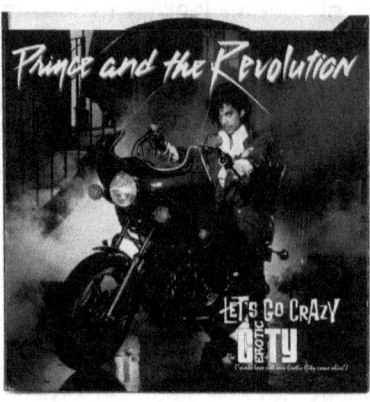

"Let's Go Crazy"

Released as the album's second single, it became his second US number one single, spending two weeks at peak and 21 weeks on the chart altogether.

"Take Me With U"

Designed as a duet for Apollonia and Prince, "Take Me With U" was to be included on the Apollonia 6 album before being snatched up exclusively for Purple Rain.

"The Beautiful Ones"

Wendy Melvoin cites this song as a moment when she knew that Prince was working at the height of his powers.

"Computer Blue"

This was edited down from a 14 minute version that was recorded in Minneapolis.

"Darling Nikki"

A deliciously explicit song made infamous by Tipper Gore (author and wife of Vice President Al Gore), who was apparently inspired to found the Parents Music Resource Center after overhearing her eleven-year-old daughter listening to the track. The Center subsequently advocated the mandatory use of a warning label ("Parental Advisory: Explicit Lyrics") on the covers of records judged to contain language or lyrical content unsuitable for minors. Needless to say, many of Prince's future albums sported the label.

"When Doves Cry"

Magnoli came up with a montage in editing to help explain the personal demons that were plaguing The Kid, and he knew that it required a song he hadn't heard yet. Prince delivered two new songs the next day. One stood out, made all the more memorable buy the decision to drop the conventional bassline from the mix entirely (prompted by singer and Purple Rain co-star Jill Jones), flying in the face of current musical style.

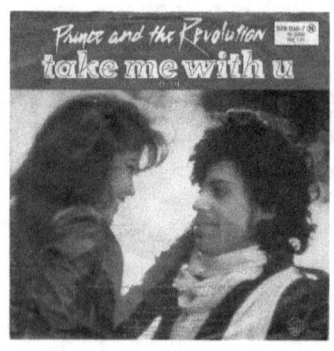

It would be Prince's first number one single, and the best selling single of 1984, and it was number one on black, pop and dance charts at the time of the album's release. It remained in the charts for over six months after its debut.

"I Would Die 4 U"

The song was recorded during a live concert at First Avenue in 1983, as part of a benefit performance for the Minnesota Dance Theatre. Peaked at #8 in February of 1985 (showing the lasting power of that album) with 16 weeks on the chart.

"Baby I'm a Star"

Also debuted at First Avenue benefit concert, along with the title track.

"Purple Rain"

Prince perceived the title song as his anthem, and possibly wrote it at the suggestion of keyboardist Dr. Fink after a conversation about, of all people, Bob Seger. Prince's act was following Seger's around the country on the 1999 tour, and he had wondered aloud why Seger was selling out arenas. Fink said it was the big, anthemic, gut-punching ballads that packed the houses. He asked for lyrical help from Stevie Nicks – she owed him one for his help with a critical keyboard assist on "Stand Back" for her album The Wild Heart.

She was intrigued by the fact it was essentially a country rock song, but was overwhelmed by the

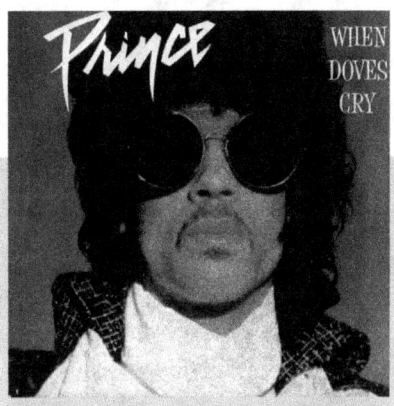

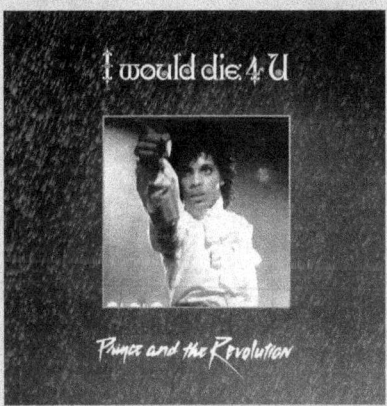

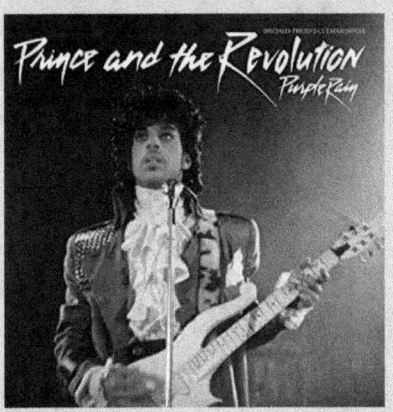

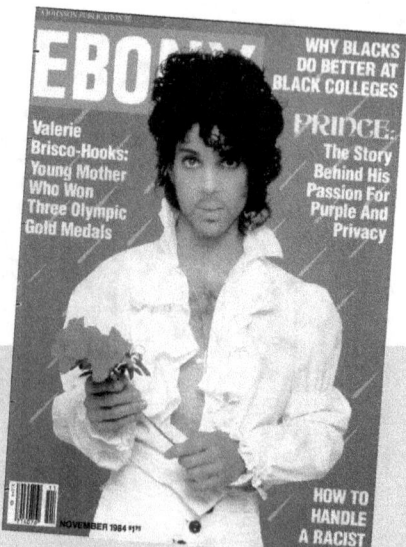

On the magazine cover:

EBONY

WHY BLACKS
DO BETTER AT
BLACK COLLEGES

Valerie
Brisco-Hooks:
Young Mother
Who Won
Three Olympic
Gold Medals

PRINCE:
The Story
Behind His
Passion For
Purple And
Privacy

NOVEMBER 1984 $1.75

HOW TO
HANDLE
A RACIST

A PURPLE PLAN

- Prince had tried making a film called *The Second Coming* during the 1982 Controversy Tour, but drove director Chuck Statler off trying to film interstitial narrative scenes. Statler referred to the endless retakes as a "gruesome drill."

- Throughout the Triple Threat Tour, Prince was seen scribbling in a purple notebook that held ideas for the film that became *Purple Rain*.

- He told Jill Jones "it was going to be bigger than *Saturday Night Fever*."

- According to Dez Dickerson, Prince said "if it's just me and Chick (his bodyguard "Big Chick" Huntsberry) in the snow with a camcorder, I'm going to make this movie."

demo's ten minute length and tapped out. Prince also feared that he had replicated Journey's song "Faithfully" too, er, faithfully, and called Journey member Jonathan Cain to ask permission to proceed. Having shared only a chord structure, Cain thought it was okay, stating "I thought it was an amazing tune, and I told him, 'Man, I'm just super-flattered that you even called... Good luck with the song. I know it's gonna be a hit.'" Prince's searing guitar solo is also inspired by Journey's guitarist Neall Schon "How much he loved Neal Schon is crazy," Cain adds. "He studied Neal for so many years, learned his licks and made them his own. You can hear it on ('Purple Rain') for real."

The song was recorded during the infamous live benefit concert at First Avenue on August 3 1983, minus some overdubs that would be recorded at Sunset Sound in Hollywood California. The runtime of that performance was a whopping 13 minutes that would be edited to the song as we now know it. Magnoli was a part of the audience that night; afterwards he told Prince he was sure it was the missing song for the end of the film. Prince considered, and asked, "If that's the song, can *Purple Rain* be the title of the movie?"

The song won the Oscar for Best Original Song Score in 1984. It failed to make it to number one but reached #2, and spent 18 weeks on the Billboard Hot 100. It would be Prince's seventh highest

Right up until release, the studio was unsure of what they had. The old hardliners at the studio were still hung up on questions like "will it play at the drive-ins?" A screening in Texas proved to the studio they had a crossover hit, when a crowd of 300 white kids was on their feet in the first three minutes.

Purple Rain opened in 900 theaters across the United States. It made back its cost of $7 million in its first weekend, and went on to clear nearly $70 million at the box office – adjust it for today's dollar and you're looking at a hit the size of a typical superhero movie. The soundtrack album has sold more than 20 million copies worldwide, and spent 24 consecutive weeks at Number One on Billboard's album chart. It won two Grammys and an Oscar, and included two Number One singles ("When Doves Cry" and "Let's Go Crazy") and another, the title track, that reached Number Two. The video cassette was priced at $29.95 and sold nearly half a million copies, putting it right behind the Michael Jackson's Thriller home video release.

Reviews were predictably condescending, such as "the flashiest album cover ever to be released as a movie" by Vincent Canby, and "a rock star's mixed-up confession and self-glorifying fantasy" by David Denby. More generous was David Ansen of *Newsweek*, who said "as a rock star he's outrageous but plausible. As a movie star, he's unprecedented."

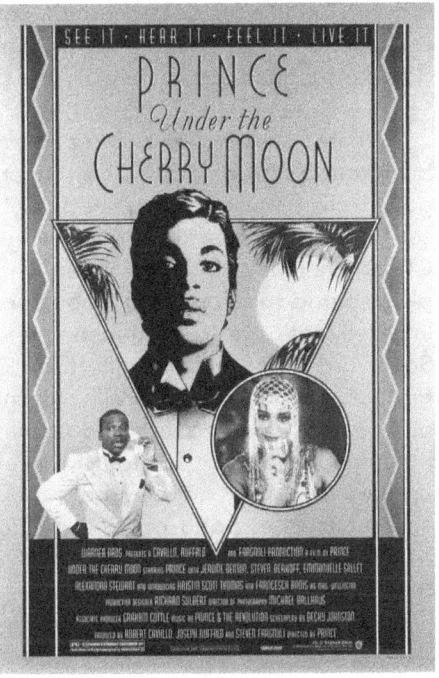

"Wrecka Stow!"

It's easy to write off *Under the Cherry Moon* as nothing more than a vanity project from an artist at the top of his game, who was given a little too much leash and put too much faith in a beginning screenwriter. The LA Times called it "Under the Cherry Bomb," but approach it with no expectations and a marginal grounding in film history and you may find something to work with. Prince may have set out to make a 1930s romantic comedy, from its black and white photography to its art deco end credits; he should probably have tried to make a 1930s musical instead. Only in his determination not to recreate the success of *Purple Rain*, does he succeed completely.

Where *Purple Rain* may have been autobiographical, *Cherry Moon* goes full 1930s fantasy (although set in the modern day). Prince plays Christopher Tracy, a musician who plays piano in a bar and smoulders in the direction of rich women in the South of France. He and his (friend? brother? cousin? lover?) Tricky, played with comic gusto and charm by *Rain*-alum Jerome Benton, have set up shop as gigolos and now have their eye set on the grand prize: a young heiress who will inherit a $50 million trust fund.

The movie is packed with lots of opportunities for the leads to mug for the camera, whether being seductive or silly. The story doesn't so much as build as wander through a sort of purloined film history, with bits of Fellini or the French New Wave, or classic Hollywood antics that might be at home in a Marx Brothers movie. Prince does a Bela Lugosi Dracula hypnosis bit (the facial muscles he uses in his guitar solos are capable of some rubbery fun), and plays a melodramatic piano score to accompany a lover's jealous husband's voice message. It's really a movie out of time, and needs to be viewed as one.

The comedy plays pretty well, but the romance is surprisingly weak, and despite Prince's on-screen magnetism nothing seems to flower. Alas, the only chemistry in the film is between Christopher and Tricky. At the time I'm sure those moments were played for (homophobic) laughs, but there seems to be a genuine love between the two, a kind that never quite gets off the ground for the film's intended romances.

Heiress Mary Sharon is played by Kristin Scott Thomas, who went on to much smarter things. It's a part that Prince wanted to give to then-girlfriend Susannah Melvoin (twin sister of guitarist Wendy). An acting test proved they needed someone with better chops, and even Madonna was briefly considered. Thomas and the rest of the cast play everything straight and give the film a veneer of respectability. Steven Berkoff, known for playing Russian bad guys in the 80s (Orlov in *Octopussy*, Podovsky in *Rambo II*), plays Mary's father. He inherited the role from Terence Stamp, who punched out early when he realized what he had gotten himself into. Victor Spinetti, rock-music movie royalty who had appeared in all three of The Beatles films, also has some screen time, which probably only serves to remind one of a much better black and white rock musical.

As director, Prince has a couple of inspired moments. A scene in the bar spins a full 360 twice: in the first pass one story is told with the background characters and in the next our expectations are reversed. A love scene ends with the couple superimposed on the palm of a hand that's just opened post-orgasm.

The film's tragic conclusion will unfortunately elicit a laugh, being as it hasn't been set up to be that kind of movie and the onus of dramatic acting falls on the comedy foil. But Prince shows that there's an afterlife, and that it's scored by The Revolution, as the end credits song features a resurrected Prince smiling and singing in the clouds for the final song "Mountains."

Prince was not originally set to direct the follow up to *Purple Rain*, but when the director departed, the Prince filled the spot. Original director was Mary Lambert, then known for making the music videos that made Madonna famous (as well as Sheila E's "The Glamorous Life"). The immensely talented Michael Balhaus put light and lenses on it. The film was shot in color, but Prince managed to convince the studio to release it in black and white, further placing it in some dreamlike Hollywood memory. The film debuted in Sheridan, Wyoming, the result of an MTV contest. The post-movie concert was held at the local Holiday Inn. The film landed at the zenith of the MTV-to-Movies crossover, sandwiched between *Labyrinth* and Madonna's *Shanghai Suprise*.

The album "Parade" came at a time when Prince was experimenting and evoking a psychedelic inspired sound, moving away not only from the Minneapolis sound he created but also from the big-hair and ruffles look that accompanied it.

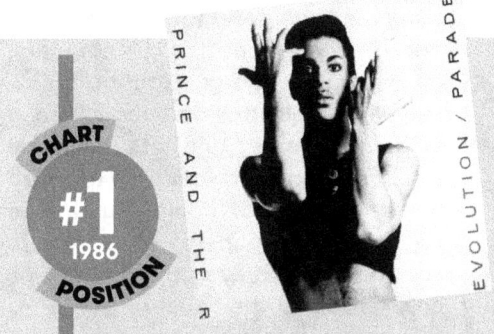

SOUNDTRACK

Christopher Tracy's Parade
New Position
I Wonder U
Under the Cherry Moon
Girls & Boys
Life Can Be So Nice
Venus de Milo
Mountains
Do U Lie
Kiss
Anotherloverholeinyourhead
Sometimes It Snows in April

NOT ON THE ALBUM

An Honest Man
Mia Boca
Alexa De Paris
Love or $
Old Friends 4 Sale

And the song "Kiss" was written by Prince as a sort of acoustic number; disappointed with it he handed it off to one of his protege bands, the Minneapolis-based Mazarati (headed by Revolution bassist Brown Mark). The demo they subsequently recorded upped the tempo and turned it into a funk song, complete with the little marimba-type part that survives in the background. Prince saw the potential, took it back, added a guitar break, sang it in falsetto, and rode it to a Billboard number one hit. The basic tracks and backing vocals of Mazarati remain, stripped down by Prince to almost emptiness in complete contradiction to everything that was on the radio at the time.

The album marks the first time Prince worked with a full orchestra, thanks to the arrangements of Clare Fischer, known for jazz and latin albums stretching back to the 1950s. Bits of the film's French location seep into songs like the out-and-out-*chanson* "Do U Lie," and as usual Prince performs most of the instruments on this album. Listen for costume designer Marie France in the seductive French-language second half of the song "Girls & Boys." The music videos from this song and others from the film are variations on the filmed portions of their respective songs, sometimes with additional footage that suggests a slightly cooler take on the movie starring the whole band.

In an interview for Yahoo, the band reminisced about Prince's experience on *Cherry Moon*. "He was really involved," says drummer Bobby Z, "and he was culturally taken by (France). He went to Versailles, and he went to see Mozart's house. He was taken by Europe and the movie reflected it." Is it time we see Cherry Moon as Prince's "European Art Film," and embrace it with all the baggage that comes with it?

Prince would break ties with the Revolution shortly thereafter.

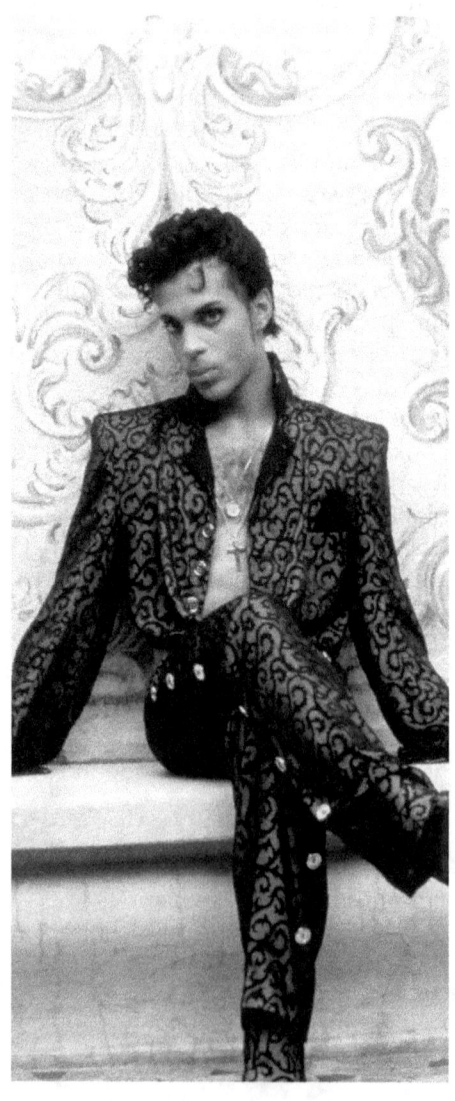

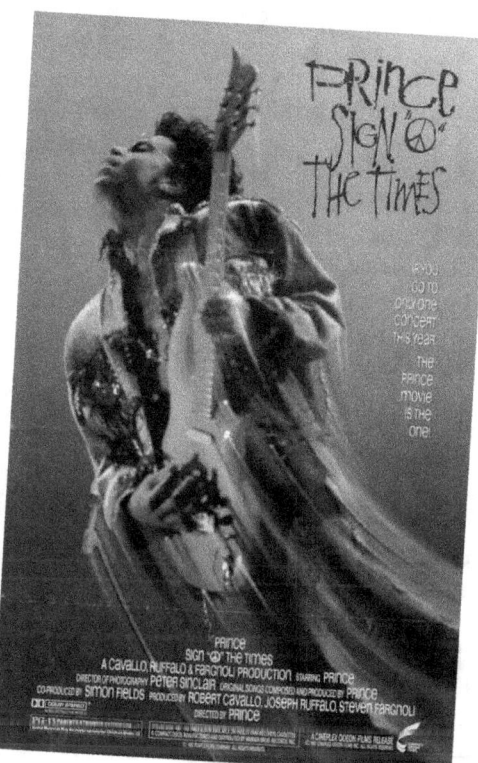

An energetic concert film seasoned with a mere tablespoon of plot, *Sign 'O' The Times* is a visual companion to the album Rolling Stone called a "capstone of his recklessly fertile Eighties period." In the album he would play with more challenging ideas (like a high-pitched female-type voice from an abandoned project in which he would play his female alter ego Camille), and get an even bigger, jazz infused sound with large horn sections. Many see it as his last great album, with parallels to the Beatles *White Album* for scope and innovation.

The accompanying film appears to have been driven by a financial need as much as a creative one. The album had done well overseas but the US market was either resistant to the new sound or feeling burnt after the previous underperformers. While touring Europe it was decided to film one of the concerts, build upon that material upon return to the states, and invade US cineplexes with a movie event to stir sales.

Live shows in Rotterdam and Antwerp were photographed, but only a portion of the footage was deemed usable – and even the audio was a technical disappointment. Returning to his enormous recording facility and soundstage Paisley Park in Chanhassen, Minnesota, the stage set was recreated and the concert filmed again. This time, with the benefit of a controlled environment, multiple takes, and unencumbered close ups, the live material would take on a music-video level of polish. Approximately 80% of the film is reshot, an estimate put forth by sax player Eric Leeds

"some say a man ain't happy truly, until a man truly dies..."

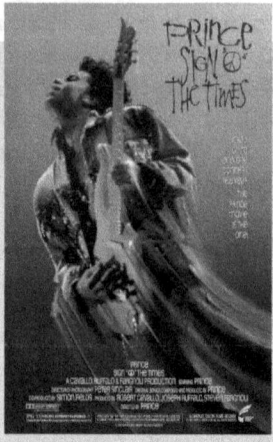

SOUNDTRACK

Sign o' the Times

Play in the Sunshine

Little Red Corvette/ Housequake

Slow Love

I Could Never Take the Place of Your Man

Hot Thing

Now's the Time (Charlie Parker cover by the band)

Drum solo: Sheila E.

U Got the Look

If I Was Your Girlfriend

Forever in My Life/It

It's Gonna Be a Beautiful Night

The Cross

(whose awesome stage costume is a black hooded robe and aviators). If so, there is no shortage of energy lost in the translation. In fact, this may be more energetic than a show in front of an audience. Unlike the linear slog of a legitimate live concert, the performers clearly paced themselves and paused between set-ups; everyone is on their a-game, all the time, and no one sweats. Lip sync to the material is totally passable, and by editing in the wide shots of the European shows a sense of reality is achieved. A small handful of audience close ups that are a little too perfectly arranged (populated as they are with perfect, albeit European-looking people) reveal the gag. The difference between the full-scale live venue and the recreation are largely blurred in the haze of smoke and lighting, and the resulting movie comes across as a beautiful dream, a long dream of a perfect seat at an impossibly good concert.

There are certain attempts at a narrative throughline in the movie that inject a level of artificiality; it's arguable whether they add or distract. Instead of playing it dead straight, Prince opts to make it a sort of a "play with in a concert movie." It opens with a scat/beat poetry type word association argument between the dynamo dancer Cat and backup singer Gregory Allen Brooks that takes place in an obviously artificial alley. Clumps of neon signs and colored gels make the whole thing look like a stage play vision of New York. Prince observes the fight, later there are implications that it's a love triangle that excuse the film's more sexual overtures as Prince and Cat "make love" on stage. Cat, Prince's *muse du jour*, gets the most spoken lines in the film (maybe a dozen). Besides Prince, she's the star of the film: her dynamic dancing is featured as prominently as any of the musicians, maybe more. Prince had recently changed his lineup, keeping Dr. Fink on keyboards and adding a host of horn players as well as one of his favorite drummers.

Sheila E is next in screen prominence is, and gets plenty of screen time both behind the drum kit (including a long solo) and out front in a wildly asymmetrical outfit. This would be around the time that Prince proposed to her (on stage, in the middle of "Purple Rain," as the legend goes), so her on-screen bits are packed with his obvious adoration for her. Though the relationship would be broken off, they would continue to collaborate, and their relationship lasted the longest, from meeting her in 1978 to playing together for the last time in 2011. As she said in an interview with Billboard, "we were together for so long I don't really know when we weren't. We always loved each other."

Sheena Easton appears in the most artificial of the sequences, performing "U Got The Look," the duet from the album. Prince had written "Sugar Walls" for her in 1985, and they sort of dated (a limo driver recalls a date in which Prince wanted to communicate with Sheena only through their eyes, she pleaded with him to speak but he stood firm to her total frustration). Here they don't even try to make it look like the concert (no microphones required!) despite the presence of the audience. It is essentially the music video, dropped in mid-show. It's gamely framed as a daydream, with Prince imagining the proceedings from his dressing room.

Like *Cherry Moon*, there are fleeting moments of cinematic brilliance. One scene with Cat in her apartment transforms as the camera flies out the window, over the audience, and towards the stage. At times the film becomes a sort of jazz funk version of *Guys and Dolls*, with the stagey environs and even a crap game erupting on stage. The nearly pornographic performance of "Hot Thing" is an eye-roaster.

Sign 'O' The Times earned a meager $3 million on release in the US – I recall my small (but hormonally charged) group of friends were the only folks in the theater at our early summer viewing.

The film went out of print on home video after a 1991 VHS release, but has popped up in international DVD editions and recently was revived on Showtime. If you're looking for a document of Prince at the height of his capabilities, raging across the stage like the love child of James Brown and Jimi Hendrix, this is it.

"I've seen the future and it will be..."

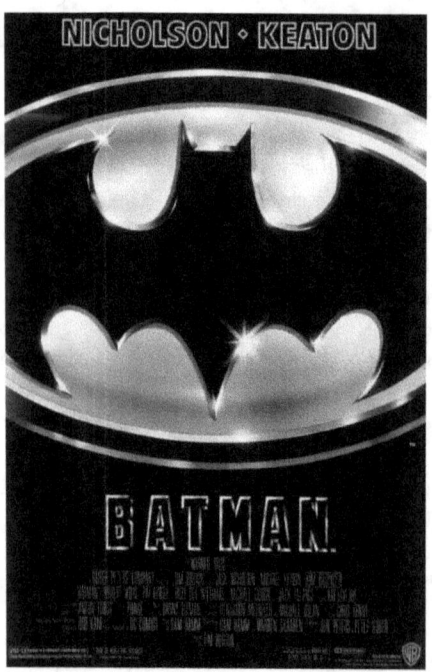

Alas, 1989's *Batman* is not a musical, but in it director Tim Burton imagines a 1940s-inspired, art deco nightmare world in which the only pop music is Prince. And thus we must grab our can of green hair spray and begin.

The film assumes you know who Batman is, who Bruce Wayne is, and

hits the ground running. Prince's slightly bonkers tie-in album has been shrugged aside, much as this version of Batman has, but both were so wildly successful that it bears discussion. Also, it's Prince, so even at his worst there's a gem or two.

Burton has said that he listened to Prince while concocting scenes for the film, especially when conceiving his take on the Joker. He included songs like "1999," and "Baby I'm a Star" as temp tracks when cutting the film, even before Prince was asked by Burton to do a song or two to fill those holes. At first unsure, Prince visited the movie's set in England to discuss it. Burton recalls meeting Prince for the first time in the Batcave and "he actually sort of fit when he walked in, it was kind of funny." Accurate enough: Prince was a mysterious, reclusive rich genius – a spiritual kin to Bruce Wayne if ever there were one. After a rough cut screening, Prince was so interested that he considered cutting short his current tour for *Lovesexy*, but the write-off would have been too costly.

Still under contract to Warner Brothers for several more albums, Prince returned with an entire album's worth of material. Was this Prince up to his usual productivity, or was he deliberately churning out material to rush his contract to completion?

One can imagine where those temporary songs were placed based on the tracks that eventually replaced them. "Partyman" is the film's ersatz "1999," as Joker and friends deface the artwork at the absurdly industrial

Fluegelheim Museum. And "Trust" has the same pace and feel as "Baby I'm a Star," used when The Joker rolls out his street parade of doom. Fans can try subbing them out at home and see for themselves – Jack Nicholson's Joker does seem to be following the beats and yelps of "I'm a Star."

The rest of Prince's contributions are heard as "source" music, playing on speakers too thin or too fat to really make them out. The effect is that, with the exception of the two "musical numbers," the film remains largely timeless. While an epic, over-budgeted hit that symbolized and lampooned the excess of the 1980s, it revels in its gleefully 1940s lighting and staging, and minus some hairstyles and some cars seems duly divorced from the era.

In retrospect, Prince seems an odd match to Tim Burton's carnival dark ride atmosphere, and in the superhero rearview mirror the whole thing's probably a little bit embarrassing. Possibly most embarrassing is the indulgent music video to the film's chart topping hit "Batdance," that depicts Prince as a kind of Two-Face – half Joker, half Batman. Dancing female Batmen and Jokers and a gaggle of Vicky Vales join in the festivities. The music video for "Partyman" fares better, as the split-faced villain returns (now half-Prince-half-Joker) and menaces or entertains a Phantom of the Opera-like group of partygoers. The two-faced character gets billing in the liner notes of the album as, appropriately, "Gemini." It's the little touches like this that make the Batman album a little more than the sum of its parts. Even director Burton refers to it as a "companion, conceptual album" that was indicative of the type of multi-level marketing that was pioneered with Batman and soon became standard for blockbuster Hollywood releases.

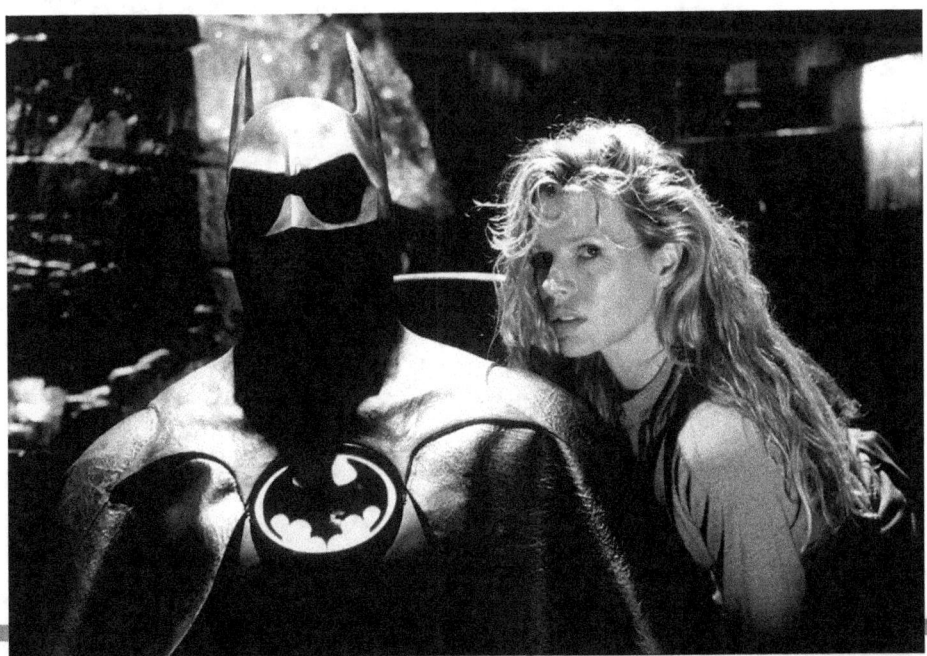

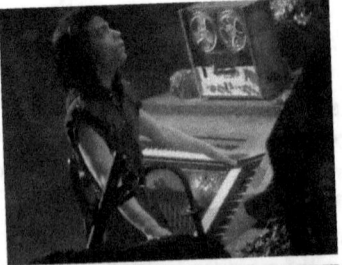

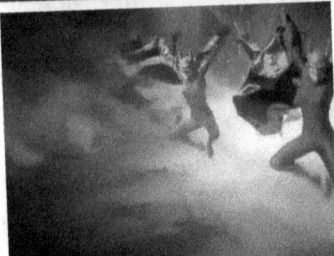

SOUNDTRACK

The Future
Electric Chair
The Arms of Orion
Partyman
Vicki Waiting
Trust
Lemon Crush
Scandalous!
Batdance

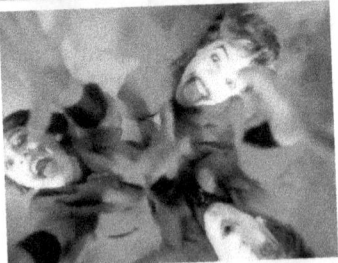

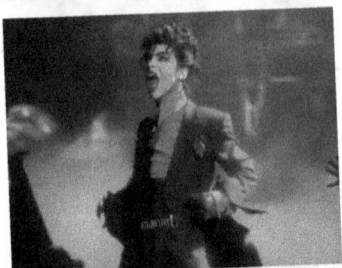

Batdance (right) – a music video that does no favors for the DC Cinematic Universe. Directed with purple verve by Albert (Purple Rain) Magnoli ©1989 Warner Brothers

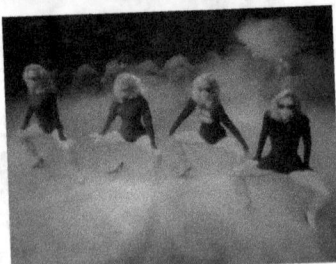

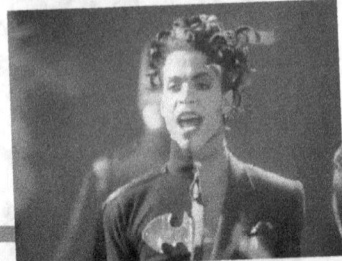

The album references itself and the movie on many occasions, pulling sound bites from the then-workprint, especially for electronic collage songs like Batdance. Bond Movie-songstress Sheena Easton also teams up with Prince again for the ballad "The Arms of Orion." You won't find any of the Batman tracks on greatest hits compilations due to licensing agreements.

As Prince was always known to produce more work than was needed, something was sure to end up on the cutting room floor. Missing from the album and the film are his first take for the parade scene, "200 Balloons," which lives on as a sample in "Batdance," and the Joker-inspired song "Dance With the Devil," which Prince himself deemed too dark. Despite all the weirdness, the album was swept up in the Batmania of 1989 and nested at number one in the belfry of the Billboard charts for six weeks.

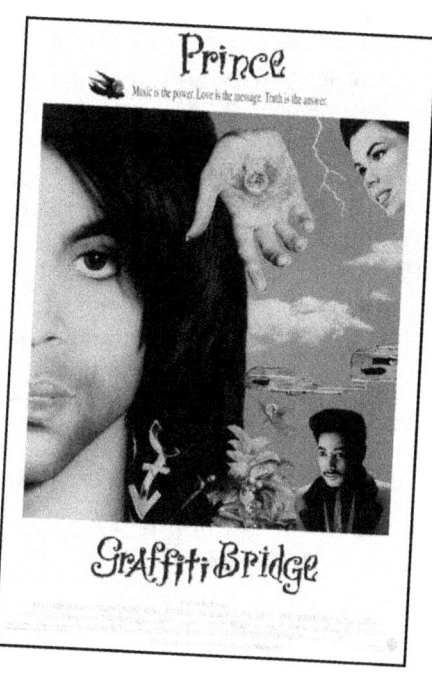

> **"Are there really angels, or are they just in our minds? It all comes out in the wash... in time."**

If the Kid and Morris from *Purple Rain* were transported to the same world that *Sign O the Times* took place (one that's probably just a couple streets down from the alley where Michael Jackson's "Smooth Criminal" club exists), you'd have *Graffiti Bridge*. Too theatrical and artificial to be a real sequel to *Purple Rain*, and with a story no deeper than a music video, it's nowhere nearly in the same league as the purple movie that started it all. Still, as a musical to run at full volume in the background while you're doing something else, it's a fine collection of music by Prince and friends with great (if wholly artificial) visuals. And Morris and Jerome keep the thing alive when no one else can, God bless 'em, even if they fail to reach the bar they set in *Purple Rain.*

Morris Day returns as "himself," a performer and impressario who owns controlling interest in every club on "Seven Corners," except the club Glam Slam, where his 50% ownership is challenged and matched by The Kid (Prince). To make matters worse, the Kid specializes in that uncomfortable musical marriage of "sex and God" that characterized Prince's music at the time, something that Morris can not abide.

MORRIS: "You making that spiritual noise again. You know I can't make no money that way."

THE KID: "If you ever gave it a chance, one day you would."

The Kid lives under the stage in the club, a funky Phantom of the Opera, and writes letters to his (dead) father on heart-shaped note paper. Circling the drama is Aura (Ingrid Chavez), a cute angel with a leather jacket, on an earthly mission *a la Wings of Desire* (1987).

The audience is allowed to hear her thoughts, likely in an effort to provide some insight into what the heck's going on. The Kid is interested in her, but this time it's more about sex than God. The Kid is visibly disappointed to find out that she belongs to not "him" but "Him," and she's come here not to fool around but to change Morris' mind.

The story meanders and is little more than showcase for the songs, which should be appealing enough, and it's full of eclectic sets, comic book lighting, and enough smoke and colored gels for three movies. They almost never leave the soundstage; Seven Corners itself has no sky, only a ceiling with a lighting grid, and there's a naught but handful of brief shots of various Minneapolis-area alleyways to occassionally open up the film.

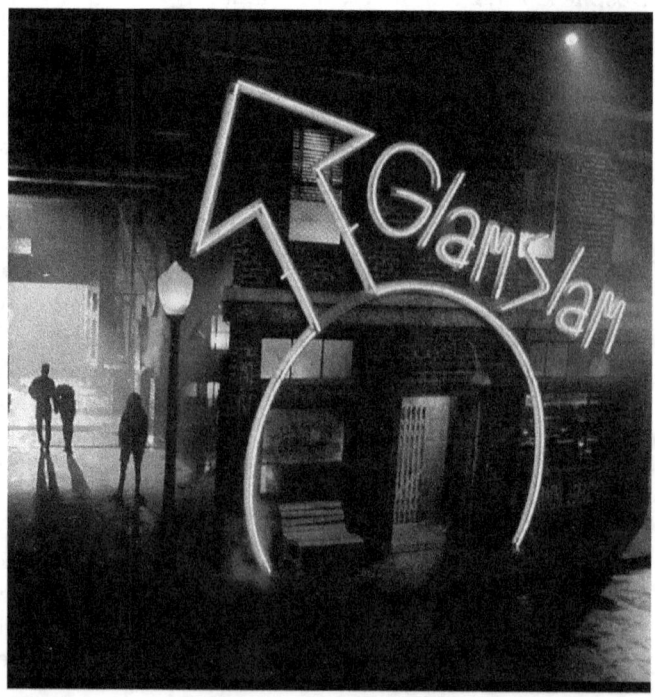

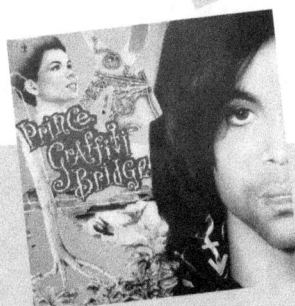

Inspired bits include a "Duelling Banjos" riff with cash instead of banjos, a too-short appearance by George Clinton, the great gospel-tinged song "Melody Cool" featuring Mavis Staples, and Quincy Jones protege Tevin Campbell. Alas, there's little chemistry between Prince and Chavez, and Prince is plagued by his worst haircut and a George Michael-type stubble beard.

Ingrid Chavez was inspired (by Prince, one would assume) to move to Minneapolis in 1986 to pursue her dream of becoming a songwriter. She met with Prince in 1987, who encouraged her to write 21 poems (a concept that made it into the film) and he would record the music for an album of her poetry. They recorded it over the next couple of years, with Chavez reading the poems over Prince's music. Warner Brothers demanded it be turned into a singing album instead, so Prince shelved it.

During the filming of *Graffiti Bridge*, Chavez went into the studio with Lenny Kravitz and co-wrote what would become Madonna's "Justify My Love," a song that sounded unlike Madonna's previous output and as such perhaps heralded the end of the 80s.

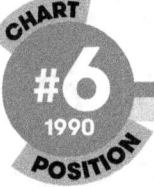

CHART
#6
1990
POSITION

SOUNDTRACK

Can't Stop This Feeling I Got
Prince

New Power Generation
Prince

Release It
The Time

The Question of U
Prince

Elephants & Flowers
Tevin Campbell & Prince

We Can Funk
Prince

Joy In Repetition
Prince

Love Machine
The Time

Tick, Tick, Bang
Prince

Shake!
The Time

Thieves in the Temple
Prince

The Latest Fashion
Prince & The Time

Melody Cool
Mavis Staples

Graffiti Bridge
Prince

New Power Generation (Pt II)
Prince and Cast

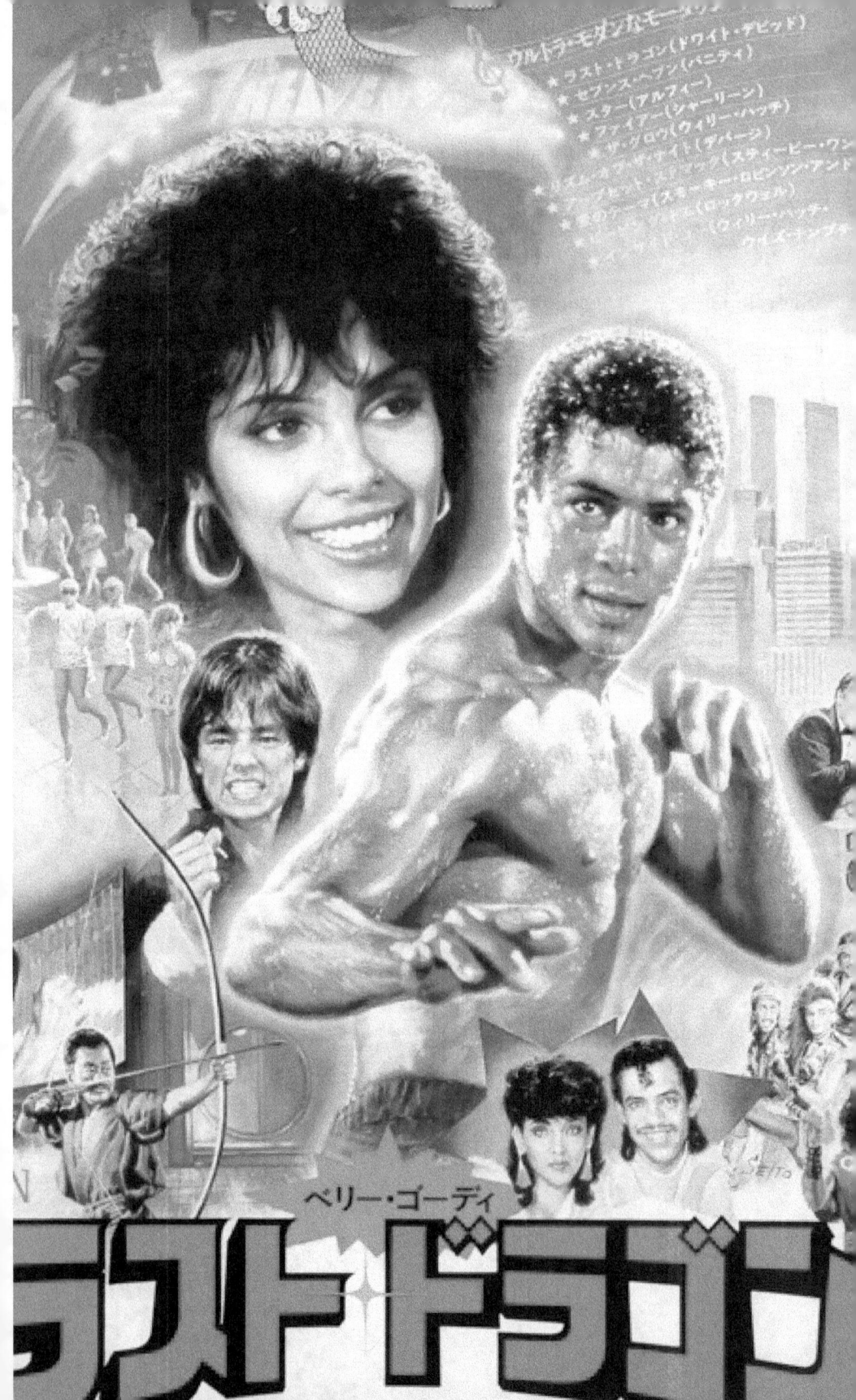

15

ODDBALL ROCKERS

MTV proved that just about any music could be combined with any imagery and end up pretty sweet. In the feature film world, that meant that you could put musical elements and musician characters in just about any story. Martial arts? Alien invasion? Madcap comedy? The genres in this chapter are all over the place.

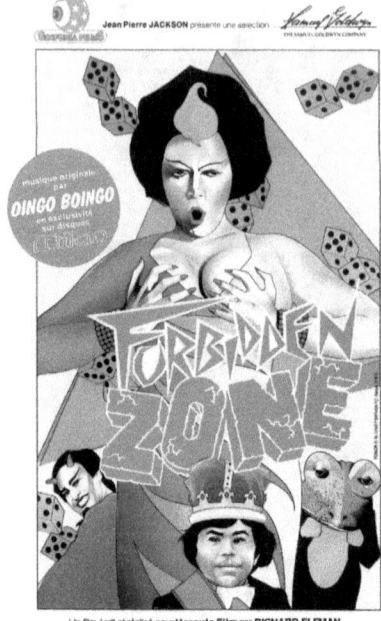

Jean Pierre JACKSON présente une sélection

Un film écrit et réalisé pour **Hercule Film** par **RICHARD ELFMAN.**
Producteur exécutif: **GENE CUNNINGHAM.** Directeur de la photo: **GREGORY SANDOR.**
Décors: **MARIE-PASCALE ELFMAN.** Animation: **JOHN MUTO.**
Interprétation: **SUSAN TYRELL, HERVE VILLECHAIZE, MARIE-PASCALE ELFMAN, VIVA, JOE
SPINELL, DANNY ELFMAN, TOSHIRO BALONEY, KEDRICK WOLFE, GISELLE LINDLEY, PHIL
GORDON, HYMAN DIAMOND,**

FORBIDDEN ZONE (1980)

Alas, the only thing new wave about this movie is the forward-looking poster, with its terrific typography and Susan Tyrell's iconic, boob grabbing Queen Doris of the Sixth Dimension, a vague mixture of Divine and the Bride of Frankenstein. Arriving as it did before the 80s aesthetic really gelled, we have another lost 70s artifact here, striving perhaps for another Rocky Horror-type midnight success. Forbidden Zone shares a love of the ugly, cheap, and scatalogical with early John Waters movies, and resembles a black and white musical version of *Pink Flamingos* by way of a 30s cartoon come to life. I might be selling you on this, but be warned:

it's truly jaw dropping and horrible in its cheap surreal antics. See now even that sounds pretty good, but I'm warning you it's not for the weak of heart!

If you love Danny Elfman you are invited to try to make it through Forbidden Zone, as some of the music is his, and shows that same songwriting sensibility that would be put to use in scores like *Nightmare Before Christmas*. The film is built around the musical theater troupe, The Mystic Knights Of The Oingo Boingo, formed by Danny's older brother Richard in the early 70s. The Knights were a post-modern musical theater act of more than 15 musicians that did music from the 1890s through the 1950s, in whiteface and clown makeup with a variety of quirky orchestrations. That group would distill down to eight members and go by Oingo Boingo by 1979. Danny became interested in ska and wanted to focus on the music instead of the theatrics, so the band morphed into the form that most people recognize in the 80s. Danny himself appears as Satan in the movie, in the film's only really good musical number, a bittersweet victory in that it's really a cover of Cab Calloway's "Minnie the Moocher." A lot of the remaining music is recycled from the past and as such makes for a wholly unique experience.

On the subject of unique, where else will you get Hervé Villechaize as King Fausto of the Sixth Dimension, a place that you reach by going through cartoon-animated internal organs before being pooped out of a giant painted ass among stuffed turd-pillows? The answer is, of course, nowhere. The non-sequiturs fly amidst horribly hand-painted expressionist backgrounds and a vaguely retro wardrobe. Ugly people abound, sandwiched between antiquey songs, cut-out animation, undercranking, backwards footage, rotoscoping, pixelation, dryhumping, blackface… It does give you that icky 1930s feeling a lot of the time, which is a rare vibe. Wait, that sounded like an endorsement. Proceed with caution.

MUSIC EXPOSÉ

DANNY ELFMAN

- **Oingo Boingo (1976-1995)**

- **Performed on-screen in 1986's *Back to School***

- **1985: Tim Burton and Paul Reubens ask Elfman to score *Pee-Wee's Big Adventure*, starting a long collaboration between the filmmaker and composer**

- **Provided the singing voice for Jack Skellington in *The Nightmare Before Christmas***

- **Wrote the theme to the *Simpsons* in 1989**

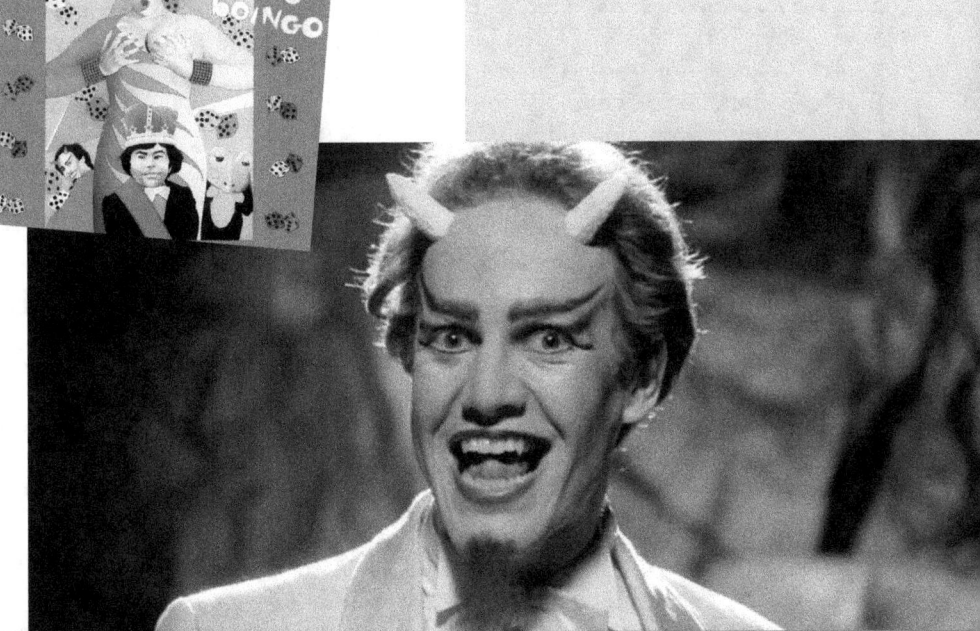

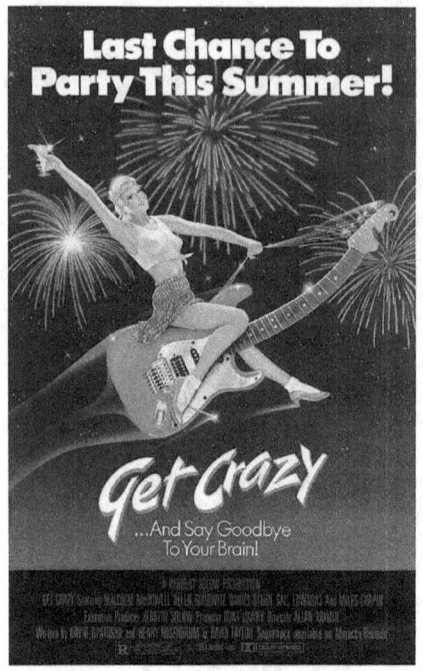

Last Chance To Party This Summer!

Get Crazy

...And Say Goodbye To Your Brain!

GET CRAZY (1983)

Director Allan Arkush tries to distill his experiences as a concert crewmember in the late 60s but ends up with "*Animal House* at a concert venue" in this 1983 comedy that grows and grows on you once you understand the rules. Caution: the rules are there are no rules.

Arkush worked at the Fillmore East from 1968-1971, one of the most important rock venues of the late sixties. Owned by rock promoter Bill Graham, one can only imagine the drug-soaked goings-on at a venue that hosted psychedelic luminaries from the Grateful Dead to Jimi Hendrix. Arkush recalls the film's origins in an episode of Trailers From Hell: "I had

had some success for Roger Corman with *Rock and Roll High School* which was a cult movie, and then I thought I was going to get my big break directing a sci-fi movie for a big studio. It was called *Heartbeeps* and it was a complete bomb on every level. After that experience I wanted to make something more personal about my life, and my relationship to rock music.... And this independent production company with their own financing – they liked it, they wanted to make it. Yes, they did, but they didn't want my personal story set in the 60s. They wanted to do something more like Airplane in a rock and roll theater so I said yes..."

Standing in for the Fillmore is The Saturn Theater, played again by the always-up-for-it Wiltern Theater in Los Angeles. According to star Malcolm McDowell, "we trashed it just before they restored it. They knew we were going to do it, so they didn't mind."

The film's conflict comes from Colin Beverly (Ed Begley Jr.), yet another one of those unscrupulous 80s real estate developers with eyes on the Saturn. He's followed around by two sycophants who add a coda to everything he says (a common joke but done here with great wordplay and rhythm and fun). He even shows a bunch of stereotypical foreign investors what he has in mind for the site with the usual scale model, but this one involves a copy of The Saturn that explodes to reveal the new project.

Mr. Beverly makes an offer to the club's current owner Max Wolfe, who is so incensed by the move that he collapses from an apparent heart attack. Max's nephew Sammy is fully willing to make the deal, though, and becomes an accomplice in a plan that involves a high tech stink bomb and setting fire to the theater.

The story takes place on New Years Eve, with the business of the celebratory concert event held together, barely, by stage manager Neil (Daniel Stern, but Arkush wanted Tom Hanks!), whose attention is split between the unlikely bill of musical acts, protecting his nubile little sister Susie (Stacy Nelkin of *Halloween III*), and love interest and former stage manager Willy (Gail Edwards).

The musical acts provide the crazy color for the film, much as the Fillmore mixed in jazz and blues acts with the rock headliners. We first catch up with King Blues, the opening blues act, at a funeral attended almost exclusively by blind blues players (and the customary slapstick that should

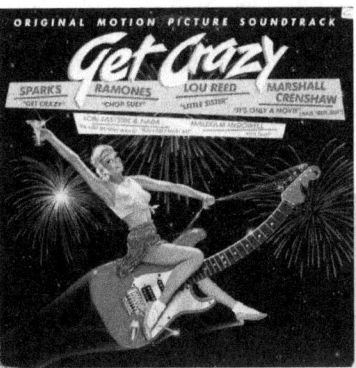

SOUNDTRACK

Get Crazy
Sparks

You Can't Make Me
Lori Eastside & Nada

Chop Suey
Ramones

It's Only a Movie
Marshall Crenshaw

Little Sister
Lou Reed

I'm Not Gonna Take It
Lori Eastside & Nada

Hot Shot
Malcolm McDowell

The Blues Had a Baby and they Named it Rock & Roll
Bill Henderson

Hoochie Coochie Man
Fear

Starscape
Michael Boddicker

Auld Lang Syne
Howard Kaylan and Cast

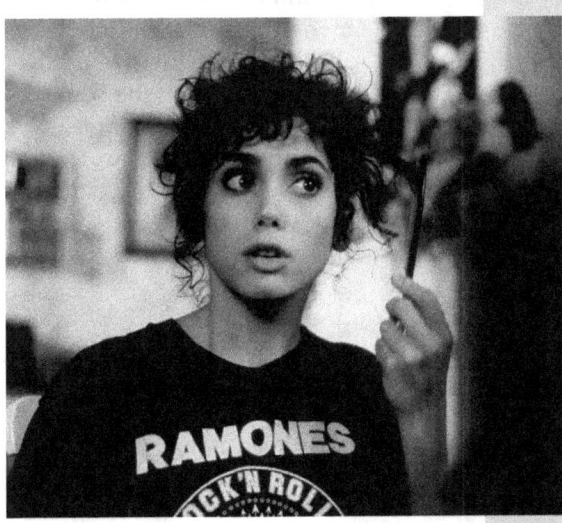

accompany such a thing). After some dangerous-looking stunt driving, they arrive at the venue to find that a Jew's band, not a blues band, has been selected to provide backing, complete with matching powder-blue yarmulkes and a harmonica-playing rabbi. Turns out they sound pretty good, so the act goes on as planned. They perform "Hoochie Coochie Man," a song that subsequently gets played two more times by other bands in their own style. As a sort of ersatz concert film, it seems a missed opportunity to trot out the same song three times. It's either lazy, clever, or it is indicative of the limited music licensing budget.

The next act is a huge, all-female group Nada, led by a Toni Basil-type and made of about 15 members playing a mix of punk/pop/slightly new wave, and really the only one of the acts that sound like they belong in 1982-3. Lee Ving plays an Iggy Pop spoof called "Piggy," who head-butts everything in sight and stage dives a lot. Soon the entire balcony section is stage-diving into the audience below in a series of hair-raising stunts that are so well edited I was genuinely terrified.

The headliner is Reggie Wanker, who Arkush describes as "a combination of Mick Jagger and Rod Stewart." Played with the expected aplomb by Malcolm McDowell, he gets to sing a couple of songs (and vocally recalls Gerrit Graham's character "Beef" in Phantom of the Paradise), and in fact has a scene in which he has a two-way conversation with his penis. The fact that Wanker Junior responds in a high-pitched English

accent is not as disturbing as the fact that he makes Doors-drummer John Densmore give him a drink.

All the while, Lou Reed plays a reclusive vaguely Bob Dylan-type character who is trying to get to the venue, taking the scenic route by cab as he tries to write a new song for the show. He's relaxed and funny, has some good physical stunt/shtick crossing the street while composing on a guitar, and the end song he performs after the audience has dispersed is great.

You can sense the 1960's DNA in the film, from the proliferation of flower children (long extinct in 1982 except for comedy punchlines), persistent drug use, and songwriting types. At times one is reminded of those 70s musical films like Rocky Horror or Phantom of the Paradise, either of which would make a terrific double bill with this one. Get Crazy must have been a great movie to see at the drive-in or midnight screening, where paying attention isn't necessarily the point. Among the more inspired things is a robot(?) drug dealer named Electric Larry, always on the spot with a briefcase full of medicinals. He's the film's strongest original image, with glowing red eyes and a pimp-hat decked out with a mirror-ball-material hat band.

What else has it got? A wacky miniature sequence of a 747 tour plane hijacked by drugged-out John Densmore, a joint mascot costume that gets smoked, undercranked fast speed action, silly sound effects, trippy opticals to represent drug effects, high pitched voices, wire flying, and SO much stunt work it's quite exhausting. The amount of dangerous activity and irresponsible behavior in this film is kind of amazing, and nothing is allowed to linger. No joke is allowed to stagnate – some scenes are five seconds long. And the entire proceedings look incredibly complicated, almost everything is a crowd scene and the stage show is always filled with performers. It's packed to the gills with musical cameos, like Fabian, Bobby Sherman, Lori Eastside, Howard Kaylan of The Turtles, John Densmore of the Doors. And yes, there's Dick Miller and Jackie Joseph, who would be teamed as husband and wife again in *Gremlins* (1984), and other Roger Corman players like Mary Worononov and Paul Bartel, and Clint Howard. Linnea Quigley is immediately recognizable in her trademark nakedness as a groupie.

The film's release was squandered, Arkush claims the producers realized they could make more money by losing money and veritably buried the film, selling off the movie as a tax shelter.

"When it opened there were no ads, no critics screenings, and the soundtrack LP wasn't promoted. Ultimately the production company went bankrupt and some of the executives were actually indicted for financial crimes but that's not the worst of it. In the transfer of the movie back and forth for these different shell companies, the negative was lost, as well as the entire soundtrack. Lost. I checked all the film vaults, it was gone, cannot be found, which is why it's never been on DVD." Music wise it's a mixed bag, but Malcolm McDowell sings his own stuff and that's interesting enough. In the studio to record his tracks, the engineer asked him to really let it go, but Malcolm said "okay, but I am an actor so I really want to enunciate the words... And John Lennon's producer, that had done his last album *Double Fantasy*, he called me and said 'I know you sang those songs in the film, didn't you?' I said 'How did you know?' 'Becuase I understood every word.'"

"*Get Crazy* was really kind of the end of my movie career. Luckily, rock videos happened right around then... and then I got work on the TV series "Fame.""

Since then, revival screenings form some surviving prints have attracted the love of directors like Edgar Wright and Eli Roth. And no wonder – the huge effort to create something like this is evident throughout, even if (as Arkush claimed) every good idea was committee-ed out of existence by the producers. If Tom Hanks had been cast, would *Get Crazy* still be a "lost" film? Regardless, the film as made, with the right audience and the right frame of mind, is quite a sight.

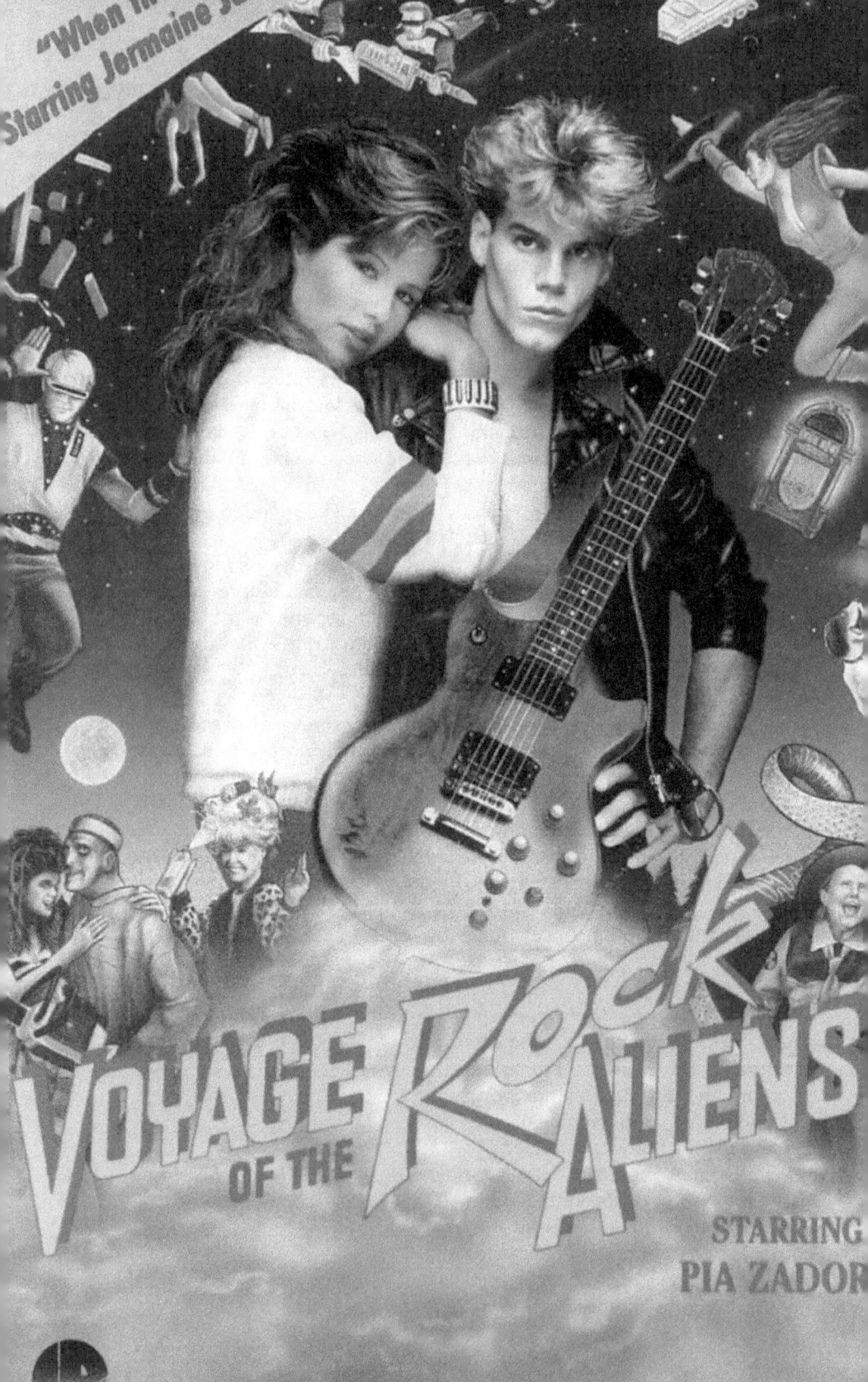

"When the...
Starring Jermaine J...

VOYAGE of the ROCK ALIENS

STARRING
PIA ZADOR

AN INTER-PLANETARY CURB PRODUCTION OF A JAMES FARGO FILM VOYAGE OF THE ROCK ALIENS

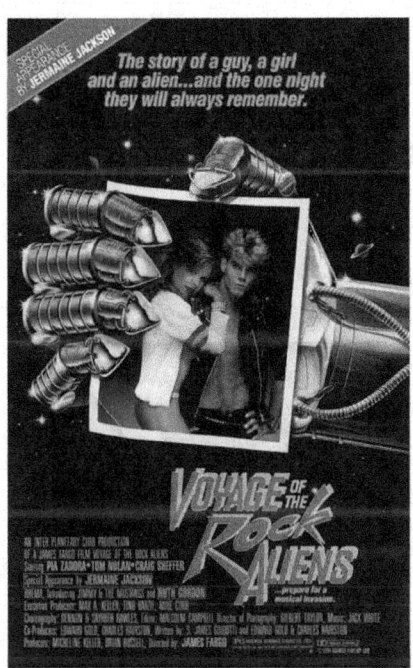

It begins with the unrelated music video for "When the Rain Begins to Fall," a duet with Jermaine Jackson. The video is about as Italian as you can get, with clearly Italian actors and locations despite the sci-fi trappings. We find out that this is a broadcast detected by the robot crew of a guitar-shaped spacecraft, searching the galaxy for rock'n'roll. The robots hilariously revive the humanoid crew (they're stored in a refrigerator at doll size, run through a pneumatic tube, and reconstituted). The alien crew arrives in a smoking phone booth to the small town of Speelburgh (shot in Georgia) and arrive at Lake Eerie, a body of water so toxic it dissolves a surfboard. The robot sidekick disguises himself as a silver fire hydrant and putts around the town like an RC R2D2.

The film borrows from all the right drive-in genres, and pulls in music appropriate to the character faction – the greaser gang gets a Stray-Cats-type treatment, the Devo-like alien crew is appropriately New Wave, and Pia's songs are sort of MTV-meets-musical-theater. The surprisingly elaborate musical routines seem plucked from a 60's beach movie,

VOYAGE OF THE ROCK ALIENS (1984)

A desperately new wave sci-fi musical, *Voyage of the Rock Aliens* is a dumb but earnest B-movie filled with shameless musical numbers, where everybody appears to be having enough fun to make the whole thing fairly forgivable.

Astoundingly, the illustrious Gilbert Taylor is credited as cinematographer, having photographed films like *Hard Day's Night*, *The Omen*, and *Star Wars*, and had worked for Hitchock, Kubrick, and Polanski.

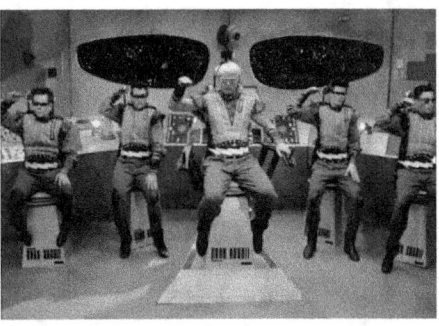

which makes sense as the leads are named Frankie and Dee Dee. When the alien leader spots Pia for the first time, his head explodes. The crew collects the pieces, print him out like a cutout and reinflate him.

Ruth Gordon plays a local sheriff with her usual naturalistic, appealing style. Michael Berryman is a chainsaw maniac who escapes from the local Speelburgh Asylum for the Criminally Insane. The aliens teleport through the toilet to join a battle of the bands, and back Pia for a typically decent 80s tune. Craig Sheffer as Frankie seethes and glowers like an angry bluejeans model as a back and forth music battle ensues between the forces of new wave and rockabilly. The film even becomes a chainsaw-killer horror movie for a moment as Berryman pursues Dee Dee's friend Diane (Alison la Placa), but true love is found when the resourceful Diane helps him repair his broken tool.

The genre flipping was an intended part of the fun and according to writer James Guidotti:

"It's a little like sitting home and watching TV late on a Saturday night, all the while switching channels from 5 to 9 to 11 and to 13, on channel 5 they're airing an old Beach Party movie; on 9 one about alien invaders; on 11 a film about a mad, homicidal maniac on the loose; and on 13 a rock 'n roll program."

PIA ZADORA

Pia is and Italian/Polish American from New Jersey that started as a child actor (appearing in Santa Claus Conquers the Martians, 1964) and grew up into an actor that looked like a child. She was panned for the inflammatory 1982 film Butterfly, considered by many to be the worst performance ever to win a Golden Globe. It is assumed that her husband Meshulam Riklis (30 years her senior) bought the award through an expensive promotional campaign. Riklis and Zadora later purchased and mostly demolished Pickfair, the Hollywood home of Douglas Fairbanks and Mary Pickford.

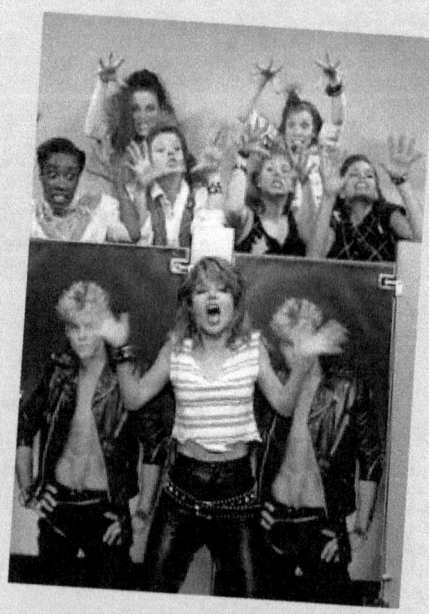

Voyage of the Rock Aliens features about half of Pia's 1984 album "Let's Dance Tonight," and the aliens are played by a real-life new wave band called Rhema. Only one of the band members was asked not to participate on the basis of what had to have been a very bad screen test. Likewise, the greaser band is a real outfit called Jimmy & the Mustangs, both of the bands appeared on Curb Records,

In the end the whole thing is put together rather roughly and the songs aren't quite good enough to elevate the film to a kooky classic. Pia is little more than a goofy, 50-cent Madonna and not compelling enough either, but it's much better than it should have been. Director John Waters is an avowed fan of the film and cast Pia in *Hairspray*, you gonna argue with him?

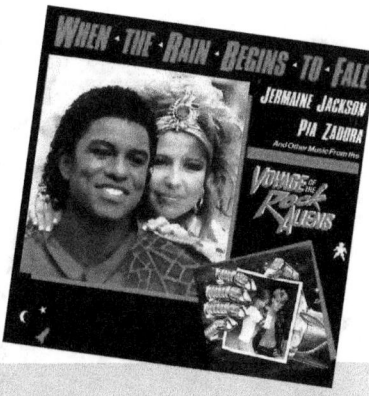

SOUNDTRACK

When the Rain Begins to Fall
Jermaine Jackson & Pia Zadora

Little Bit of Heaven
Pia Zadora & Mark Spiro

Real Love
Pia Zadora

Nature of the Beast
Michael Bradley

Let's Dance Tonight
Pia Zadora

Back on the Street
3 Speed

Openhearted
Real Life

She Doesn't Mean a Thing to Me
Mark Spiro

21st Century
Rhema

Justine
Jimmy and the Mustangs

My World is Empty Without You
John Farnham & Rainey

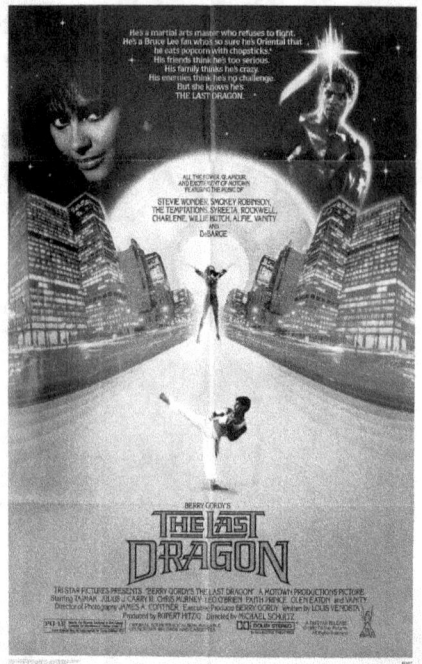

THE LAST DRAGON (1985)

In that strange middle ground between *Purple Rain* and The *Karate Kid* lies *The Last Dragon*. Berry Gordy, the founder of Motown Records, is the name above the title on this afrocentric martial arts film, as much about the power of music and music video as it is an homage to Bruce Lee and kung fu films. Gordy was an executive producer and music supervisor for the film who was reportedly deeply involved on set for this film that was a financial hit, a critical miss, and developed into a cult classic.

Leroy Green (Taimak) is a young martial artist in the advanced stages of his training and seeking to unlock

the final mystery of "the glow," basically a super power of ultimate enlightenment. At a lively screening of *Enter the Dragon* (people shouting at the screen, a sudden outbreak of breakdancing silenced by an angry Asian patron who "kills" the boombox as Bruce Lee would) is interrupted by the arrival of the samurai-like Sho-Nuff, the Shogun of Harlem (Julius Carry). Leroy prefers to remain undisturbed, eating his popcorn with chopsticks. But he is identified as "Bruce Leroy," and is singled out as "the only guy that stands between Sho-Nuff and total supremacy." Leroy avoids conflict with the super-gangster here, and over and over again, to Sho-Nuff's dismay.

The film's primary conflict revolves around singer and music video show host Laura Charles, played by Vanity. Diminutive promoter and "Video Game King" Eddie Arcadian (Christopher Murney) is threatening the producer of her show (an early appearance by William H. Macy) unless he plays a video by his girlfriend and protege. You might want to take him seriously, as he keeps some kind of flesh-eating monster in a murky aquarium.

Faith Prince plays the singer Angie Viracco as a cut-rate Cyndi Lauper, or a New York version of Julie Brown, and we get a humorous look at two of her intentionally-bad music videos. Gordy's son Kerry, who handled some of the music production, was tasked with creating songs that were obviously bad but could still have been hits, and the songs he made for the film ("Dirty Books" and "Test Drive") hilariously fit the bill. Father

Berry was apparently so impressed with Faith Prince that he was ready to put his resources behind her and turn her into a real music star if she wanted. She demurred, and became a star on Broadway instead.

Laura's Video HotPix show is a combination of Soul Train and a music video program, with an elaborate system of projection screens and a set so impressive that Diana Ross, one of Gordy's many visitors to the set, offered to buy it for her next tour. The film's breakout hit song "Rhythm of the Night" by DeBarge is featured prominently on the show, and we see almost the whole video played out full screen in the film. Vanity performs her song "7th Heaven" "live" in the studio, descending from the ceiling. When Leroy saves Laura from Arcadian's thugs, they become romantically entangled. Leroy's cooler little brother Richie (Leo O'Brien) is fully prepared to school him in the art of romance, "moves," making love, but the threats from the Shogun keep rolling in. One encounter at Leroy's school gives us the immortal line that could exist in no other film:

"Yeah coolie, kiss my Converse!"

Leroy makes a ninja-style rescue, Laura romances him with a montage of Bruce Lee clips on her bigscreen system. An all-out war breaks out on the set of Hot Pix, as Richie pops and locks his way out of the ropes that bind him and a 12-year old Ernie Reyes Jr mops the floor with assorted novelty bad guys. Escaping with the girl, Sho-Nuff reveals his own master

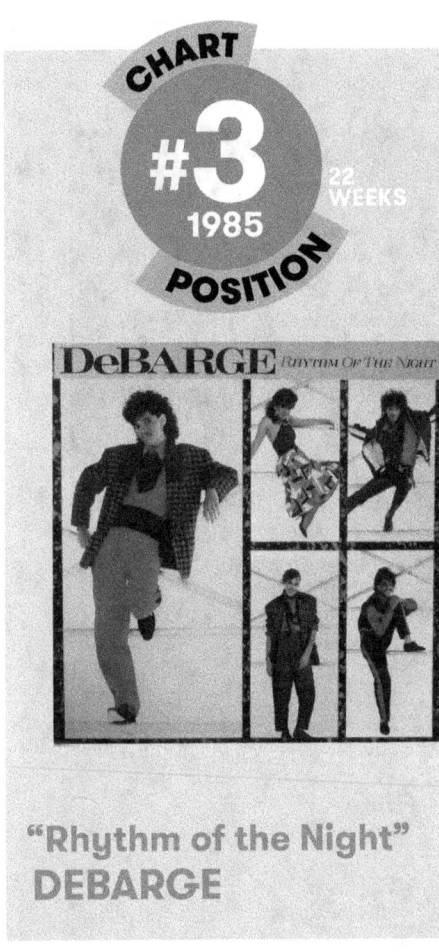

CHART

#3

22 WEEKS

1985

POSITION

"Rhythm of the Night"
DEBARGE

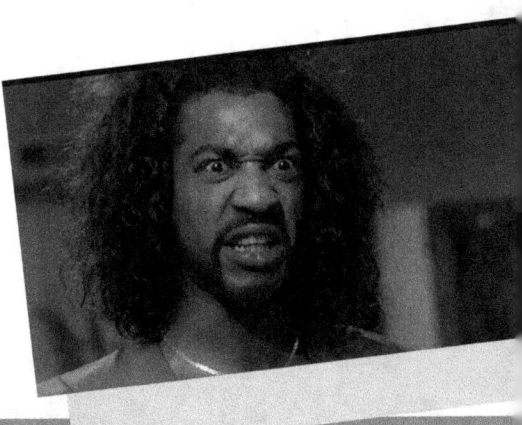

SOUNDTRACK

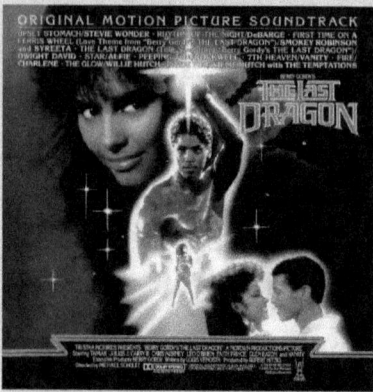

The Last Dragon
Dwight David

7th Heaven
Vanity

Star
Alfie

Fire
Charlene

The Glow
Willie Hutch

Rhythm Of The Night
DeBarge

Upset Stomach
Stevie Wonder

First Time On A Ferris Wheel
Smokey Robinson And Syreeta

Peeping Tom
Rockwell

Inside You
Willie Hutch With The Temptations

status (glowing hands and powerful blows) in a showdown in a warehouse. Leroy finds his strength, glows gold and channels Bruce Lee to win the final battle. The film's denouement is pure glorious cheese, with the whole studio audience of Laura's show dressed in white, and slow motion and freeze frames galore.

The film is an ode to NYC's cultural blender, as screenwriter Louis Venosta explains:

> "I always thought it was funny, in this particular case you had these black and Hispanic guys who had embraced this Chinese hero (in Bruce Lee). You'd walk through Chinatown and you'd see Chinese guys breakdancing. It was New York but it was also my particular eye for this kind of cultural phenomenon of the culture swapping."

Venosta wanted to create a black equivalent of Lee, who was more positive than the blaxploitation heroes. "I was friends with guys like Mario Van Peebles at the time. We were all sort of part of a little group. We always talked about those blaxploitation films; there was always that dialogue. And I went, but they're all bad guys. There really should be a young black kid superhero-type figure who kids can look up to with a positive aspirational thing."

Berry Gordy made a career out of identifying and cultivating young talent, from Diana Ross to Michael

Jackson. Gordy took it upon himself to coach Dragon's star Taimak, who was new to acting, and the results are wonderful and charming. The goal of creating a positive "black superhero" role model succeeded, as an entire generation of performers and martial artists cite it as a key influence. *The Last Dragon* has since grown to a cult hit for martial arts fans and 80s music fans alike.

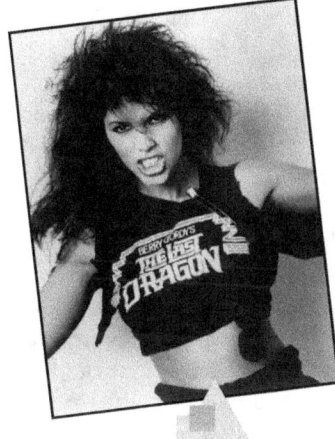

MUSIC EXPOSÉ

VANITY

- **Canadian pageant queen and model**
- **Small role in Terror Train (1980)**
- **Met Prince at 1982 American Music Awards (she was Rick James' date)**
- **Romantically linked to Adam Ant and Billy Idol**
- **Prince renamed her Vanity, positioning her as his female equivalent**
- **Vanity 6 album (1982)**

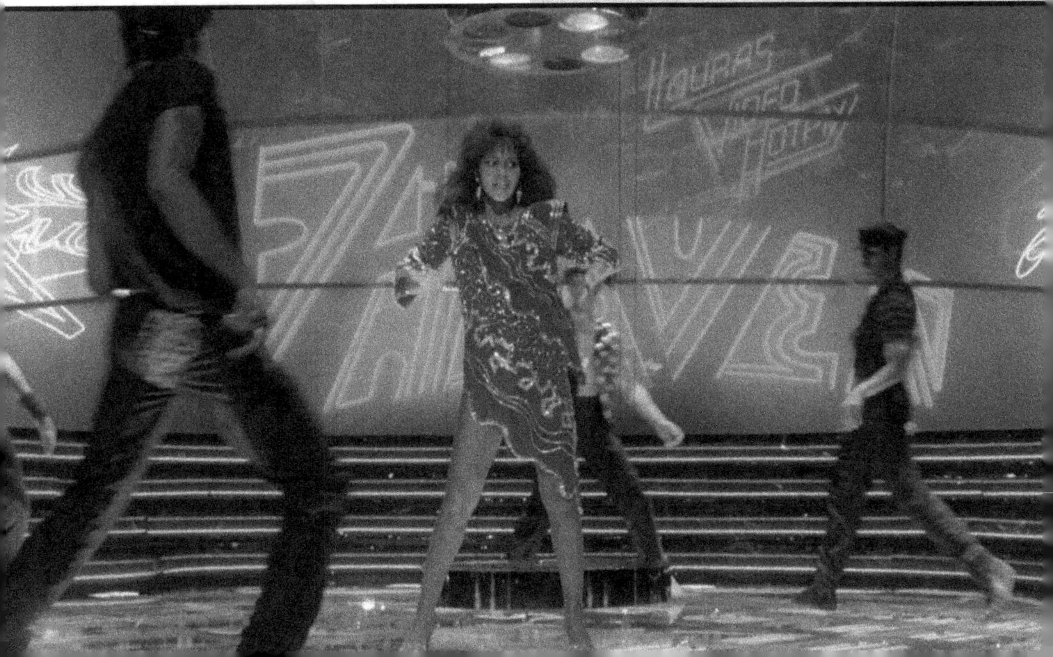

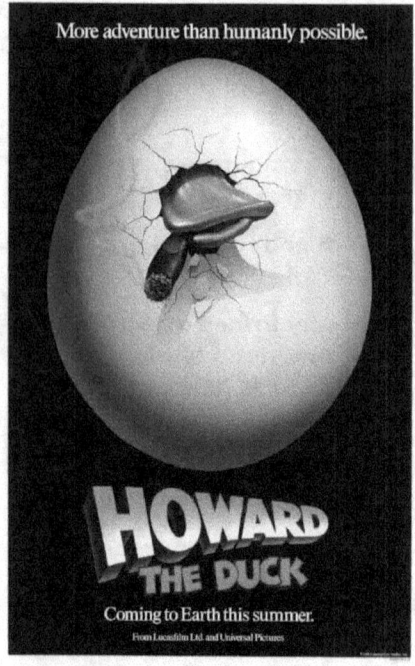

More adventure than humanly possible.

HOWARD
THE DUCK

Coming to Earth this summer.
From Lucasfilm Ltd. and Universal Pictures

HOWARD THE DUCK (1986)

While there are some who would have preferred it never arrived at all, *Howard the Duck* merely had the misfortune of arriving about thirty years too soon. That Universal didn't know how to market it was certainly partially to blame, for how could it be a family friendly adventure romp from the people who brought you *Star Wars* and *Raiders of the Lost Ark*, when the film's lead is a duck who lists as his interests cigar smoking and sex? It has everything in common with other more successful comic book adaptations that would follow, but audiences weren't ready for its mix of action, immaturity and adult themes. Compare this to something like 2014's

Guardians of the Galaxy (another Marvel Comics adaptation with an easter-egg-sized cameo by Howard): in both you have foul mouthed, tough-talking midget-sized anthropomorphic animals who fight intergalactic bad guys, and both films feature pop music prominently.

Howard the Duck's music fits into two categories: the score by John Barry and the songs by Thomas Dolby appearing as "Dolby's Cube." Barry, who provided iconic background music for the James Bond films, veers between noirish orchestration and some fantastic, unmistakable Bondian bombast.

Hot off a gig with David Bowie at Live Aid, Thomas Dolby had seen his second studio album get buried by a regime change at Capitol Records. Dolby's agents had submitted him as a composer for the entire film, which called for several original songs, and someone who could coach the actresses in the realities of on-stage rock performance. He met with producer George Lucas to review the storyboards, and went as far as setting up shop at Lucasfilm's San Rafael facility. Unlike a lot of stars who get pulled into a film, Dolby was a fan of the comics, and recognized the big budget as a chance to stretch out creatively.

Unfortunately, as he laments in his book "The Speed of Sound," "the more money that was sunk into production, the more homogenous Howard seemed to become... It became a common sight to see groups of suited, worried-looking Universal execs milling about the set. I tried in my small part to restore some coolness to the project by contributing quirky left-field music cues with names like "Duck Paté" and "Mutant Disney."

His eclectic approach was too much for the suits, however, and Dolby was let go for being "too subversive," but the songs remain. Dolby's songs include "Don't Turn Away," a song that he performs, as well as all the songs that are performed on stage by the all-girl band in the film, Cherry Bomb. Dolby wrote the songs with a dose of funkiness from George Clinton, and with the aid of Joe Walsh on guitar & Stevie Wonder on harmonica. Watch for Dolby as the bartender at the club, disguised as a Frenchman or an anarchist or something.

As a consolation, he was allowed to direct his own video for his song for the film, which sported a budget ten times that which he had for his video "She Blinded Me With Science," (which was also conceived and directed by Dolby and largely credited with his breakout success). He then discovered that the inflated budget was in fact a way for the label to launder the money that needed to change hands as part of the industry's standard practice of pay for play, and it added to his discouragement at working in the music profession at the time.

At one point in preproduction it was considered that casting a real musician in the role of Beverly would be best, with Cindy Lauper, Belinda Carlisle, and a rising Tori Amos in consideration. Lea's sudden and recent success with *Back to the Future* was deemed a more appealing package. All the vocals are performed by the actors, including

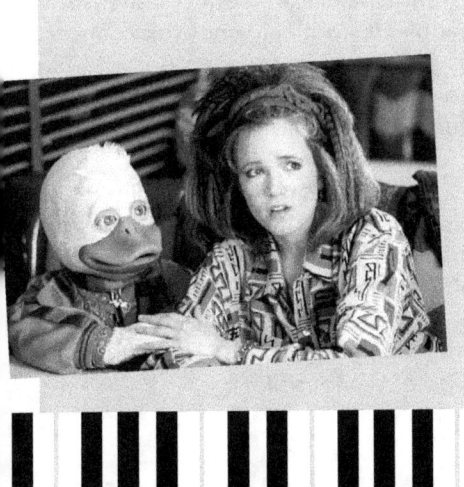

THE TRAGIC TALE OF MR. DOLBY'S WOODY

While scoring the film in San Rafael, Thomas Dolby purchased a surfer-style 1972 Morris Minor woody convertible, complete with surf decals. While it was intention to take it home to England, he never got around to filing the paperwork. It remains at Lucasfilm today, and has become the source of many sound effects in major films, beat with crowbars and baseball bats to create mechanical mayhem.

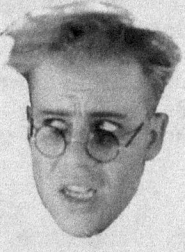

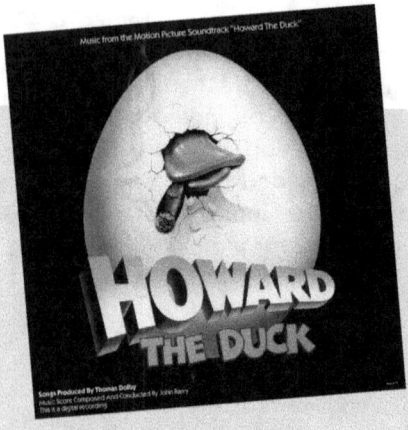

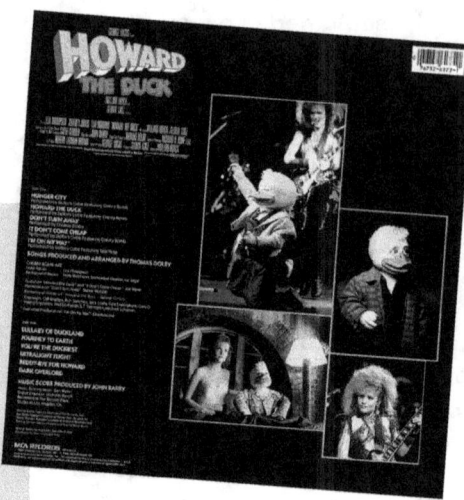

SOUNDTRACK

Hunger City
Dolby's Cube featuring Cherry Bomb

Howard the Duck
Dolby's Cube featuring Cherry Bomb (lead vocals: Lea Thompson, background vocals: George Clinton, guitar: Joe Walsh)

Don't Turn Away
Performed by Thomas Dolby, Harmonica: Stevie Wonder

It Don't Come Cheap
Performed by Dolby's Cube featuring Cherry Bomb (lead vocals: Lea Thompson, guitar: Joe Walsh)

I'm On My Way
Performed by Thomas Dolby

**Lullaby of Duckland
Journey To Earth
You're the Duckiest
Ultralight Flight
Beddy-Bye for Howard
and Dark Overlord**
by John Barry

Lea Thompson, Dominique Davalos, Holly Robinson, and Liz Sagal. The results are admirable, and it not only sells the scenes but makes you invest emotionally in Beverly's situation.

At the film's conclusion is a curtain-call musical number, as Cherry Bomb performs the theme song to a crowd of what looks like about two thousand people. It's a nicely shot fake concert as far as movie concerts go, with big hair a-plenty, and Beverly and Howard duck-walk a guitar solo to cap it off.

Thompson recalls the film as a disaster from day one ("I cried the first day of shooting."), and the box office failure that followed convinced her to take what she felt was the less interesting role in John Hughes' *Some Kind of Wonderful*.

CHERRY BOMB
FOR BEGINNERS

1 K.C. (Holly Robinson)
2 Beverly Switzler (Lea Thompson)
3 Ronette (Liz Sagal)
4 Cal (Dominque Davalos)

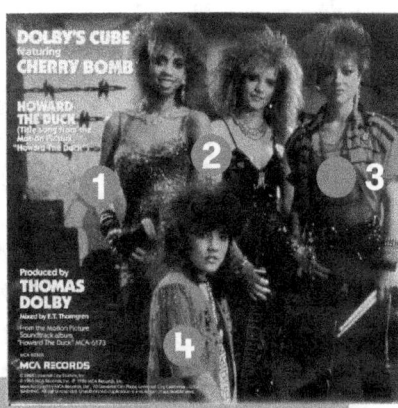

A SIMMONS SDS DRUMS

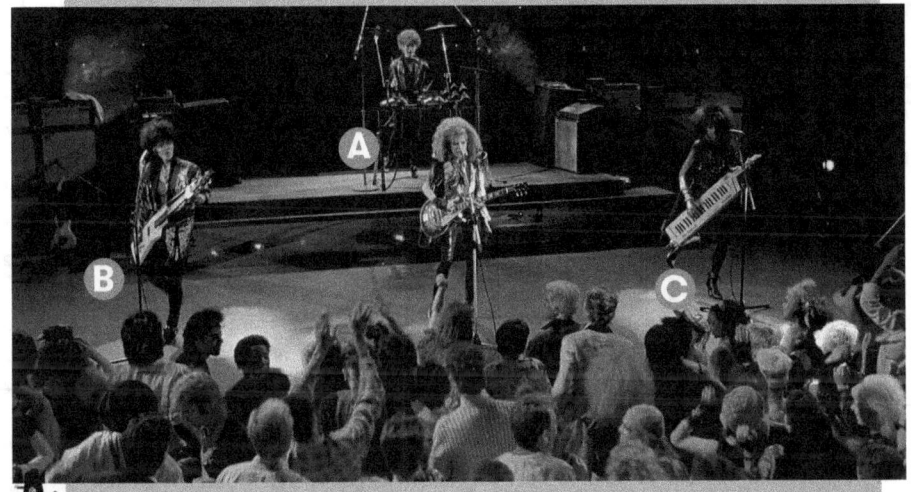

C ROLAND AXIS

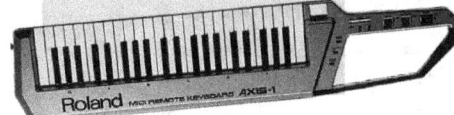

B ROLAND G-77

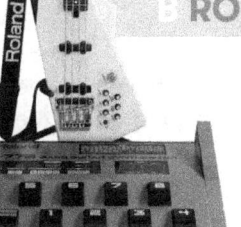

There's some great instruments pulled out for Howard's finale, like the totally hot and 80s Roland G-77 synth bass and Roland AXIS "keytar" keyboard controller.

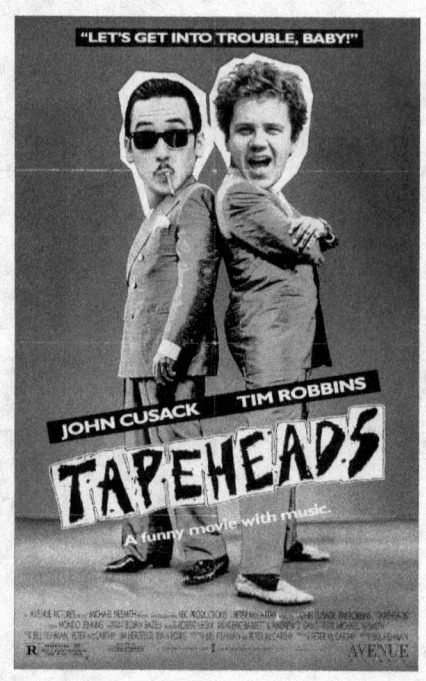

"LET'S GET INTO TROUBLE, BABY!"

JOHN CUSACK   TIM ROBBINS

TAPEHEADS

A funny movie with music.

AVENUE

TAPEHEADS (1988)

John Cusack and Tim Robbins are two best friends of that wacky, irresponsible man-child type that seemed borne of the 80s. They lose their jobs as security guards after creating an impromptu and destructive music video on the closed circuit system at work, and decide to go into business as music video directors under the name Video Aces. Their parents are less than excited by the possibility, including Lyle Alzado who (even though he works in the entertainment industry as Conan at Universal Studios) knows that they will fail.

"Look dad, video is the future. It can't lose."
"Ha!"
"...I'm going to make him eat that syllable."

To reach their goal, they have to take on some odd jobs, including an ad for Roscoe's Chicken and Waffles, a pet seance, a funeral, and a living will recording that goes horribly awry. After canvassing all the major record labels (and running into a mean Weird Al Yankovic in the process), Ivan teams up with Fuzzball Records owner Mo Fuzz ("Soul Train's" Don Cornelius). Mo has them do a few jobs on spec, including a music video for an allegedly Swedish act performing Devo's "Baby Doll" (with Mothersbaugh singing in Swedish) as they are pelted with paint, glitter and feathers.

Before long, the boys have come into possession of a blackmail-worthy videotape of presidential candidate Norman Mart (Clu Gulager).

A fiasco of a video for the heavy metal band Blender Children becomes suddenly hot when the bands members are killed by falling space junk. A dubbing mistake results in the funeral tape being broadcast with the music video's audio and becomes a smash hit for the Video Aces.

Video Aces meet their heroes the Swanky Modes, played by real-life soul and recording legends Sam Moore and Junior Walker. Sam was half of Sam & Dave, Junior had a number of chart busting songs in the 60s and provided the unbeatable sax solo on Foreigner's 1981 hit "Urgent." Their songs for the film, in a classic Motown style, were produced by Blondie's Nigel Harrison. Thrilled beyond belief, they stop everything they're doing to help the Swanky Modes.

The film was one of several quirky projects fronted by former Monkee Michael Nesmith, among them the punk classic *Repo Man*. Many of the actors from that film and its companion piece *Straight to Hell* appear here, such as Sy Richardson, Zander Schloss, Xander Berkeley, Jennifer Balgobin, Ed Pansullo, Courtney Love. While it is not as outrageously surreal as *Repo Man*, there are some inspired, irreverent bits and tons of quotable lines, and a crazy cool cast that also features Mary Crosby, Doug McClure and Connie Stevens, music stars galore (Ted Nugent, Doug E Fresh, Michael Nesmith, Jello Biafra, punk band Fishbone appearing in cowboy drag as "Ranchbone") and MTV VJ Martha Quinn as herself.

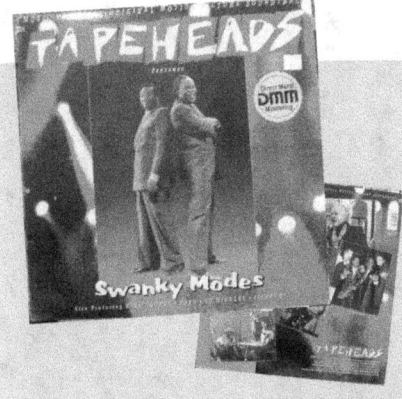

SOUNDTRACK

Ordinary Man
Swanky Modes

Roscoe's Rap
King Cotton

Surfer's Love Chant
Bo Diddley

You Hooked Me Baby
Swanky Modes

Betcher Bottom Dollar
Swanky Modes

Baby Doll (Swedish)
Devo

Slow Bus A-Movin' (Howard's Beach Party)
Fishbone

**Audience For My Pain
Language of Love
Ordinary Man (Can't Keep a Good Man Down Mix)**
Swanky Modes

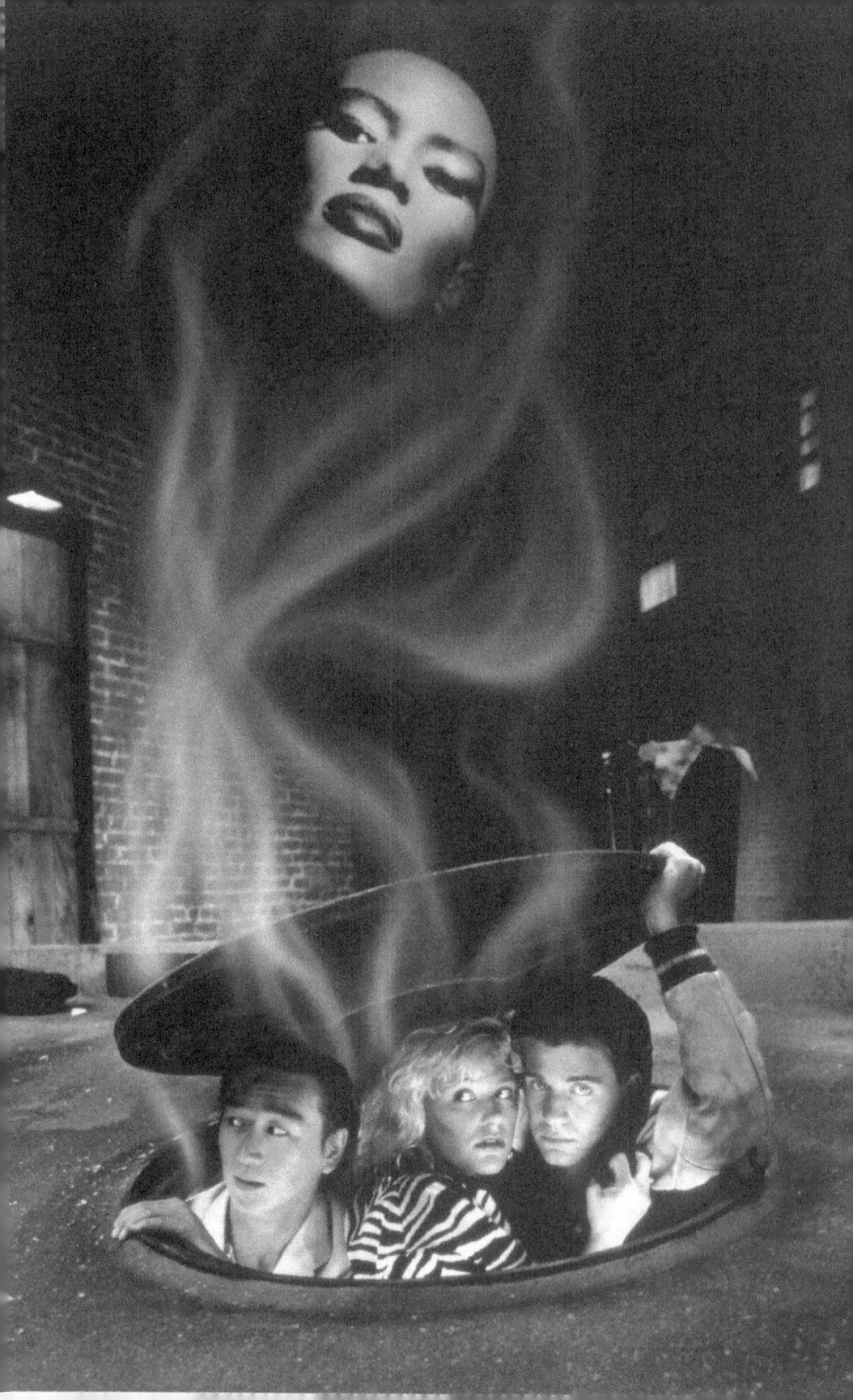

16

MONSTERS OF ROCK & HEAVY METAL HORRORS

On the strength of 1981's American Werewolf in London, director John Landis was recruited to create a promotional film for one of the biggest pop songs of all time. "Thriller" proved that 80s pop music and 80s rubber horror could work together. And the darker the music, the likelier the marriage between the creatures of the night and 80s rock and roll.

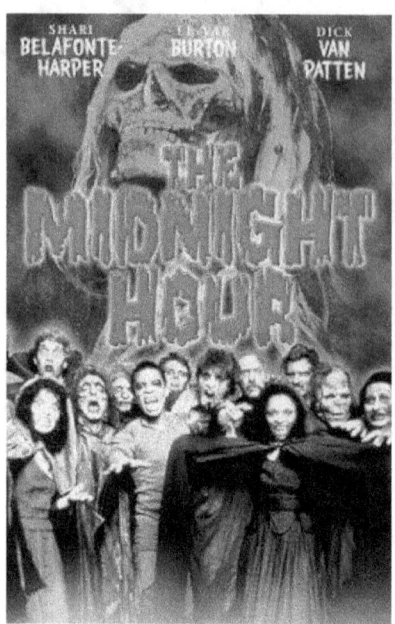

THE MIDNIGHT HOUR (1985, TV)

This ABC TV-movie follows the success of John Landis' long-form music video for Michael Jackson's "Thriller" and traffics in some of the same elements: ghouls rise from the tomb (and perform a choreographed dance number) in a 50s-nostalgia-steeped setting.

The film works best as a star-spotting exercise, as it is ripe with performers known for bigger and better things, including a bunch of high-school students played by Lee Montgomery (the kid from Ben), Shari Belafonte, Peter Deluise, LeVar Burton, and Dedee Pfeiffer. The film takes place on Halloween in the idyllic former witch-haunted town of Pitchford Cove, 300 years to the day after some hullaballoo with a witch named Lucinda. In Nightmare on Elm Street-style, some of the kids are descendants of the witch and the witchfinder general, and are rowdy and horny in that TV-safe kind of way. Phil (Montgomery) has the looks and build of the hero of the group but since he wears glasses and knows some stuff he's the ousted nerd who can't get ahead with the ladies.

As a prank, the kids steal some pilgrim costumes from the local witchcraft museum. Among the purloined items is an old parchment (or is it human skin?) that they read aloud in the cemetery as one does in situation such as these. The dead rise in a distinctly "Thriller-esque" manner, including the witch Lucinda, a dwarf, a well-preserved cheerleader, and an enthusiastic werewolf. Jonna Lee (Making the Grade) plays the cheerleader-out-of-time, an innocent ghost who has returned to the living to accomplish something she couldn't while she was alive – fall in love. Phil picks her up in his '54 Cadillac while the ubiquitous Wolfman Jack doles out 50s and 60s music on the soundtrack like the titular Wilson Pickett song. Before long the whole town is dead or undead, including dentist Dick Van Patten, drunk judge Kevin McCarthy, sour cop Kurtwood Smith, and even substitute (hot for) teacher Cindy Morgan (who chaperones the central plot's Halloween party dressed as David Bowie from the music video for "Modern Love").

There's some lightweight, dumb fun to be had, like a newspaper reading ghoul who seems lifted from an episode of *The Munsters*, and a funky midget ghoul down for some dancing. Phil makes silver bullets out of dentist's fillings, and a couple of dogs are among the town's citizens who come to report wrongdoings to the police. A horny LeVar Burton and Cindy Morgan in Bowie drag should be worth something, even if the proceedings might grind to an uncomfortable halt for the film's original song and dance number "Get Dead," performed by Shari Belafonte and a gang of choreographed ghouls.

Apart from the one original song, the film's music is rooted entirely in the 60s, except for the notable and outstanding use of The Smiths "How Soon is Now." An evocative song under any circumstances, as the backing song for a slow motion vampire scene on an ABC-made-for-TV movie it becomes a diamond in the rough, as exploding wine bottles stand in for geysers of blood. The film's score, composed and performed by Brad Fidel the same year he did *Fright Night*, features a lot of the same synth patches he uses in that score. By comparison, the work here seems rushed, with arrangements that sound like he might have simply played along in one pass. Still, a couple are right out of the *Fright Night* and *Terminator* playbook

The Midnight Hour answers the burning question "who would make a better zombie, Dick Van Patten or Peter Deluise" (it's Deluise), and features some fine Tom Burman make-up work throughout. It is largely loved by anyone who saw it in its original run, and hated by anyone after that, but if you love *Thriller* you'll probably dig it. Some better writing in the song department might have elevated the movie to a seasonal classic.

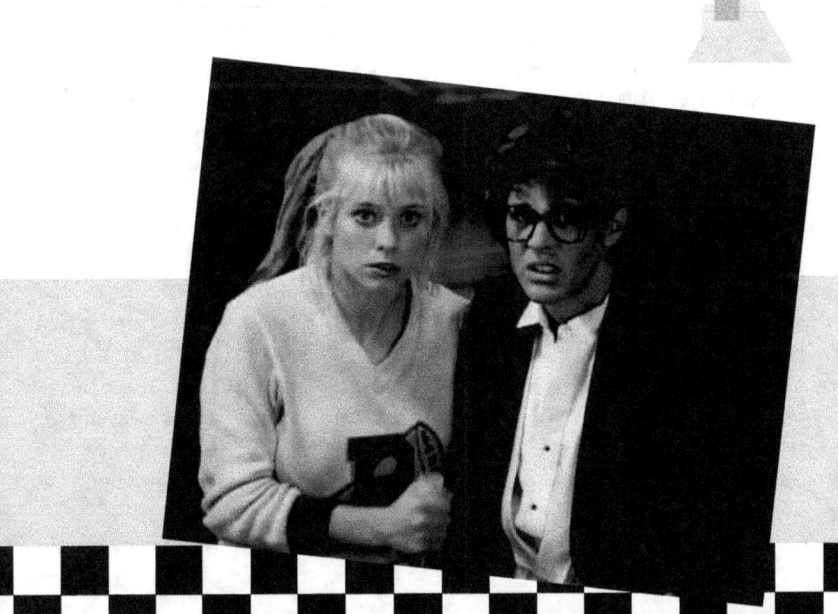

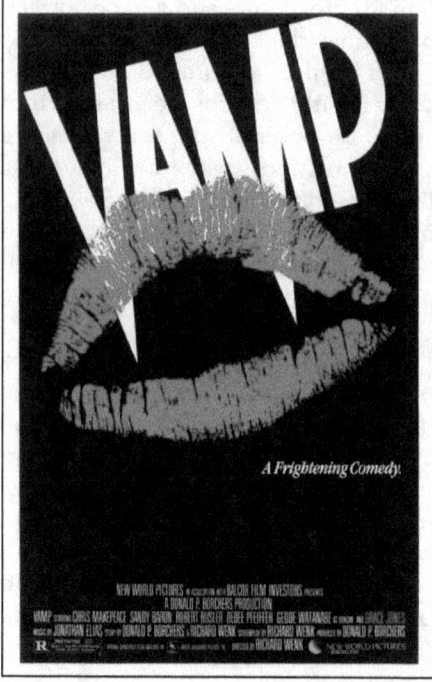

A Frightening Comedy.

NEW WORLD PICTURES A ACQUISITION BY A BALCOR FILM INVESTORS PRESENTS
A DONALD P. BORCHERS PRODUCTION
VAMP STARRING CHRIS MAKEPEACE SANDY BARON ROBERT RUSLER DEDEE PFEIFFER GEDDE WATANABE AS DUNCAN AND GRACE JONES
MUSIC BY JONATHAN ELIAS STORY BY DONALD P. BORCHERS RICHARD WENK SCREENPLAY BY RICHARD WENK PRODUCED BY DONALD P. BORCHERS
DIRECTED BY RICHARD WENK NEW WORLD PICTURES

VAMP (1986)

By 1985, Grace Jones had started appearing in high profile screen roles like *Conan the Destroyer* and *A View to a Kill*. All of those roles seem custom fit and indistinguishable from her stage persona, but none allowed her the raw rock and roll opportunities of 1986's *Vamp*. In a role absent from dialog, she comes across as a lithe, predatory, otherworldly creature of the night that is seductive and terrifying in equal doses. Here she's Katrina, an ancient (Egyptian?) vampire queen who runs a skid row strip club that specializes in "waste disposal" – ridding the city of the "sickies, the degenerates, the forlorn, the lowlifes, the fucking dregs of humanity."

The gothic opening scene of a sacrificial ritual turns out to be a fraternity pledge that our heroes see right through. Still, students Keith (Chris Makepeace, *Meatballs*) and AJ (Robert Rusler, *Nightmare on Elm Street 2*) are extremely motivated to get out of the dorms and into this fraternity, and if their frat brother sponsors want them to get a stripper for a party, then a stripper they will retrieve. Rich student Duncan (Gedde Watanabe, *Sixteen Candles*) will loan his wheels for the quest if they "pretend to be my friends for a week!"

When their car spins out in a stretch of downtown Los Angeles, there's a sense that the doomed trio has entered another time and place. They find themselves on the wrong side of town, where the nightclub emcee, bouncer, bus driver and seedy hotel clerk seem transported from a 1960s Vegas. There's a preoccupation with old musical standbys like "Volare" and "That Old Black Magic."

Bubbly Allison (DeDee Pfeiffer, *The Midnight Hour*) is an innocent server at the club, and knows Keith from a small town teenage game of Spin the Bottle. While a bevy of themed beauties take the stage at the club (such as the "Builder of major erections, our construction engineer... Hard Hat Hannah") it is Jones' Katrina that is the headliner. Her haute couture tease includes pantomimed oral sex with a Keith Haring sculpture to one of her own songs, "Seduction Surrender."

Distinguished by its lurid comic book colors, the whole thing is an

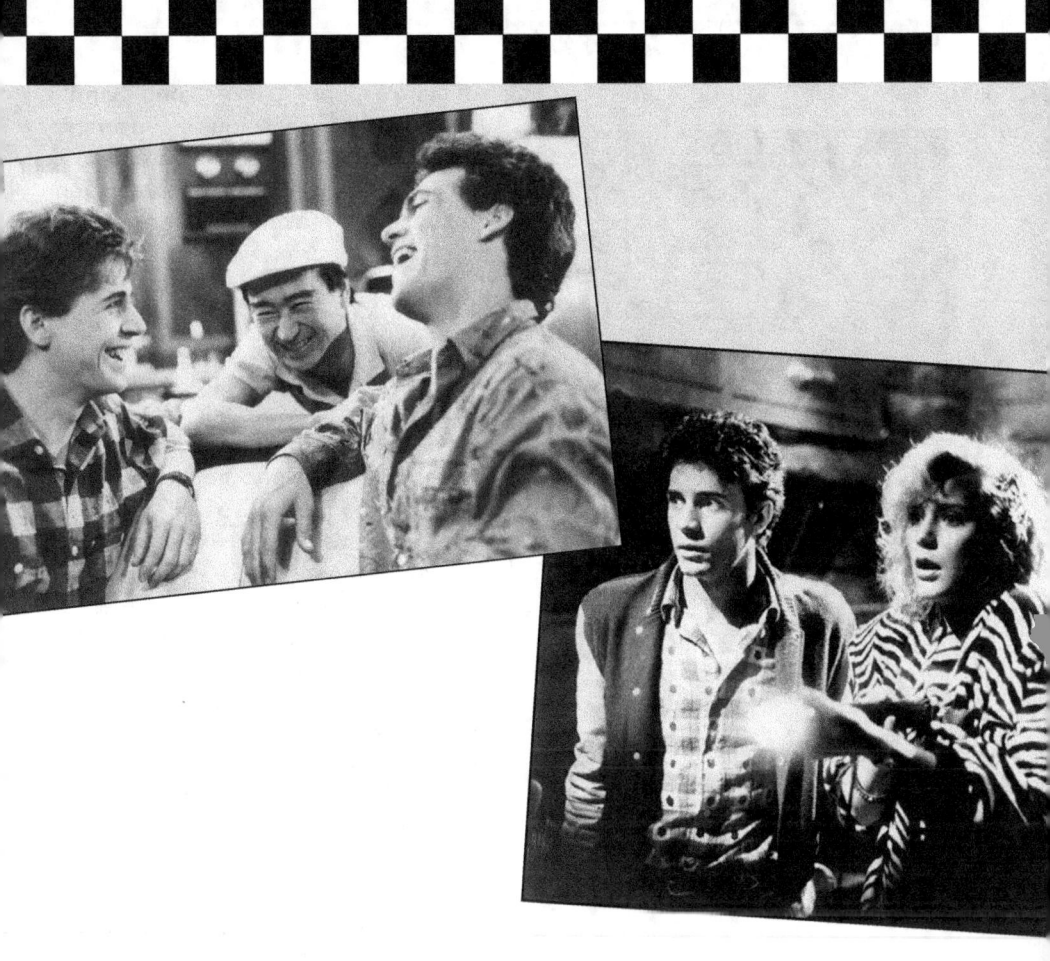

entertaining, monster-movie take on Martin Scorsese's *After Hours* (1985). Watanabe's character is funny and self-deprecating, all without the crutch of the Asian stereotype that Watanabe was constantly asked to provide for comedies like *Sixteen Candles* and *UHF*. Rusler and Makepeace have an easy rapport that hooks you right away. No soundtrack was released at the time, but the film features some evocative rock tunes and a percolating synth score by composer Jonathan Elias (known for crafting the rocking stinger for MTV's quintessential 1983 ad bumper "Moon Landing.") Keen viewers will note that Quentin Tarantino's script for *From Dusk Till Dawn* certainly seems to borrow conceptually from this fun horror entry.

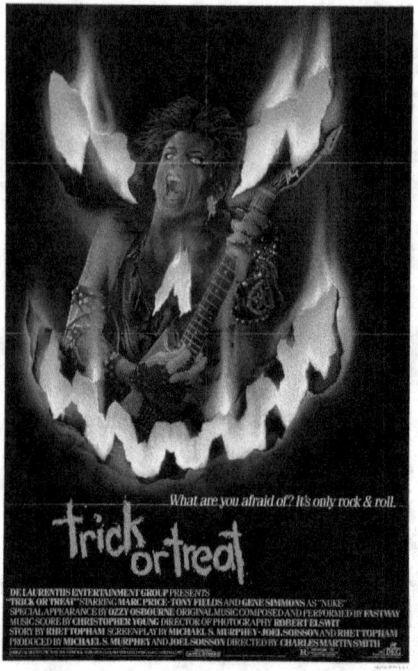

What are you afraid of? It's only rock & roll.

Trick or Treat

DE LAURENTIIS ENTERTAINMENT GROUP PRESENTS
"TRICK OR TREAT" STARRING MARC PRICE·TONY FIELDS AND GENE SIMMONS AS "NUKE"
SPECIAL APPEARANCE BY OZZY OSBOURNE·ORIGINAL MUSIC COMPOSED AND PERFORMED BY FASTWAY
MUSIC SCORE BY CHRISTOPHER YOUNG·DIRECTOR OF PHOTOGRAPHY ROBERT ELSWIT
STORY BY RHET TOPHAM·SCREENPLAY BY MICHAEL S. MURPHEY·JOEL SOISSON AND RHET TOPHAM
PRODUCED BY MICHAEL S. MURPHEY AND JOEL SOISSON·DIRECTED BY CHARLES MARTIN SMITH

TRICK OR TREAT (1986)

Simply the best of the small handful of heavy-metal-meets-horror movies that were made in the 80s, with real horror trappings (if not exactly full of the scares or the gore) and a wall-to-wall fist-pumping soundtrack by Fastway. Metal fans may say the music isn't good enough, and horror fans may say it's not scary or gory enough, but I think it's got enough of the trappings to be a contender. And when you try to get through those other horror-hair-metal pictures, you'll see why.

This one landed hot on the heels of the infamous PMRC (Parents Music Resource Center) and Senate Hearings of 1985, a music-censorship group that succeeded in creating a music rating and warning label system but failed to make much of a change to rock, pop, or rap music. Opposing the panel and speaking out against the potential for censorship were musicians as varied as Frank Zappa, and John Denver (who has repeatedly had to clarify what he meant by a "Rocky Mountain High"). Twisted Sister frontman Dee Snider also spoke, and proclaimed he was not going to take it because "the full responsibility for defending my children falls on the shoulders of my wife and I... there is no one else capable of making these judgments for us." And *Trick or Treat* takes the question "what if you play the record backwards?" to its logical, Freddy-Krueger-like conclusion. If the intent is to point out the absurdity of Satanic panic, it likely succeeds.

Eddie is a quiet kid who favors denim jackets and listens to heavy metal on his Walkman. Everyone who came of age in the 80s knew one of these marginalized kids, and actor Mark Price plays it to perfection, a lovable loser like the signature role you might know him for: Skippy on Family Ties (if the idea of Skippy as a metalhead is intriguing to you, proceed). If his bedroom is any indication he likes a lot of different metal artists, but he is a superfan of one in particular: Sammi Curr. Sammi graduated from the same high school, you see, and has since gone on to become a giant, if controversial, metal star. Eddie refers to Sammi as "Rock's Chosen Warrior," and writes him long, introspective and confessional fanmail under the penname "Ragman."

"Why not just end it? Be done with it all? Dead. Gone. But the one thing that holds me together is you." This is intercut with scenes of Eddie's abuse at the hands of school bullies, notably Tim (Doug Savant), and if you don't feel sympathy for Eddie at this point you aren't going to.

Sammi was due to play a concert his alma mater but was shut down by pressure from local conservatives – and a televangelist played by Ozzy Osbourne, railing against the devil's music! If that weren't enough, Eddie is crushed to learn that Sammi Curr died in a hotel fire. He tears down all the posters in his attic bedroom in a fit of rage, but stops at Sammi's sinister, sneering portrait.

Eddie seeks solace from his friend and local DJ, Nuke (Gene Simmons, who wisely plays it with an air of mystery suggesting he may be the devil in disguise). Nuke presents Eddie with an acetate demo copy of Sammi's last recording – the only copy in existence, save for the tape Nuke made to play on Halloween night. "He's in here," Nuke intones, suggesting that while Sammi lives on in his music, this disc may be even more significant.

Surprisingly, Eddie shows great restraint and attends school instead of running straight home and putting on that record.

There, the school's only nice girl Leslie (Lisa Orgolini), who feels bad about all the bullying, invites Eddie to an illicit teen get-together that the cool kids are putting on at the school's swimming pool. He attends, naively expecting it to go well, and for his trouble is sunk in the pool fully clothed with a weight in his backpack. Rescued by Leslie, he vows revenge and storms off.

He retreats to his bedroom angrily and puts on the record, which is strange and filled with backwards sounds. Falling into a kind of trance, he has a vision of Sammi's demise at the hotel, which appears to have been part of a fiery Satanic ritual. He wakes to the sound of the record

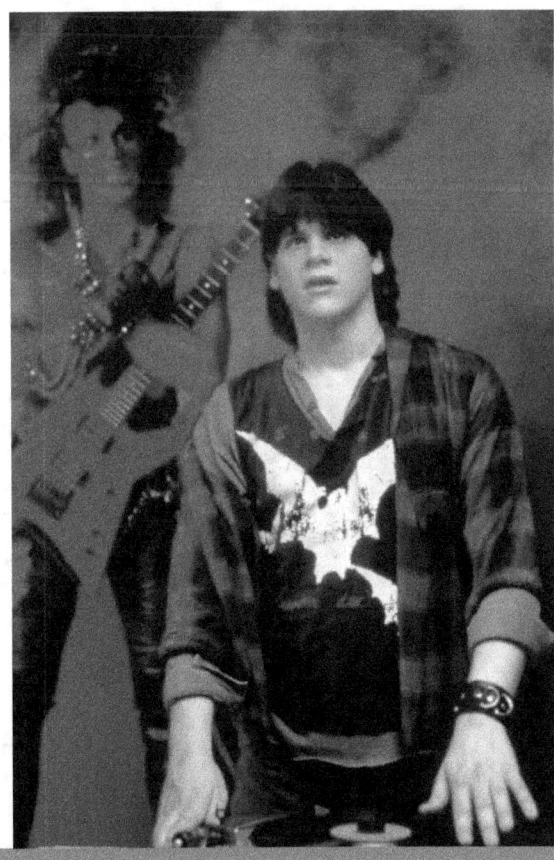

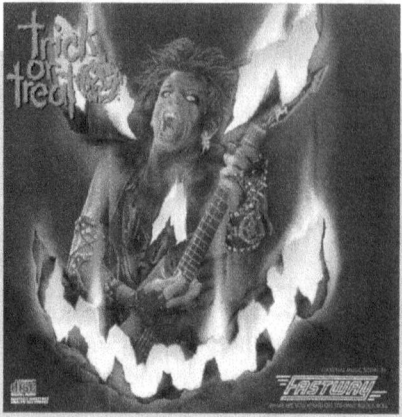

SOUNDTRACK

Trick Or Treat

After Midnight

Don't Stop The Fight

Stand Up

Tear Down The Walls

Get Tough

Hold On To The Night

Heft

If You Could See

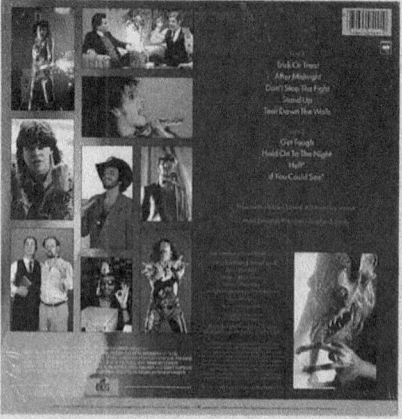

skipping, he manually reverses it to hear a message goading him on to his revenge. He sets up an elaborate trap at the school and gets Tim in a load of trouble.

Inspired by the turn of events, Eddie tries to make a tape of the backwards message to show his friend Roger, but the record starts speaking - way too clearly and way too specifically. It suggests a room number at the school, where Eddie lies in wait for his tormentors. When Tim and his buddy arrive, they must face a woodshop that has taken on a dangerous life of its own. Eddie saves Tim - slowly - from being punctured by a drill, who declares that this isn't over.

This new found power has Eddie hooked, such that he dubs the doomed song onto a special chrome tape for Tim as a "peace offering." But when Tim's girlfriend gets a listen first, she ends up supernaturally molested in the back of Tim's car, her clothes undoing themselves in a cleverly done bit of special effects. When the girlfriend is hospitalized, Eddie decides that it's gone too far but has trouble convincing the demonic album itself, which has started mutating his stereo system and seems determined not to quit. Before long, Sammi himself incarnates in a storm of little electrical bolts, looking like a sort of Satanic Stephen Pearcy with a half-burned face.

Eddie destroys the LP, but his dubbed tape of doom is still out there. He sends pal Roger to get it and destroy it. Sammi materializes to threaten Roger, demanding that he play the tape at the high school Halloween dance. Roger caves, and sneaks the tape in during the party preshow, allowing Sammi to appear from inside an amplifier (and threaten the live band's guitarist, played by 80s horror makeup hero Kevin Yagher). Eddie rushes to the school to try to stop it but it's too late. Sammi spins and whirls and flips about the stage, seducing the audience before taking up a guitar and electrocuting students, teachers, and the band itself. Bully supreme Tim gets the personal treatment from Sammi, as does pal Roger when he tries to shut down the power.

When a bunch of kids ID Eddie as the person responsible, he is forced to evade the police as well, and Leslie follows. They must now keep disc jockey Nuke from playing the midnight tribute on the air; in the process they discover that Sammi (being made of electricity as he is) is susceptible to water. They hightail it to the radio station where all manner of supernatural shit is going down. Eddie finishes off Sammi spectacularly, and takes to the radio mic to celebrate.

Trick or Treat is directed by Charles Martin Smith, who knows a little bit about the nerdy underdog, having portrayed "Terry the Toad," one of cinema's great geeks in the seminal *American Graffiti*. You can also spot him, under Groucho glasses, as the teacher at the microphone in the Halloween dance scene. The movie strikes two tones: early on you get the sense that this will be played straight and played for pathos, so

cruel is the treatment of Eddie. But when the supernatural shit hits the fan, the film feels free to crank up the laughs in sync with the absurdities. It is probably a good choice, given the fantastic nature of the material, but I'm a sucker for a good underdog and they probably could have kept up the sincerity and I would have bought it.

Producer Joel Soisson admits that Dino De Laurentiis was looking to hit Freddy Krueger gold (Would that be Krugerrands?) "(De Laurentiis) kept going, 'I want Freddy Krueger!' That's where this whole Sammi Curr idea came from … He didn't come out your dreams, he comes out of a record. Yet the way he infiltrates the real world was similar to Freddy (and) the scarring on his face was derivative in that way.'" Sossion remembers beginning the movie with the set being blessed by a Catholic priest. "Dino was ferociously Catholic. We were happy to take it."

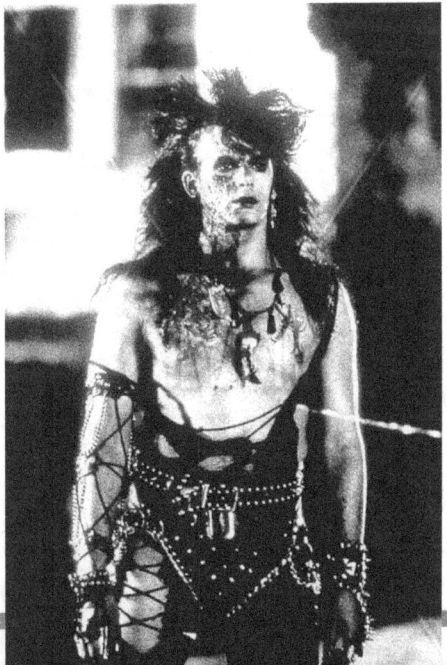

Sammi Curr is played with gusto by Tony Fields, who was a Solid Gold Dancer from 1979 to 1984, and puts those moves to great use here. While purists may look at it as an untraditional and not very "metal" performance, Fields moves approach the supernatural in their ability. He was also known for having appeared in Michael Jackson's "Thriller" and "Beat It" music videos, and starred in the 1984 film of A Chorus Line, before his untimely death in 1995.

Music-wise, the soundtrack was the fourth album by Fastway, which featured "Fast Eddie" Clarke of Motorhead on guitar, bassist Pete Way of UFO, and vocals by Dave King. King would cite this as a reason for quitting metal and later forming the band Flogging Molly. "We were commissioned to write basically the soundtrack for this movie and I felt, you know, this is not what I wanna be doing in my life. It has nothing to do with my life, so I said this is it for me."

Is the music, which was more or less commissioned by the film's producers, formulaic? Yes, which is why it works so beautifully as a stand-in for "everyman's metal." Two songs are from previous Fastway releases, "Heft" from Fastway (1983) and "If You Could See," from All Fired Up (1984).

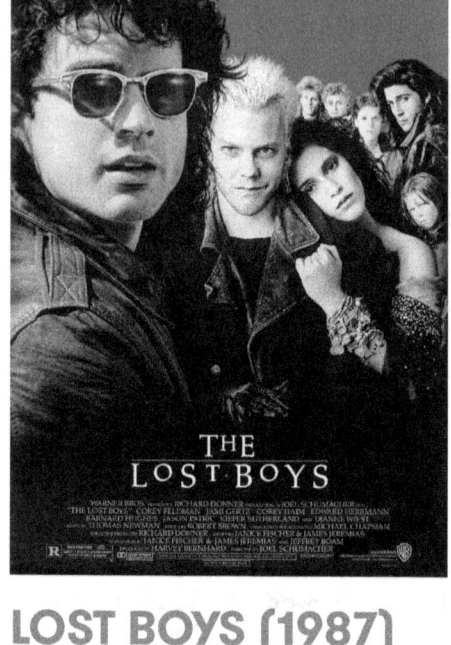

LOST BOYS (1987)

Sure, there were plenty of vampire movies in the 80s that reimagined the undead as rockstar-stylish and cool – *The Hunger, Fright Night, Vamp* – but few embraced the MTV-ness of the coffined creeps in Joel Schumacher's *The Lost Boys*. Taking visual cues from everything from British goth-rock to American heavy metal, these vamps held court over a soundtrack that was just as eclectic as they were, and a movie whose visual style was tailor-made for MTV.

Taking place in the fictional California town of Santa Carla, Lost Boys follows brothers Sam (Corey Haim) and Michael (Jason Patric) as they navigate a post-divorce relocation to a new town that

happens to be inhabited by a gang of vampires. When their mother (Dianne Wiest) starts dating the owner of a cool video rental store (Edward Herrmann), young Sam suspects he's a vampire and fights back.

Rock music and rock imagery pervades the film, the town seems stuck in a perpetual party – whether it's the boardwalk amusement park with the free concerts, the post-hippie businesses and arcades, comic book stores, or video rental outlets. The vampires, led by Kiefer Sutherland's punky David, have taken over the ruins of a seaside hotel and decorated it in late 60's California, complete with a huge Jim Morrison poster. Sexually speaking there's something for everybody in the film – if you like them hunky or brooding or even bad-boy beautiful, there's Michael and the vampires. There's a touch of the homosexual about young Sam, whose Rob Lowe poster and flashy outfits (including a shirt that says Born to Shop) are likely intentional, given director Schumacher's openly gay orientation. And that's nothing compared to the oiled-down sexy sax man Tim Cappello and his muscular cover of The Call's "I Still Believe." Jami Gertz (Sixteen Candles) is the ethereal girl Star, who Michael finds irresistible. The original script featured much younger kids and more specific Peter Pan references (we still have the lost boys and Michael but lost Wendy and John, the dog "Nanook" is a riff on Nana).

The soundtrack features some covers and some predictable entries, but occasionally rises above the norm,

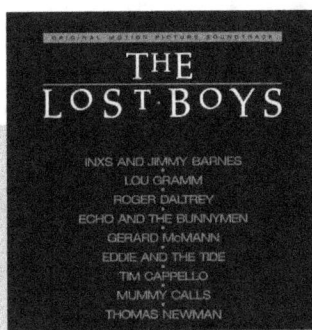

SOUNDTRACK

Good Times
INXS & Jimmy Barnes

Lost in the Shadows (Lost Boys)
Lou Gramm

Don't Let the Sun Go Down On Me
Roger Daltrey

Laying Down the Law
INXS & Jimmy Barnes

People Are Strange
Echo & The Bunnymen

Cry Little Sister (Theme from The Lost Boys)
Gerard McMann

Power Play
Eddie and the Tide

I Still Believe
Tim Cappello

Beauty Has Her Way
Mummy Calls

To The Shock of Miss Louise
Thomas Newman

particularly with the theme "Cry Little Sister." Written by Gerard McMahon and Michael Mainieri rapidly and without seeing a frame of the film, says McMahon:

"I had gotten a call from Gary LeMel, President of Music at the Warner Bros. film studio... They sent me a script to read. Up to that point I'd always looked at a cut of the film before I'd write the music, but as it turned out I got inspired by reading the script and the events in my own life and wrote the song. The co-writer, jazz musician Michael Mainieri, came up with that beat and we were off!"

"I always say that if I'd have seen the film first, I would probably not have written 'Cry Little Sister'. I didn't want the song to be specific to the vampire. I wanted it to be about the longing for family from a rejected youth's perspective, which I went through myself and that many of us have felt. Knowing much about the origin of vampires, they're a lonely yet lusty sexual being that mortality leaves in a world hunting in their loneliness. That's what The Lost Boys spoke to me; youth gone rebel-without-a-cause, with a great deal of angst and sexual lure."

Of 80s music, McMahon has this to say: "There was a great sense of adventure in music in the '80s; so much diversity. Its impact has carried over into artists today."

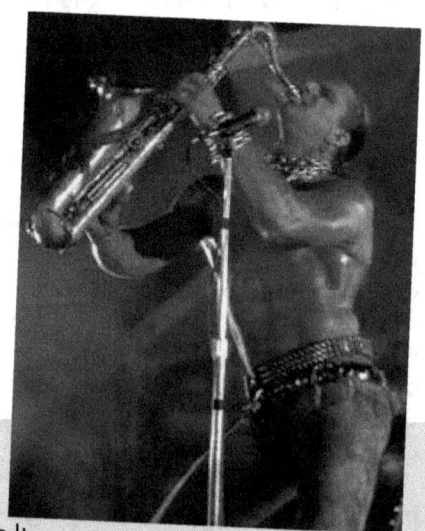

MUSIC EXPOSÉ

TIM CAPELLO

- Started studying music at Age 4
- Dropped out of high school at 15 to pursue music
- Played piano for Billy Crystal's early standup performances
- Touring in the 70s, fought drug addiction
- Recorded and/or toured with Peter Gabriel, Carly Simon, Ringo Starr
- Created a "Porn Pop" band called the Ken Dolls, performing in a g-string
- Tina Turner's sax man for 15 years (much of that was two shows a night 4 and 5 days a week)
- "We Don't Need Another Hero" and "One of the Living" from Mad Max: Beyond Thunderdome
- TV: The Equalizer, Miami Vice
- Film: Hearts of Fire (1987), Tap (1989)

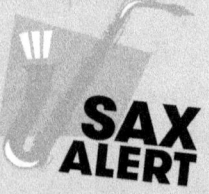

SAX ALERT

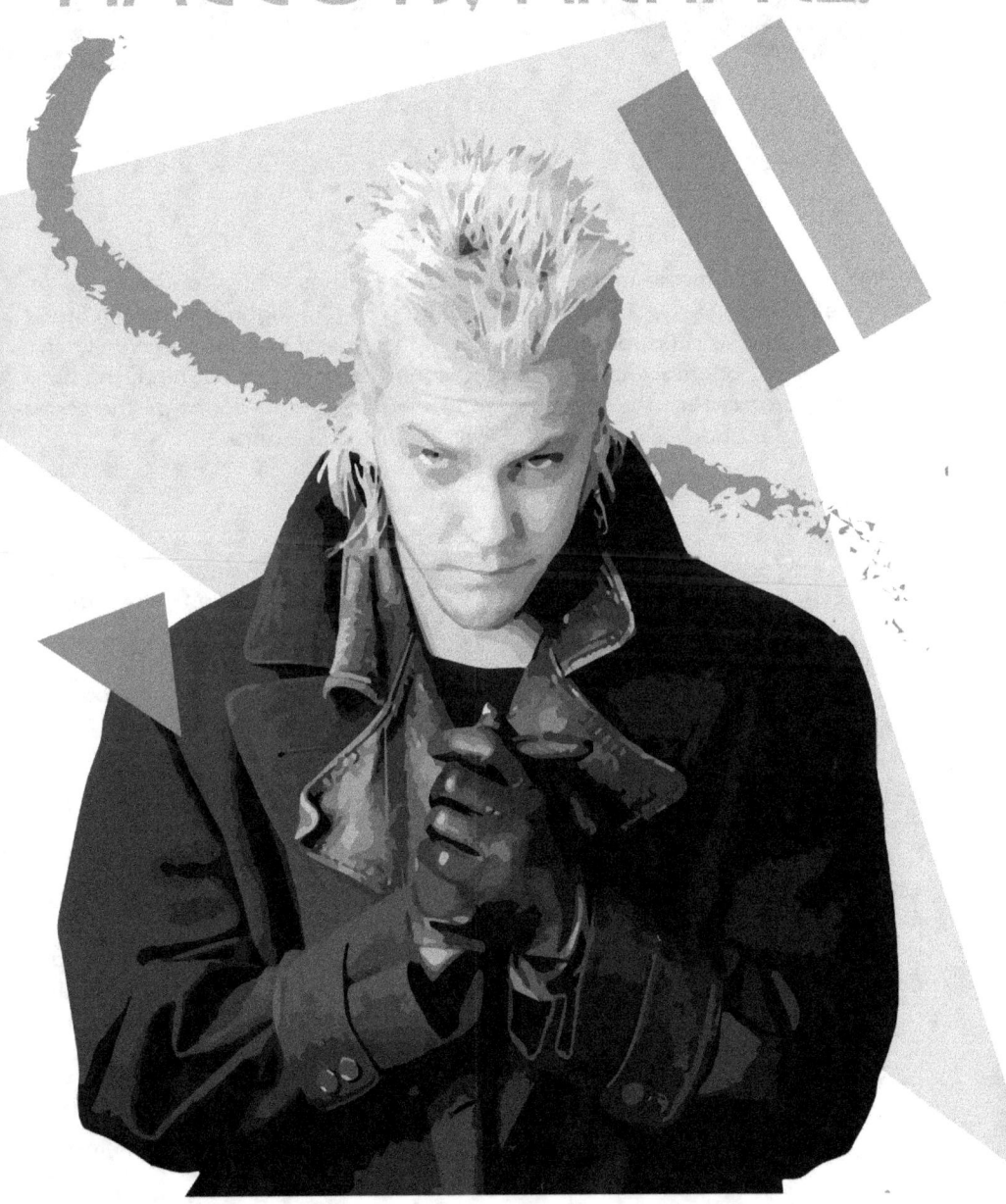

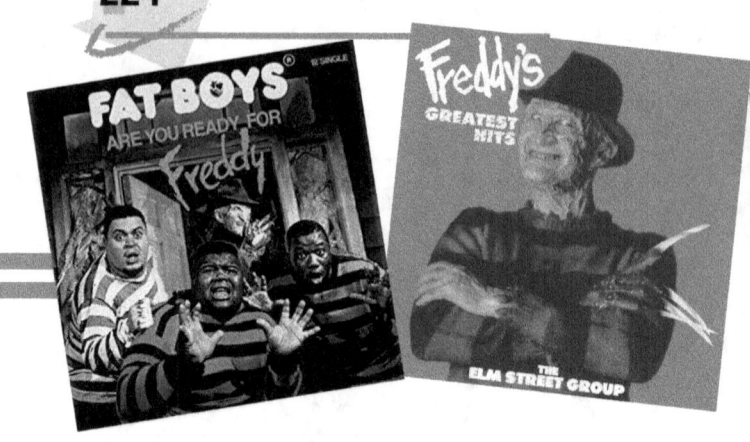
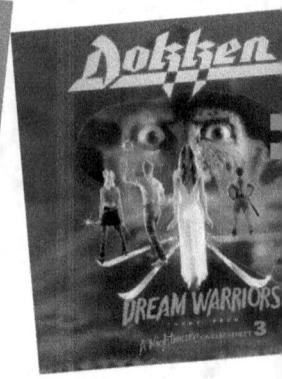

RAPPIN' & ROCKING WITH FREDDY K.

No other 80's movie monster inspired more songs than the nightmare on your street, Freddy Krueger. While the original 1984 film *Nightmare on Elm Street* takes place in a world apparently free from the joys of pop music (even Glen's (Johnny Depp) boombox is used to play sound effects, not hot hits), the films eventually cranked up the use of soundtrack songs – no doubt as the series enjoyed bigger budgets and stunning pop culture dominance.

DREAM WARRIORS (DOKKEN, 1987)

Undoubtedly the glorious, hair-sprayed love child of pop-metal and pop-horror, "Dream Warriors" enjoys prominent placement in what could be the crowning glory of the multi-film series, *Nightmare on Elm Street 3: The Dream Warriors*. Dokken's manager was good friends with creator Wes Craven, and the band worked from a copy of the script to create the operatic hit.

The music video illustrates the power of Hair Metal against evil, as Don Dokken's powerful voice and steady hand pushes Krueger (Robert Englund) right the fuck out of the dream dimension. "Erk! What a nightmare!"

The release of the film pushed Dokken's fourth studio album, "Back for the Attack," to platinum status in only three weeks.

FREDDY'S GREATEST HITS (THE ELM ST. GROUP, 1987)

Riding the crest of Kruger-mania is this nine-track novelty album sporting covers like "In the Midnight Hour" and original tunes like "Do the Freddy" and "Down in the Boiler Room," all with Robert "Freddy Krueger" Englund himself laughing manically on top.

ARE YOU READY FOR FREDDY? (FAT BOYS, 1988)

Englund joins Prince Markie Dee, Kool Rock-Ski, and Buff Love for a rap homage to everyone's favorite four-fingered slasher, which was used as an end credits song for *Nightmare on Elm Street 4: The Dream Master*. In the music video, the Boys must spend the night in their "Uncle Fredrick's" house in order to get their inheritance. In short order, they are hounded by Krueger, who alternately raps along and slashes while samples from the first film are used as counterpoint.

NIGHTMARE ON MY STREET (DJ JAZZY JEFF AND THE FRESH PRINCE, 1988)

A jokey rap song written with *Nightmare 4* in mind, sporting great rhymes like "He wears the same hat and sweater every single day, And even if it's hot, outside he wears it anyway!"

When studio and copyright owner New Line opted not to use the song by rising star Will Smith, record label Jive/RCA attached it to their album "He's the DJ, I'm the Rapper." New Line didn't stop the use of the song, but did prevent a music video from being released, and subsequently the album was stickered to clarify that the song was "not part of the soundtrack and is not authorized, licensed, or affiliated with the *Nightmare on Elm Street* films."

The music video surfaced years later; while there is no Freddy or anything resembling him, Will Smith does appear in a bizarre Frankenstien makeup.

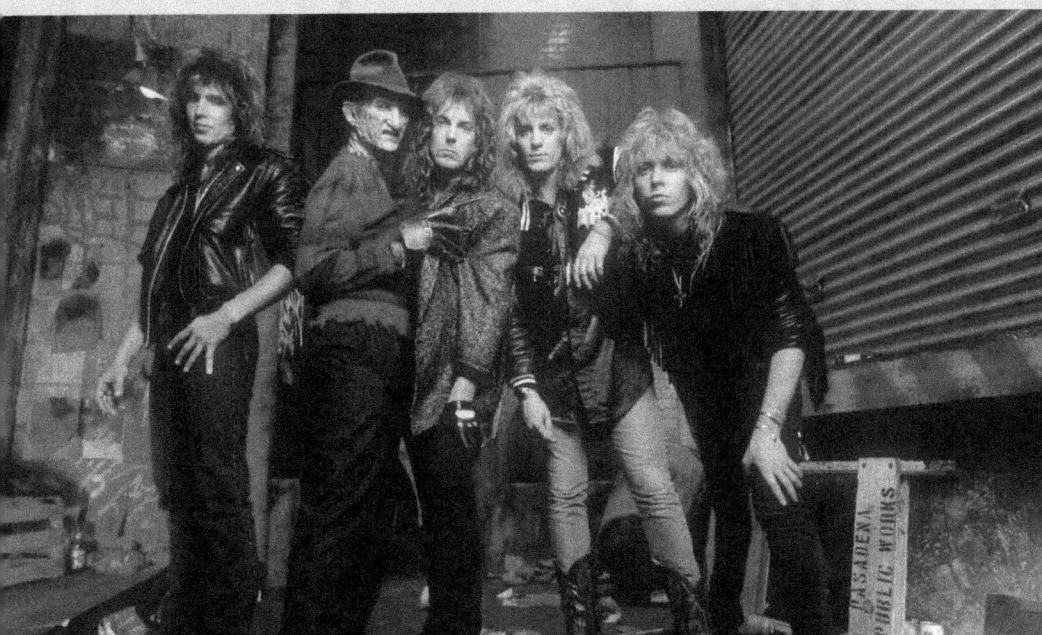

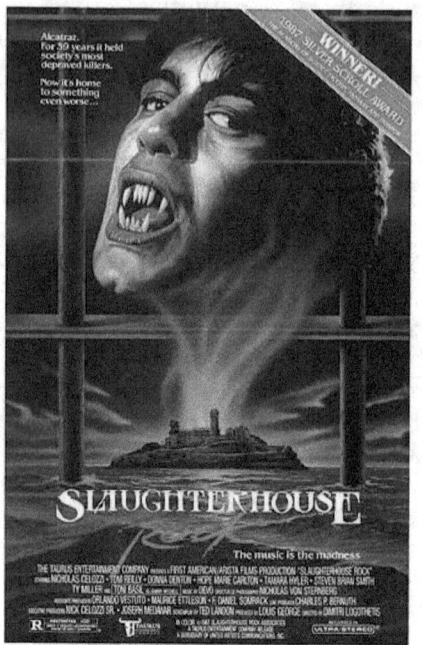

SLAUGHTERHOUSE ROCK (1988)

If a female heavy metal singer gets killed at Alcatraz investigating a cannibal ghost for use in her own rituals, you'd think you'd be in for some on-screen heavy metal mixed with the horror. Not so much with *Slaughterhouse Rock*, for a variety of surprising reasons. First, the singer is played by Toni Basil, who doesn't perform any songs on screen. Second, the film's music is entirely by Devo, not the most metal 80s band. Still, this one's kind of a neat cheapie.

A good portion of the film takes place on Alcatraz, and the on-location exteriors seem to have been shot in a perpetual wispy misty rain made all the more palpable by the 80s-blue-gel lighting. The plot is in the mold of Freddy Kruger's antics, where a killer from the past is haunting a young man's dreams, manifesting as real phenomenon like causing him to float above his bed in a column of light or setting his bedroom on fire. With the aid of sexy professor-and-paranormal investigator Donna Denton, they connect the dots to a Civil-War-era cannibal nutcase. One night, they trek to the island to confirm the source of the supernatural dreams. A couple of gory makeups, some contact lenses and fangs, and a kind of demon thing in a hallway are the extent of the manifestations but make for a diverting VHS-era distraction.

On the subject of the music, there are some attempts for a metal-type guitar-driven horror score as well as a Halloween-eque theme from composer Mark Mothersbaugh. Toni Basil gets to chime on on the very fine end credit song "The Only One" that combines, yes, metal guitars, Devo style keyboard and bass, and Mothersbaugh on backing vocals.

The film itself, however, is ripe with missed opportunities. Basil's character Sammy Mitchell, wearing her own (magically changing) wardrobe for her appearances as the ghost, gets one attempt to show off her skills in a choreographed ritual dance. The bit is too short and static, she spends the whole thing in one spot and in several shots you can see her chalk mark of where she needs to stand for optimum lighting. Her heavy metal bandmates (the band is aptly called "Bodybag") appear as slaughtered corpse ghosts, a la *American Werewolf in London*, make a couple jokes, and leave.

There is no music performed on screen, but the wall-to-wall Devo on the soundtrack makes it the first film scored by Mothersbaugh, who has since scored over 170 TV shows and films. Their connection to this film is convoluted. Devo played on and provided songs for Basil's debut album "Word of Mouth." Prior to *Slaughterhouse Rock*, Dean Stockwell had procured Devo's assistance and songs for Neil Young's film *Human Highway*. Dean had dated Toni Basil, and so had Devo member Gerald Casale. Toni suggested Devo for *Slaughterhouse Rock*. At the time, according to Mothersbaugh, Devo wrote collaboratively on the albums and tried to apply that method to the film score. Finding that the world of film composing required faster turn-arounds than they were used to executing on their albums, Mothersbaugh opted for a one-man writer approach that he maintains to this day. *Revenge of the Nerds* would be the last film scored by Devo-as-committee.

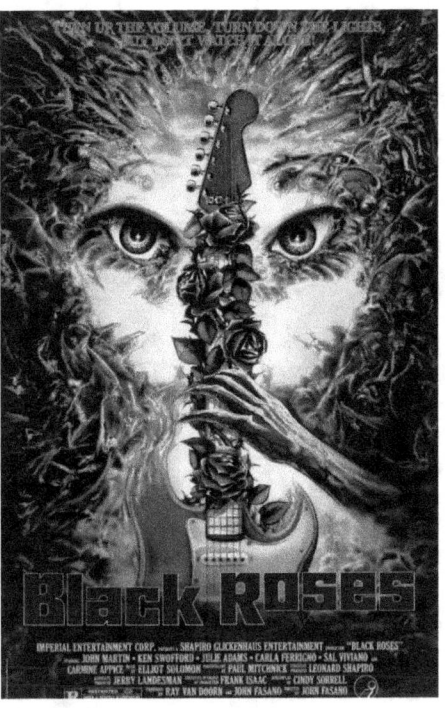

BLACK ROSES (1988)

An alternately slick and low-rent movie that should have been a lot more fun, but when one is faced with such a short list of heavy metal horrors one must not be too picky. It's sometimes billed as a comedy, which appears to have not been on the actor's minds when production ensued, and in watching the film the tone is not immediately apparent until the increasingly silly deaths ensue. Even then, such on-screen executions as "death by a giant speaker insect" might have been earnest Freddy-Krueger-esque attempts. Fans of rubber and puppets should not come up short.

SOUNDTRACK by DEVO
The Only One
Man Turned Inside Out
Part of You
Set Me Free
Slaughterhouse Rock Theme

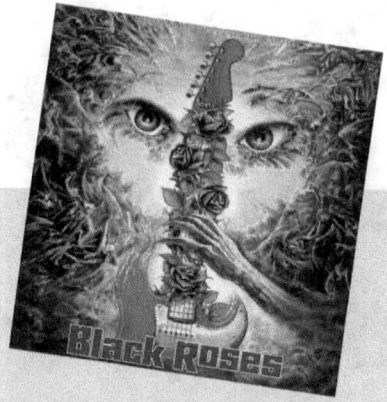

SOUNDTRACK

Dance on Fire
Black Roses

Soldiers of the Night
Black Roses/Masi

I'm No Stranger
Bang Tango

Rock Invasion
Black Roses/Masi

Paradise (We're On Our Way)
Black Roses

Me Against The World
Lizzy Borden

Take It Off
King Kobra

King of Cool
David Michael Phillips

Streetlife Warrior
Tempest

D.I.E.
Hallow's Eve

An unfortunate tip-of-the-hat prologue shows us what the conclusion of the film might look like, as demon-undead dudes rock the hair metal before a moderate-sized crowd of enthusiastic youths. Spoilers are irrelevant: the iconic lead-singer's makeup was emblazoned on the back of the VHS box (and the rental version of the film was one of the few to feature an elaborate embossed plastic cover, so it's probably all about suckering you into a first (and only) viewing anyway).

Two scissor-door Lamborghinis pull into small town Mill Basin in 1987. Inside are members of the metal band Black Roses; presumably their extensive collection of gear and smoke machines is packed on another truck. Apparently the band is aiming to start its tour in a small town (filmed in Hamilton and Dundas, Ontario, which explains the US and Canadian flag sharing the stage at the town hall meeting).

As date of the first of four (?!) Black Roses concerts in town approaches, high school English teacher Matt Moorhouse uses the opportunity to frame a discussion of Walt Whitman in the context of heavy metal. Yes, the hero of the film is the high school English teacher, which is indeed not very metal, and he is often accompanied by an overzealous musical score that positions him as a member of the A-Team or something. Indeed, his action exploits leave much to be desired, such as battling a demon with a tennis racquet (and shoving a ball down its throat too).

This is little more a set of gory set-pieces strung together, with a bit of social statement about the corrupting power of heavy metal on today's youth. Other films of this genre did it better, though, and this one misses opportunities for atmosphere and opts for dialog-driven exposition and unconvincing character building. Without spoiling too much of the fun, there's a mutating LP and a speaker that gives birth to a giant centipede puppet, a school counselor pushed out a window and a student-teacher seduction that ends in a demon fight. When the band plays, a few kids get fried down to emaciated zombie puppets (with eyeballs and big hair still intact).

Enthusiastic makeup and rubber puppets abound, but are marred by too much light and too much screen time. Sal Viviano plays lead singer Damian with a fair serving of charismatic swagger, and lipsyncs convincingly to Mark Free (singer of King Kobra). With his cape and tall haircut he passes for a prettier Ozzy Osbourne. The band also features Carmine Appice on drums (who has played with everyone from King Kobra to Pink Floyd, Rod Stewart, Paul Stanley and Ozzy Osbourne). Mark Free came out as Marcie Free in 1993 and has since retired from music to spend more time with her family.

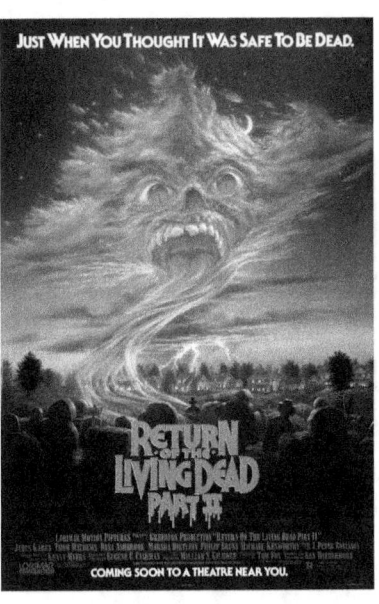

JUST WHEN YOU THOUGHT IT WAS SAFE TO BE DEAD.

RETURN OF THE LIVING DEAD PART II

COMING SOON TO A THEATRE NEAR YOU.

RETURN OF THE LIVING DEAD 2 (1988)

"Look, they're ugly and they're dirty and they're dumb, and I don't even care if they are dead. I hate 'em, there's no way they're touching me!" – Brenda

It's metal instead of punk for *Return of the Living Dead 2*, if only because punk had run its course and heavy metal hair bands ruled the airwaves by the time this sequel arrived.

Young Billy has fallen in with a couple of dumb neighborhood bullies, who come across yet another lost canister of the failed army experiment 245-Trioxin, complete with its own pickled inhabitant. Meanwhile, Thom Matthews and James Karen have

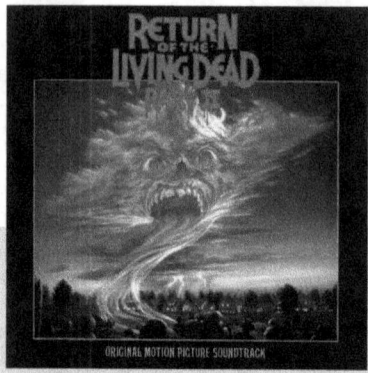

SOUNDTRACK

Space Hopper
Julian Cope

High Priest of Love
Zodiac Mindwarp and the
Love Reaction

I'm The Man
Anthrax

Big Band B-Boy
Mantronix

Monster Mash
The Big O

Alone in the Night
Leatherwolf

ADI/The Horror of it All
Anthrax

Flesh to Flesh
Lamont

The Dead Return
Peter Robinson

been resurrected as graverobbers (!) collecting heads from a nearby cemetery. If it all seems familiar, it certainly does to those two, who admit outright to the strange feeling of cinematic deja vu.

When the trioxin is released and the cemetery pops to life it's business as usual with thinly written but likable leads. Colonel Glover (Jonathan Terry) returns, unable to rest until the last container is recovered. The "Tarman" zombie is back, too, who's lost some of his charm and all of his element of surprise by this point. Brian Peck, who was Scuz in *ROTLD1*, plays no less than five featured zombies including the Michael Jackson zombie that gets electrocuted front and center with the rest of the mob.

A heap of dumb, rubbery puppets and strange makeups don't get a chance to be very scary, but everybody gives it their enthusiastic all as the dead invade a new suburban development. Horror movie royalty Forrest J. Ackerman makes one of his over-200 film appearances here as an undead fellow, and Suzanne Snyder, who was all over the 80s (*Weird Science*, *Night of the Creeps*, *Killer Klowns from Outer Space*) joins the all-caps acting troupe as squirmy redhead Brenda.

NOT ON THE ALBUM:
"Bad Case of Lovin You,"
"Looking for Clues" by
Robert Palmer

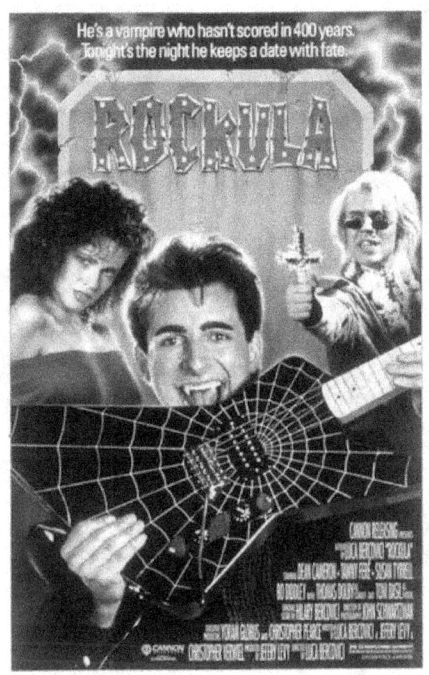

He's a vampire who hasn't scored in 400 years. Tonight's the night he keeps a date with fate.

ROCKULA (1990)

Let's be fair, for a film that was released in 1990 you don't get more of an 80s sensibility than *Rockula*, a film which star Dean Cameron calls "a fever dream of a movie that they only made in the 80s," and the director terms an "oddball piece frozen in time at the end of the 80s." And the film's release date on home video in August of 1990 doesn't tell the full story of a film that was completed much earlier, at a time when Cannon Films was surrendering to bankruptcy.

That director, Luca Bercovici (a name that sounds like a vampire himself, though he's actually a very soft spoken American man), had been developing a dark romance about a couple set against the LA underground music scene. It was Romeo and Juliet with Romeo as a vampire, and Bercovici sold it to Cannon Films where it languished for some time. At a fortuitous meeting with the monumentally multitasking Menahem Golan (who was simultaneously watching Van Damme dailies, eating lunch, and doing an interview), Bercovici asked for a couple million to do the film. Golan said, "you're in pre-production, and make it a comedy." Like his previous effort *Ghoulies*, the slide from a dramatic piece to a comedic one was relatively easy. With *Ghoulies*, the creature effects inspired a sillier take on the material, and in the case of *Rockula*, it was going to be hard to take that title seriously.

Dean Cameron plays Ralph, possibly the least threatening vampire in history. He wears a retainer, is repulsed by blood, and remains a virgin due to an unfortunate curse. Every 22 years, he is doomed to repeat the same fated romantic encounter, fall in love, and lose the poor girl to a pirate with a rhinestone peg leg. And if he doesn't at least try, the girl ends up dead anyway. It's happened 14.5 times so far, and Ralph has had enough, but he has two persuasive people in his life that urge him to give it one more try: his mother Phoebe (Toni Basil), a voluptuous vampire who rocks a Betty Page hairdo and an outrageous wardrobe, and his reflection. That's right, not only does this vampire have a reflection, it's got a more outgoing personality than him and he argues with it constantly. The film makes great use of the mirror gag with some elaborate staging involving careful camerawork, a reflected set, and a body double.

Mona (Tawny Feré) is the 1980s reincarnation of the girl, she's a musician working with a music-producer-slash-coffin-salesman Stanley (Thomas Dolby playing it with cartoony aplomb). Stanley's Death Park is the source of many a running gag about the funeral business, with home-grown tv-ads that offer discount coffins to models that literally allow you to roll in your grave, all set to a quirky Thomas Dolby jingle. And Stanley's car is the Munster's Koach, the insane custom car designed by George Barris for the 60s TV show.

And try as he might to avoid the curse, Ralph is run over by Mona's car on a busy LA street and is of course swept away. When he discovers she's a musician, he dons a healthy dose of sunblock and roams the big-hair streets of late-80s hair-rockin' Los Angeles in pursuit. He finally catches her act at Club Hell, featuring the jungle-noise-sample-packed song "Break These Chains." One of the strengths of the movie is its low-budget but emotionally-correct music, actually sung with some skill by the actors. They're not hits but they're not entirely embarrassing, and the film isn't afraid to let the whole thing play out. Mona's single bandmember is Robin, (Nancye Ferguson) sort of a sexy Edith Head on keyboards.

Ralph lies about being a musician to sustain an after-show conversation with Mona, and depression sets in. Checking in at a dive bar with the only people who know him, Chuck the Bartender (Susan "Forbidden Zone" Tyrell), Raphael (Kevin Hunter of the band Wire Train), and Ax Man (Bo Diddley, who provides some guitar textures), he decides to pose as a musician and recruits them as the backup band to see his plan through.

Ralph performs a novelty rock song "He's Rockula," written by Jefery Levy, one of the film's producers and writers. Dean Cameron performs all his own music, having played guitar and written songs in high school bands, and while he's not rock star material he holds his own and is good enough to impress Mona. Romance blooms to the song "By My Side," written by David Aronson and performed with gusto by Cameron and Feré.

Meanwhile, Ralph's mother Phoebe is working her own agenda, posing as a fortune teller and convincing Stanley he must murder Mona to keep her. He provides him with the specifics: it must be a ham bone, he must dress as a pirate, the peg leg must be rhinestone, and thus the curse will continue. She also invites Mona over for dinner, regales her with tales from history, and entertains the group (which includes a pro wrestler played by Rick Zumwalt from *Over the Top*) with another musical number. Any chance to get Basil dancing should be seized, and her sharp, vampy, proto-hip-hop movement is put to great use here.

Ralph decides to tell Mona the truth, and reveals himself as a vampire when he turns into a huge bat, or a midget with wings, dubbed "Bat Dork" in the credits. Upset, Mona

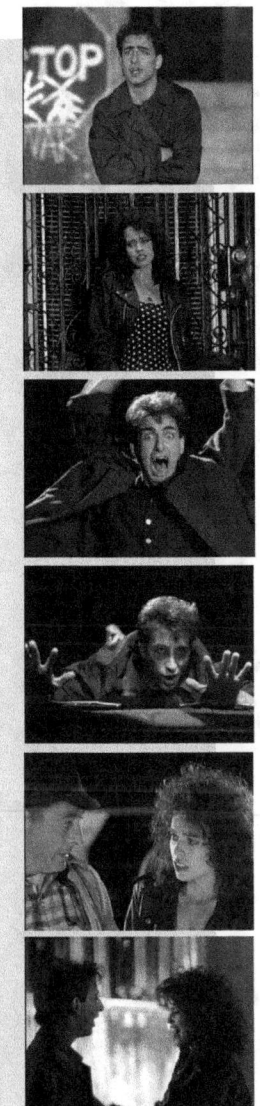

tries to leave him but ends up drawn back to the Halloween concert at Club Hell where the curse starts to come to fruition. Mona's partner Robin must step in and perform on stage. Actress Nancye Ferguson, a filmmaker and songwriter in her own right, appears with one of her music projects called Visiting Kids (a collaboration with Mark Mothersbaugh – married to Ferguson at the time – with Mothersbaugh's niece Alex among the tiny girls dressed in First Communion dresses). Stanley makes his move but it's Ralph to the rescue and the curse is finally lifted. Mirror Ralph is left behind as Real Ralph leaves with Mona, so he magically exits the mirror with a trio of backup singers and performs an Elvis-meets-Bo-Diddley end credits song "The King is Back," written and performed by Dean Cameron on vocals and guitar.

Why watch *Rockula*? There's a lot of inspired laughs, great costumes, Dean Cameron brings the same appealing spirit as he provides as "Chainsaw" in *Summer School* (and here he's really providing two very different roles), Tawny Feré is a fine singer and actor, Basil and Dolby are entirely entertaining, and the music is dumb fun.

MONTAGE FROMAGE
"By My Side" Cameron/Feré

A kiss in the rain triggers a musical number, scarcely interrupted when half of the duet is hit by a car...

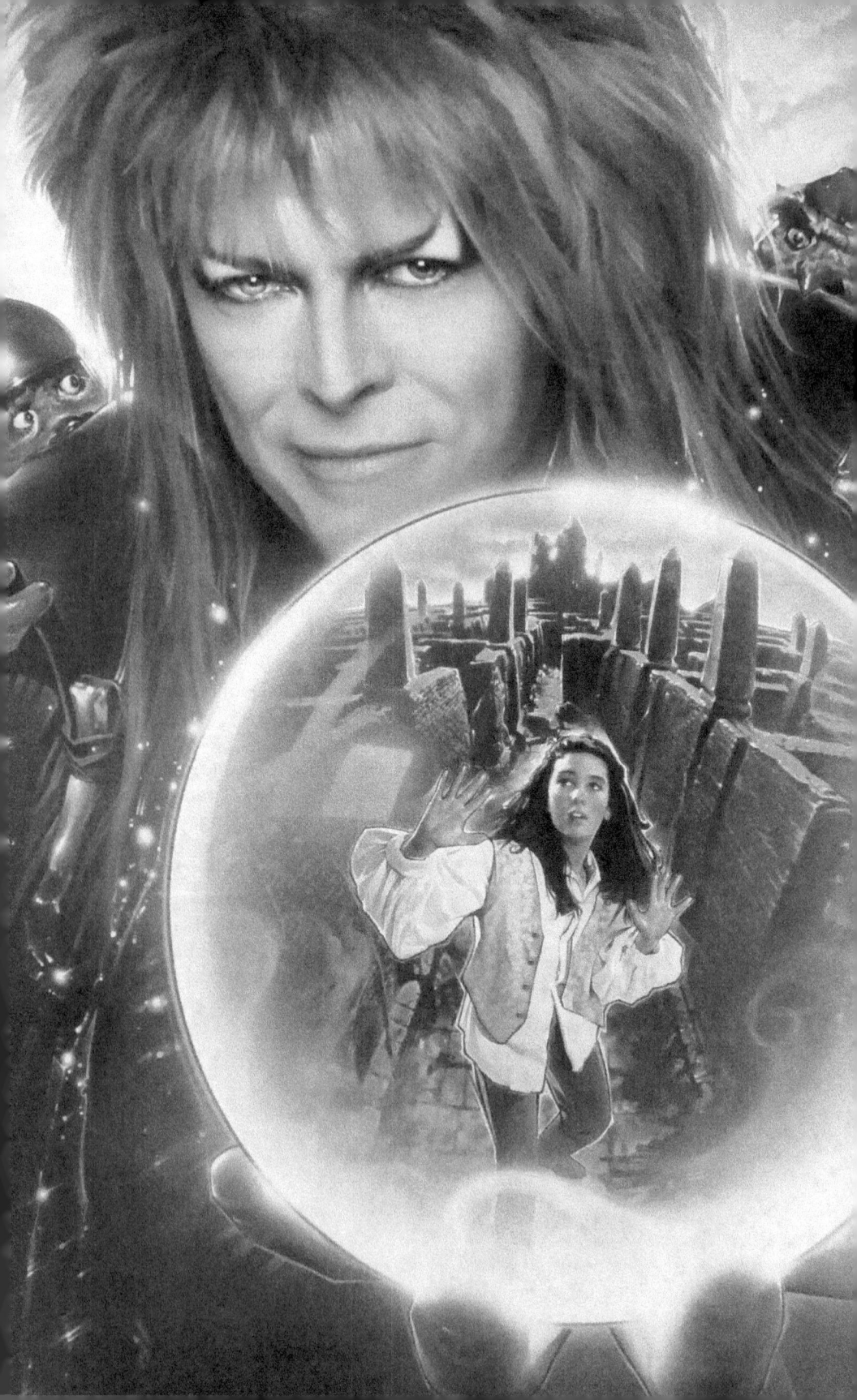

17

LABYRINTH'S MAGIC DANCE

Labyrinth is a fantasy film of the kind they stopped making in the 80s, and a musical with the kind of music they stopped making in the 80s. Yet the audience for it has grown and grown ever since, even if they haven't exactly grown up.

"It's only forever Not long at all..."

A timeless fairytale done in a very time-specific way (pure 80s, packed with rubber puppets and synthy pop songs), *Labyrinth* is a film starring a shape-changing singer-songwriter who re-emerged in the time of MTV to renew his title as a rock legend. Mention the film to people of a certain age and you'll surely get something about "The Pants." It's a dark quest, populated with challenging obstacles, enemies and allies, and yes, David Bowie's prominent package. (You know it's formidable, when people lose sight of the accompanying wig, which has its own zip code.)

British illustrator Brian Froud, who provided the design work for Jim Henson's *The Dark Crystal*, floated a basic concept during a limo ride after a screening of that film. When Henson asked, "what should we do next," talk turned to goblins, a labyrinth, and a child in danger. The film was written by Monty Python alumnus Terry Jones, with rewrites galore by Henson, Dennis Lee and Laura Phillips of *Fraggle Rock*, Elaine May, (and probably some George Lucas in there too). In Jones' hands, the film would change greatly following the dictate from Henson that a rock star would play the Goblin King Jareth, and that there would be songs. (And when Bowie got ahold of the revised script,

he personally saw to it that some of Terry Jones missing laughs were reinstated.)

With *The Dark Crystal*, Henson had been missing the comedic opportunities and songs – basically all the things that made The Muppets such a joy to watch (and to make!). And so he set out to do a fantasy film, mixing puppets and humans (he was dissatisfied with the stiff performances of the nearly-human Gelflings in *Crystal*). And he would do so without the default musical fallback of an orchestral score, but with contemporary music. He proposed a list of charismatic rock stars that could star in the film: Michael Jackson, Sting, Bowie, David Lee Roth, Mick Jagger, Rod Stewart, Roger Daltrey, Freddie Mercury, Prince, and Ted Nugent. Keen readers, take a moment to close your eyes and imagine those "what if," alternate universe versions of the film!

Henson needed a consummate performer who could be in on the joke of Goblin King as Ultimate Rocker. Of those choices, David Bowie had the most proven screen acting experience (and as we run down the list of the other options, perhaps that choice has aged the best as well). Henson and son Brian had seen Bowie in a Broadway production of *The Elephant Man* a few years earlier, and were sold. Brian recalled "I think my dad was really impressed at how courageous David was. The biggest concern that you have when you cast a music artist in an acting role is whether or not they are scared of being completely vulnerable... It was clear that David was completely comfortable onstage."

Jim Henson met with Bowie while he was on the American leg of the Serious Moonlight tour in 1983, tempting him with scripts, Brian Froud's artwork for the film, and a tape of *The Dark Crystal*. "I could see the potential of making that kind of movie with humans, with songs, with a more lighter comedy script," Bowie said. "I'd always wanted to be involved in the music-writing aspect of a movie that would appeal to children of all ages, as well as everyone else, and I must say that Jim gave me a completely free hand with it. The script itself was terribly amusing without being vicious or spiteful or bloody, and it also had a lot more heart than many other special effects movies. So I was pretty well hooked from the beginning."

Bowie was no stranger to fantasy (his song "The Laughing Gnome" from 1967 is a novelty song about a wee man, complete with a chipmunk-like accompaniment), or to elaborate dress-up. So it may come as no surprise that he reportedly had a wonderful time making the film (Brian said it was like he was on vacation), always polite and open with even the lowest ranking crewmembers. Surely, the pace of filmmaking (characterized as it is by long periods of waiting) would seem a vacation after a prolonged spate of recording and touring.

"Every age group really has a whole thing about David, and he himself is a very normal, well-grounded, straightforward person that is absolutely professional,"

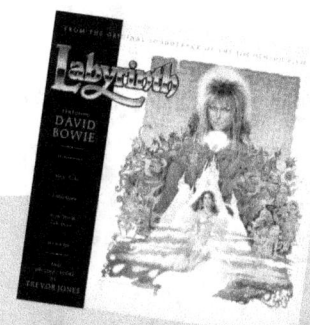

SOUNDTRACK

Opening Titles/Underground
Trevor Jones/Bowie

Into the Labyrinth
Trevor Jones

Magic Dance
David Bowie

Sarah
Trevor Jones

Chilly Down
David Bowie

Hallucination
Trevor Jones

As The World Falls Down
David Bowie

The Goblin Battle
Within You
Thirteen O'Clock
Home At Last
Trevor Jones

Underground
David Bowie

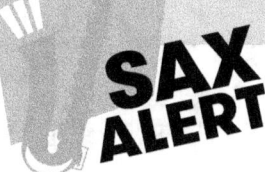

SAX ALERT

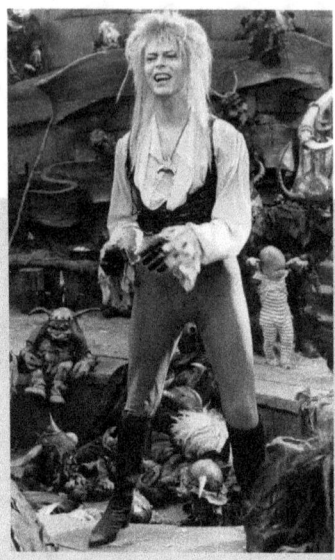

ON BOWIE'S PANTS

Any similarity between the Goblin King and real rock stars is intentional. As American author Chris O'Leary points out: "Labyrinth's designer took Bowie's conceit that Jareth was a failed rock star ("a young girl's dream of a pop star"), who was stuck ruling a backwater goblin kingdom that no one ever visits, while all he wanted to do was hang out in a nightclub somewhere. So Bowie's outfits are burlesques of a rock star's garb: he's a pantomime satyr." The character is a potent mix of "rock star, and he is also a leather jacket guy – a classic "bad boy" – and he's Heathcliff, and also a ballet dancer," according to designer Froud. "He's an amalgam of the inner fantasies of this girl." Popular opinion suggests that The Goblin King may have single handedly jump-started womanhood for an entire generation of female viewers.

the elder Henson gushed. Lucas added: "Jareth is like the devil. He's completely alluring, a character that draws people in, that people are infatuated with. And what better person to play the part than a rock star, because that's what they are. But at the same time, David Bowie was very, very smart and very talented."

Playing the lead opposite Bowie is Jennifer Connelly, a talented New York actress who was 14 but playing 16 in the film. She came in with little prior David Bowie knowledge but found in him a patient teacher and partner.

Sarah (Connelly) is an adolescent girl with a rich fantasy life, torn between the worlds of childhood and adulthood (with responsibilities like getting home on time, looking after her baby brother, or pressure from her stepmother to start dating). In a moment of frustration at not being able to quiet baby Toby, she wishes the goblins would take him away. And it works. Goblin King Jareth appears and insists that a deal is a deal, but offers her one chance: if in thirteen hours she can reach the center of the Labyrinth, she can get her brother back.

Aside from a few exteriors in the state of New York, the film shot from April to September of 1985 in completely manufactured environs at Elstree Studios in England. The film stands the test of time as a masterpiece of traditional effects work, with every pre-digital filmmaking trick (and one very early computer graphics sequence) put to great use. In today's age of film trickery, it's easy to lose sight of how complicated such a project is, with up to 50 performers coordinating their efforts on screen at once. Indeed, most of the lead puppets are the work of multiple performers, each handling one aspect of the character in practiced synchronization.

For the music Bowie was given free reign, and while the production expected him to return with rough demos of the songs, all were suitably surprised when he returned with fully formed studio songs. American author and Bowie-expert Chris O'Leary suggests that we "think of Bowie's five *Labyrinth* songs as a secret mid-Eighties Bowie album. It finds Bowie in his typical scrapper mode, using pieces he had considered for a "proper" album and repurposing them for the soundtrack of a fantasy movie. Bowie reworked old themes, looking for flashes of life, still trying to write himself out of his funk. So a rousing singalong goofy kid's song ("Magic Dance") is also a pop trope as old as "Love Potion No. 9"; the ballad "As the World Falls Down" is one of his loveliest, saddest pieces of the era."

While composer Trevor Jones wrote most of the synth-based score, Bowie wrote and recorded five songs for it: "Underground," "Magic Dance," "Chilly Down, "As The World Falls Down," and "Within You."

MAGIC DANCE

This was the film's big production number, with dozens of performers playing through holes in the set, marionettes, and little people in costume dangling from wires. The refrain "You remind me of the babe," is a riff on a Cary Grant/Shirley Temple film from 1947. On the album, the five-plus minute edit of the song outstays its welcome, but it works great as a three-minute scene. The song was titled "Dance Magic" while in production.

CHILLY DOWN

"Chilly Down" was the first piece Bowie wrote for the film. The rhythm tracks were cut during the *Absolute Beginners*/"Dancing in the Street" sessions in late June 1985, and Bowie cut a guide vocal that careful listeners will still detect in the mix. The song is performed, finally, by those who lent voices to the puppets (though not all puppeteers): Danny John-Jules ("Cat" in the UK-sci fi comedy Red Dwarf), Kevin Clash (who played the career-defining Elmo on Sesame Street) Charles Augins and Richard Bodkin.

AS THE WORLD FALLS DOWN

Given a drugged peach, Sarah is transported to a fractured Venetian ballroom, where either the goblins take human forms, or the depraved gentry play at being goblins. Either way, Sarah is out of her league in the grown up, sexual world. Lust or terror or both can be read on her face; that it can be read in a number of ways makes the performances so great. Lyrically, this one plays it straight and could have been a hit single; Bowie would hold out releasing it in favor of his darker upcoming album *Never Let Me Down* (1987).

WITHIN YOU

This song is featured when Sarah faces off with Jareth in the Escher-like recesses of the labyrinth. It's a complex piece in several different time signatures that would be impossible to sing on your way out of the theater (a job that's reserved for the end credit song).

UNDERGROUND

An epic, rousing end-credits song, "Underground" featured a who's who of backing singers: Luther Vandross, Chaka Khan, Cissy Houston, Fonzi Thornton (Chic, plus Roxy Music's Avalon), Eunice Peterson (backup for Aretha Franklin), Renelle Stafford (backup for Paul Simon) and members of the Radio Choir of the New Hope Baptist Church. On lead guitar is the master bluesman Albert Collins.

The film was not well received at the time and only earned back half its budget, but has since gained a cult status. A theatrical re-release and recent 4K transfer for home video shows off the film's detail, artistry, and sheer scope of the undertaking; a flurry of licensed tie-ins from toys to board games suggest that the audience for Labyrinth has grown immensely since its disappointing theatrical run. All of this is well-deserved recognition of the collaboration between a Python, the man who created Star Wars, the man who created the Muppets, and the Man who fell to earth.

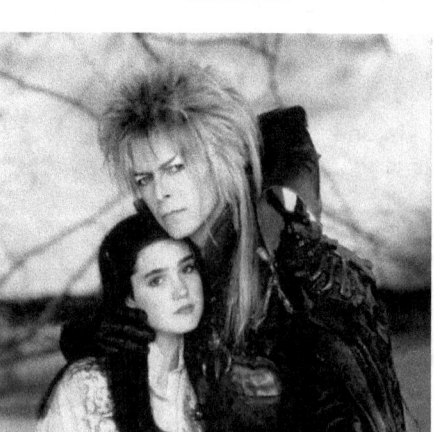

18

LADIES AND GENTLEMEN, THE PUNKS

Punk rock was a subculture that rose in the late 1970s and then scattered, but 80s cinema loves a punk. Whether it's a punked-out henchman, or a quirky sidekick character in a teen comedy, there's always room for some leather and spikes.

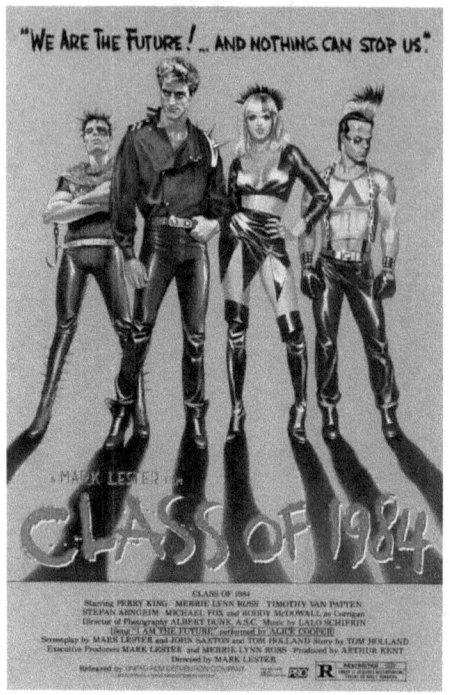

"WE ARE THE FUTURE! ... AND NOTHING CAN STOP US."

CLASS OF 1984 (1982)

There's not a ton of on-screen punk music in the punk-themed *Class of 1984*, which depicts a school system so far in decay that the teachers must carry weapons. Director Mark Lester (*Commando*) self-distributed this potboiler (inspired by 50s exploitation films like *Blackboard Jungle*) when the studios wouldn't touch it, and between the persistent cruelty of the main gang and the violent final act, one can see why. The screenplay by Tom Holland (*Fright Night*) keeps the tension building to it's operatic conclusion.

Perry King plays the new teacher on the block, who gets schooled by a pistol-packing Roddy McDowall on how the place works: don't get involved and you might make it through the day. An impossibly-young Michael J. Fox barely survives the proceedings, doled out by a gang led by Timothy Van Patten. Gang members include a lot of actors from the filming location in Toronto, including Stefan Arngrim (whose bonkers 1981 film *Fear no Evil* is a blast) Keith Knight (*Meatballs*), and Lisa Langlois (*Happy Birthday to Me*). Every one of them is so consistently horrible to the people around them that the film's inevitable revenge should have you rooting for their comeuppance.

The film opens with the song "I Am the Future," written by composer Lalo Schifrin and sung by Alice Cooper, which is not your average musical match-up and the rather indescribable results are even less punk than that combination suggests. Punk music is suggested as one of the sources of the kid's aggression, in a nightclub scene presided over by Canadian punk band Teenage Head. Timothy Van Patten wrote his own piano piece for the film in which we learn he is much more than a mindless thug.

While it was supposed to be cut down to reach an R rating, Mark Lester has claimed that he accidentally delivered the X-Rated cut to the lab that made the prints. The film sometimes played as what can only have been an exhausting double bill with *Mad Max 2: The Road Warrior*.

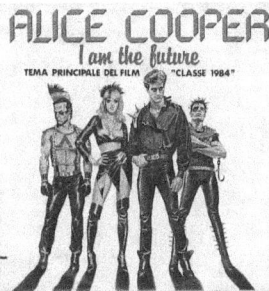

SOUNDTRACK

I Am the Future
Alice Cooper / Lalo Schifrin

Fresh Flesh
Fear

Let's Have a War
Fear

Ain't Got No Sense
Teenage Head

Stegman's Concerto
Timothy Van Patten

Suburbanite
Jeffrey Baxter / Lalo Schifrin

You Better Not Step Out of Line
Schifrin / Baxter / Randall Bramlett

Little Boxes (Alimony)
Teenage Head

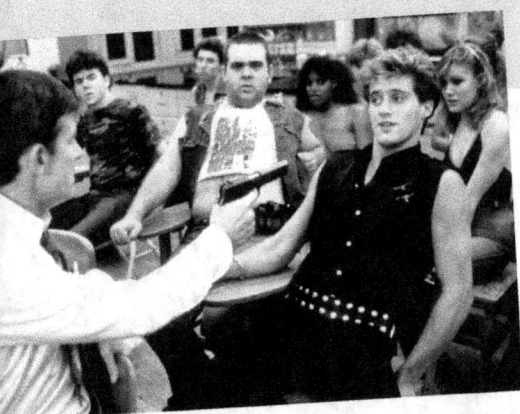

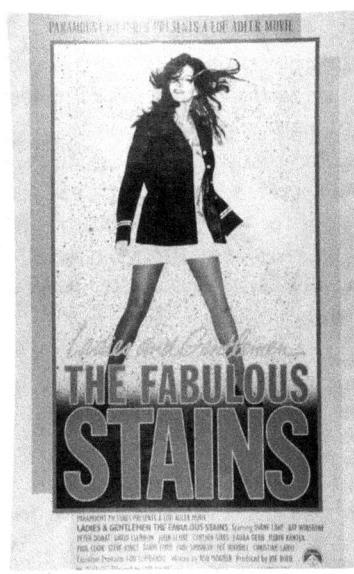

LADIES AND GENTLEMEN, THE FABULOUS STAINS (1982)

Imagine a supergroup consisting of Sex Pistols Paul Cook on drums, The Clash's Paul Simonon on bass guitar, and fellow Pistol Steve Jones on guitar... Now imagine that you don't have to imagine such a thing! Now put a fresh-faced Ray Winstone, shortly after his appearance in Quadrophenia, on the microphone in a performance that distills several of the classic punk frontmen, and you have The Looters, the best sounding band in a film about a concert tour on the nascent punk wave through an America that might not be ready for it.

Corinne Burns (Diane Lane) is an angry sixteen year old orphan in the industrial dump of Charlestown PA (which appears to be as British a condition as you probably can muster in the states, and a ripe breeding ground for a punk attitude). Lane, who had been acting since 1979 but was about to break out for roles in The Outsiders, Rumble Fish, and Streets of Fire, positively smolders as Corrine. A series of TV interviews sets her on her rise to fame, starting with one where she quits her job (her boss is Brent Spiner in the one remaining shot of a much longer prologue), and another interview where she emerges as a teen role model noting she has changed her name to "3rd Degree" and insists she doesn't put out.

She's in a band with her sister Tracy (Marin Kanter) and cousin Jessica (a 13-year old Laura Dern, who was able to skirt her mother's objections to her involvement in the film by suing and winning emancipation). When Corinne sees the punk energy of The Looters at a local concert appearance, she asks singer Billy for an audition. Billy's promoter Lawnboy, a rasta who also drives the tour bus, agrees to put them on the bill, which is already a mixed bag thanks to the past-their-expiration date headliner the Metal Corpses (including two members of The Tubes).

The death of the Metal Corpses bass player opens up two more doors of opportunity: not only do the Stains move up the bill, but Corinne seizes the chance for another self serving TV appearance and claims to be the bass player's lover. The sum effect of all this press coverage is that a growing group of underage girls have started to imitate her nonconformist look of skunk-colored hair and see-through blouses. Eventually they are playing to a sold-out house made up entirely of Corinne clones, and when The Looters get a cold reception it's Billy who calls out the crowd as being the real sell out. When the crowd realizes they've been sold a bill of goods, they rebel against The Stains. The business spits them out as fast as they could consume it.

At this point in their careers, Paul Cook and Steve Jones were recording and touring as The Professionals, their post-Sex Pistols, post-Malcolm McLaren project. Steve Jones was conveniently in Canada, where the

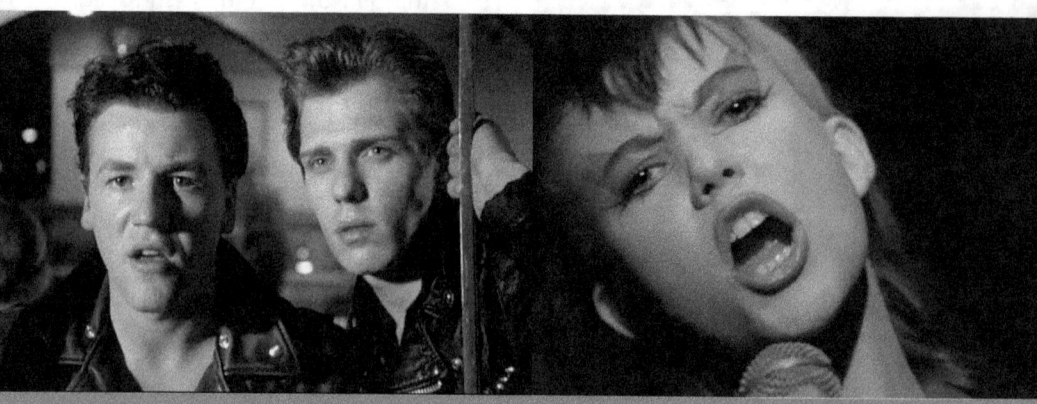

film was shot, detoxing and getting off drugs. All punk songs are credited to "Cook 'N' Jones," with The Tubes performing the Metal Corpses song "Roadmap of My Tears" and Barry Ford (Lawn Boy) as composer on everything else.

The film was directed by Lou Adler, whose connection to music and film is long and strong, although at this point he had only directed one other picture: *Up in Smoke*. He co-managed Jan & Dean with Herb Alpert, founded Dunhill Records, produced the hits of The Mamas & the Papas and Carole King. He was responsible for the Monterey International Pop Festival of 1967 and produced the film that chronicled it. Hell, the guy was the "A" in A&M Records. Perhaps most importantly for a discussion about cult music movies, he obtained the US rights for *The Rocky Horror Show* and executive produced the film based on it and its sequel *Shock Treatment*. The screenplay for Stains was by Nancy Dowd (*Slap Shot*, which takes place in the same fictional town, and *Swing Shift*), credited under her pen name Robert Morton after she weathered horribly sexist conditions on-set.

Adler and the producers don't much understand or embrace punk but are merely positioning the story in that milieu as a bit of colorful background. It's set in an unlikely media world where the only news show appears to be this strained pair of anchors who have only Corinne's story to report on. The male anchor starts skeptical and ends up repulsively dismissive, in what would have been the film's depressing conclusion. But a tacked-on sequence

that imagines the Stains as a great success was shot nearly two years later, made in response to the rise of MTV that occurred during production. In a nice twist of fate for most of these kinds of things, the girls suddenly look older when the cut occurs, and you genuinely get that passage of time most films lack. Laura Dern looks to be about twice as tall, and the hairstyles look appropriately updated.

The costumes and makeup of The Stains was a "hands off"

SOUNDTRACK

All Washed Up
Lawnboy / Barry Ford

The Professionals
The Looters

Roadmap of My Tears
The Metal Corpses

La La La
The Looters

Curfew
Lawn Boy

Waste of Time
The Stains

All Washed Up
Lawn Boy

Professionals
The Stains

Don't Blow It All Away
The Looters

Conned Again
The Looters

Professionals (Video Version)
The Stains

statement devised by London-born artist Caroline Coon, who began creating sexually charged and revolutionary work in the sixties. She also designed and photographed cover art for album singles by The Clash and The Police.

Stains was another 80s example of a film that failed to generate interest on its initial release but gained a new lease on life thanks to cable. In particular, Stains got traction thanks to USA Network's "Night Flight" block of weekend programming, and was re-released in specialty theaters in 1985. Despite Adler's connection to multiple music publishing platforms, the soundtrack was not released though it is promised on Ode Records in the film's end credits.

NIGHT FLIGHT

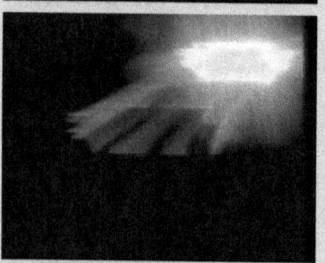

USA Network's NIGHT FLIGHT ran from 1981 through 1988 in massive four hour blocks on Friday and Saturday nights, redefining late night TV for an entire generation of cable owners.

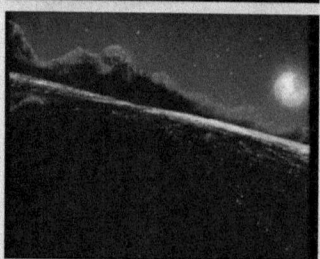

At a time when cable nets were struggling to fill broadcast days (with decades-old sitcoms and all-too-familiar syndicated titles as the primary fodder), NIGHT FLIGHT arrived with a format that defied classification. It was a smorgasbord of independent films, B movies, music videos, short films, and interviews with musicians, artists, and filmmakers.

Not suprisingly, the show's Director of Programming Stuart Samuels was a historian and author of the book "Midnight Movies." Samuels said Night Flight was the first show to place director's names on the videos, interview the bands, create band profiles, air uncensored videos, and to air longform 12" remix videos.

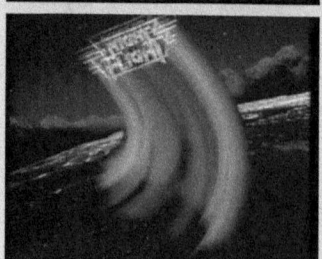

Recurring segments included themed music video blocks ("Take Off"), standup comedian profiles ("The Comic") Cold War instructional films ("Atomic TV"), and comically dubbed versions of public domain movies.

The show was replaced by "Up All Night."

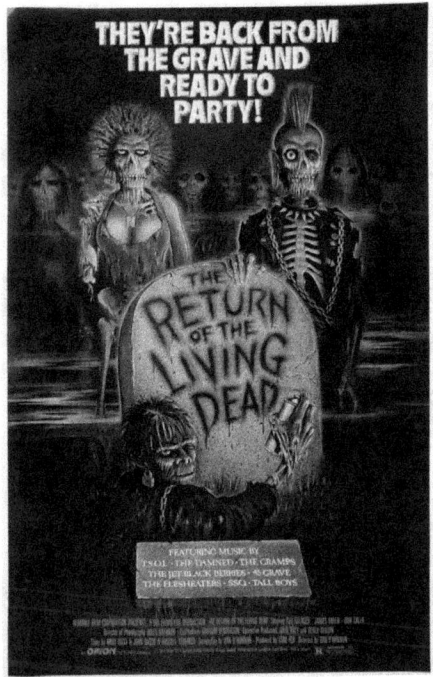

RETURN OF THE LIVING DEAD (1985)

The first post-modern zombie movie, and maybe the best, *Return of the Living Dead* is an eager-to-please collision of underground music and over the top 80s horror.

Young punk Freddy (Thom Matthews) just started working at the Uneeda Medical Supply warehouse, where he gets sage advice from long-time employee Frank (James Karen). Freddy asks Frank "what's the weirdest thing he's seen come through the warehouse," and Frank tells him about the spooky story of an Army shipment of lost chemical-soaked cadavers – and what's more, the bodies are still here. One

unfortunate case of show and tell later, they've accidentally opened the case, unleashing the chemical (245-Trioxin!) into the air. Meanwhile, a motley gang of types (with names like Spider! Trash! Scuz! Suicide!) descend on Freddy's warehouse waiting to party with Freddy. They picked the wrong time to play in the nearby Resurrection Cemetery, though, as the toxic fumes from the canister have seeded the rain clouds and promptly bring the dead back to hungry life. And in a cinematic first, the only thing that can satisfy them is – human brains. In a fun twist, the zombies aren't the lumbering George Romero brand, but smart, speaking, resourceful, and speedy as hell.

The wall to wall music assails your ears like an underground 1984 mixtape (the film's release was delayed almost a year), combining some of the best the period had to offer in American punk, along with LA synth pop group SSQ (later known under the singer's name Stacy Q). Unlike most horror movies, this horror-comedy opted to emphasize a party style barrage of songs instead of traditional score. This was a choice that fell to the movie's editorial staff – the production had commissioned an electronic score in a deal with the publishing company that would have made the music free of cost. The score arrived as a hunk of music without any specific visual cues. One story puts the tape's length at only 15 minutes of music, O'Bannon claimed it was hours and hours of improvised noodling; either way the problem fell to music supervisors Rob Randles and Budd Carr.

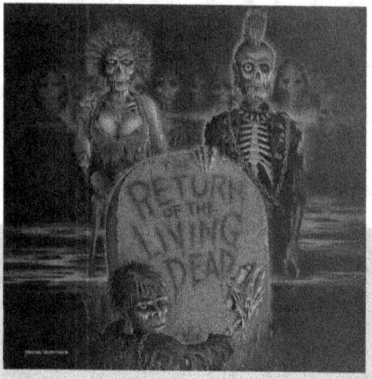

SOUNDTRACK

Surfin' Dead
The Cramps

Partytime (Zombie Version)
45 Grave

Eyes Without a Face
The Flesh Eaters

Burn the Flames
Roky Erickson

Dead Beat Dance
The Damned

Take a Walk
Tall Boys

Love Under Will
The Jet Black Berries

Tonight (We'll Make Love Until We Die)
SSQ

Trash's Theme
SSQ

According to Carr, he and Randles agreed there wasn't enough music to go around. They ran the picture "playing songs along with it... The songs were working great and we were really enjoying ourselves, laughing and having a good time." That spirit would translate to the viewer, as the songs injected a laugh-along energy that defined the horror comedy of that period. The film's producer John Daly demanded an early look and was immediately convinced it was the way to go. He wanted as many songs as possible, where director O'Bannon was more dubious. "(Daily) thought that because these were youth oriented pop songs," said O'Bannon, "that he could make a bundle with an album. I didn't give a rat's ass about some fucking record album, I was making a movie."

As common practice for a picture of the period, Carr had been asked to find songs for the film. The presence of a boombox throughout the opening dictated a picture-specific need, and seizing upon the themes and characters of the film Carr had skewed toward the nascent punk scene from act like The Cramps and LA acts 45 Grave and The Flesh Eaters (names that also afforded some serious horror credibility as well).

"So how do I figure out how to get what Dan (O'Bannon) is looking for in relation to punk, and get what John (Daly) is looking for in relation to not paying for it. My solution was to call Bill Hein, who ran a company called Green World which was a big independent distribution company. And he said 'we've got this label,

Enigma, we've got a lot of great bands, and this will be great." According to Engima's Steve Pross, they had two weeks and $20,000 to put together the soundtrack. Lucky for them, the LA punk scene was big – in part because local radio station KROQ would actually play independent music; a band could sell 25,000 records in southern California alone.

All of the Enigma-signed bands proved to be huge fans of horror and cult movies, so there was never a question about getting them enthusiastic about a moderately budgeted zombie movie. The Cramps were excited to be offered the end-credits song slot, a position that would instead be given to 45 Grave's all-too-perfect theme song "Partytime." According to band leader Dinah Cancer, the song's more metal approach was the result of their strictly-punk band getting accidentally booked at a metal show. As a way to fit in, the group decided to play the song at half-speed – the reaction was so positive the song stayed that way.

The band T.S.O.L. provided "Nothing for You" for the first appearance of the punk kids. At the time the band was managed by Mike Vraney, who started a cult movie home video label Something Weird Video. Synth outfit SSQ was also on Enigma, and since the score was going to be electronic they were asked to provide a couple of horror-themed songs for source music as well as versions of those songs that could be employed as score. Through various releases of the film the soundtrack varied; notably The Damned's track is absent from some home video versions.

With *Return of the Living Dead*, both the directors and the producers were proven wrong one one decision or another. The producers hated the idea of fast zombies, the director hated the idea of a punk and rock and psychobilly score, yet these are the enduring elements of the movie and set it apart from the pack. It's a horror film that acknowledges other horror films (now a commonplace idea), and that forges an all-new mythology for the living dead.

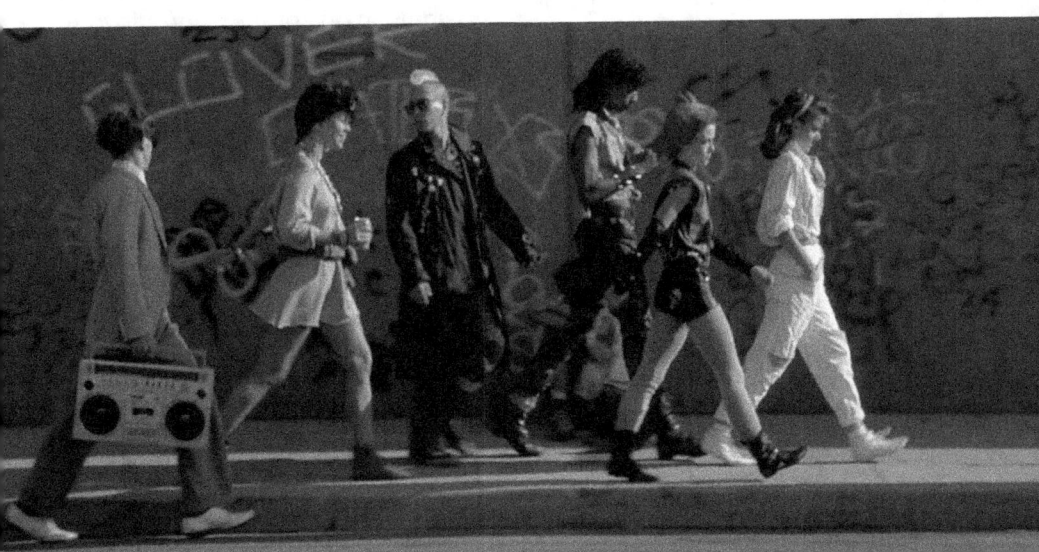

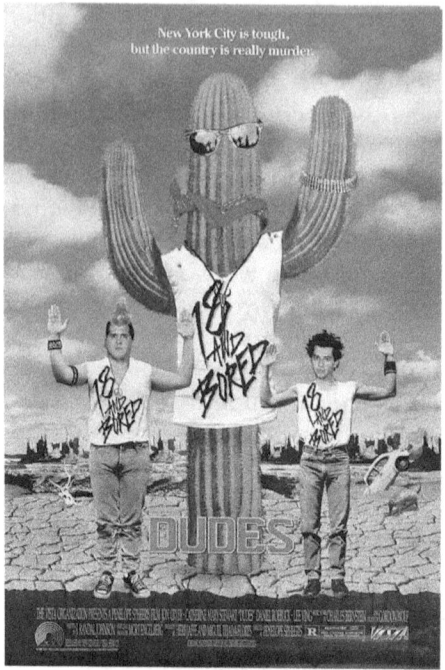

DUDES (1987)

"I wanna be a cowboy. I was born to be a cowboy."
– The Vandals

A trio of New York punk rockers who are "sick of waiting for the world to end" set out on a road trip adventure that includes ghost cowboys, hallucinogenic hooch, an Elvis-impersonating rodeo clown, and a shocking murder.

Grant (Jon Cryer), Biscuit (Daniel Roebuck) and Milo (Flea) are punk kids whose aimless nights are divided between mosh pits and late-night Chinese restaurants. Fed up, Milo offers up a thousand bucks of his own money to get them out of town,

off to the apparent punk paradise of California. They set out in a powder blue VW bug, apparently teleport across the entire midwest, and promptly arrive in the picturesque West of the John Ford films.

Along the way, they come to the aid of Daredelvis (Pete Willcox) an Elvis-impersonator and a whole lot more (horse trader, snake charmer, marriage counselor, divorce lawyer, musician, poker player, stunt driver, dowser, clairvoyant, actor, and poet).

Daredelvis: What's your line of work?
Grant: Survival.
Daredelvis: Man, that's the slowest form of suicide.

Along their journey, Grant may or may not be hallucinating – cryptic glimpses of a mythical cowboy figure haunt the landscape. When they stop for the night, they are harassed by a group of rogue, rural bikers led by Missoula (ubiquitous punk-rocker-actor Lee Ving). Missoula's crew usually just picks on border-crossing Mexicans, but when our heroes put up camp in one of the gang's favorite night spots without permission, things quickly escalate. When Grant and crew attempt an escape, things take a surprisingly dark turn – the child-like Milo is shot square in the head by Missoula.

An appeal to the local sheriff falls on deaf ears, and there will be no investigation into Milo's murder. Instead, Biscuit and Grant are arrested and run out of town. Grant won't stand for the injustice and vows to avenge Milo's death, and they soon pick up the trail of Missoula and gang.

A chance encounter at a roadside diner with tow-truck driver Jessie (Catherine Mary Stewart) gains them one more supporter – even if they don't take her initial advice not to go into the diner dressed as they are (resulting in a comically knock-down drag-out bar fight). She takes them in, and proves to be a whiz with a single-action revolver and on horseback. She's the cowboy they've been looking for, but the script doesn't let her join the quest.

While romance blooms between Grant and Jessie, Biscuit dreams of an Indian massacre, one in which he is a tribesman and Missoula leads the cavalry. He awakens a changed man, adopting full native garb and a terse, cliché "Indian" accent. He's gone native, and insists they continue the chase. Grant gets a full cowboy upgrade (complete with punk trimmings), and they upgrade to a huge car that sports as a hood ornament a full-size set of bull horns. Eventually, they corner Missoula in a one-street town and Grant must assume the mantle of modern cowboy.

Directed by Penelope Spheeris (Wayne's World) the film mixes some grisly action (Milo's execution, the gory death-by-bull of one of Missoula's gangmembers) with loads of offbeat humor – anyone in 1987 expecting another teen comedy with Jon Cryer were undoubtedly put off by the radical, genre-busting blend of elements. The film's grip on reality is tenuous, mixing dream sequences and impossible visions with the otherwise straightforward revenge action, and eventually succumbs to mostly film western tropes including a jailbreak and shootout. Doors drummer John Densmore plays a small town cop and Peter Kent (a frequent Schwarzenegger co-star) plays a road-warrior-esque punk rocker.

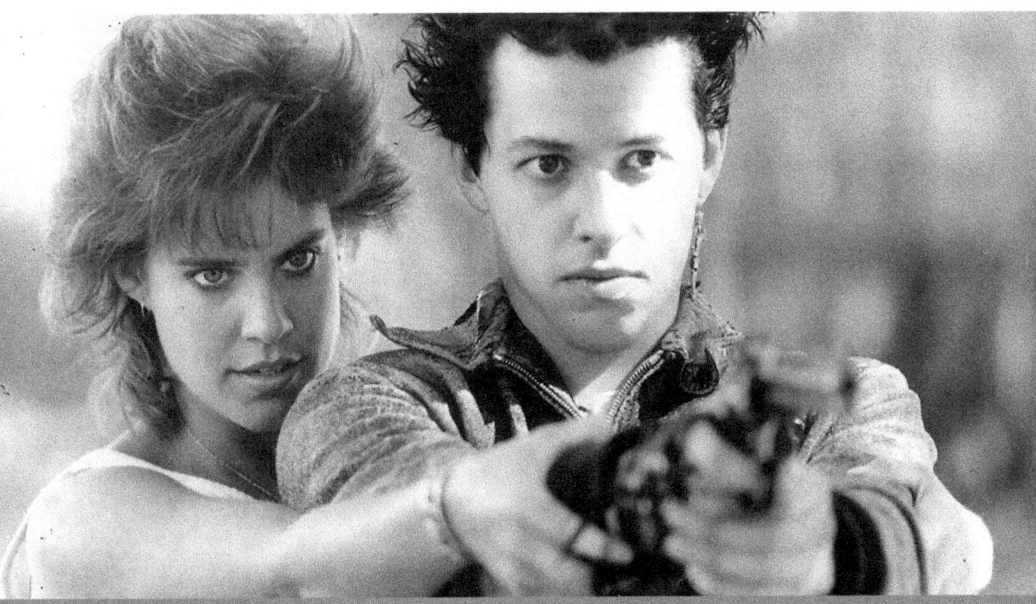

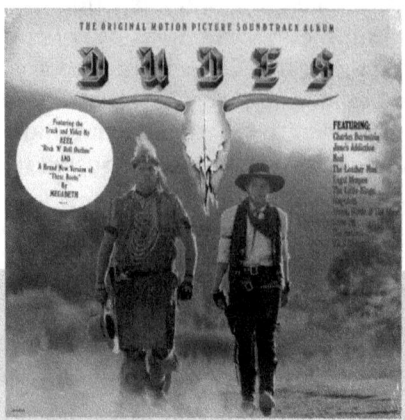

SOUNDTRACK

Rock and Roll Outlaw
Keel

Urban Struggle
The Vandals

Show No Mercy
W.A.S.P.

Vengeance is Mine
Simon Steele and The Claw

These Boots Are Made for Walkin'
Megadeath

Time Forgot You
Legal Weapon

Jesus Came Driving Along
The Leather Nun

Mountain Song
Jane's Addiction

Lost Highway
The Little Kings

Dudes Showdown
Charles Bernstein

Amazing Grace
Steve Vai

The soundtrack on their journey is wall to wall guitars, a potent mix of metal, countrified rockabilly, and punk that perfectly fits the epic western spaces. In the same way that California surf music influenced the spaghetti westerns of the 60s, LA's early 80s punk scene had toyed with western music. The film's music and style acknowledges that connection throughout, and manages to distance itself from the UK punk scene while still embracing certain visual elements. Cinematographer Robert Richardson was hot off Oliver Stone's films *Salvador* and *Platoon*, and offered to do the film for whatever the production could afford. He would go on to do most of Oliver Stone's films, as well as titles for Martin Scorsese and Quentin Tarantino.

At risk of being typecast as following his turn as Duckie in *Pretty in Pink*, Cryer jumped at the opportunity to play a hero in the film, but was worried about being seen as a fraud when it came to playing a punk rocker. Cryer's musical tastes, like his co-star Roebuck, veered towards musical theater – Cryer was Matthew Broderick's understudy for productions of *Brighton Beach Memoirs* and *Torch Song Trilogy*. And both were thrown to the wolves in the film's opening (and real) mosh pit scene. Much more at home in the pit was Flea, who had been cast in director Spheeris' film *Suburbia* and took his acting opportunities very seriously.

19

ALEX COX: PUNK PROPHET

Born in England, Alex Cox studied film at University of Bristol and UCLA before he became one of the most consistently bizarre filmmakers of the 1980s. He wrote the screenplay for Repo Man with the intention of making it for $70,000; when producer Michael Nesmith became involved the budget shot over the $1 million mark. His punk credentials led to a series of surreal movies about and starring members of the alternative music scene.

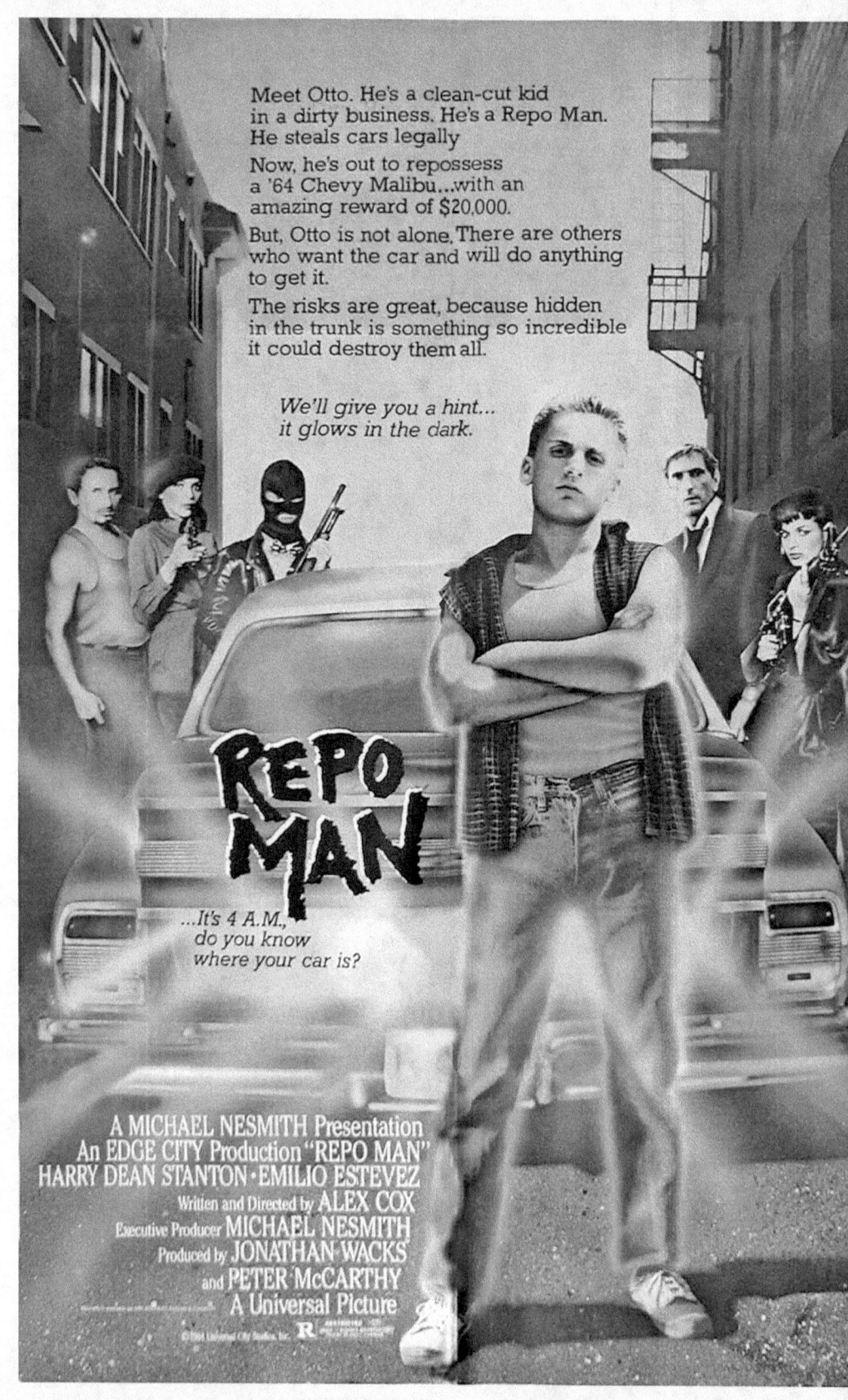

> ## "as Buñuel and Dali knew, there's something particularly empowering and exciting about telling stories that resemble dreams..."
> ~ ALEX COX

REPO MAN (1984)

If the breakdancing movies helped bring street dance to the midwestern kids, then Repo Man delivered punk to the suburbs almost simultaneously. It's not a musical but the music is woven right into the texture of it, and sports a soundtrack album that raised awareness of the LA punk genre and saved the movie from disappearing completely on arrival.

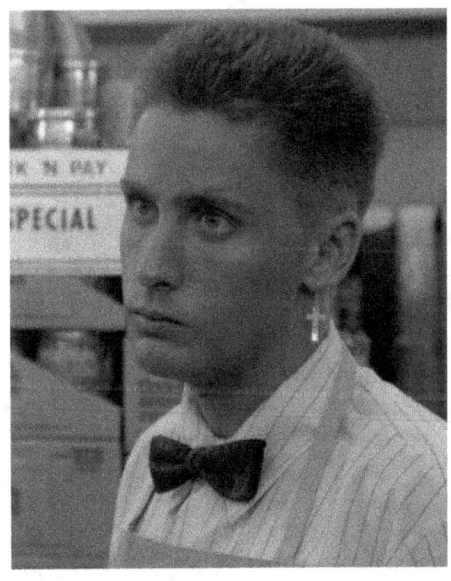

The music hits you right from the get-go with low-tech opening credits set to Iggy Pop's threatening theme song, and the film never lets up with wall to wall music, from the surf-spaghetti-western Peter Gunn guitar score to an endless parade of source music of every genre coming from car radios. We immediately learn that Repo Man is science fiction of a sort, because there's something lurking in the trunk of a 1964 Chevy Malibu that vaporizes people instantly, leaving nothing a pair of smoking boots when the car is stopped by a nosy highway patrolman.

The main character is Otto, a white suburban punk downplayed by Emilio Estevez in a role originally meant for the film's writer Dick Rude (who instead plays his disaffected friend Archie). Otto is working at a local grocery store, where he stocks shelves with his nerdy pal Kevin. Otto finally snaps and walks out of his job only to be recruited by repo man Bud (Harry Dean Stanton).

Bud is one of a team of repo men named after beers (Oly, Lite, and Miller) working out of a shoddy lot somewhere in the wastelands of LA, always depicted with oppressive, dusty grubbiness by cinematographer Robby Muller (and post-production pickups by Bob Richardson). Otto trades in his back alley mosh pits for a shirt and tie, riding shotgun with Bud and the cool-as-steel Lite (Sy Richardson) and absorbing the "repo code."

Never broke into a car, never hotwired a car. Never broke into a truck. 'I shall not cause harm to any vehicle nor the personal contents thereof, nor through inaction let the personal contents thereof come to harm' It's what I call the Repo Code, kid!

When the supernatural Chevy surfaces with a $20,000 reward, it becomes a target for not only the repo men, but a crypto-government organization led by a woman with a robotic hand, and car thief/revolutionaries Los Hermanos Rodriguez (Napo and Velez, who are secretly working with repo-office girl Marlene, played by Blacula's Vonetta McGee).

The film is filled with little off-screen audio asides and packed per director Cox's request with tiny visual easter eggs for the observant viewer. Films that do this illustrate the care and attention to detail of the filmmakers, in that they are layering in entertainment value from the production designer's desk all the way through the sound mix. Nothing escapes Cox's 80s political agenda in this film, skewering television evangelism, conspiracy theories, Spielberg movies, Reaganomics, US influence in Central America, and the impending threat of nuclear annihilation. His book "X Films: True Confessions of a Radical Filmmaker" goes deeply into the challenges of making a studio film, contrary to his loose 16mm style he had developed at UCLA, and a lot of insight is there for the taking. "We weren't playing the film like a comedy. Our strategy was to make Repo Man as downbeat dingy and normal-looking as possible: so that if you saw a still from it you'd think it was a contemporary thriller, not a comedy."

This was one of the oddball films produced by former Monkee Michael Nesmith, who got the script and accompanying lo-fi comic book adaptation drawn by Cox and was interested in getting a bigger budget for it through a big studio. Cox states "we were going to do it super low budget with all four members of Fear, but it never came about. We tried to raise $100,000 to make the film on the low road and couldn't raise the money. Then, Michael Nesmith, Executive Producer comes along and says he can take it to the studio and get more money. Then we had to cast people who were names."

Bud was written with Dennis Hopper in mind, but when he proved too expensive Harry Dean's agent recommended – nope, not Harry Dean Stanton, but Mick Jagger, because

Harry Dean's career was on the down slide. Director Alex Cox knew this was ridiculous and insisted on Harry, who soon after gained the late-career recognition he deserved for *Paris, Texas.*

Alex Cox moved to Los Angeles from his native England at the very moment of punk's rise. He states that though he never saw any of the punk acts in England he was privy to groundbreaking shows by Devo and Latino punk band The Plugz (who contributed their distinctive, indelible sound to the score). Cox reports punk was more than just a style: "I was into the scene, properly; I liked the music a lot, back in the late 1970s and early 80s. I think the punk thing was rather like the surrealist movement; the dadaists. It wasn't just a style of painting or a style of music. It was an attitude: there was a rebellious thing to it that gave it the quality of a movement."

"The punk score came about gradually. It appeared as source music ("Pablo Picasso") existing songs were sung by characters ("TV Party"). The Circle Jerks appeared in sequinned jackets doing a lounge act and we showed the film to Iggy Pop hoping he'd write our title music.... Iggy felt it should resemble the Batman theme. I thought this was an excellent idea... His guitar player was Steve

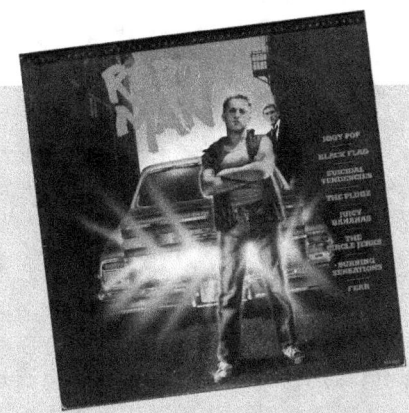

SOUNDTRACK

Repo Man
Iggy Pop

T.V. Party
Black Flag

Institutionalized
Suicidal Tendencies

Coup D'Etat
Circle Jerks

El Clavo y La Cruz
The Plugz

Pablo Picasso
Burning Sensations

Let's Have a War
Fear

When the Shit Hits the Fan
Circle Jerks

Hombre Secreto/Secret Agent Man
The Plugz

Bad Man
Juicy Bananas

Reel Ten
The Plugz

Jones late of the Sex Pistols another recent LA arrival. These were all edgy thoroughbred musicians. It could, in other circumstances, have been a horrible disaster."

Musicians abound in the film. In addition to the Circle Jerks appearing as lounge versions of themselves, the LA-based mod/ska band The Untouchables appear as a scooter-riding band that becomes the target of one of Otto's repos. Jimmy Buffett makes a blink-and-you'll-miss-it cameo as a government agent; all the other agents are blond and mustachioed too you're likely to miss it.

Kevin is played by Zander Schloss, who was the sometimes-bass player for the Circle Jerks. Schloss inherited the role from Chris Penn after his firing – he was on set anyway as a PA and Penn's wardrobe fit him, so he was swiftly recruited. Any similarity between Kevin and Napoleon Dynamite appears to have been no accident, as Zander himself believes Jon Heder's portrayal is a direct rip off. "That's exactly what I was like in high school... When I watched the movie, it was kind of disturbing. My reaction was pretty visceral, it was like looking in a mirror."

Their main contact at Universal left before the film was finished, and the new regime didn't see much merit in a wry punk surrealist sci fi movie. Reviews were mixed – and in the case of *Variety*, quite literally mixed, as they accidentally reviewed it twice (once for the daily and once for the weekly) with contradictory results! To Cox's dismay, Universal's fly-postering campaign in Los Angeles featured the logo, in black, on a nearly black background. Cox made a stencil, bought 20 cans of red spray paint and drove around town fixing them himself, which is undoubtedly the most punk solution possible.

The film went straight to cable and then to video, but the tale didn't end there. It seems that MCA's release of the soundtrack was doing well, and the head of the record label asked "is there a movie to go with this?" A limited second release of the film grossed four million dollars in the summer of 1984.

Cox's experiences only confirmed his distrust of the corporate filmmaking system and would grow increasingly and vocally independent in films to come.

"Talking to students and younger people now I get the impression that they think a film is given to a filmmaker by a studio or a production company. This is not so – if you're a real filmmaker a film is something that you personally conceive and then in partnership with similarly minded colleagues make yourself."

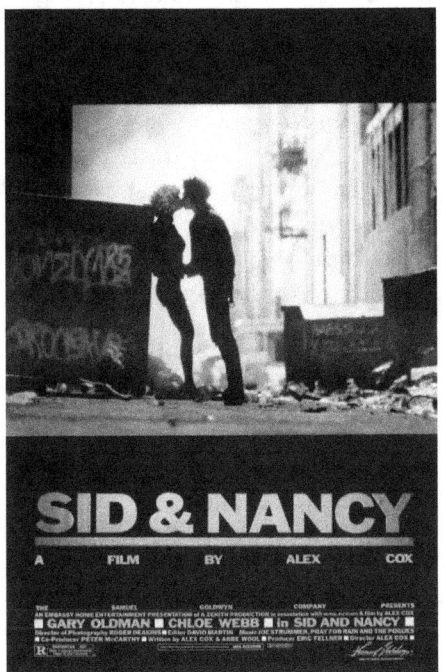

SID & NANCY
(1986)

Sid & Nancy is a gruelling bio film about the Sex Pistols bassist and bad boy Sid Vicious. Beautifully and heartbreakingly played by Gary Oldman in his first lead role, this can be a tough one to watch despite quirky surrealist touches by director Alex Cox.

The film lovingly recreates a few 70s musical scenarios, playing at clubs, touring the US, failing to record much of anything. Originally titled *Love Kills*, the film chooses to focus on the relationship between Sid and American groupie Nancy Spungen, and the destructive influence of her and her heroin. Was Nancy to blame, Yoko-style, for the fall of this flashpoint band? That, or Sid's stupidity, or more charitably, his naive innocence? But the period reenactments, then only ten years after the fact, and the ever-chameleonic Gary Oldman make it a should-see for music enthusiasts.

The film began as a retaliatory strike, of sorts, against the threat of another Sid and Nancy film that would have starred Rupert Everett and Madonna. Cox was given the opportunity to direct that project, but was sitting on half of a Sid Vicious script of his own (or more correctly, an apocalyptic script called "Too Kool to Die," about a rich American family that hires a blind detective to rescue their daughter from the clutches of an English bass player named Ringo Shiv, all in a flooded futuristic London). Cox was convinced his script could never get made so he began interviewing people who had known Sid or Nancy, including a dominatrix, Sid's mother, Malcolm McClaren, and the remaining Pistols. Cox teamed with producer Eric Fellner, who till this point was known for some high profile music videos, as Cox related in his book:

"For his sins, he'd just produced a series of high-gloss pop videos in the style of the Emanuelle films, featuring sexy models crawling through the jungles and Venetian blinds. His strategy had been to use these glassy images to sell faux bands like Duran Duran, and it succeeded – nailing shut, in the process, the coffin lid of Punk."

Daniel Day-Lewis was auditioned for Sid, but in a bit of reverse-classism Cox championed Oldman, because he had grown up in the same Bermondsey neighborhood as Sid. And though Courtney Love was interested in the role of Nancy she was too young to play opposite Oldman (who had banked about ten years more on the planet than Sid ever lived to see).

Enter John Lydon, aka Johnny Rotten of the Pistols, who was brought in after a screenplay was fashioned to get his opinion and ersatz stamp of approval. Cox said that Lydon was gracious and positive about the script, and interested to see Drew Schofield, a Liverpudlian, playing Rotten (a Londoner). "He was pleased Drew was a scouser and thought the actor should play 'Johnny Rotten' as one." In retrospect, Cox detected Lydon's efforts were made to further fictionalize the Sex Pistols, elevating their story to almost-mythical status. When the film debuted Lydon railed against it in the press, suggesting it was a blatantly capitistic feast on the corpse of their fame. All the negative press served to help the film, and Cox believes that was Lydon's intention all along, really operating by the old Sex Pistols playbook and exploiting the latent tendencies of the media. Lydon's next album, "Album," featured a cover that evoked *Repo Man's* generic product line – an irony that was not lost on Alex Cox.

With biographical films like *Sid & Nancy*, there is inevitably the need to prioritize drama over fidelity to the facts. Those with intimate familiarity of the London punk scene in 1976 would see through the artificiality of any endeavor to put it on film, and to any critique of the documentary aspect of the film necessarily puts Cox on the defensive:

"Memory plays tricks, makes good things great. It was these memory tricks that I was emulating in a re-creation of London Punk, a scene I'd never seen. Real London Punk in 1976 or 1977 was a couple of skinny, spotty boys bouncing up and down. Ours was a mob of tattooed skinheads and mohicans, slamdancing in a mosh pit. It looked like California Punk, circa 1984, because that's what I knew, and it was visually more exciting. I wanted to show the movement's heroic, epic side, so the viewer would understand the tragedy of its destruction."

At the London wrap party for the film, Cox happened upon a gate-crashing party-goer in the men's room who would become an important collaborator on this film and others: Joe Strummer of The Clash. An offer to make a song for the film turned into a real soundtrack collaboration, with Strummer visiting the cutting room for inspiration and vanishing for a day, only to return with a bit of incidental music for the scene in question. His record company (Epic) insisted he could only provide two songs for the film, but he quickly exceeded his quota with cuts both diegetic and non-diegetic. Cox recalls conversations like "you could do with some reggae here, playing over the speakers," and Strummer would reappear with a cassette of the piece the next day. He would continue to produce music, and kept the record company in the dark by providing them under assumed names. He would go on to make several songs in a variety of styles (including country-western!) all credited to non-existent performers.

No Sex Pistol music is on the official soundtrack album, although the film recreates live Sex Pistol examples of "God Save the Queen," "Anarchy in the UK," "No Feelings," "Pretty Vacant," and "Problems" as well as a cover of Paul Revere and the Raiders' "I'm Not Your Stepping Stone." Much of the score is by Dan Wool, a San Francisco-based composer operating under the band name Pray for Rain. That collaboration with Cox would continue into his next film *Straight to Hell*, as would the contributions of The Pogues who are also featured prominently.

The film is gorgeously shot by Roger Deakins, who asked Cox why he didn't just hire Robby Müller again, but Cox assumed he was on permanent call with Wim Wenders. This was Cox's biggest budget film and it shows, with complicated reenactments and a production that spans England, France, and the US. For fans of *Repo Man* and *Straight to Hell*, it can be a fun challenge to watch for Cox's repertory of actors who reappear throughout, especially Miguel Sandoval as an American music promoter with a song suggestion for Sid.

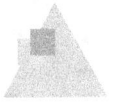

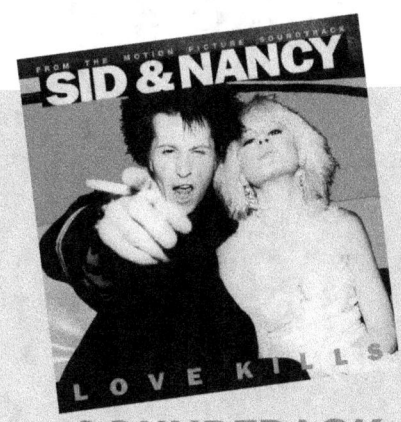

SOUNDTRACK

Love Kills
Joe Strummer

Haunted
The Pogues

Pleasure and Pain
Steve Jones

Chinese Choppers
Pray for Rain

Love Kills
Circle Jerks

Off the Boat
Pray for Rain

Dum Dum Club
Joe Strummer

Burning Room
Pray for Rain

She Never Took No For An Answer
John Cale

Junk
The Pogues

I Wanna Be Your Dog
and **My Way**
Gary Oldman

Taxi to Heaven
Pray for Rain

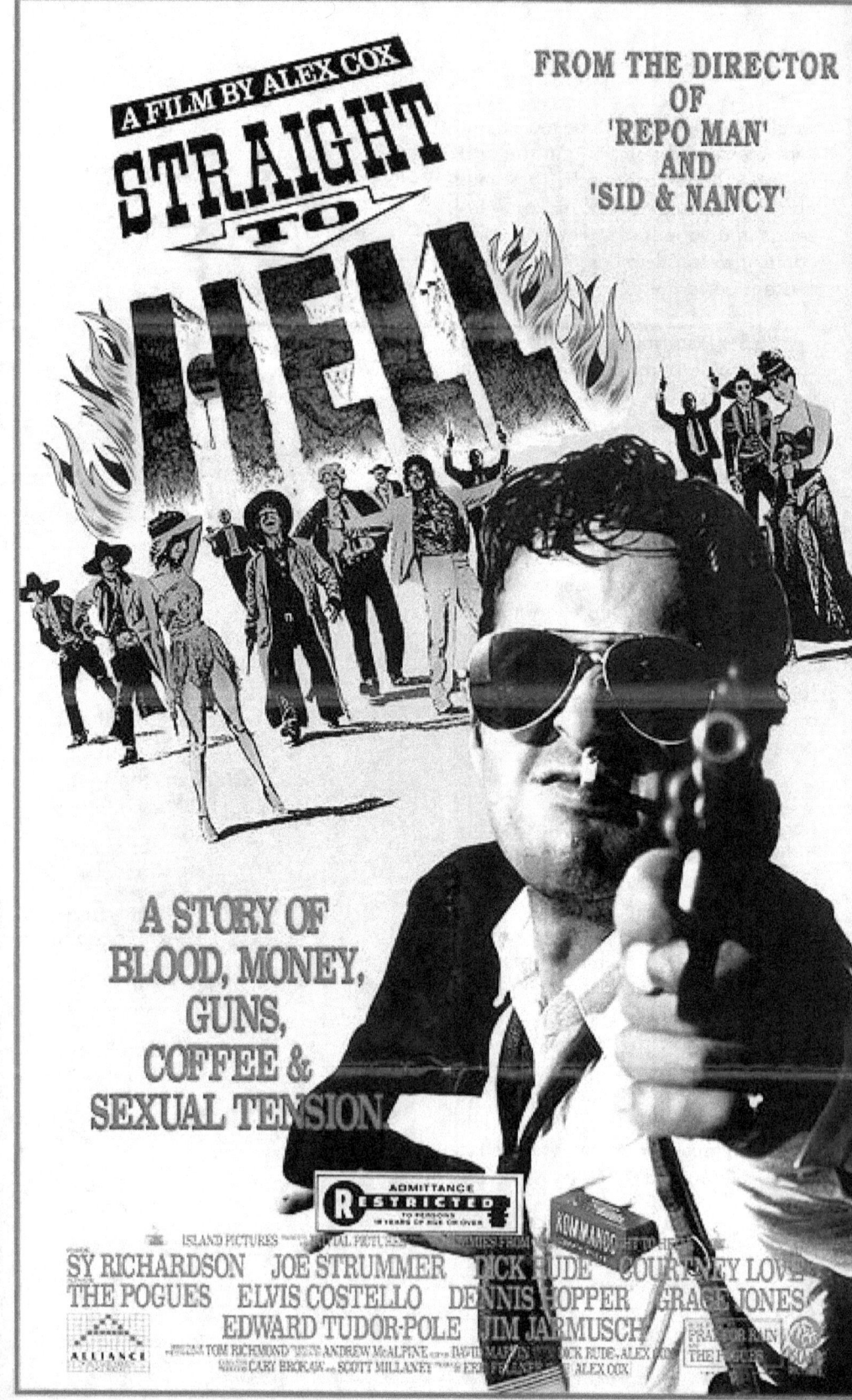

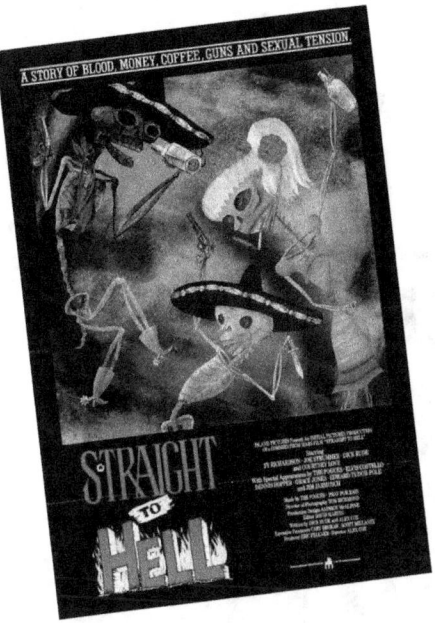

"They look like coffee addicts to me, boys..."

STRAIGHT TO HELL (1987)

A word of caution – I have an unhealthy affection for this movie. It is not for everyone. Viewer discretion is advised.

Very quickly, a trio of hitmen evade authorities after a botched job and end up in a town ruled by a sadistic family addicted to coffee and cruelty. But that doesn't begin to explain *Straight to Hell*, the same way "some repo men search for a Chevy Malibu" fails to synopsize *Repo Man*.

I first encountered *Straight to Hell* the way most people probably did: a lurid VHS with Joe Strummer in aviator sunglasses aiming a pistol at me, his smirking lips adorned with a cigarette. I was working at a video rental store in college, the film may have just come out on tape, and somehow it followed me home. Perhaps it was on the strength of *Repo Man*, perhaps it was the French New Wave allure of Joe Strummer doing a Jean Paul Belmondo. What followed was a combination of British surrealist comedy and spaghetti western, starring British punk icons, with sex and violence and no swearing. Repeat viewings only served to permanently etch the dialog into my subconscious, and I spread the disease to my filmmaking friend Troy.

The film emerged out of a benefit concert in 1985 for the FSLN (Sandinista National Liberation Front) in Nicaragua and against the US-backed war there. The concert featured The Pogues, Joe Strummer, and Elvis Costello, and played to a packed house at The Fridge, a movie-theater-turned nightclub in Brixton in which Strummer was an investor. Strummer proposed a follow-up concert in Nicaragua, which Alex Cox would film and release on videocassette; they could presell the tape to pay for the trip. All the companies that producer Eric Fellner shopped it to said no, but the bands had already committed to keeping a month open for the tour.

Fellner came back with the proposal to do a feature instead, which they could sell on the strength of the rock stars and promote on the back of the success of *Repo Man* and *Sid & Nancy*. Strummer and Cox had recently been to Almeria, Spain, to shoot a promo video for his *Sid & Nancy* track "Love Kills," in which a bearded, bedraggled Gary Oldman wanders into a Mexican town run by an Elvis-obsessed military leader (Strummer). The idea of a spaghetti western appealed to Cox, although given the acting chops of the musicians he wisely doubted Strummer's hope that it could be played dead serious.

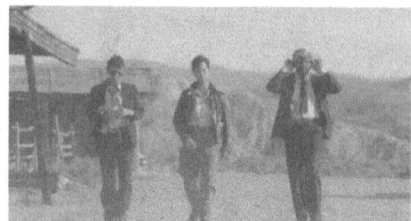

Dick Rude and Alex Cox took up residence in an LA hotel to write the screenplay, which emerged from the question, "who would the hero be?"

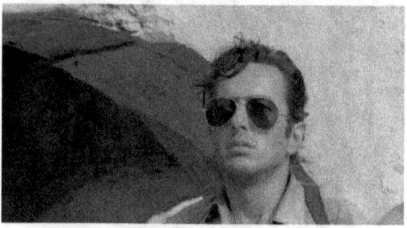

"Joe was the obvious candidate, but he was an untried actor whose enormous stage charisma might not translate onto film. The Pogues were innate rivals: the group would kill any of its cohorts rather than let him play the lead. Elvis (Costello) had a great look, but it wasn't the square-chinned, pale-eyed killer of Eastwood, Franco Nero, or Henry Fonda. Should an actor play the lead? Sy Richardson was the obvious protagonist: commanding, credible, experienced. But he wasn't one of the rock'n'rollers. Unknown to me, he was currently working as a bank manager."

-- ALEX COX

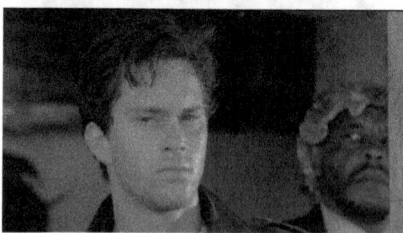

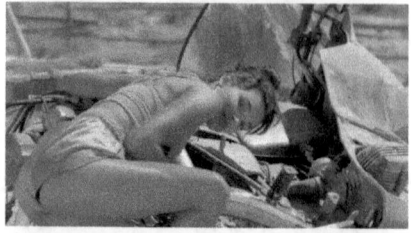

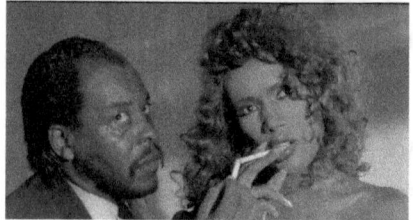

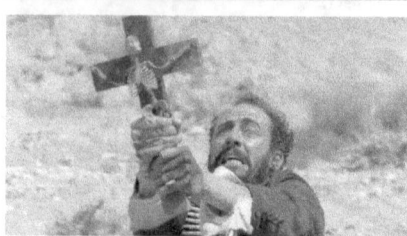

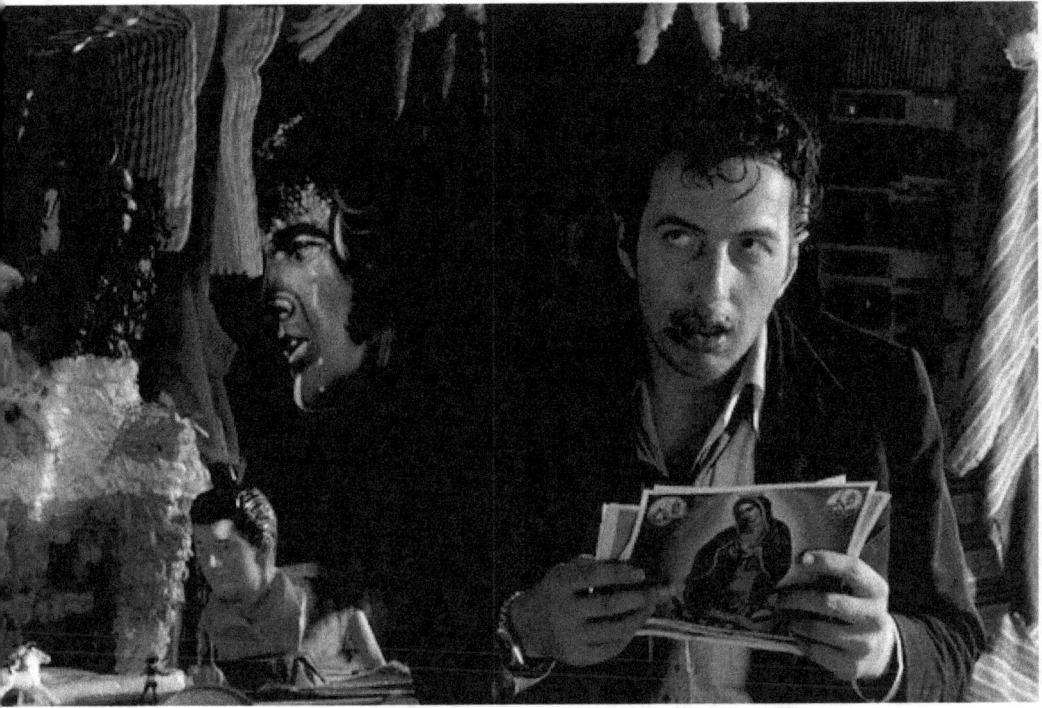

In the writer's hotel room, Cox and Rude drank bad coffee and stared at one of the hotel's bikini-clad, perpetually suntanning denizens. And, for some reason, the resulting screenplay melds the classic themes of the western with coffee addiction and unreleased sexual tension.

A strong initial image – the killers parked outside the hotel pool – had come from the trip to Cannes to promote *Sid & Nancy*, when Dick Rude and Joe Strummer hung out poolside in black suits after an all-nighter.

The script emerged in three days, which is not terribly surprising, when you consider it is the sum of some long-brewing ideas and writing to the strengths of the actors they had. And in a few ways they were saddled with keeping folks happy. They were asked to include a part for Grace Jones and Dennis Hopper, amends would have to be made to Dick Rude for having lost the lead on *Repo Man*, and his Repo co-star Zander Schloss had his own demands. As if that weren't enough, the film also had to contain the considerable and emerging screen presence of one Courtney Love.

The film is shot in an area of Almeria where there were several standing sets built for the Italian western boom of the 1960s, all right off a freeway that can be seen in the background of most wide shots.

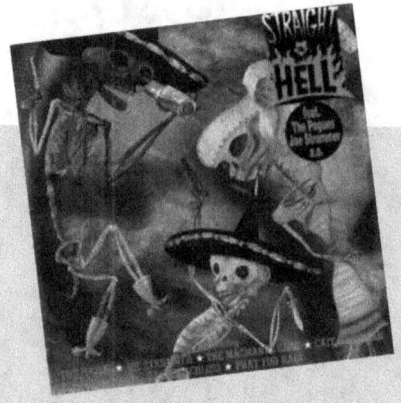

SOUNDTRACK

The Good, The Bad And The Ugly
The Pogues

Rake at the Gates of Hell
The Pogues

If I Should Fall From Grace With God
The Pogues

Rabinga
The Pogues

Evil Darling
Joe Strummer

Big Nothing
The McManus Gang

Money, Guns and Coffee
Pray For Rain

Ambush At Mystery Rock
Joe Strummer

Salsa Y Ketchup
Zander Schloss

The Killers
Pray For Rain

Danny Boy
The Pogues, Cait O'Riordan

While one might think such a shoot would be a like an extended vacation with a bunch of rock stars, the truth was somewhat difference. The abuse that Zander Schloss withstood as Weiner Boy Karl soon became too real, writhing in burning coals and the like, and the actor asked for some kind of restitution. Rude and Cox ran through some options, and settled on a redemptive death scene and and implied sex scene.

Strummer dispells any romance about filmmaking: "People think, "oh, what a lark," but at 6am every day, for three weeks and six days. Everyone was on set, in the middle of the blazing desert, wearing full clothing like suits and stuff. And working till sundown. And back on the set at 6am. Sometimes some of The Pogues would fall asleep drunk in the gulley. We wouldn't be able to find them and they'd just sleep in the gullies all night, and we'd find them the next day. I mean it was a pretty wild set, but people worked really hard and for scale pay."

Contrary to expectation, the main crew remained drug-free the whole time, according to cinematographer Tom Richmond, who relished the "little kids in a sandbox" mentality, coupled with the freedom: "we could do whatever we want, fast and on time and it looks beautiful." Del Zamora and Luis Contreras said that some actors were upset when they found there wasn't any cocaine on set, but rather plenty of wine and coffee. Joe Strummer's despise of Courtney Love was genuine and well-earned, as she had a habit of talking during rehearsals and direction, something that grated on her screen-husband Richardson as well.

If the film is a musical at all, it's largely due to Strummer's influence, who kept adding songs like "The Weiner Song" co written with Zander and Miguel Sandoval, and the last-supper number of "Danny Boy." The score by Dan Wool / Pray for Rain is appropriately in the mold of the Leone westerns. The Pogues and Strummer provided songs and additional cues, including "Evil Darling," a Strummer song that didn't make it into the film.

The character's doom, which is sealed in three days in the final film, originally took four days to unfold. When screenings of the four-day edit were met with shrugs and a dismissive "not funny enough," the picture was shortened by about ten minutes. Strummer even proposed a reshoot and voice over, framed around Miguel Sandoval's character George as a survivor of the apocalypse. One Cox collaborator suggested the film be cut down to feature Strummer's Simms almost exclusively, which is an understandably tantalizing idea.

Alex Cox seemed on a typical Hollywood trajectory after *Repo Man* and *Sid & Nancy*, but it was not to be – he turned down the chance to direct *The Three Amigos*, and chose *Straight to Hell* instead. Cox stands by the film, noting its great Sy Richardson performance, "good music and photography, some demented and sadistic humor, and a sustained spaghetti western homage. But this was 1987: there was no vogue for jokey films about black-suited professional hitmen." So what do you think, did Quentin Tarantino knowingly rip off *Straight to Hell* for *Pulp Fiction*? Remember, he worked in a video store too.

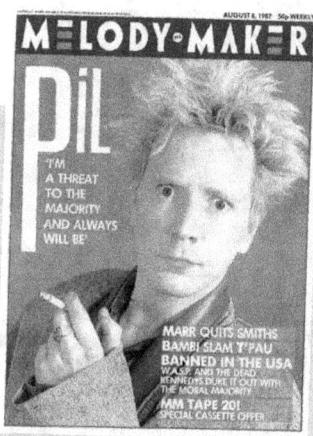

ROTTEN SPEAKS

"I cannot understand why anyone would want to put out a movie like Sid and Nancy and not bother to speak to me; Alex Cox, the director, didn't... To me this movie is the lowest form of life... All of the scenes in London with the Pistols were nonsense. None bore any sense of reality... It was all someone else's fucking fantasy, some Oxford graduate who missed the punk rock era. The bastard. When I got back to London, they invited me to a screening. So I went to see it and was utterly appalled. I told Alex Cox, which was the first time I met him, that he should be shot, and he was quite lucky I didn't shoot him..."

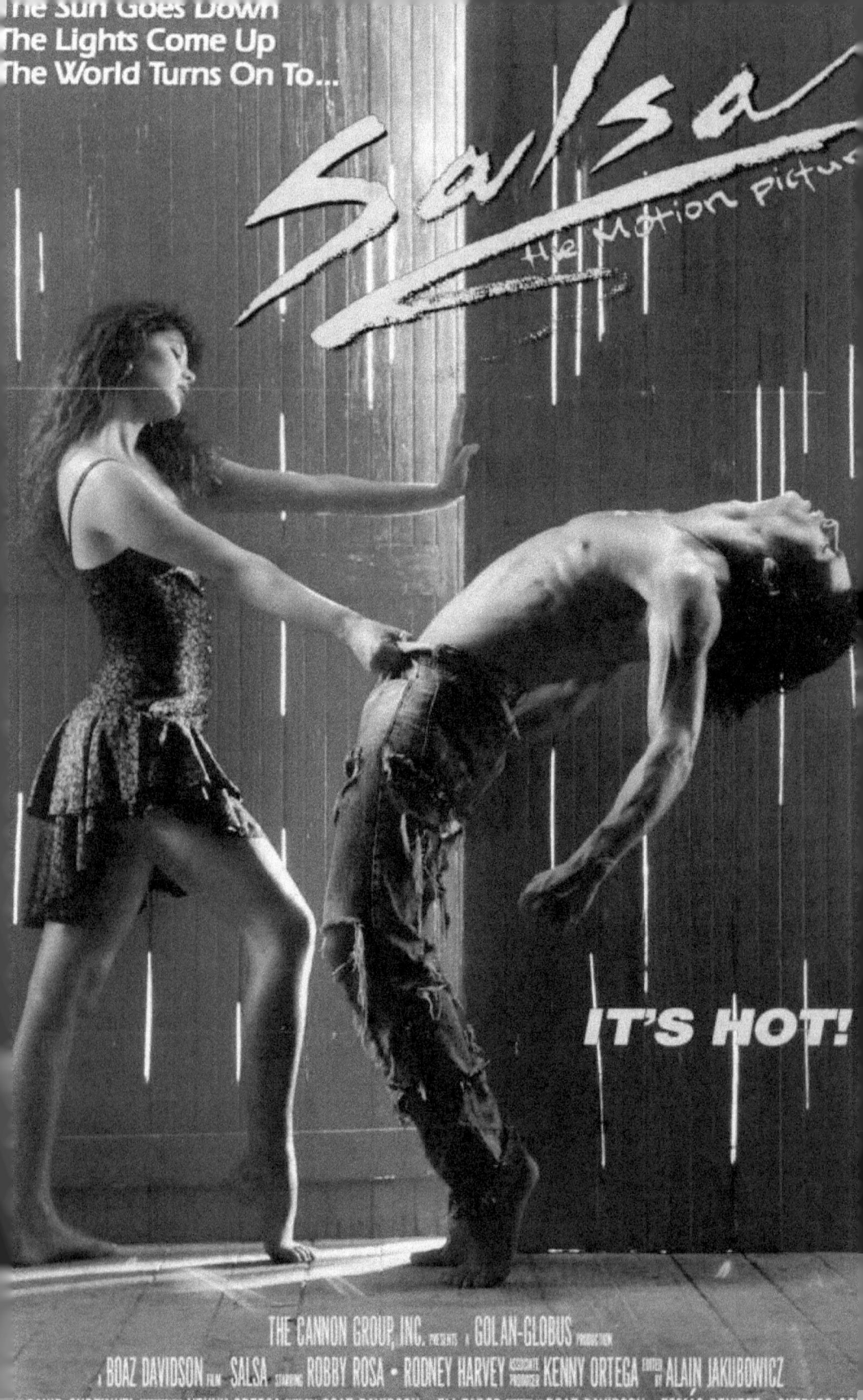

20

THERE WAS DANCING. IT WAS DIRTY.

Where Footloose and Flashdance were about the individual expression of dance, these movies know that the dance is merely foreplay for something else.

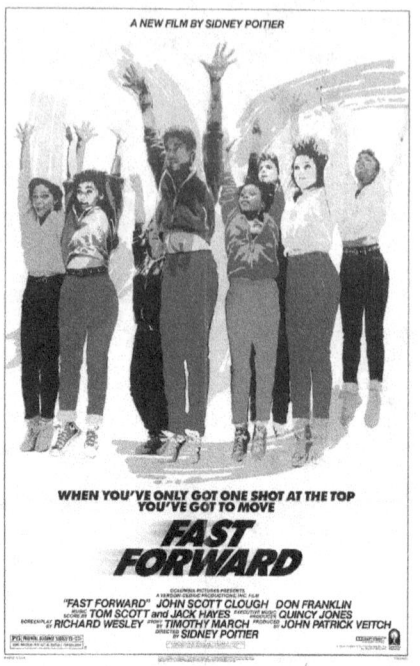

A NEW FILM BY SIDNEY POITIER

WHEN YOU'VE ONLY GOT ONE SHOT AT THE TOP
YOU'VE GOT TO MOVE

FAST
FORWARD

COLUMBIA PICTURES PRESENTS
A VERDON-CEDRIC PRODUCTIONS INC. FILM
"FAST FORWARD" JOHN SCOTT CLOUGH DON FRANKLIN
MUSIC TOM SCOTT and JACK HAYES EXECUTIVE MUSIC QUINCY JONES
SCREENPLAY BY RICHARD WESLEY STORY BY TIMOTHY MARCH PRODUCED BY JOHN PATRICK VEITCH
DIRECTED BY SIDNEY POITIER

FAST FORWARD (1985)

Eight high school students from Sandusky Ohio are very serious about their musical dance group the "Adventurous Eight." For example, if the teacher takes a break in band class, they quickly whip out the song they're working on. After school, they meet in their abandoned warehouse dance studio for an illicit practice session. And after harassing an aging bigtime New York talent agent disguised as waiters, they try to wrangle an audition. The 3 white kids and 5 black kids agree not to tell their parents, hop a bus to NYC, and arrive at the agency, only to discover the old man has passed on and the company is in new hands. The new manager, Friedkin (Sam McMurray, Raising Arizona), tells them to come back in three weeks for a possible shot. Instead of returning to Ohio with their tails between their legs, they try to tough it out in the big city.

After securing a shared ramshackle apartment, they make ends meet by dancing anywhere they can, including a fancy restaurant, an upscale garden party, and the tough streets themselves, where they run afoul of a street/dance gang. A dance showdown at a NY hotspot does not go as well as they wanted (it looked like a draw to me), so the kids decide they need to up their game if they're going to compete against big city acts. They absorb "street" moves at clubs and work it into their high-energy, jazz and ballet-styled routines. Returning to the agency, they are given a firm "no" by Friedkin. They decide to take up the matter with the agent's widow played by Ida Sabol, who sees firsthand the young people's enthusiasm and skill. She agrees to help them, and sneaks them into the big talent show. She's been told to stay out by Friedkin in a contentious meeting, so she dons a black leather punk outfit and spikes her hair up, complete with blue tips, going to the theater incognito. Using her long list of contacts backstage, she gets the songs to the sound guy, the instructions to the lighting guy, and the microphone from the emcee. The Adventurous Eight go on stage and wow the audience, who demand an encore. Ida tells Friedkin she's going to resume her position and oust all the young guys he's brought on in an effort to return the company to her husband's original vision.

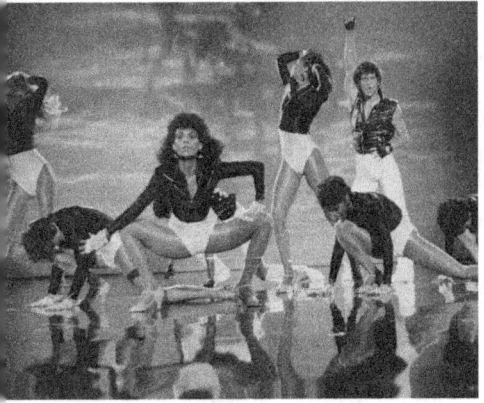
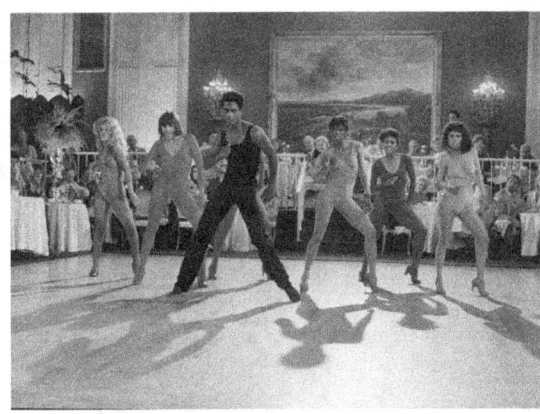

Fast Forward is light, TV-movie fun. None of the characters really emerge as the main character, and some get a little lost in the shuffle. The songs come with predictable frequency and are not as good as they should be coming from Quincy Jones as executive music producer. The real in the trenches production work of the soundtrack was done by John "Jellybean" Benitez and Narada Michael Walden (a frequent 80s soundtrack contributor). Siedah Garrett, known for her work with Michael Jackson (duet with Michael on "I Just Can't Stop Loving You," co-wrote "Man in the Mirror") handles the lion's share of the vocals. The closest thing to a music hit in the movie is the kids apartment, plastered with posters of Prince, Michael Jackson, and The Police.

Fast Forward was directed by Sidney Poitier, who'd directed several films and had a hit with Stir Crazy in 1980. He calls the film "as much about self-sufficiency as it is about dance, it is a movie about young people who have taken hold of their lives and taken responsibility," he said in Jet Magazine (3/4/85) "They go out using the pleasure principle of dancing, but they use it to mold their destination, to captain their own ship." In casting the film Poitier looked at 3000 dancers, selected eight of the best who could also act, most of whom would go on to TV and low budget movie roles. That the cast skews in favor of people of color is appropriate for Poitier, whose career arc pushed the presence of black actors in Hollywood.

Karen Kopins (Once Bitten) appears as the rich girl love interest. Boy George is mysteriously in one shot at a nightclub. But the hero of the production is the choreography, headed up by Rick Atwell and a number of others, none of whom had other film credits (except Felix Montano who would appear in *Earth Girls Are Easy*). The dance numbers, coupled with the harmless "aw-shucks-y" enthusiasm of the performers, make it a typical if forgettable 80s pic. Dancing, yes, dirty, no.

PATRICK SWAYZE · JENNIFER GREY

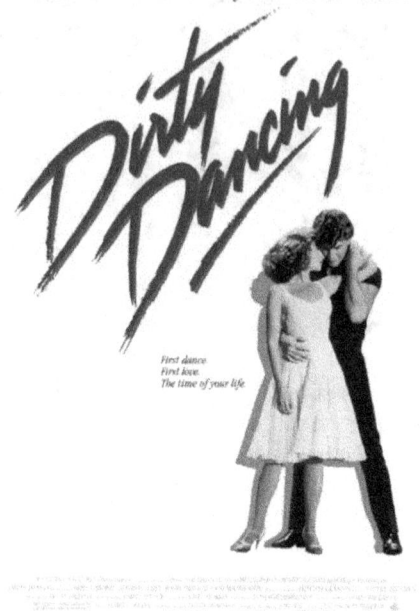

First dance.
First love.
The time of your life.

DIRTY DANCING (1987)

Sometimes you strike at just the right moment with a song or a film, and such is the case with the runaway hit Dirty Dancing, which was the first film to sell more than a million copies on home video. It's a period picture through an 80s filter, with a classic story that couldn't miss. Like *The Big Chill* and a few other 80s films, this one mined the 60s for musical nostalgia, but this one had its share of enormous radio hits too. Period film purists will balk at the distinctly 80s touches (that typography in the opening title is more *Purple Rain* than Bay of Pigs), and a lot of people must have imagined the chemistry between the romantic leads, but popular taste is hard to predict.

It's 1963, and the Housemans make their annual summer trek to Kellerman's, a resort in the Catskill Mountains. Dad is a doctor, mom is a mannequin, and they have two daughters with radically different personalities. Baby (Jennifer Grey) wants to join the Peace Corps and help in Southeast Asia (maybe a little early for that train, but good intentioned), sister Lisa is untalented and looking to score an upscale husband.

Baby wanders the resort grounds and gets swept up and swept away – the resort's dance instructor Johnny Castle is an almost-mulleted Patrick Swayze, hunky and bursting from tight-outfits; his dance partner Penny is a knocked-up Barbie doll that needs rescuing. Baby scores the money to pay for Penny's delicate matter, and volunteers to cover for Penny at a required stage performance with Johnny. Thus begins the requisite race to teach Baby how to dance. Given the amount of shirtlessness that ensues, you can imagine where that goes.

The film is set in 1963 as a sort of crossroads out of the idyllic 50s and into the turbulent 60s. Even the resort's out-of-touch manager knows that things are changing. It also marked a period when dance was changing from the ballroom-style hands-on approach to the 60s club-style of dancing a few feet away from each other. At the time, director Emile Ardolino told The Los Angeles Times "it's about partner dancing. In *Flashdance*, only women danced on that stage and they did it for themselves. Even in *Footloose*,

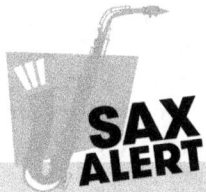

SAX ALERT

SHE'S LIKE THE WIND & TIME OF MY LIFE

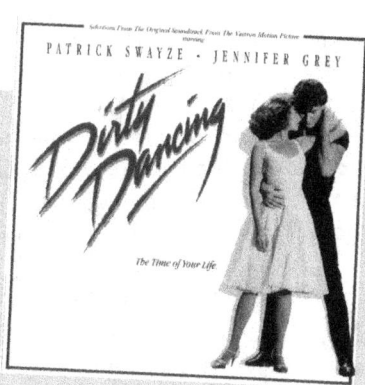

SOUNDTRACK

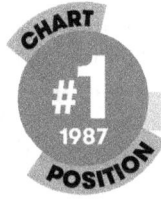

CHART #1 1987 POSITION

(I've Had) The Time of My Life
Bill Medley & Jennifer Warnes

Be My Baby
The Ronettes

She's Like The Wind
Patrick Swayze

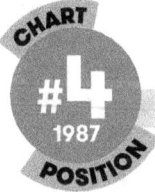

CHART #4 1987 POSITION

Hungry Eyes
Eric Carmen

Stay
Maurice Williams and the Zodiacs

Yes
Merry Clayton

You Don't Own Me
The Blow Monkeys

Hey Baby
Bruce Channel

Overload
Zappacosta

Love Is Strange
Mickey and Sylvia

Where Are You Tonight
Tom Johnston

In The Still of The Night
The Five Satins

the kids don't dance with each other. In *Saturday Night Fever*, the basic thrust was a guy being satisfied when he danced alone." Dirty dancing itself as seen in the film is a combination of Mambo and Cuban motions choreographed with spine-bending gusto by Kenny Ortega.

The film uses a ton of period-60s music to good effect, and the soundtrack album (and it's follow up

"More Dirty Dancing") is ripe with old standards and modern hits with a 60s streak. No one could have predicted that teenagers in 1987 would want a record brimming with old 60s tunes and Latin instrumentals, nor were the artists that performed the modern songs hot new acts – the biggest name was Bill Medley, the surviving half of the Righteous Brothers!

The entire music budget for the film was a paltry $200,000, less than most major labels spend producing a new band's debut album. Jimmy Ienner was the executive producer of the soundtrack, and had set out to break away from the mold of other mid-80s soundtrack records by not only embracing period-correct songs, but infusing the new songs with a 60s DNA. Ienner has said "we're dealing with 31 years of music in this soundtrack from '56 to present day, and we decided all the songs belong with each other, not segregated."

The album that would sell 11 million copies and hang on to the number one spot for over four months almost didn't happen, as Music Supervisor Michael Lloyd recalls: "The movie was being made by a new studio (Vestron Pictures) that no one had heard of, and the stars weren't big stars, so I couldn't get anybody to sing on it." That desperation for new material opened the door for Swayze himself to contribute a song he had written called "She's Like the Wind," which through association with the film did gangbusters business too. The gargantuan hit from the picture was "(I've Had) The Time of My Life," and when it was released prior to the film had withered on the charts. When the movie exploded, the song burst to life.

The Academy Award-winning "(I've Had) The Time of My Life" was turned down by numerous duos (Donna Summer and Lionel Richie, Daryl Hall and Kim Carnes), and turned down

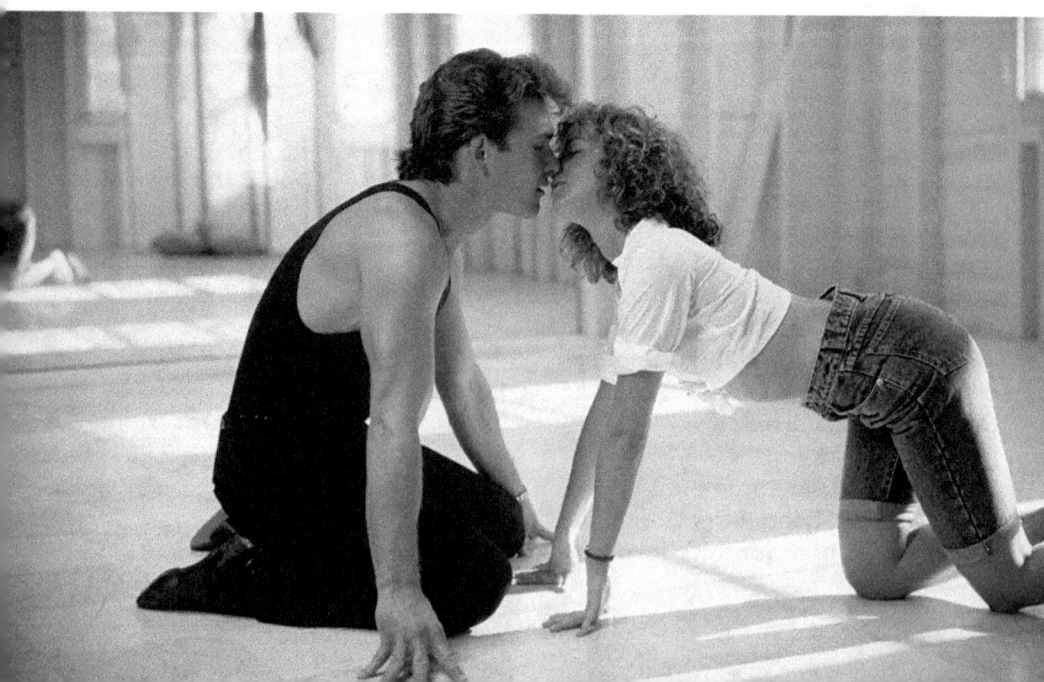

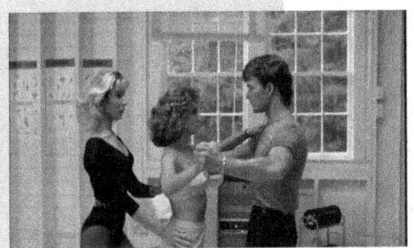

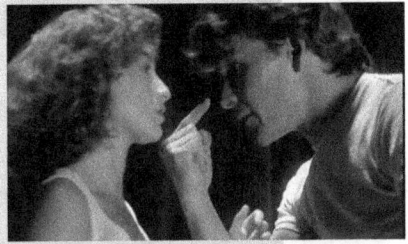

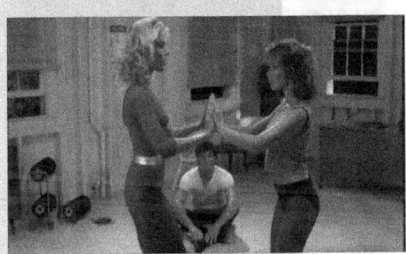

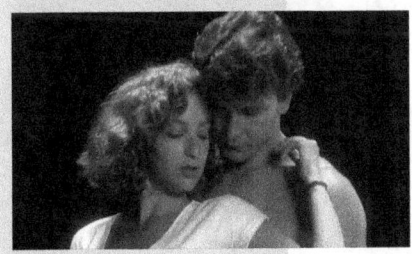

repeatedly by singers Bill Medley and Jennifer Warnes. Medley thought the movie's title sounded like a porno, Warnes was cautious about any song needing three or more writers. Song producer Jimmy Ienner cast the performances for the singers to type: "I'm kind of supposed to be Swayze on the record, and Jennifer's voice kind of fit Jennifer Grey's character," says Medley. "Jimmy really knew what he was doing."

The original songs have a different mix in the film: the guitars were dropped substantially to give them a more correct period sound, as the early 60s was a sound dominated by vocal and saxophone.

MONTAGE FROMAGE

"Hungry Eyes" Eric Carmen

"Head up. Lock eyes. Look, spaghetti arms!" Hmm, could be a threesome going on here.

**RATING
6/10**

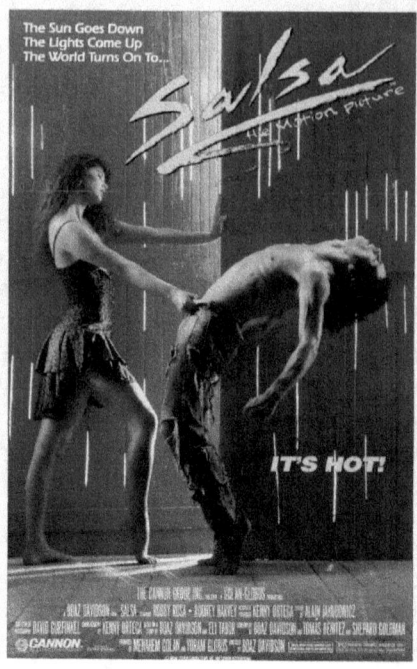

The Sun Goes Down
The Lights Come Up
The World Turns On To...

salsa
the motion picture

IT'S HOT!

SALSA (1988)

By 1988, Cannon had proven again and again that they could make cheap films, fast, that looked good and could be turned into a decent trailer. Cannon will never be accused of overthinking it. Inevitably disposable, yes, but like many exploitation companies before them they were capable of hopping a popular trend and releasing it fast (see *Breakin'*, 1984). Salsa is clearly meant as a low-budget response to the popularity of *Dirty Dancing*, and targets the underserved Latino portion of the movie going audience. It landed at a time when Cannon was reeling from the high-profile failure of *Superman IV: The Quest for Peace* and the underperformance of *Masters of the Universe*.

Rico (Robi Draco Rosa, formerly of Menudo) is a Puerto Rican mechanic who is in a perpetual state of enthusiastic exuberance. He dances when he works, he dances in the shower, he slithers down the stairs with a towel on and leaps on his piano. Rico constantly looks like he just won the lottery, except when he's having to play dad to his younger sister Rita (Magali Alvarado). She's a Catholic school girl who looks old enough to sneak into the club that Rico dances at, La Luna. Run by fading salsa dance star Luna (Miranda Garrison), La Luna is a cool night spot with freeway signs, neon, and full-size cars sticking out of the walls. Rico is a good salsa dancer, good enough to catch the eye of Luna, who sees in Rico an opportunity to win a prestigious dance competition one more time.

Salsa takes place in a world where ordinary people break into joyous dance without provocation, where shirts are frequently optional and hair is large and tightly curled. It has a harmless teenage sensibility (the dirtiest moment comes from an imaginary dance sequence perched atop a large travel billboard, in which Rico is grabbed by the junk and led around by his partner Vicki). Bad behavior includes eating ice cream cones on a motorcycle in LA traffic.

The film is pretty but filled with obvious padding throughout (a birthday party? A run to get beer for the birthday party?), but some of it is fan service with appearances by salsa celebrities like Mongo Santamaria, Celia Cruz, and Tito

Puente. Slightly weirder but relevant is Michael (Maniac) Sembello appearing on screen. Strangest of all is choreographer Kenny Ortega, unfortunately, an accomplice to murder in a cover song massacre of The Young Rascals "Good Lovin'." The inclusion of that song, plus Ben E. King's "A Rose in Spanish Harlem," does remind one of the similar 60s-nostalgia cuts on *Dirty Dancing*'s soundtrack. There's loads of music throughout, they were definitely looking out for that *Dirty Dancing*-sized hit, but in the end it's specialty music that would have a hard time breaking out in 1988.

Draco Rosa evaded the trap of some 80s boy bands, forming the brilliant one-shot band Maggie's Dream in 1990, capitalizing on the hard-funk sound that was popular at the time. He would provide songwriting and producing for fellow Menudo Ricky Martin, including "La Vida Loca" and "She Bangs." He returned to singing, putting out a number of successful, Latin Grammy-winning Spanish-language rock albums. Actor Patrick Warburton was a production assistant on the film.

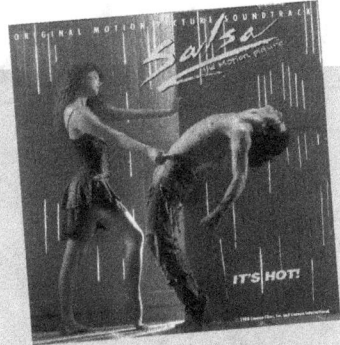

SOUNDTRACK

Margarita
Wilkins

Chicos Y Chicas
Mavis Vegas Davis

Cali Pachanguero
Grupo Niche

Your Love
Laura Branigan

Good Lovin'
Kenny Ortega & Chain Reaction

Under My Skin
Robby Rosa

Oye Como Va
Tito Puente

I Know
Marisela

Spanish Harlem
Ben E. King

Puerto Rico
Bobby Caldwell, Marisela,
Michael Sembello, Wilkins,
Mongo Santamaria

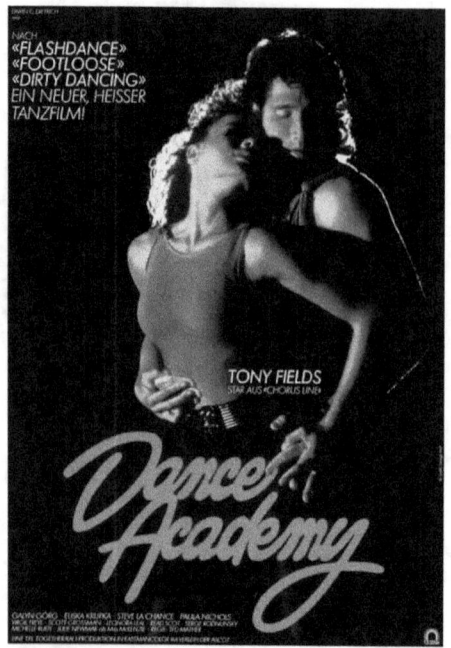

NACH
«FLASHDANCE»
«FOOTLOOSE»
«DIRTY DANCING»
EIN NEUER, HEISSER
TANZFILM!

TONY FIELDS
STAR AUS «CHORUS LINE»

Dance
Academy

DANCE ACADEMY aka BODY BEAT (1988)

While this Italian-American co-production looks poised to capitalize on the success of *Dirty Dancing*, *Dance Academy* appears to have been shot in 1986 (note *Crocodile Dundee* on the movie theater marquee) which makes the *Dirty Dancing*-like marketing a smart afterthought. Where *Dirty Dancing* traffics in plot and a hit soundtrack, this film's chief export is comedy in the first act (which fails to land any punches) and contrived, chemistry-free sensuality in the second. The matter-of-fact direction and an unimaginative script typical of a quick money grab results in a

lack of surprises and a lot of missed opportunities. Yet, I'd argue that any opportunity to get Tony Fields (*Trick or Treat*) dancing on camera is worth it, and while there's not much of him, he fairly ignites the screen here.

Fields is the cocky dance instructor David Bronson, also known in rock circles as "Moon." The edgy, volatile teacher (who's fresh out of jail!) has been chosen to head a jazz dance program at the once prestigious McKenzie Academy of Dance, run by Miss McKenzie (*Batman*'s Julie Newmar, sadly underused here). McKenzie has been running the Academy as a ballet school for years but has been overruled by the new owners, and immediately takes steps with her sycophant Percy (Serge Rodnunsky, a former member of the American Ballet Theater and cast member of *Cats* and *Fame*) to oust David by any means necessary.

The story centers around knockabout Vince (Steve LaChance, *Girls Just Want to Have Fun*), who we first see being fired from his job at a produce shipping company. Covered in crushed tomatoes and chased off the site by the foreman, he hops by chance into the car of rich dancer Jana (Galyn Gorg, *Point Break*). She's on her way to the Academy, and Vince has nowhere better to go. It's lucky for him – and for the prospects

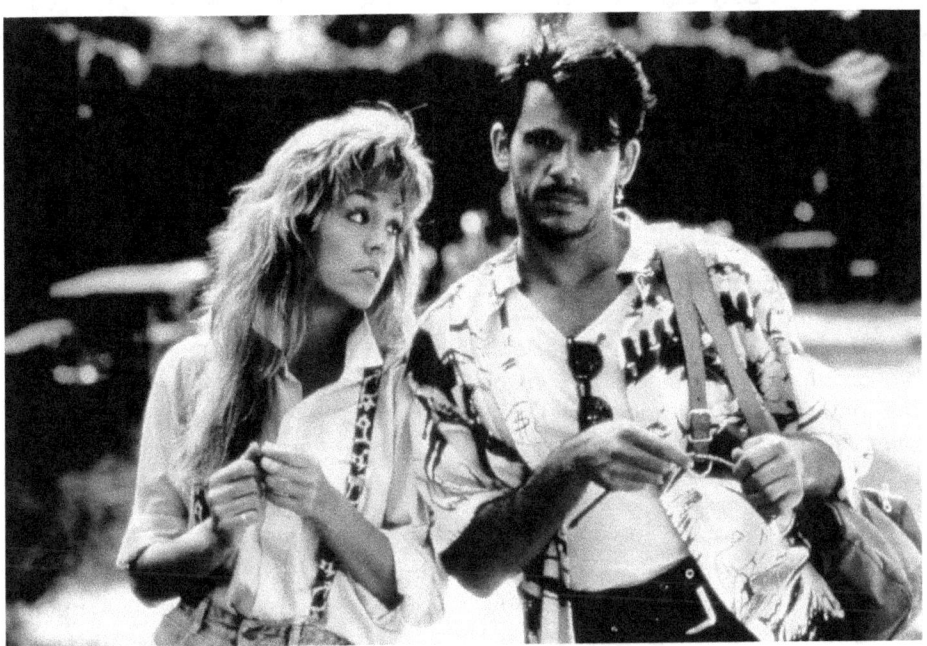

of the story – that he's a highly skilled dancer, whose martial-arts-inspired histrionics are pretty cool.

Students arrive at the academy and break into dance – and song, as one of the students, Paula (Paula Nichols) is also a songwriter. Before long the entire student body is dancing in the mansion-like common room of the Academy, including party-crasher Vince. Miss McKenzie calls a halt to the festivities and is about to throw Vince out on his ear, but David arrives and vouches for him, claiming him to be a pet project. Vince's piano-top workout seems to have sold the new instructor, and they're off and running.

The soapy drama focuses on a few characters, none of whom are fleshed out deeper than a simple sketch. Vince wants Jana, David wants Paula. Vince can't afford to take Jana to dinner so he snags a job as a valet at the restaurant they're attending. He sneaks out in the middle of the date to park cars, and it doesn't go well. The sentiment does not go unnoticed. When another dancer, Maggie (Michelle Rudy, *Captain EO*), wants to seduce Vince, she uses the school's improvisatory class workshops to take advantage of him, much to Jana's dismay.

David and Paula collaborate on a song, and record a duet together. The romance blooms. The filmmakers seem unaware of how songs are written, because as Paula seems to be writing at the piano, she plays along with a boombox with complete backing tracks already on cassette.

Finally, Percy succeeds in framing David and threatens to bring the evidence to the attention of the school's board of directors. At an investor performance however, the boys get their revenge by waxing his dance floors and lubricating his shoes, bringing his efforts to a halt. At the big Hollywood showcase, one big costumed number is the sum of the show. The performance is met with the customary standing ovation, and David is named the head of the new program.

Overall there's not much of a tone, swinging between teen comedy and adult romance. There's a strange running gag about people running into each other with enough violence to knock the person over, and there's a mysterious groundskeeper who trains chickens to dance. And the chickens wear pants. As mentioned, there's some great work by Fields, exhibiting the same swagger that worked so well in *Trick or Treat*. His tough dialog comes across like a young Travolta, wringing what emotion he can out of the sappy material. He is most convincing playing the tough instructor, and given his skill at the art one suspects he'd seen his share of that type in his life. Tony Fields actual name was Campos, of Portuguese origin, and he died in 1995 of AIDS-related cancer at age 36. Had he been in higher-profile films, I believe he would have emerged as a star.

The film boasts wall-to-wall music, mostly mediocre, and takes every chance it can to get people dancing, often with long uninterrupted takes that telegraph the film's budget but go a long way into showcasing the dancer's skills. There's one elaborate sequence that erupts outside of a theater on Hollywood Boulevard where the climactic show will take place, but any chance meeting or rehearsal is grounds for a number. For a music movie, however, there's often a disconnect between the onscreen action and the chosen songs, sometimes undercutting the dance performances when it's clear they were choreographed to a different energy of music. Most of the choreography is embarrassing but the dancers execute it with enthusiasm. No soundtrack album was released in the US, there were multiple European releases. Songs were performed by actor Paula Nichols, with further contributions by Ted Mather and Guido de Angelis, the film's director and writers. Mather would follow the film with a film that was sometimes marketed as a sequel, *City Rhythms* (aka *Dance to Win*) in 1989.

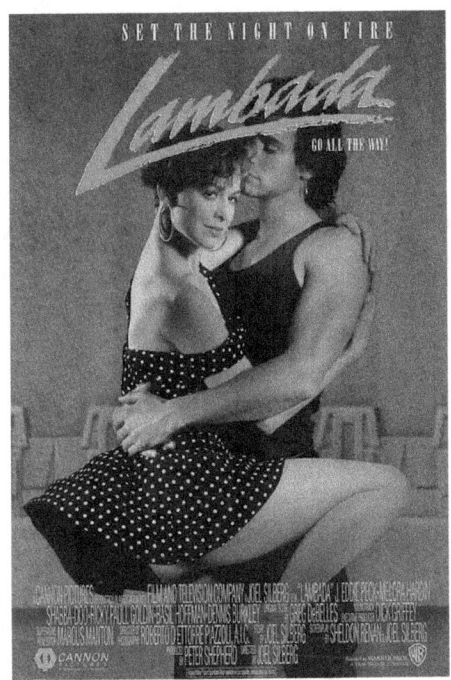

LAMBADA (1990)

Joel Silberg, the writer-director who brought us Breakin' and Rappin', delivers one of two lambada-themed movies to land in theaters on exactly the same day in March of 1990. The story of how two films fought for the miniscule audience of a flash-in-the-pan dance craze is more interesting than either movie could be.

Lambada was a sexy dance craze that emerged out of Brazil and briefly became relevant in 1989 with French pop group Kaoma's worldwide hit song "Lambada." That same year, as Cannon films reeled from its bankruptcy proceedings, Yorum Globus split from the company he founded with cousin Menahem Golan to form his own company, the (wishfully) titled 21st Century Film

Corporation. Cannon was taken over by Pathé Communications, where Globus remained. The two men would not speak to each other for three years; so fierce was the animosity that Golan was known to spit on the ground at each mention of Globus.

Cannon had made a career out of spotting a pop trend and issuing a film fast enough to take advantage of the "first to market" philosophy, so Globus rushed a lambada film into production. Meanwhile at 21st Century, Golan set about on his own take on the dance phenomenon. Was this a coincidence fostered out of years of working together, or direct jab at his former partner? Things certainly took a turn towards revenge when Globus announced a May 4 release date for his film, and Golan responded that his would be out on April 6. Then Globus petitioned the MPAA to refuse Golan the use of the word "lambada" in the title. Golan, now stuck with a lambada film without the word lambada in the title, countered by beating Globus to the exclusive use of the Kaoma song, forcing Globus to rely on a handful of forgettable knock-off tunes.

On March 8 Golan took out a two-page ad in Variety attempting to clear the confusion about the films once and for all: "I am proud and honored to have had the opportunity to create the one and only original Lambada film that truly depicts the lambada dance." In response, Globus announced that his film was coming out March 16. It had finished shooting on March 5th.

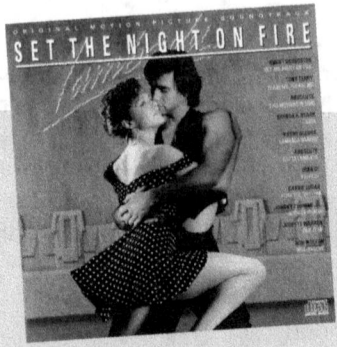

SOUNDTRACK

Set Night On Fire
Sweet Obsession

This Moment In Time
Absolute

Perfect
Dina D!

Tease Me, Please Me
Tony Terry

Lambada Dancing
Kathy Sledge

Gotta Lambada
Absolute

I Like The Rhythm
Carrie Lucas

Rock Lambada
Johnny Thomas Jr.

Wes Groove
Billy Wolfer

Sata
Brenda K. Starr

Give It Up
Judette Warren

In The Heat Of The Night
Soul II Soul

Surprisingly enough given the ambitious schedule, the resulting film is only narrowly less-watchable than the average Cannon film, and snagged almost $3 million on its opening weekend, probably from folks who had worn out their Dirty Dancing tape and were looking to recapture the magic. The poster for Lambada boldly claims "The Original" beneath a double tagline of "Set the Night on Fire" and "Go All the Way" (exactly neither of which is achieved in the film). It is only barely about the lambada itself and never ever sexy, which makes Globus' victory to the Lambada title a rather hollow one.

Mister Laird (J. Eddie Peck) is a mild-mannered high school mathematics teacher and loving father by day. But by night he leaves his family at home, dons tight jeans, a leather jacket and an earring, drives a motorcycle and goes by the name Blade (not the vampire killer). Turns out he's going to his "special job" at night – as a mild mannered teacher in a leather jacket helping inner-city kids get their GED. His impromptu school is called "Galaxy Program," and takes place in the back billiards room of a warehouse nightclub called No Man's Land (that, like other Silberg clubs, features a lot of automotive imagery, not the least of which is an upturned police car hanging from the ceiling, complete with rotating red lights). It's run by a big white biker named Uncle Big (ubiquitous biker-type Dennis Burkley), but attracts a typically latino East LA crowd who dance erotically in varying states of sweaty undress.

"What IS that," asks out-of-place high school student Sandy (Melora Hardin). "THE LAMBADA!" exclaims her amazed friend, as if they've discovered an exotic lost artifact. The central move of the lambada appears to be the male dancer placing his knee between his female partner's legs, followed by as much grinding as you can get away with before you are kicked out of the dance club. If the music has a dose of Brasilia-tropicalia, and you have no shame and four legs between the two of you, then you have what is required.

Sandy recognizes her teacher from class, whose athletic buns she was fawning over earlier in the day (it's a missed comedic opportunity that she doesn't first recognize him from from behind). This only serves to throw more fuel on the fire of her sexual fantasies about him, and she daydreams a sexy dance scene involving Blade, a motorcycle, and a vintage convertible. He's clearly a math teacher because there's no chemistry in sight – but now she's got it in her head that she must have him. Soon her implausibly horny actions put him in danger of losing his job.

J Eddie Peck was known for his work on the big three "D's": Days of Our Lives, Dynasty, and Dallas. Melora Hardin played Baby in the short-lived Dirty Dancing TV series, making her one of the more qualified people for the film, but is known for her turn in the US version of The Office. Adolfo "Shabba Doo" Quiñones does double duty as the film's choreographer and as wild-eyed heavy Ramon, a kid from the club who has "potential... College potential!" Alas, any potential for some good Shabba Doo choreography is squandered by clunky photography and editing.

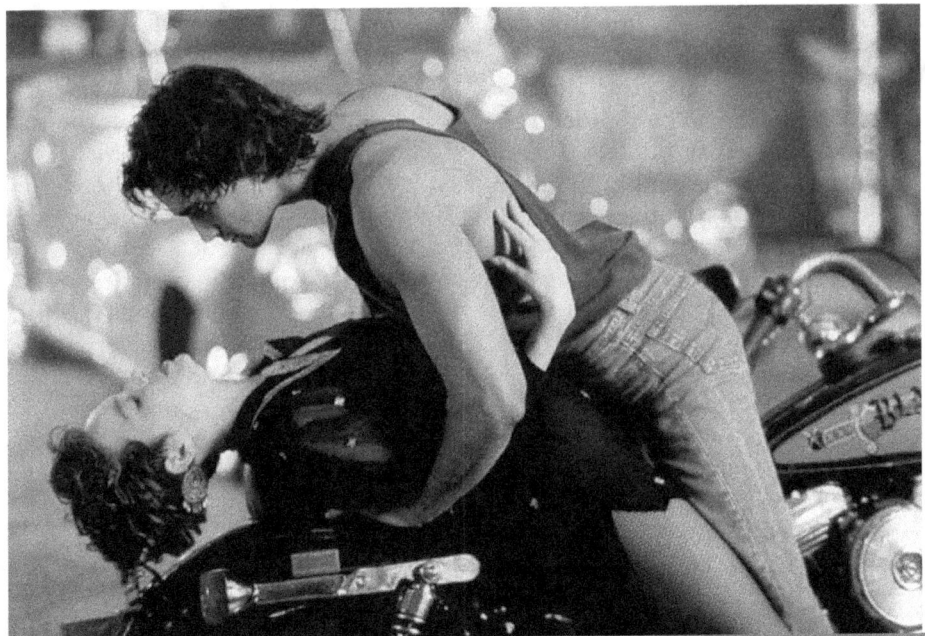

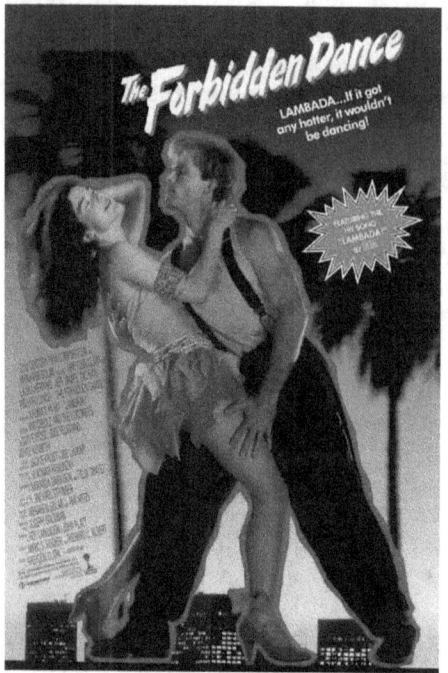

THE FORBIDDEN DANCE (1990)

Menahem Golan's take on the Lambada craze is even crazier, and therefore a lot more fun. This one positions the female character as the lead, and is ostensibly an action adventure film (probably force of habit for Menahem at this point) with a moral stance stuck between a lot of titillation and more than a little dancing.

Nisa (Laura Harring) is an Amazonian princess whose village is invaded by the sleazy Benjamin Maxwell (direct-to-video staple Richard Lynch). As an emissary of the multinational corporation Petramco, he's going to raze the village to make way for progress. His explanation is so on the nose it sounds more like a notecard than a finished screenplay: "It's a shame to clear this jungle, it's so pretty, but business is business." Nisa heads to the United States with her giant witch doctor pal of few words, Joa (the incomparable Sid Haig), with the hopes of convincing the company to stop its evil ways. Following a magical altercation at the corporation in which Joa shoots sparks around the lobby, he is arrested and Nisa escapes. Befriended by hispanic maid Carmen (Angela Moya), she gets a housekeeping job at the home of rich layabout Jason (Jeff James). To his racist parents' dismay, the 20-something Jason is always rolling in late after a night of dancing, and is about to get kicked out if he doesn't straighten up. When he sees the new maid partake in an earthy, sensual nighttime ritual to some exotic tribal club music (gyrating in a nightie, to be exact), it's off to the races.

She schools him in lambada ("It's not my type of music," he quips, "it's more East LA than Beverly Hills") and angers his on-again off-again girlfriend. According to Nisa, the government of Brazil banned the lambada fifty years ago "because it was too sexy," but it causes a stir at the the nightclub Jason frequents. His parents scold him, and fire Nisa, who finds a job dancing for money at a sleazy Hollywood dive. The club's owner Mickey (Miranda Garrison yet again) would be hit with some serious harassment lawsuits today, but before you can say "caramba" Nisa is billed as "Queen of the Jungle" and fending off horny businessmen.

Of course there's also a dance competition. If the couple can get on camera at the Kid Creole and the Coconuts show, they can bring the village's plight to the attention of the masses. One training montage later and the couple has their routine down, and when they get a chance to audition they get the whole crowd participating through the (magical jungle) power of Lambada. They're in the big show, but Maxwell kidnaps Nisa and forces her to dance for him in an abandoned theater. Jeff swoops in for the daring rescue, and like most of these things, the filmmakers check their watch and realize they have to wrap it up. At the show, they haul the king of the tribe on stage, Kid Creole declares the jungle worth fighting for and offhandedly tells the entire viewing audience to go ahead and boycott that darn company.

The script for The Forbidden Dance was commissioned on December 7, 1989, and five editors worked around the clock to meet the film's March 16, 1990 release date. This one definitely puts the exotica and action up front, in contrast to the unremarkable sister Lambada film. Soundtrack cuts are appropriately used throughout, and the on-stage antics of Kid Creole and the Coconuts are a good match for the material, with their Latin American sound, with a dose of Cab Calloway and LL Cool J thrown into the mix. Any similarities between the zoot-suited Creole (August Darnell) and Prince won't be accidental; around this time he was working with Prince on the Creole album Private Waters in the Great Divide.

No soundtrack album was released, but there's a semblance of notable artists, including Exposé ("Stop Look Listen and Think"), José Feliciano ("Lambada the Forbidden Dance"), and that Kaoma track everybody was fighting over which gets its own title card in the opening of the film. Arriving the same day as Lambada, this one took in a mere $1.8 million ensuring the end of the lambada craze.

MIRANDA GARRISON
OUR WONDERFUL, BITCHY GODDESS OF THE DANCE

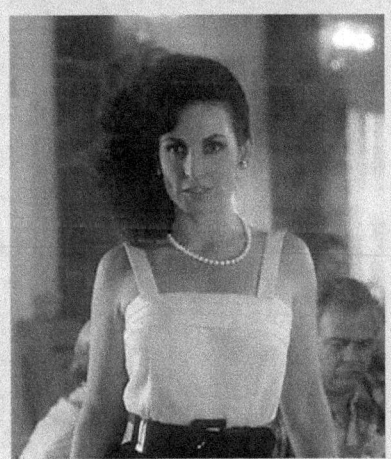

Dancer in Xanadu

As actor and choreographer: Dirty Dancing ("Vivian Pressman"), Salsa ("Luna") and The Forbidden Dance ("Mickey")

Choreographer on Selena (1997), Dirty Dancing: Havana Nights (2004)

FINAL TALLY:

Best Choreography: Dance Academy

Dirtiest Dancing: Lambada

Best Drama: Dirty Dancing

Best Dancer Male: Tony Fields, Dance Academy

Best Dancer Female: Cynthia Rhodes, Dirty Dancing

Spirit Award: Draco Rosa, Salsa

Best Soundtrack: Dirty Dancing

Most Eco-Conscious: The Forbidden Dance

Most Ritual Magic: The Forbidden Dance

21

MODERN EARTH GIRLS THAT DESPERATELY WANT TO HAVE FUN

In a decade dominated by female performers, it seemed a natural to make some movies that put the music from those gals front and center. Sometimes, even the singers themselves got in front of the camera.

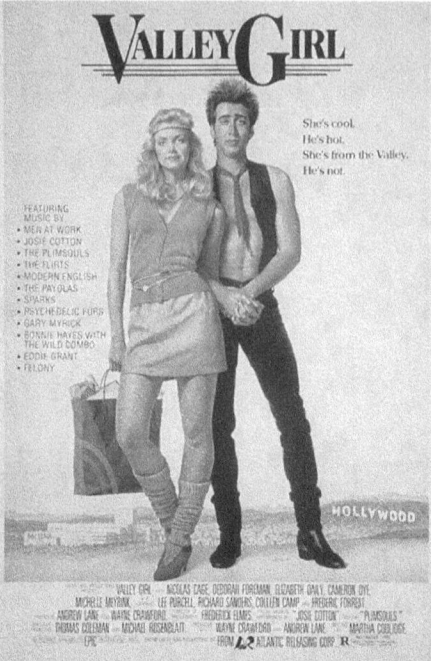

VALLEY GIRL (1983)

For a brief moment, the female denizens of California's San Fernando Valley were vilified as the worst the decade had to offer – shallow, ditzy teens with a shopping addiction. In 1982, Frank Zappa's song (featuring daughter Moon Unit) became his biggest hit and, like, totally defined the stereotype and the specifics of the vernacular, fer sure. While director Martha (*Real Genius*) Coolidge's film may have been designed to capitalize on the trend (Zappa sued unsuccessfully), it is a surprisingly affectionate retelling of Romeo and Juliet with little cynicism in sight.

Randy (Nicholas Cage) is a Hollywood punk who crashes a Valley party and falls in love with a Val named Julie (Deborah Foreman, *April Fools Day*). When Julie's on-again/off-again boyfriend Tommy (Michael Bowen, *Night of the Comet*) kicks him out of the party, Randy sneaks back in through the bathroom window and waits for her in the shower. He liberates her from the party and they share a night cruising Hollywood Boulevard with tagalong couple Fred (Cameron Dye, *Last Starfighter*) and Stacey (Heidi Holicker).

Unlike fated Romeo and Juliet, however, Julie's idealistic hippie parents (Colleen Camp and Frederic Forrest) are supportive and Randy's are nowhere to be seen, and the drama focuses exclusively on the social class differences of the couple, and peer pressure from the friends. The real message of the film comes from hippie dad Steve: "The point is, what difference does it all make? The way you look, the kinds of clothes you wear on your body… It's what you are that counts, what's inside you, what you stand for. Not what other people want to make you."

The Valley Speak in the film is handled naturally and with very little condescension, the fact that the girls are humanized and not plays for laughs legitimizes the drama. Any subplots that manifest do so without conclusion and are mostly there to crowbar in some sex scenes – director Coolidge was reportedly working with producers who enforced a quota of four scenes with bare breasts. There's a lot of laughs – a "driver's education class gone wrong" bit here was co-opted with some success in 1995's *Clueless*. Cage is adorably mopey

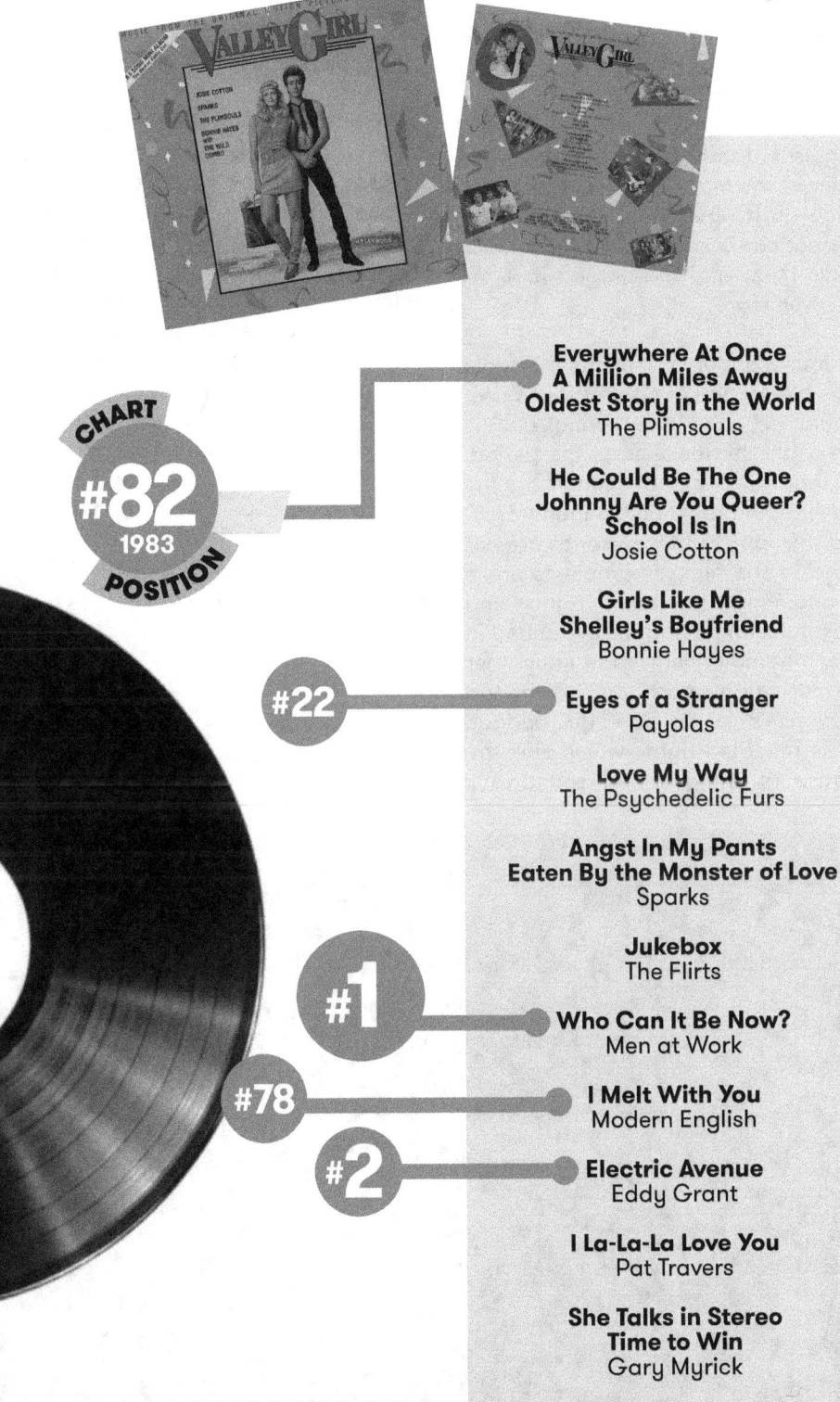

**Everywhere At Once
A Million Miles Away
Oldest Story in the World**
The Plimsouls

**He Could Be The One
Johnny Are You Queer?
School Is In**
Josie Cotton

**Girls Like Me
Shelley's Boyfriend**
Bonnie Hayes

#22 Eyes of a Stranger
Payolas

Love My Way
The Psychedelic Furs

**Angst In My Pants
Eaten By the Monster of Love**
Sparks

Jukebox
The Flirts

#1 Who Can It Be Now?
Men at Work

#78 I Melt With You
Modern English

#2 Electric Avenue
Eddy Grant

I La-La-La Love You
Pat Travers

**She Talks in Stereo
Time to Win**
Gary Myrick

as Randy; in true Cage form, he buys in completely to the role. When Julie turns Randy away, he starts inserting himself back into her life in various disguises (carhop at the drive in, usher at the movie theater) which lets Cage rip it up a little. The fact that he's not cut from the strict hunk mold works here, and makes you root for him even more.

Music supervisor Michael Papale does a great job of pairing songs with sequences, and the soundtrack is one of the better ones of the period. The end credits show songs by the Clash, Culture Club, Bananarama, and the Jam, but those songs are not heard in the film, as problems arose in acquiring the music rights and substitute songs had to be dubbed in after the credits were made. Altogether the music rights cost $250,000 on top of the film's original $350,000 budget. Those muddled rights would sink the release of the planned soundtrack album, and a six-song EP became a highly prized collector's item.

Quite a bit of music is performed on stage in the film: at Randy's favorite night club (The Central, later to be renamed The Viper Room), they see The Plimsouls perform a number of songs, including minor hit "A Million Miles Away." Retro act Josie Cotton performs at the Valley High Prom, and does their version of the Go-Go's song "Johnny Are You Queer," and "He Could Be the One." The film makes good use of punk band Modern English's only non-punk song and hit "I Melt With You." The song charted at #78 US in 1983 after it was first released. When Modern English re-released it in 1989, it did a little better, placing at #76.

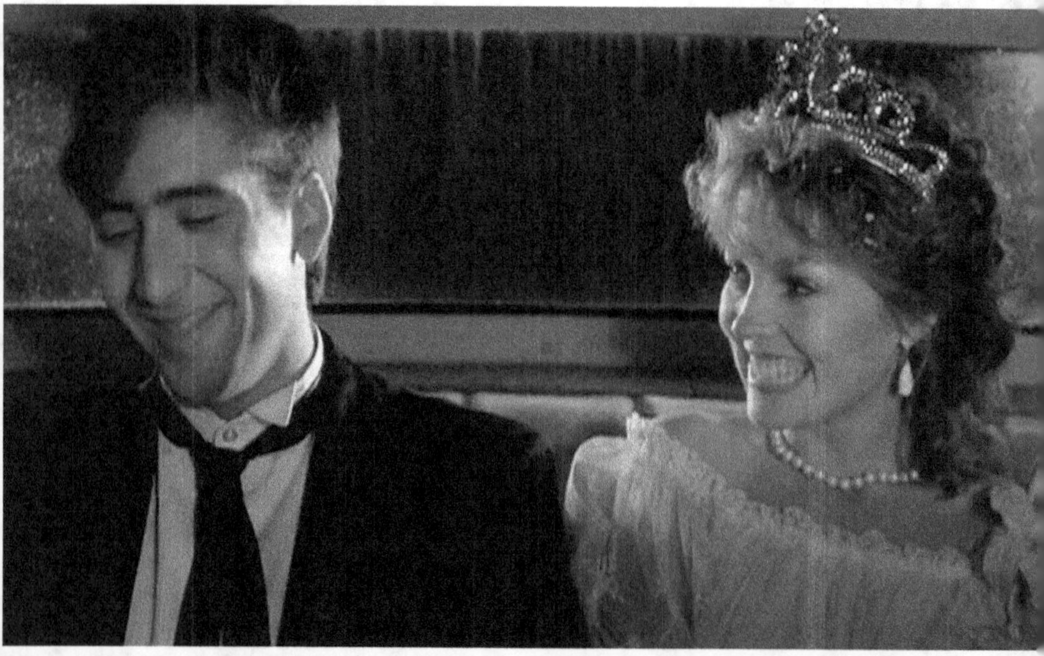

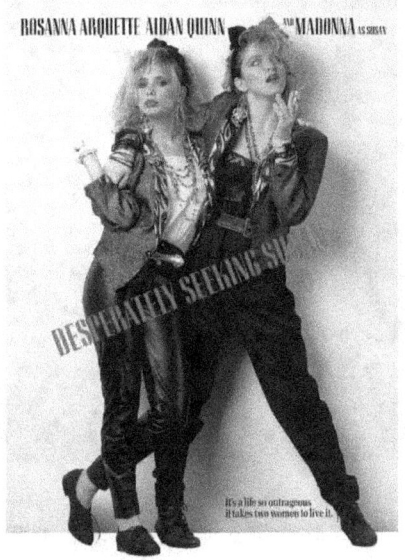

DESPERATELY SEEKING SUSAN (1985)

Madonna's iconic Manhattan street style erupts on the big screen and causes a deadly case of mistaken identity in Susan Seidelman's fluffy comedy.

Bored housewife Roberta Glass (Rosanna Arquette, herself a kind of 80s icon who, while dating keyboardist and songwriter Steve Porcaro, inspired the Toto song that share her name) is married to a rich hot tub salesman (Mark Blum) but is addicted to the personals section of the newspaper and dreams of a more exciting life. She follows the mysterious personal ads as one would follow a soap opera, and is especially interested in one name that pops up with tantalizing frequency: "Susan."

"Desperately Seeking Susan. Keep the faith. Tuesday 10 am Battery Park Gangway 1…" As she explains to sister-in-law Leslie (Laurie Metcalf), "You see, Jim follows Susan all over the country. Last January she was in Mexico City, and then Seattle. They send messages back and forth, that's how they hook up!" She imagines such a life to be romantic, and indeed it appears so when we see Susan, playfully writhing on the floor of her upscale hotel room in a distinctive pyramid-emblazoned jacket, taking Polaroids of herself while last night's mobster boyfriend is stone-cold crashed out in the bed. From a table littered with telling detritus (postcards from Atlantic City, playing cards, a bag of puffed cheez doodles beside emptied liquor bottles, and an incriminating but non-descript Polaroid of Susan in the aforementioned jacket), she steals some poker chips, and moves on to his suit coat. Helping herself to the contents of his wallet, she discovers a pair of enormous jeweled earrings which she claims for herself. She loads up her skull-bedecked punk-rock luggage and her petite red boombox and hits the road, but is spotted leaving by a sinister man (Will Patton) sent to kill the boyfriend. When the boyfriend ends up dead on the front cover of the local tabloids, Susan tries to lay low.

On the fated Tuesday, Roberta stakes out Battery Park and sees Susan meeting musician Jim (Robert Joy), spying on their long, passionate kiss until the money runs out of her coin-operated telescope. Following her downtown, Roberta loses Susan in a vintage clothing store. She settles for

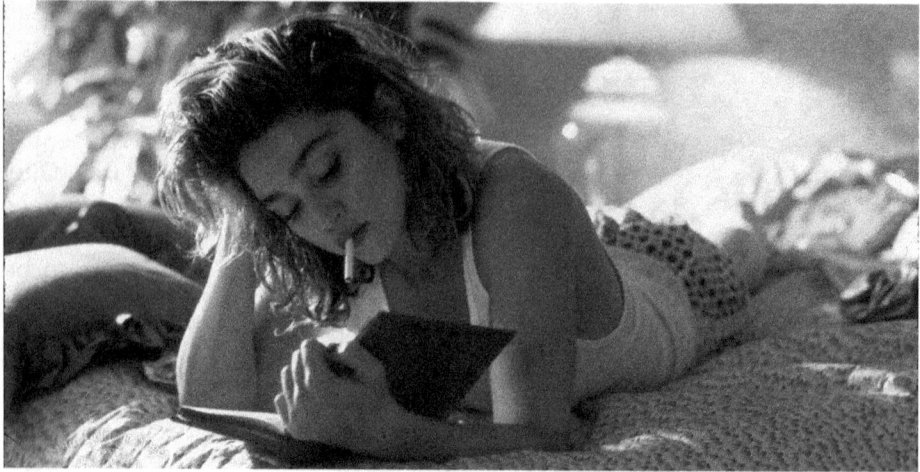

buying the now-abandoned pyramid jacket, which coughs up some clues, not the least of which is a Port Authority locker key. Roberta tries to lure Susan out into the open with a "Desperately Seeking" personal ad that is signed "A Stranger." The wording spooks rocker boyfriend Jim, who calls in a favor with movie projectionist Dez (an effortlessly hunky Aidan Quinn) to protect her. Soon everyone is looking for the blonde in the pyramid jacket, and a run-in with creeper Wayne (Will Patton) results in an amnesia-inducing bonk on the head. In a case of mistaken identity, Dez has Roberta believing she is Susan herself.

The film bursts at the seams with a veritable encyclopedia of cult actors ranging from comedian Steven Wright to Cohen Brothers regular John Turturro, with John Lurie and American punk rockers Richard Hell (of the band Television) Richard Edson (original drummer Sonic Youth) and Rockets Redglare (a punk scenester and bodyguard/drug dealer for Sid Vicious). Great

grungy location work with a touch of theatrical lighting elevates a film that veritably erupts with Madonna's undeniable star presence. Plenty of funny side moments and some nice directing choices can be found throughout, and the performances are uniformly engaging. While she was clearly the film's lead, Rosanna Arquette won the BAFTA Award for Best Actress in a Supporting Role for the film, and was nominated for a Golden Globe for Best Actress in a Comedy or Musical. Trashy-chic has never looked so compelling as when Madonna air-dries her armpits with an upturned hand drier in a bus station.

There was a bidding war for the screenplay, but once it was snapped up by a studio interest had waned. As producer Sarah Pillsbury recalled "When we circulated the script, only women and gay men liked it... But at the time, there was no female executive who could greenlight a movie." After a couple of years languishing on a shelf, Orion pictures set it up with director Susan Seidelman, who was fresh off a 1983 debut feature *Smithereens*, about a young woman in the punk scene.

At under $5 million the film was a cheapie, and at the time of her signing to the film Madonna was not a known commodity, with just two early MTV hits and a cameo in *Vision Quest*. More expensive actors such as Goldie Hawn, Melanie Griffith, Kelly McGillis, Jennifer Jason Leigh and Ellen Barkin had circled the role of Susan. Even less hip producers in Hollywood were suggesting Diane Keaton and Barbra Streisand, when the script was a little more hippie. Credit goes to director Seidelman for bringing in the young, hip, and New York attitude, and the film remains a snapshot of a lost New York.

Seidelman "pulled for Madonna — I knew her from living downtown," she recalls. "Studio execs had never heard of her, so Ed Lachman [the film's director of photography] and I went to Union Square to shoot her audition reel. I remember someone walking by, pointing at her and saying, 'That's Cyndi Lauper.'" But the confidence in Madonna proved smart. "On the first day, when Madonna walked down the street, only a few people turned their heads. By the last week of shooting, *Like a Virgin* had dropped and we needed security. Her rising fame overshadowed many aspects of the film."

Arquette was drawn to the female line-up: "I loved the idea that the producers, director, screenwriter, and studio executive all were women. I liked the fact that Roberta had a character arc, that she changed and grew." Seidelman stated at the time that she dealt with Arquette as an actor and Madonna as a personality, focusing on getting her "not to act, but to be." Mads herself said "Sometimes what

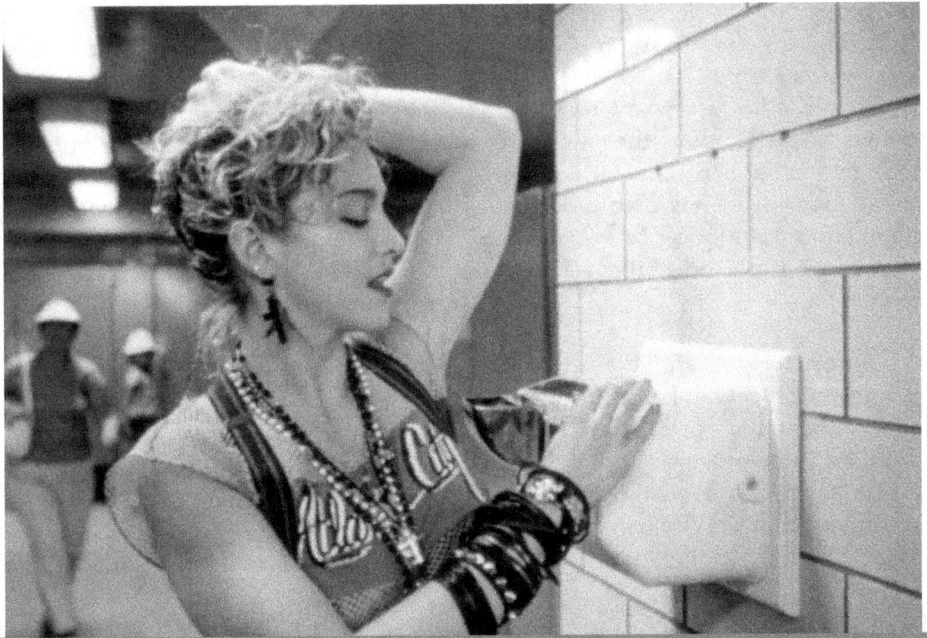

I do has nothing to do with acting — it's cheating for the camera while remembering to perform all these choreographic moves." Producer Midge Sanford remembered any on-set arguments with affection "There should be more crying on movies sets. It's the female version of yelling. People should feel passionate about what they're doing."

There were three major production crews in New York at the time: Woody Allen, Sidney Lumet, and Mike Nichols' gangs. Allen's group was the quirky one, and had just been released from *Purple Rose of Cairo* and became available for *Susan*. Costume designer Santo Loquasto rummaged through Madonna's closet to select some of her own clothes for the film. The infamous pyramid jacket sold at auction for $225,000 in 2014, and a single one of the "Egyptian" earrings fetched $34,000.

The studio had no idea how to market the project; some in the department feared that a poster with two women on it would suggest it was a movie for lesbians. A marketing genius seized upon the Madonna look and produced pins, lace gloves, and rubber bracelets as promotional items, and the movie poster with two women on it proved nothing short of iconic.

Surprisingly, there was no soundtrack album released, since the film prominently features Madonna's hit "Into the Groove" by collaborator Stephen Bray, a song that was later attached to *Like a Virgin* in its reissue. That song was originally intended for her New York DJ friend Mark Kamins to release with another singer, but Madonna snatched it back to put into the film instead. As there were already five Madonna videos in rotation on MTV at the time of release, it was determined that another new video would risk oversaturation, so the music video is comprised exclusively of film clips and was produced by Parallax Productions (a company that was among the first to specialize in movie-tie-in videos). Bray described the collaborative process with Madonna at the time thusly: "I've always kind of made the rib cage and the skeleton of the song already – she's there for the last things like the eyebrows and the haircut. She writes in a stream of mood really." This may undersell her contributions, however, as sections like the bridge seemed to flow fully formed from the singer (in which she uses her more natural lower register of singing). It may be a pitch-perfect 80s dance floor anthem, but it only reached 19 on the Billboard Top 100 in America. It fared better in the UK, where it was her first number one single.

Of the film, Seidelman rightfully defends the work, "*Susan* said you can be a woman filmmaker and make a commercial movie and said that you can have female leads in a movie and that men would see it."

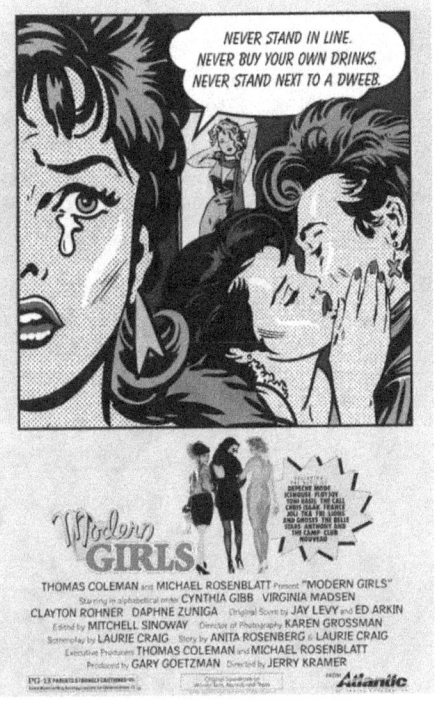

NEVER STAND IN LINE.
NEVER BUY YOUR OWN DRINKS.
NEVER STAND NEXT TO A DWEEB.

THOMAS COLEMAN and MICHAEL ROSENBLATT Present "MODERN GIRLS"
Starring in alphabetical order CYNTHIA GIBB   VIRGINIA MADSEN
CLAYTON ROHNER   DAPHNE ZUNIGA   Original Score by JAY LEVY and ED ARKIN
Edited by MITCHELL SINOWAY   Director of Photography KAREN GROSSMAN
Screenplay by LAURIE CRAIG   Story by ANITA ROSENBERG & LAURIE CRAIG
Executive Producers THOMAS COLEMAN and MICHAEL ROSENBLATT
Produced by GARY GOETZMAN   Directed by JERRY KRAMER
Atlantic

MODERN GIRLS (1985)

Three shallow young Los Angelinos live for the nightlife in this thinly plotted but music-packed film that manages to jam every genre of LA club between one sunset and sunrise.

Margo (Daphne Zuniga) is failing as a telemarketer, Kelly (Virginia Madsen) works a pet store and on sheer sex appeal she sells heaps of kittens to young men who don't want them. 80s-fashionable Cece (Cynthia Gibb) tries new wave makeup on the old matrons at her department store job and is promptly fired, but nothing stops these girls from their main goal of nightclubbing in LA's hopping underground scene.

"You do this every night?" "No, last Tuesday I had a cold."

Clifford (Clayton Rohner) arrives to pick up his date Kelly, but when the other girls learn Kelly's ditched them and left them without a car, they hijack Clifford's night (and his sweet but borrowed convertible). That Clifford is a dead ringer for edgy rockstar Bruno X (Rohner again, with different hair) provides most of the drama.

They find Kelly at the club, she has forgotten about Clifford's date and is caught kissing the the jerky DJ Brad (Stephen Shellen) before she notices her friends. Cliff is ready to bail but the girls convince him to stay. When Bruno X comes in the club, Cece literally throws herself at him from a go-go dancer's perch.

Kelly's attempt at reconciliation with the horndog DJ fails, but Cece wins the rockstar's heart before the cops break up the club for a license violation. Cece and Margo lead Cliff on a wild goose chase through after-hours Los Angeles in search of Bruno, and various adventures ensue. At a grim gothic club Cliffy gets a hip makeover that mostly consists of messing up his hair and clothes. Infiltrating a music video set results in Cliff getting recruited as a Bruno stand-in, but when the real Bruno calls to say that he's searching for the love of his life Cece, the video is cancelled and the chase is back on. Cliff unintentionally steals a bit of Bruno's wardrobe, resulting in some mistaken identity later.

Milo (ubiquitous LA edgy-weird guy actor Josh Richman, making wonderfully oddball choices with props) drugs Kelly, and while sprawling stoned on a pool table at a redneck bar she's nearly devoured by unsavory types, but Cliff rushes in claiming she's contaminated from a power plant spill.

The final club is a tropical voodoo themed joint, where Cliff is rendered drunk by fruity drinks and Kelly makes a last ditch pass at Cliff, to Margo's dismay. A run-in with slimy DJ Brad sets Kelly off on a round of bad judgement calls once again, hopping in the car of a strange man with a violent reputation. The gang rushes to the rescue, beat up the guy in a public fountain, and spend a while at the police station sorting things out.

Margo's search for the perfect guy blinds her to the fact that she and Cliff have the most in common of anyone in the movie. "I have my standards," she claims; Cliff counters "sure, no reason you should have to settle for a human being."

The female-centered screenplay by Laurie Craig does rely on men for its conflict, and resolution, so the film isn't exactly ahead of its time. Packed full of quotables and great songs, this is a comfort food retro movie to either embrace your lost youth or laugh at somebody else's ill-begotten style. Sometimes the questionable behavior of the girls looks scary

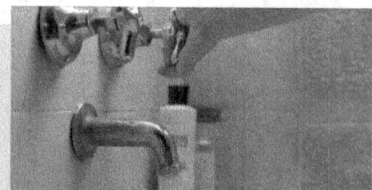
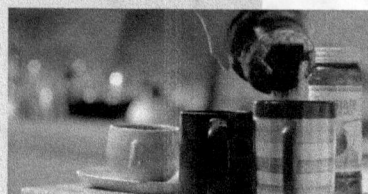
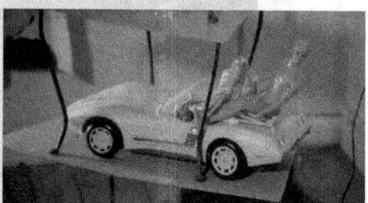
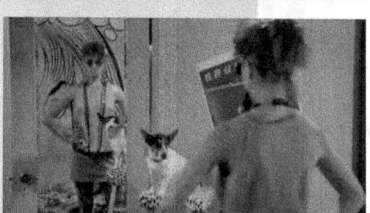
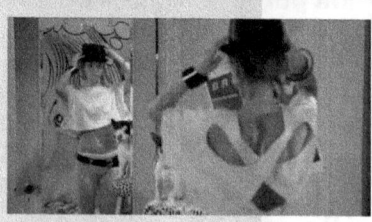

MONTAGE FROMAGE
"Girl's Night Out" Toni Basil

The ultimate getting ready mix. Toni Basil pulling a Madonna co-written with hit songwriter Franne Golde.

RATING
6/10

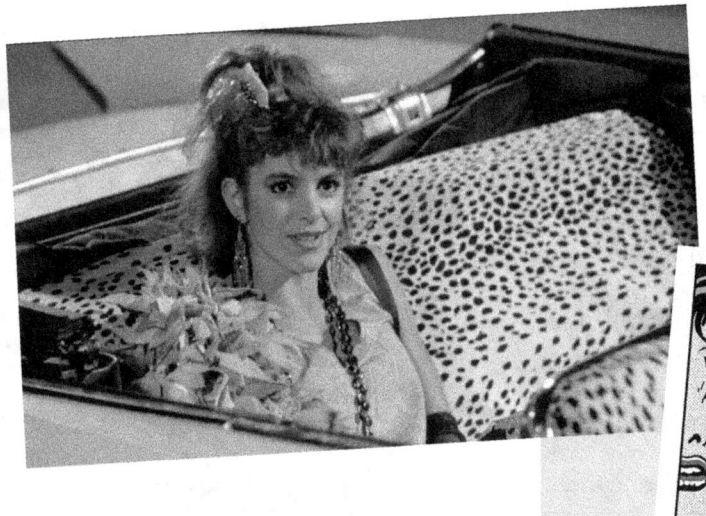

NOT ON THE ALBUM

Don't Think Twice – France Joli

Safare – Scott Rogness

Roof's On Fire – The Band of...
Blacky Ranchette

Angels in the Night – France Joli

Game I Can't Win – Dennis Quaid

Eyes of Fire – Chris Nash

Passion – Lions and Ghosts

Dancin – Chris Isaak

Bond of Addiction – Scott Rogness

Everywhere I Go – The Call

Something Inside Me Has Died –
Kommunity FK

Iko Iko – Belle Stars

Love Changes – Jackie Warren

SOUNDTRACK

But Not Tonight
Depeche Mode

How Many Lovers
Anthony and The Camp

Weak in The Presence of Beauty
Floy Joy

The Girl Pulled a Dog
Female Body Inspectors

Girls Night Out
Toni Basil

Concentration Breakdown
George Black

Jealousy
Club Nouveau

No Promises
Icehouse

One Way Love
TKA

Some Candy Talking
The Jesus and Mary Chain

through today's lens as they repeatedly put themselves in harm's way in search of a good time (one wonders if Kelly survived to see 1990), and the feel-good resolution is pretty laughable. NY Times critic Janet Maslin said "it might be worth putting in a time capsule, right beside *Ferris Bueller's Day Off*. Twenty years from now, no one will believe life was ever lived this way."

The girls live in a great apartment with decor that should have been anybody's hip design goal, and there's nice footage of Hollywood Boulevard and Melrose Avenue in the heyday. The casting director worked overtime to deliver nightclub extras that are a encyclopedia of LA styles circa 1985, and the rock and alternative-heavy mix of songs are among the era's best (if lesser known) college radio tunes. Pamela Springsteen, daughter of that Springsteen, plays one of Kelly's friends.

MODERN RULES

Q: Which of these is not mentioned in the film?

1. **Never pay for parking.**
2. **Never carry cash (Bad luck).**
3. **Never buy your own drinks.**
4. **Never wait in line.**
5. **Never stand next to a dweeb.**

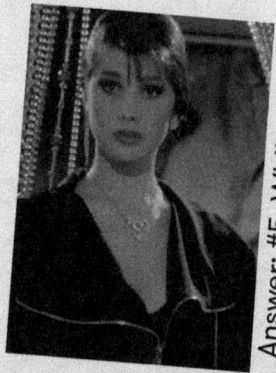

Answer: #5. While not in the film's dialog, it is on the poster.

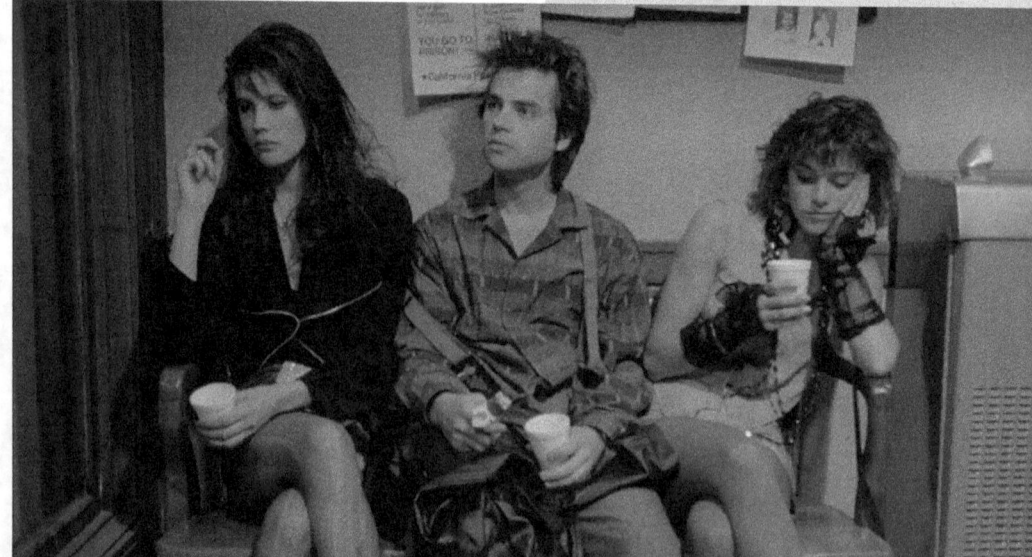

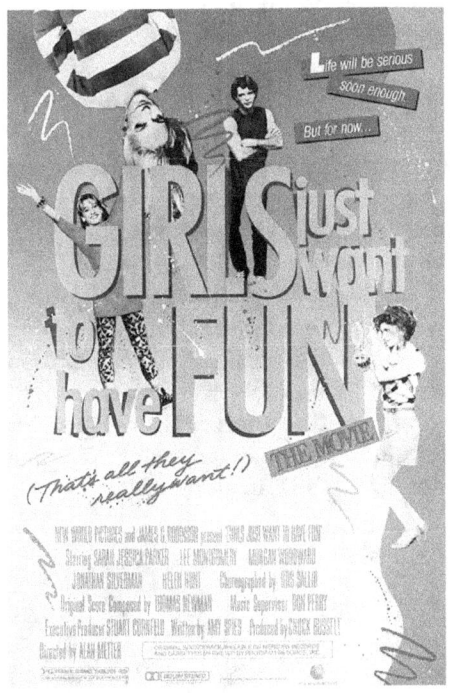

GIRLS JUST WANT TO HAVE FUN (1985)

Catholic school girl Janey (Sarah Jessica Parker) moves to Chicago, where her favorite popular music and dance program, Dance TV, is produced. Buddying up with class clown and troublemaker Lynne (Helen Hunt), she vows to get on the show despite the resistance of her military father (Ed Lauder, whose career is founded on thankless roles like these). Janey ends up paired with beefy boy next door Jeff (Lee Montgomery), whose bad boy muscle rock style contrasts with her gymnastics-dominated style. There's a chatty jokey Jewish kid (Jonathan Silverman, *Weekend at Bernies*) and a cartoonishly mean rich girl (Kristi Somers) who also wants to compete for the winning dance slot.

Many audition to be on the show, with a wide variety of styles unlikely to be featured on a trendy TV show. So much flipping and jumping figure into the winning dance routine that you would be forgiven for mistaking this for a gymnastics movie (the nun on the pommel horse contributes to the feeling as well). Screenwriter Janis Hirsch worked on Parker's new-wavey nerd sitcom *Square Pegs*, and the material here is similarly safe. But there's a subversive oddness that peeks in from the corners of the film occasionally, as when a punk samurai somersaults through the window of a teen debutante ball, unleashing a horde of choreographed punks into the fray. Helen Hunt wears a hat with plastic dinosaurs on it and a school uniform that can convert to cool by ripping off the velcro sleeves and reversing the skirt to the black leather version. The film features one of the most unhip looking night clubs in 80s cinema, with some kind of neon basketball theme. Hidden in the antics are Robert Downey Jr amongst the party crashing punks, Cindy Lauper in the diner, and Gina Gershon amidst the dancers. Frequent Alex Cox collaborator Biff Yeager (*Edward Scissorhands*) plays Jeff's understanding dad. The host of Dance TV is Richard Blade, who was the host of KTLA's music video program at the time. He has since become a keeper of the new wave flame for SiriusXM radio.

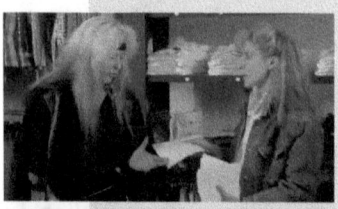

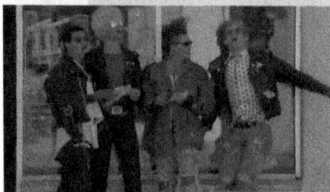

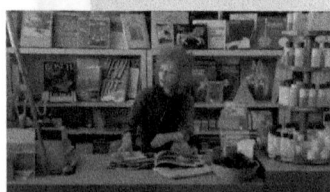

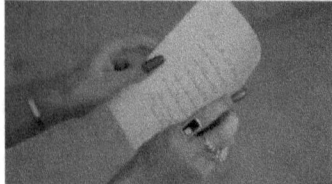

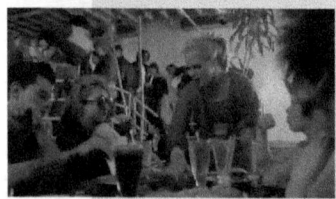

Girls Just Want to Have Fun was a staple on numerous cable networks for years, affording it much more exposure than it might have deserved. The title song is a loose cover version of the Cindy Lauper hit by the same name, and the other songs from the film are derivative or dull (one is a dead ringer for "Fame," complete with "remember remember" in the refrain). For a film about dancing, the choreography leaves much to be desired, but the framing action is harmless fun. If you were a thirteen year old girl when this came out, it might have been spot on (and prepared you for the slightly more adult version of the same concept in 1987's *Dirty Dancing*).

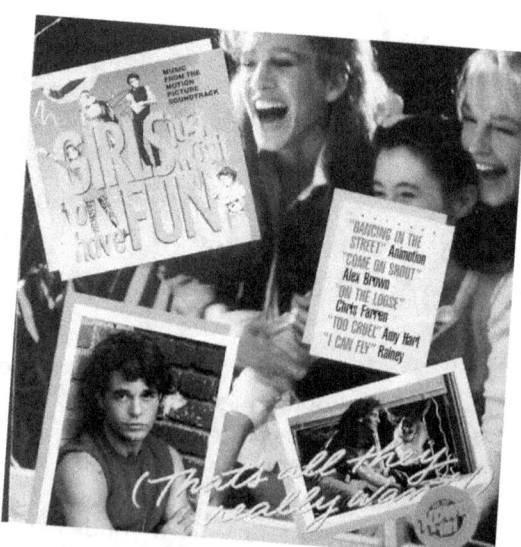

MONTAGE FROMAGE

"Girls Just Want to Have Fun,"
Deborah Galli (Written by Robert Hazard)

Punks, cross-dressers, shop attendants, female body builders, and an icognito Cindy Lauper are invited to sabotage mean girl Rikki's debutante ball.

**RATING
5/10**

LAUPER ALERT! WHEN ARE GOONIES GOOD ENOUGH?

Lauper wrote the theme song to the 1984 film *Goonies* with the simpler title "Good Enough," figuring that including the word Goonies wouldn't do it any favors on radio – and it didn't. While popular with fans, it was ignored on commercial radio. Lauper says "I was so bothered that they ruined the name of that song, that I refused to sing it for years." Producer Steven Spielberg had stripped a lot of the songs from the film (perhaps in reaction to what

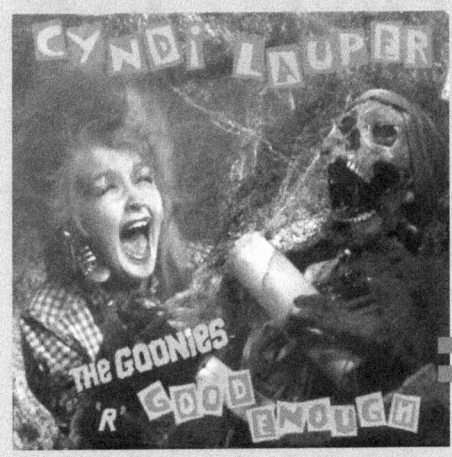

the rest of the industry was doing at the time), so even the soundtrack album lacked relevance to audiences.

When it came time for a promotional video, however, this one took the cake. Lauper had gotten involved with pro-wrestling at the behest of her manager/boyfriend, who saw it as another promotional opportunity. The massive, two part, adventure-style video was shot on the sets of the film and included members of the *Goonies* cast, but was built around a slew of the biggest names in wrestling. Andre the Giant, Captain Lou Albano, Rowdy Roddy Piper and the Iron Sheik all appear.

Spielberg himself appears between the two "chapters," responding to Lauper's call for help "Steven Spielberg, how do I get outta this one?" The answer, by the way is "well the first thing you sh---" before he breaks off sheepishly to admit "I don't know..." And among the pirates at the end of the video are the pre-fame female band The Bangles.

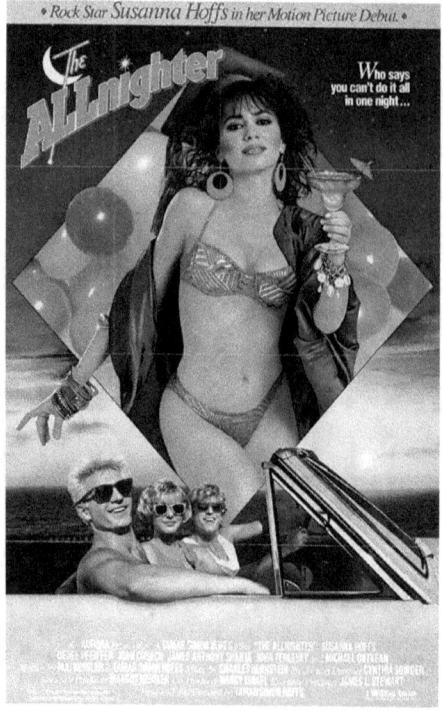

• Rock Star *Susanna Hoffs in her Motion Picture Debut.* •

THE ALLNIGHTER (1987)

Somewhere somebody loves this movie, maybe even you. Maybe it's because you had a similar experience at a California college situated way too close to a beach. Maybe Susannah Hoffs was your first crush, or maybe you're still crushing (okay, guilty). With its come-hither poster art and sun-kissed subject matter there was a lot of potential, but this collection of missed opportunities lands somewhere between a *Beach Party* movie and a PG-13 *Sex Lies and Videotape*.

Among those whose skills are squandered are the great Joan Cusack (Gina, an artsy student with no discernable love life), the impossibly cute Dedee Pfeiffer (Val, a party gal who's engaged to an overbearing golf ball salesman but is still playing the field), and that aforementioned pint-sized rocker Susanna Hoffs (Molly, the shy school valedictorian). That Cusack doesn't get to be funny and Hoffs doesn't play any songs are among the film's central shortcomings.

It's the night before graduation at Pacifica College. Molly regrets not having that one earth shattering collegiate romance, even though she appears to be romantically involved with Ken doll surfer boy C.J. (John Terlesky, *Deathstalker II: Duel of the Titans*). Maybe it's because he's distracted by bitchin' waves, and drawn to the beach by his philosophizing bud Killer (James Shanta), where the two surf and speak in that familiar, Spanish-laced Baja patois.

At the big end of the year party, Molly tries to tell C.J. how she feels; unfortunately he ends up being snatched up by Mary Lou (Janelle Brady, *Class of Nuke 'Em High*) before she can. But when Molly finds out that fading rock star Mickey (Michael Ontkean) used to go to their school, and used to live in their beach-side house, AND happens to be back in town looking for romance, she seizes upon the opportunity and meets him at his hotel.

Unfortunately for her, one of her school advisors is also one of Mickey's former flames, and the two cross paths at the Hotel Playa Del Mar. Molly ends up trapped on Mickey's hotel room balcony, and calls Val and Gina for assistance. A pair of overzealous hotel detectives mistake the girls for hookers and they're carted off to jail. Before the sun is up, many wrongs are made right, and Molly makes it back in time to give the speech at graduation.

At first blush, this looks like a vehicle to take advantage of Susanna Hoffs' musical popularity and make a kind of teen sex romp, what with the eye-opening key art and tagline ("Who says you can't do it all in one night..."), not to mention a long scene in which Molly prepares for her date, dressed down to her underwear and swaying before a mirror. But hold the phone: *The Allnighter* was directed and co-written by Tamar Simon Hoffs, Susanna Hoff's mother.

How did we come to this? Rewind to 1975: Susanna Hoffs attended the same preschool as the children of Ben Gazzara and Leonard Nimoy. Socializing with film industry people led Tamar Hoffs, a fine artist, to consider film writing. Meanwhile, young Susanna set her sights on being an actress, appearing in school plays. But at Berkeley she quit theater and earned an art degree because as a 5'2" brunette she felt overshadowed by the hordes of tall California blondes. "I wouldn't get parts because of the way I looked," she said, and

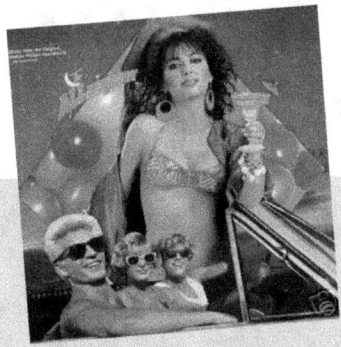

SOUNDTRACK

Dangerous
Monalisa Young

No TV No Phone
Price-Sulton

Love Is You
Redd Kross

The Girl in a Sweater
Hard-Ons

Respect
Funky Lips

Take a Mile
Louis & Clark

Boo Hoo
Angie Jarree

Dangerous
Exploding White Mice

Pipeline
Agent Orange

(Sittin' On) The Dock of The Bay
Chronic Disorder

NOT ON THE ALBUM:
"The Future's So Bright, I Gotta Wear Shades" (Timbuk 3) & "Respect" (Aretha Franklin).
Plus absolutely nothing by Susannah Hoffs. Explain that one.

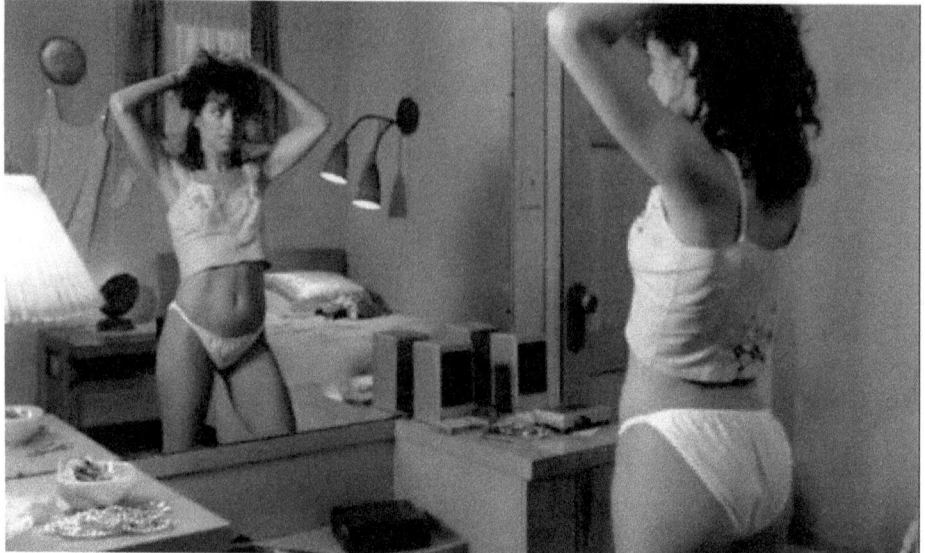

eased into music instead, connecting with the three Bangles (then The Bangs) through a want ad. "My father instilled a sense of creativity and adventurousness in me and my two brothers," Susanna explained, "but it was my mom who picked up on the fact that I loved to sing and dance when I was a kid, and she's always encouraged me. I think we've always known we'd work together one day."

During the making of the film (and indeed the Bangles height of popularity), Susanna was living at home, or more precisely in the converted garage. Mom Tamar Hoffs had made award winning short films and directed a handful of videos (including Bangles "Going Down to Liverpool") before making her feature film debut with *The Allnighter*.

"Movies are never 100% accurate because they're one step away from reality," Tamar told the LA Times, "but I think this is an accurate depiction of young people--and not just kids in Southern California in 1987. I went to Yale and the experiences depicted in the film are very much like experiences I had at school. In fact, the three female leads are loosely based on myself and my two roommates... There are certain stories you can tell over and over, and it's possible to have enormous amounts of content buried in a film like this. Being in school delays having to deal with certain aspects of life and these kids are still a bit innocent, so on one level the film is about the end of innocence. It's also about the relationships that develop between people when they live together at a certain point in their lives."

"I've always felt oversensitive to life," said Susanna, 27 years old at the time. "When does the rite of passage end?" When asked why she didn't sing in the film, she explained, "This movie isn't a musical, and it would've confused the audience if I'd sung in the film--particularly since that's not what the character I portray is about. I play a vulnerable, cautious, self-protective girl--adjectives that describe me pretty well, by the way. I identified with this character quite a bit. On the other hand, she's a beach girl and that's something quite foreign to me. Even though I grew up at the beach and love it there, I can remember looking at surfers and surf bunnies and thinking 'Wow! Who are these people?! They're so cool they're like creatures from another planet!'" Mother Hoffs may have felt the same way, and proves equal opportunity when it comes to fetishizing the surfer boys and girls in the film.

Add to the short list of disappointments the fact that the soundtrack, supervised by Mike Gormley (Bangles and Oingo Boingo manager) and Susanna Hoffs, is devoid of Bangles songs nor any of the members' spin-off bands. *The Hollywood Reporter* claimed *The Allnighter* "borders on child abuse," and The New York Times called it "outstandingly dim... The principals are three bubble-headed women who room together, and the film could be accused of sexism if their male counterparts were not equally dumb." I wouldn't go that far, but one can imagine what should have been; a teen sex comedy that let Joan Cusack cut loose, co-starring Hoffs as a cute, pint-sized rocker with a giant Rickenbacker guitar.

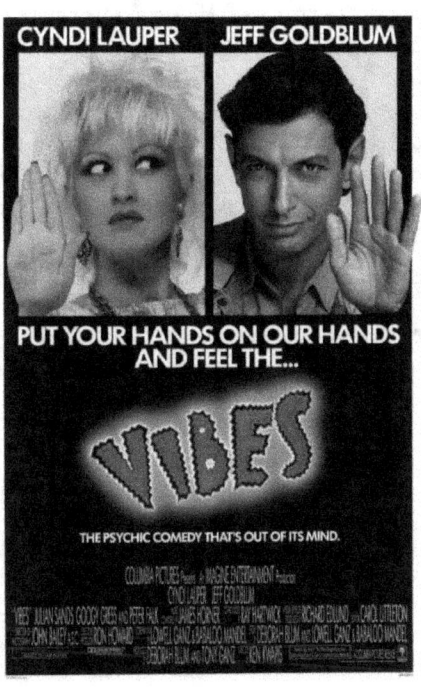

VIBES (1988)

Psychic Cindy Lauper takes direction from her spirit guide Louise and Jeff Goldblum's outsized hands can feel the history of an object in this comedy written by the comedy team of Lowell Ganz and Babaloo Mandel. The two writers made a career first in television for *Laverne and Shirley* and *Happy Days*, then as writers for projects directed by their alumni including Ron Howard and Penny Marshall (ranging from *Night Shift* and *Splash* by Howard to *A League of Their Own* by Marshall).

Nick Deezy (Goldblum) is a psychometrist, who can determine the history of an object by touching it. At the New York Department of Para-

Normal Studies Testing Laboratory (right next to NYU, one imagines it a business successfully spun off from *Ghostbusters*), he reveals the history of a series of knives laid out on a table, and then proceeds to the table ("Someone has had sex on this table," he proclaims as the scientists hurriedly wrap up the study with guilty expressions). His unsatisfying job as a curator at the museum is exploited by everyone in the building for their own gain, and his long-time girlfriend is having an affair.

Sylvia Pickel (Lauper) with the accent on the "KEL," is desperate for some lasting emotional attachment. She's certainly not getting any from gambler Fred (Steve Buscemi) as he uses her for betting tips and dumps her for Jennifer Balgobin (*Repo Man*).

Enter Harry Buscafusco (Peter Falk), who approaches the couple claiming to search out his lost son, but is revealed to be working with some unscrupulous treasure hunters who disappeared mysteriously in Ecuador. Despite being psychically equipped, the two bumble their way through Spanish Ambassadors and sexy hired assassins on their way to finding a lost city of Incan gold.

Shot in Ecuador (with a soundstage-based climax), Lauper told the director in her inimitable Queens accent, "Jeez I'm glad we're here, because the weather's nice, the food is great, and the coffee is sensational!"

The leads are good in a classic Hollywood-caper, slightly-theatrical kind of way, and the dialog is Marx-Brothers clever and similarly screwball. Character quirks (Goldblum packs his own water supply for the trip) are exploited and exaggerated (at a fancy cocktail restaurant, he sips from a five gallon plastic drum with a paper umbrella jauntily sticking out). Some *Raiders of the Lost Ark*-style effects are provided by the man who did the effects for *Raiders of the Lost Ark*. Even if it's a *Romancing the Stone* knock off, it does so on its own fun terms. The last act trades in some of the charm for some rote supernatural adventure action, but makes up for it with Cindy Lauper speaking in ancient tongues. Pop music is limited to a Lauper-performed end credits song, James Horner's film's score is appropriately South American tinged, full of ancient-world mystery and adventure.

As Lauper said during the filming: "it's funny, it's sad, and it's got mystery, I get to speak a lot of different languages, you know, the next language I'll probably learn is English, it's very exciting for me."

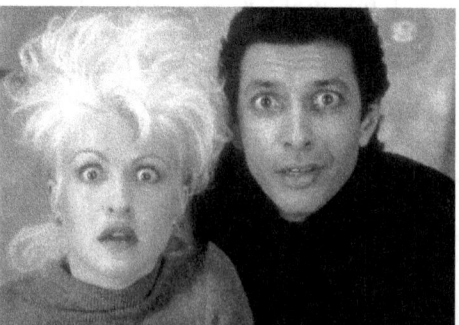

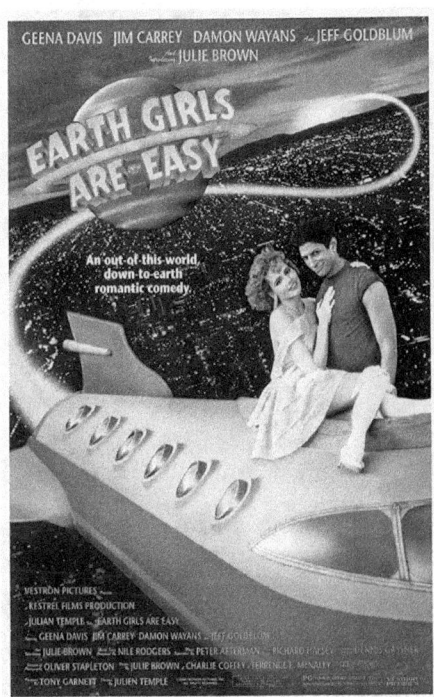

GEENA DAVIS JIM CARREY DAMON WAYANS and JEFF GOLDBLUM

with JULIE BROWN

EARTH GIRLS
ARE EASY

An out-of-this-world,
down-to-earth
romantic comedy.

VESTRON PICTURES
A KESTREL FILMS PRODUCTION
JULIAN TEMPLE film EARTH GIRLS ARE EASY
GEENA DAVIS JIM CARREY DAMON WAYANS and JEFF GOLDBLUM
music JULIE BROWN music NILE RODGERS director PETER AFTERMAN RICHARD HASHI
director OLIVER STAPLETON by JULIE BROWN , CHARLIE COFFEY , TERRENCE E. McNALLY
producer TONY GARNETT director JULIEN TEMPLE

EARTH GIRLS ARE EASY (1988)

Aliens Mac (Jeff Goldblum), Wiploc (Jim Carrey), and Zeebo (Damon Wayans) are brightly colored, hairy humanoids who speak in a backwards language, fawning & fighting over the nubile bikini clad women whose images they're picking up from Earth's terrestrial transmissions. Their 1950s-style spaceship is a bright, retro-toy-like thing that proves to be smaller than it looks when it crash lands in the backyard pool of Valerie (Geena Davis). Valerie (an epithet here which surely means "of the Valley") works

as a manicurist and is engaged to philandering doctor Ted (Charles Rocket). When the aliens emerge, Valerie is more curious than terrified, and watches with bemusement as they absorb what passes for English by consuming television pop culture.

They will have to remain on earth until their ship can be repaired, which necessitates draining the pool, a task for pool boy and aging surfer Woody (Michael McKean). In the meantime, they'll have to blend in. Valerie enlists the help of stylist friend Candy Pink (Julie Brown) who seems nonplussed by the alien's fuzzy forms. "Well I see split ends are universal. Lost in space with no conditioner, huh?" A shave and dye job produces some hunky results, with Wiploc emerging as a California surfer dude, Zeebo as a hip black guy with great moves, and leader Mac as a studly nerd (or nerdy stud, depending on your stance on Jeff Goldblum). Valerie is attracted to Mac, but after all, she argues, "I'm from the Valley, you're an alien, we might not even be anatomically compatible."

Turns out they are compatible in that area, and Wiploc and Zeebo are also deemed desirable by the nightclubbing Valley girls. The breast-obsessed aliens have definitely come to the right place, where pneumatic gals come onto them at stop lights and absurdly-proportioned LA-celeb Evangelyne refuels her pink Corvette at the local gas station. The rambling plot varies between genuinely funny fish-out-of-water moments with the aliens, to less-memorable musical numbers. In fact, the film waits about ten minutes before establishing itself as an outright singing-into-the camera musical, and when it does is mostly structured around a trio of tunes by Julie Brown who wrote the screen story.

"Miss" Julie Brown was known at the time for her half-hour MTV program *Just Say Julie*, in which she lampooned videos in her Valley Girl persona, a show that (along with *Beavis and Butthead*) was likely one of the nails in the coffin of taking music videos seriously. Prior to that she had gained recognition for a series of comedy music albums that positioned her as a novelty-songstress, and songs like "'Cause I'm a Blonde" gained popularity on the syndicated radio show Dr. Demento. That song was added to the film late in the game when another scene was cut.

Earth Girls was made around the same year as Davis' star role in *Accidental Tourist*, and in one of these she was nominated for an Academy Award for Best Supporting Actress (I'll leave it to you to guess which one). That she was married to Goldbum at the time surely made such matters as on-screen romance easier and more convincing, and their relationship here pays homage to the much more indelible performances from David Cronenberg's 1986 *The Fly*.

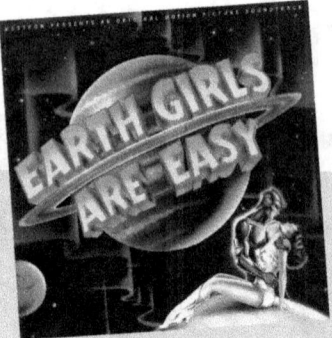

SOUNDTRACK

Love Train
Daryl Hall & John Oates

Baby Gonna Shake
Royalty

Hit Me
Information Society

The Ground You Walk On
Jill Jones

Earth Girls Are Easy
The N

Shake That Cosmic Thing
The B-52's

Route 66 (Nile Rodgers Mix)
Depeche Mode

Who Do You Love
The Jesus & Mary Chain

Throb
Stewart Copeland

Brand New Girl
Julie Brown

'Cause I'm A Blonde
Julie Brown

NOT ON THE ALBUM:
Summer of Love (The B-52's)
I Like 'Em Big And Stupid (Julie Brown)
Body to Body (Nile Rodgers)
Animal Attraction (Angelyne)

Director Julien Temple was one of the key figures in the rise of music video, directing seminal MTV spots for acts like Stray Cats ("Rock This Town" and "Stray Cat Strut"), ABC ("Poison Arrow") The Kinks ("Come Dancing"), Dexy's Midnight Runners ("Come on Eileen"), and David Bowie ("Blue Jean"), who he cast in his film *Absolute Beginners*. He is most known for chronicling the early years of the Sex Pistols, both in short promos and the film *The Great Rock and Roll Swindle*.

Temple's work here has been compared to Frank Tashlin's (from his animation work for Warner Brothers to his 1950s features like *The Girl Can't Help It*) and traffics in bright colors and Cinemascope framing. The film takes place in a quirky, postcard Los Angeles situated under the Hollywood sign, a world in which even the Griffith Observatory can be reimagined as a nightclub. It's a postmodern delight that relishes in recycling – from *Buckaroo Banzai* Lectroid aliens to the cars from *Death Race 2000*; from Robby the Robot to M*A*S*H's Larry Linville.

Nile Rodgers is credited in the opening titles as composer of the musical score, although that may be somewhat of a misnomer. Rodger's fingerprint is on many of the background songs (a couple from his work on B52's album *Cosmic Thing*, his production work on the Hall & Oates song "Love Train," his remix of Depeche Mode's "Route 66"), and he produced the front-and-center performance songs "The Ground You Walk On," and "Brand New Girl."

There's some clever visual effects from Dream Quest Images – notably a completely convincing "growing" scene in which the aliens grow to human size, a wild "love touch" effect reportedly produced using a four-lensed camera, and of course some lovingly fake spaceship shots.

Warner Brothers had developed the project but when such bigger box office draws as Madonna and Molly Ringwald declined the lead role, Warner got cold feet, but De Laurentiis Entertainment Group picked it up shortly before declaring bankruptcy. It was left to Vestron to distribute where it largely tanked despite mostly positive (if dismissive) reviews.

Film critic Jonathan Rosenbaum sums up the pitfalls of music video direction versus Temple's film work in the following way: "The negative side of [postmodernism] can be seen in the average rock video, where the entire history of cinema ... is represented, but with all of its meaning and effect stripped away. Through a process of equalizing and synthesizing all sorts of contradictory materials, what tends to emerge is a kind of nerveless mush, easy to consume and often impossible to remember. But the positive side of this kind of mix, which the work of Temple illustrates, is the elimination of all the snobbery and condescension about culture and class that modernism often entails– and the implication, more pragmatic than pathetic, that if we have to eat mush, it might as well be tasty."

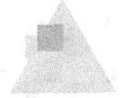

FINAL TALLY:

The Best Dressed – Madonna, Desperately Seeking Susan

The Least Dressed – Susanna Hoffs, The Allnighter

Biggest Hair – Cindy Lauper, Vibes

Biggest Hands – Jeff Goldblum, Earth Girls Are Easy

Best Apartment, Location Location Edition – The Allnighter

Best Apartment, Interior Decorator Edition – Modern Girls

Best Car –Modern Girls

The Most Girl Drama – Modern Girls

Best Boyfriend – Nicholas Cage, Valley Girl

Best Soundtrack – Valley Girl

Shoulda Been a Double Album – Modern Girls

22

CRAZY FROM THE HEAT: THE DAVID LEE ROTH MOVIE

For music fans of a certain age, there is a divisive moment in the 80s, when one had to decide whether they could still enjoy Van Halen – you know, in the years AD (After Dave). Most assumed it was the in-fighting, drug use, and years of touring that had left everybody tired of the power struggles in the seminal rock band, leading to his replacement by (the controversial, but eminently qualified) Sammy Hagar. But Diamond Dave was aiming only to take a break and get a film project made. This is the story of the totally bonkers film that could have been.

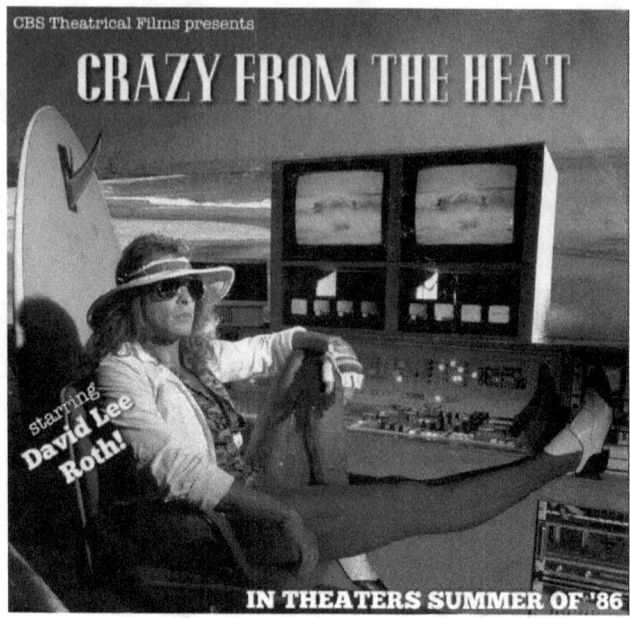

CBS Theatrical Films presents

CRAZY FROM THE HEAT

starring David Lee Roth!

IN THEATERS SUMMER OF '86

While *1984* was Van Halen's most commercially successful album, frontman David Lee Roth felt that he was losing creative control over the recording process to the band's co-founder and guitarist Eddie Van Halen. As early as 1979, band tensions began to flare around Roth's apparent need to be the center of attention (no, really?).

On tour, Dave liked to get up early to go roller skating, Eddie liked to stay up late writing to keep up with the songwriting load. Dave wanted the band to lie about their ages, and ignore Eddie's marriage to Valerie Bertinelli to maintain the non-stop party image of the band. He may have know that his days were numbered from the start. In January 1985 he told Billboard, "Since my very first days in with the band 11 years ago, I have always had the feeling that one day I

would wake up in a cold hotel, all the rooms would be empty and I would be stuck by a phone with a busy signal. From the first day. Nothing has changed."

As evidenced by his post-Van Halen output, Dave wanted to be more than just front and center, he wanted to be a complete entertainment icon, a dionysian master of ceremonies for bikini-babe-infested concept videos. Dave had two midget bodyguards with him on tour. Hell, he released his solo album on a July 4th weekend. This was a man who genuinely aimed to be no more or less than the All-American Clown Prince of Party.

And more: he wanted to act, to write and direct a feature film for himself, without Van Halen but with Eddie doing soundtrack duties. Roth asked EVH to participate, he declined.

Eddie told Rolling Stone in 1986 that the discussion was over, with Roth declaring, "I can't work with you guys anymore. I want to do my movie. Maybe when I'm done, we'll get back together." Eddie's reply: "I ain't waiting on your ass. See you later. Good luck."

The 90 page script for *Crazy from the Heat* was completed in 1985 for an intended 1986 summer release, and would be produced under CBS Pictures. In his autobiography, also titled *Crazy from the Heat*, Roth says "the idea for the movie was basically a musical with a very left of center plot. There were a number of rewrites, but the general script for *Crazy from the Heat* was a story about Dave (and keep in mind all these characters are right out of "California Girls"). Landed a 10 million dollar budget for the movie, and there was to be a couple million-dollar director's fee. It was a huge deal, especially since I was first time everything".

CBS was looking to pare down costs during a takeover by Ted Turner's network, and so disbanded their film production arm. "The entire album of *Eat 'Em and Smile* was designed to match up to the scenes for the movie that never came to be because, unbeknownst to us, CBS Pictures was in trouble," says Roth. "We had a cast. We had everything made, all the costumes, et cetera. Every shot was storyboarded. But CBS was changing hands, parts of it were being eliminated. They [killed] the movie division, decided that they didn't want to be in the business anymore. There were some eight pictures I think that were green lighted and setting up to go, ours being one of them."

Roth took CBS to court for the writing and directing fee of $3.5 million, claiming that the studio told them they would continue production despite the impending merger. "CBS told us that [its decision] would in no way affect production," Roth told Billboard magazine. "But a week before shooting began, they dragged their feet and basically turned off the money." He won the fee and took off with his new all-star band on a year-long tour. "I sued CBS. I went to court, got the director's fee. Never did make the picture-- made semi-efforts at shopping it to a couple of other movie companies, but it was something that was born out of imagination and vision."

Could the spirit of "Dave TV," with over-the-top videos like "Just a Gigolo" and "California Girls" be sustained for ninety minutes? Certainly, dumber things were done in that decade. It's got the irreverent 80s tone of shows like UHF and Strange Brew, and one can only imagine what the filmed results could have been.

In it, Dave invades the house of his manager Bernie to tell him he's going on vacation. To determine their travel plans, Dave throws a globe across the room toward a well-endowed statue; whatever location is impaled by the erection is their destination. The group heads to the tropic paradise of the Dongo Islands where there's Marx Brothers-type wordplay and tall tales, jokes about fat girls, jokes about underage girls, jokes about naked girls, and the most uses of the word "schlong" in a feature length screenplay.

"He's young, he's wild.. A Libra whose moon is in the House of Pancakes. He won't go down in history but he will go down on your little sister. Heeerrre's Dave!!"

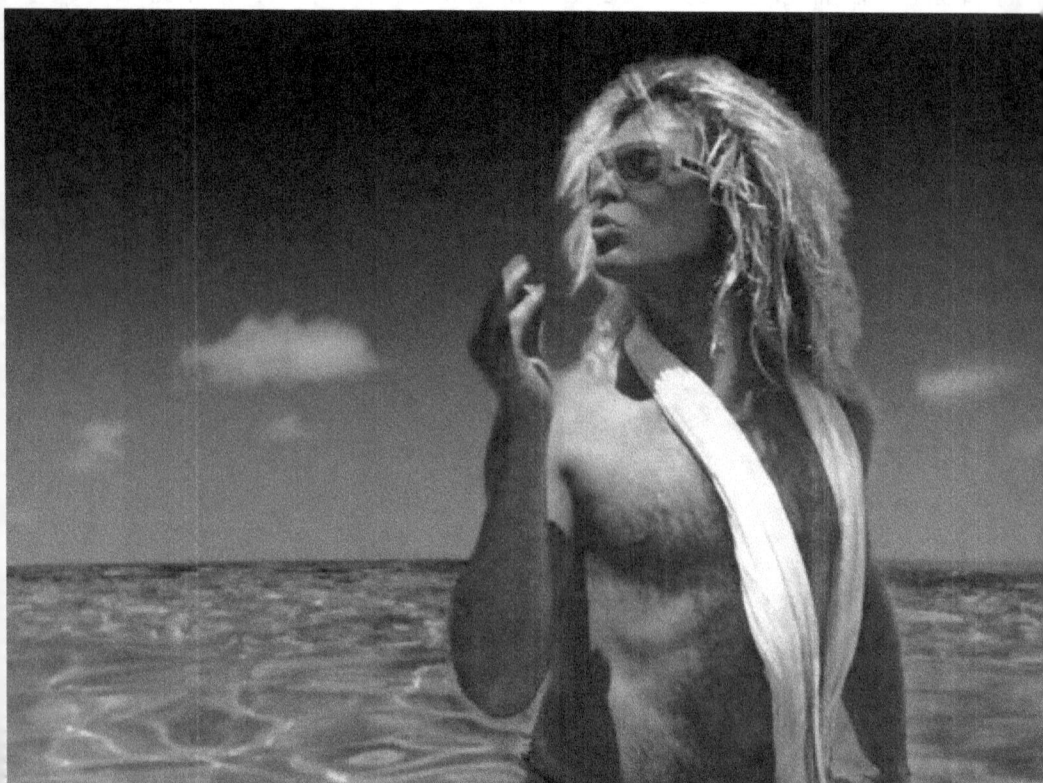

23

DID MTV RUIN MOVIES?

Anyone with eyes on MTV's inauspicious roll-out in August of 1981 would have been underwhelmed. A handful of uncharismatic jockeys introduced less-than-groundbreaking music clips, interspersed with dead air. For MTV's first two years, few American homes were wired for cable. And many of the major markets where film directors tended to live, like New York and Los Angeles, were slow to receive it. It's hard to pinpoint whether the early years of MTV influenced filmmaking or whether MTV was mimicking them. The music video itself, however, could not be ignored.

For a period in the 1980s, films may have shared a partial aesthetic with MTV, but they could only do so on a scene by scene basis. Mainstream films were still constrained by the format's particulars and audience expectations – it had to have a story and it had to have dialog. No mainstream films were 100% musicals, or dialog-free. While there was little non-traditional storytelling to be found in mid-80s movies, there was plenty in the music video arena.

The artistic idea of songs and image working in tandem was no new concept – it was almost as old as film itself. Likewise the popular 80s crossover of rock stars as actors was not new, as the films of the 60s proved cheap movies with rock stars made money. And the benefit of a successful soundtrack album had been perfected in the 1970s with films like *American Graffiti*, *Grease*, and *Saturday Night Fever*. Putting the cart (album) before the horse (movie) was not a new idea, but turned into big business in the 80s through the calculated release of the single before the film. *Back to the Future*'s "The Power of Love" is a good example: the song was released in the US and rose to number one just as the film was released. The song made money, the song drew attention to the movie, the movie made money, the soundtrack made more money. When the film opened overseas, the song introduced the band to a whole new audience, such that Huey Lewis himself cites the release as being crucial to the band winning in the overseas market. If anything, the 80s soundtrack tie-in was a by-product of the media corporations becoming more and more integrated.

To understand music video's impact on film, let's differentiate between three basic generations of MTV –

Initial Phase, or "Stone Age" 1981-1982 – directors are testing the waters, videos themselves are largely studio-bound promo pieces, often shot on video, with some then-new Paint-box type video effects. Buggles, Gary Numan, type stuff.

Second Phase, or "Golden Age" 1983-1985 – Classic MTV, that give us filmed promos with stories and locations. The works of Michael Jackson, Madonna, and Duran Duran are among the gold standard.

Third Phase "Maturation" 1986-1994 – bigger budget, more conceptual phase like Peter Gabriel's "Sledgehammer" but culminating in the slick 35mm movies of Aerosmith, Tom Petty, and Guns N Roses.

After 1994, the introduction of reality programming sent the cable network down the fourth path, and along with other media influences put us in the cultural handbasket we're in now. That's another story, mercifully this book is not about that.

In the world of film criticism of the early to mid-80s, the phrases "MTV-look" or "MTV-editing" quickly became a way to write off a certain sort of mainstream movie making. Upmarket critics who had come to power in the 1970s had lived through a real renaissance of film art, so when commercial film of the 80s failed to live up to that standard, it was just easier to blame the new kid on the block. What exactly was the MTV look? And how is MTV editing different than other editing? And should a cable channel – one that didn't actually produce any of the content that aired on it – be blamed for a shift in motion picture style?

THE LOOK

If there's one "MTV look," the directors involved must not have gotten the memo. The visual style of most videos, although they could be parcelled out into a handful of obvious genres, were as varied as their artists' music. What critics may have been responding to was an overall shift in the style of filmmaking as popular trends waxed and waned. Thinking again to the 1970s film aesthetic and the kind of films that typified the period, you'd likely cite visual realism as the main style. *Exorcist, Taxi Driver, Jaws,* all appear to take place next door – and are all the more powerful because of it. With the arrival of filmmakers like Ridley Scott (who had made a name for himself in big-budget TV advertising), a more theatrical approach begins in which lighting and production design become stars in their own right. *Blade*

Runner was inspired by the early 80s punk and new wave music scene, to be sure, and in turn impacted a huge swath of MTV.

A unapologetically MTV-look movie might be *Streets of Fire*, but by necessity (of story, of budget, of convention) even a large part of that is shot realistically. Practically speaking, no one could embrace the MTV look and sustain it for the length of a whole film. And the door swung both ways, "Hungry Like the Wolf" is just a sexy, three-minute *Raiders of the Lost Ark.*

THE EDITING

So what's MTV Editing? Is it merely a case of more cuts? Film history had plenty of examples of rapid cutting (the silent-era Russians made an art of it). But the generation that grew up with MTV (and by that token 80s Saturday morning cartoons, home video, and Atari) became immersed in it, their ability to process visual information was accelerated. Speed was a factor in 80s editing, but just as important to the MTV aesthetic is

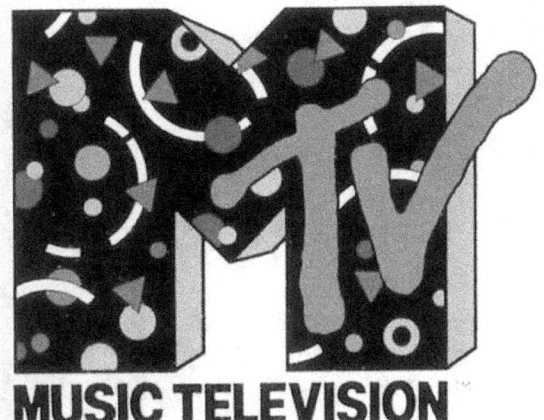

MUSIC TELEVISION

"what we cut to." Is the next shot a direct storytelling moment, or does it go to a parallel place? The nature of a musical performance demands parallel cutting to see the different performers at work, and when a narrative is introduced on top of that you have yet another layer to draw from. In the case of narrative story, we may also leap forward in time, as in the ubiquitous 80s training montage.

A montage sequence like "Never" from *Footloose* (by the appropriately titled band Moving Pictures) is a prime example of what film critics of the 80s responded to, mostly negatively. Of the film's music video-like sequences, Roger Ebert said at the time:

"these scenes may play well on TV, but they break what little reality the story has, and expose *Footloose* as a collection of unrelated ingredients that someone thought would be exploitable."

Footloose's "Never" sequence combines the idea of cross-cutting performance with narrative. Kevin Bacon arrives at an empty, backlit warehouse space – itself an ideal music video location. The music is motivated initially by a cassette he shoves angrily into his car stereo, very quickly elevating to non-diegetic music. Before the song even gets to the first lyric, we cut away to footage of the Reverend: the reason Bacon's character Ren is angry. But the cutting

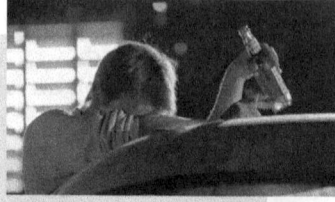
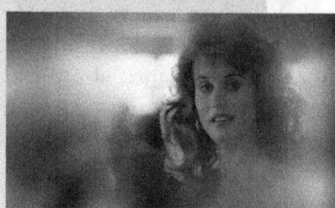
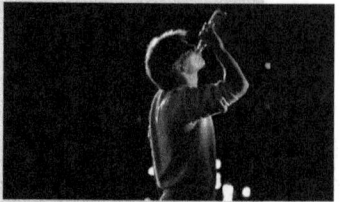
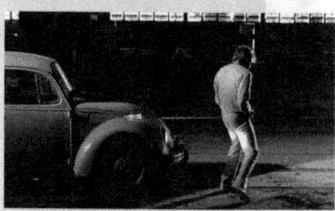
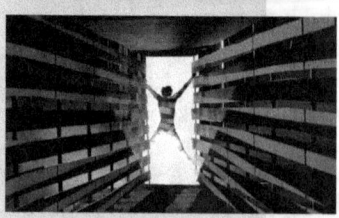

MONTAGE FROMAGE
"Never" Moving Pictures from *Footloose* (1984)
Angry dancing, punch dancing, whatever you call it it's a good one.

RATING 8/10

creates a call and response effect: he turns his head and sees a flashback of girlfriend Ariel, and the technique of matching eyelines puts them in the same space. When he begins dancing, the camera cuts to a series of views (first from his left in a wide shot, then his front in a close up, his right in a close up, his right in a long shot) that follow all the rules of filmmaking to establish space. The pace is rapid but we never lose the geography of the scene. The flashbacks are separated visually by the use of a fog filter so they appear different from the "now."

Silly? Sure. Motivated? The sequence is a brief, energetic and visual way of delivering some character insight and get the pulse up.

One of the first films accused of an MTV-type aesthetic in editing was 1983's *Flashdance*. But it takes a couple of years to push a project through the Hollywood machine, and while the film was in production MTV had really only started to achieve a kind of mainstream awareness. So films prior to that weren't so much influenced by MTV as they were responding to the same things MTV was. Trends in pop music, technology, and big budget advertising were as much to blame for the look and sound of early 80s films like *Flashdance*. By the time of 1984's *Footloose*, the give and take was more obvious. Ten years later, the idea of a musical montage in a movie was passé. And twenty years on, it made for one of the best jokes in the film *Team America* ("It takes a montage! Show a lot of things happenin' at once, remind everyone of

what's goin' on!") Possibly the hand-in-glove relationship with MTV peaks with films like *Top Gun*. And after that, the trend slowly waned.

Whether or not the art of film was doomed forever by MTV's influence, the folks counting the coffers saw the trend as a positive boom. MTV never paid for programming, just as the studios never paid for radio airtime when songs from their films – a great ad for the movie itself – entered heavy rotation. In *Variety*, Gary LaMel had said "Hollywood sees a way to get a lot of advertising and marketing for its target audience. The target audience for MTV is the same (as the) target for pictures. You need the twelve to twenty-five demographic." With films like Flashdance spawning multiple music video clips, and those songs entering the Top 40, there was a free and legal means to getting the movie message in front of more people than ever. If you had a hot soundtrack and could get your free three minute advertisement for it running endlessly on MTV, your movie was in for a serious uptick in business.

Some well-known directors tried their hands at music video (notably John Landis and Martin Scorsese, both for Michael Jackson). And conversely, some of the directors who got their start in music videos were beginning to make their way to feature-length Hollywood projects. But flashy directors were just as likely to come out of TV advertising, like Adrian Lyne, Tony Scott, Michael Bay.

Not many of the Golden Age music video directors made it big

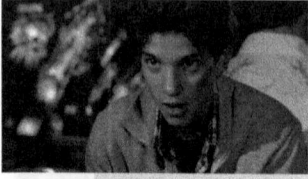

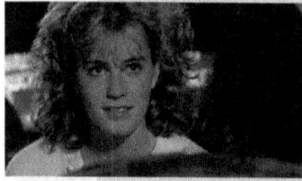

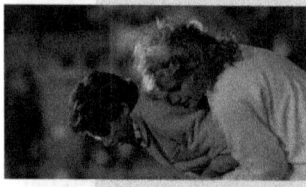

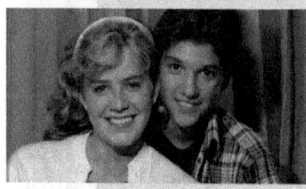

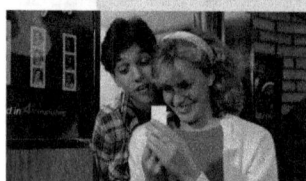

as filmmakers – folks like Steve Barron, Russell Mulcahy were hardly household names. Late-era music video directors, including Tarsem Singh, sometimes fared better. "My generation of directors – me, Fincher, Spike Jonze, Mark Romanek – we ruined your visual world," offers Singh. "We grew up on a completely visual culture, and we brought our candy video eyeballs to cinema. It'll always be looked down on, shat on, and they accuse us of being bad for the film world. There's a saying: politicians, prostitutes, and ugly buildings all get respectable if they last long enough. The same is true for film movements. Shitty or not, in twenty years it will seem valid."

Whether music videos had a positive or negative effect on the culture of movies, they will be remembered fondly by fans, filmmakers, and the artists themselves. In the book "I Want My MTV" by Craig Marks and Rob Tannenbaum, Red Hot Chili Pepper bassist (and busy 80s actor) Flea recalls:

"when they were great, music videos on MTV were like a short film festival for housewives in Nebraska... I was talking to the film director Milos Forman. He said 'I loved MTV. All those short little films... How great.' And it dawned on me how right he was. And now that it's gone, I really miss it."

MONTAGE FROMAGE

"Feel the Night" Baxter Robertson*
from *The Karate Kid* (1984)

Daniel and Ali play at "Golf N Stuff" arcade – perfectly captures that summer night innocence of the 1980s

*written by Bill Conti

RATING 7/10

24

THE GREATEST 80S SOUNDTRACK SONGS

A countdown is a tricky thing. I've avoided rating the movies in this book because it's very hard to compare unlike things. You can compare breakdancing movies against each other (a small sampling over which to deliberate), or argue which lambada movie is better (flip a coin). But there comes a time when we must face the music.

The value of a movie song can be boiled down to the following factors:

1. How well the songs sold during the period surrounding the films' release, whether as singles, part of the soundtrack, or as part of a regular studio album.
2. A song's popularity and longevity, possibly earned after the film and soundtrack had long gone. Cable and home video helped in the interim, and of course the internet is known to revive interest in a lot of lost things.
3. The song's significance to the film. Can you separate them from the picture? Were they substantially tied to the plot?
4. How quintessentially 1980s they are, in sound or sentiment.

Here is a stab at comparing some of the essential 80s film songs, and a final chance to share the love with some songs that might not have been represented elsewhere in the book.

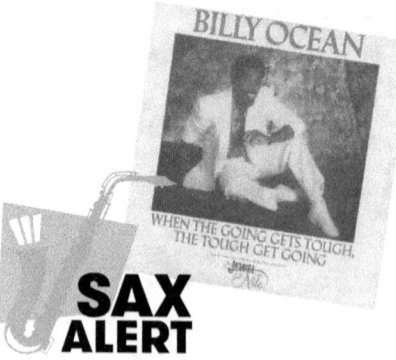

SAX ALERT

#25 – When the Going Gets Tough The Tough Get Going – Billy Ocean (Jewel of the Nile, 1985)

British by way of Trinidad, Billy Ocean excelled at vocals-driven pop songs with long names ("Caribbean Queen (No More Love on the Run)" "There'll Be Sad Songs (To Make You Cry)" and "Get Out of My Dreams, Get into My Car" among them, each #1 hits). Hot on the heels of Robert Zemeckis 1984 hit *Romancing the Stone, Jewel of the Nile* reunites Michael Douglas, Kathleen Turner, and Danny DeVito. In the music video, the three stars appear in matching white tuxedos and lipsync with the backing vocals – which apparently is a violation of musicians union rules in England, where the video was summarily banned on that basis. This song made it to Number 2 in America, but Number 1 in the UK despite the fact that the video had been nixed.

In a career with so many notable hits, it's somewhat surprising to know that he considers the song and its video one of his favorites. "I guess my fondest memory would be making the video for 'The Tough Get Going' and working with Michael Douglas, Danny DeVito and Kathleen Turner. It was great to have them involved and I thought it was very big of them, very humble of them, exceptional. I never thought they would do it but what a great job, the three put in so much energy and vibrancy. The timing was also spot on and the video was one of my favorites from that era."

Ocean loves the association with upbeat and hopeful songs like "The Tough Get Going." As he said in an interview, "Although what I'm doing is a job, I'd like to think that a part of that job is to inspire people - in a positive way, not in a negative way. I'll never write a song and tell somebody to pick up a gun and shoot somebody, but I will write a song that says 'Get up and do something positive' because no matter what you're going through, it's not over yet."

#24 - Dream Warriors - Dokken (Nightmare on Elm Street 3: the Dream Warriors, 1987)

If there were only one metal song on the countdown, it would have to be this one. As operatic and fun as Freddy Krueger himself.

#23 - Rhythm of the Night - DeBarge (The Last Dragon, 1985)

Cut from the same cloth as "All Night Long" and other feel good tunes of the decade, it's a relentlessly cheery pop bonbon. Consisting of a variable number of siblings from the DeBarge family, this Detroit group inevitably drew comparisons to the Jacksons. Singers El and Bunny were lured away after the 1985 album, and the band soon dissolved.

#22 - You're The Best Around - Joe Esposito (The Karate Kid, 1984)

If you need a confidence boost, just remember the immortal words of Joe Esposito: "Try your best to win them all, and one day time will tell. When you're the one that's standing there, you'll reach the final bell... You're the best around. Nothing's gonna ever keep you down."

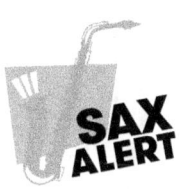

#21 - On The Dark Side - John Cafferty and the Beaver Brown Band (Eddie and the Cruisers, 1983)

Sure, it might be second-hand Springsteen, but it had a great hook and was impossible to avoid on the radio during the peak 80s soundtrack charting years.

#20 - Burning Heart - Survivor (Rocky IV, 1985)

Is it as good as "Eye of the Tiger?" Better? Let's put them in some boxing trunks and let 'em duke it out.

#19 - On Our Own - Bobby Brown (Ghostbusters 2, 1989)

Unlike poor Ray Parker, Jr, songwriters L.A. Reid, Kenneth "Babyface" Edmonds, and Daryl Simmons did not have to crowbar the word "ghostbusters" into their song

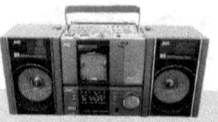

MIKE'S PICKS: SEXY CUTS

The Beautiful Ones
Prince
from Purple Rain

Come To Me
Brad Fidel
from Fright Night

Love on a Real Train
Tangerine Dream
from Risky Business

Moving in Stereo
The Cars
from Fast Times at Ridgemont High

No Place to Hide
Madonna
from Who's That Girl?

Cry Little Sister
Gerard McCann
from Lost Boys

She Talks in Stereo
Gary Myrick and The Figures
from Valley Girl

Eyes of a Stranger
Payolas
from Valley Girl

Heaven
Bryan Adams
from A Night in Heaven

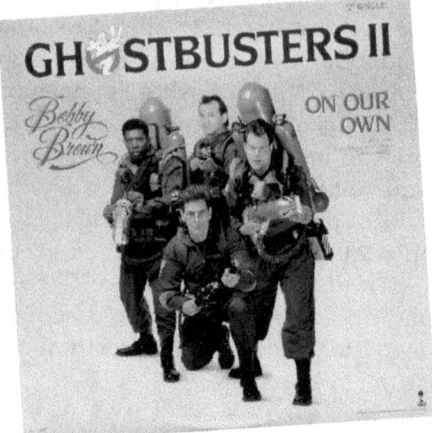

for the 1989 sequel *Ghostbusters II*. Former New Edition performer Bobby Brown was riding high (on the charts, that is) with his solo song "My Prerogative" when the film's music supervisor Kathy Nelson suggested Brown for the job.

While not the movie's theme song, nor featured as prominently in the film as Parker's original tune was, this one managed to peak at #15. Brown's inclusion in the soundtrack was motivated by a bit part in the film, as a doorman who asks the Ghostbusters if he can get a proton pack for his kid brother. Egon responds dryly, "a proton pack is not a toy." Alas, Brown's later fame came not from his music but his tumultuous personal life.

#18 - A View to a Kill - Duran Duran (A View to a Kill, 1985)

The boys of Duran Duran were longtime Bond fans - bassist John Taylor has cited watching a fateful double bill on his sixth birthday for starting his obsession, and singer Simon Le Bon a screening of *Thunderball* on his sixth as well. And indeed, one of Taylor's first rockstar indulgences was his very own Aston Martin. John was attending a party for the Wimbledon tennis final held at Michael Caine's house where he was introduced to Bond producer Cubby Broccoli. Taylor boldly asked him, "when are you going to have a decent theme song again?" Broccoli's response: "Well, do you want to write the next one?"

At Broccoli's Mayfair office, Taylor set up a meeting in Manhattan with his idol, longtime Bond composer John Barry. The band met and sussed out a song in a day in Paris. In the studio, keyboardist Nick Rhodes and Barry didn't click; both had specific conflicting visions of how to proceed, putting Taylor in the middle as a negotiator. Bernard (Chic) Edwards, who was producing The Power Station album, offered to act as producer. Duran's rhythm section made great efforts to impress him; drummer Roger Taylor copped a beat from the Rolling Stones "Honky Tonk Woman" to start. Barry's orchestral parts were recorded in London.

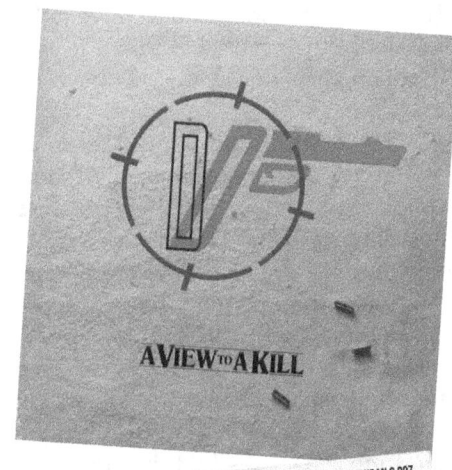

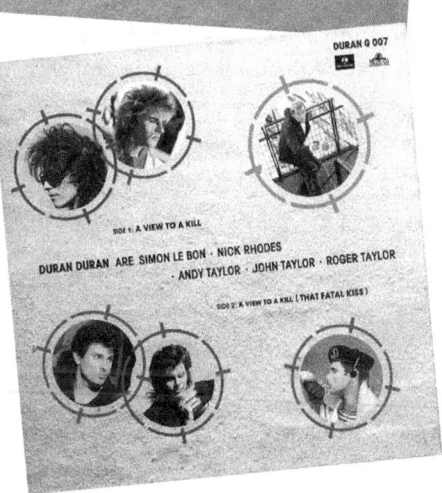

On Good Morning America in June of 1985, John Taylor and John Barry appeared to promote the song and discuss its making. "We had an approach we wanted to take, in the way we did the music for it," said Taylor. "Which was our style. We really didn't give any thought to what had come before us. We wanted to give it something very contemporary and very Duran Duran. We didn't really think about what we had to follow.

If we had thought about the acts we had to follow, we'd have never been able to do it... It puts you onto some kind of legendary status, I think."

In retrospect, Taylor's instincts were well founded. As he said in a 2012 interview, "Bond songs have to be big songs, don't they? They have to have the grandiosity. It's like designing a Rolls-Royce. You want it to be completely state of the art, but it's always going to have the honking great radiator grill on the front. There's certain criteria that have to be fulfilled. But I think we nailed it with that song."

"A View to a Kill" injected some modernity and energy into the theme songs for the series, which had spiralled into yawn-inducing adult contemporary tunes (perhaps more suitable for the aging Roger Moore than any kind of new, MTV-savvy audience), and in so doing became the first Bond theme to hit #1 on Billboard's Top 100. The band played the song live for the first time together at Live Aid, opening their set with it, and it would be the last time they would perform as that line-up for 18 years, for they splintered shortly after.

#17 - St Elmo's Fire (Man in Motion) - John Parr (St. Elmo's Fire, 1985)

British singer John Parr had already climbed the charts in 1984 with his hit "Naughty Naughty," when he was called upon by Canadian movie producer David Foster to write a song for the film *St. Elmo's Fire*.

In an interview with Carl Wiser for the website Songfacts, John Parr explained that while the song appeared to be written for the movie, the ambiguity of the lyrics worked

MIKE'S PICKS: SAPPY, BAD, BUT HUGE

#1 Endless Love
Diana Ross & Lionel Richie
from Endless Love (1981)

#1 Say You, Say Me
Lionel Richie
from White Nights (1985)

#1 I Just Called to Say I Love You
Stevie Wonder
from The Woman in Red (1984)

#1 Up Where We Belong
Joe Cocker & Jennifer Warnes
An Officer and a Gentleman (1982)

#1 Hard to Say I'm Sorry
Chicago
from Summer Lovers (1982)

#1 Separate Lives
Phil Collins & Marilyn Martin
from White Nights (1985)

#1 The Glory of Love
Peter Cetera
from Karate Kid II (1986)

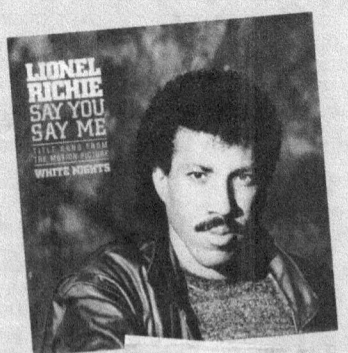

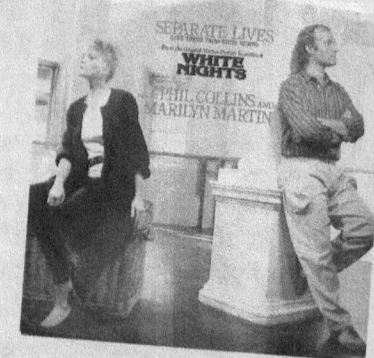

in his favor as he was more directly inspired by the life of Canadian wheelchair athlete Rick Hansen. "David [Foster] showed me a video of Rick Hansen and I was inspired to write the story of his planned epic journey to circumnavigate the globe in his wheelchair. I wrote the lyric ambiguously, so the film company would think "all I need's these pair of wheels" referred to Demi Moore's jeep when actually I am referring to Rick's wheelchair, or "for once in his life a man has his time" actually refers to when Rick would end his journey wheeling back into Vancouver with a million people lining the streets." Parr says that not seeing the film before writing the song really worked to his advantage, and his take on the material proved much more soaring and inspirational than the film.

Once again, the music video teams the film's leads and the song's creator, and Parr embarrassingly recalls trying to give the young Brat Pack actors (who were unknown in England) some performing tips. "When we were shooting it seemed like they weren't doing anything, so I was stupid enough to offer them the benefit of my experience. After all I had done a few school plays."

Parr's other music-to-film contributions include "Through the Night" with Marilyn Martin for 1986's *Quicksilver*, "The Minute I Saw You" from *Three Men and a Baby*, and "Restless Heart" from *The Running Man*, both from 1987. His take on songwriting is modest: "Great songs are given to you. Yeah you can craft them, but the great ones are gifted. As soon as you start thinking it's you... it's over."

#16 – I Can Dream About You – Dan Hartman (Streets of Fire, 1984)

In a decade obsessed with 60s music, this was a fair approximation of the real thing. In the context of the movie, it provides some light at the end of the tunnel in a town that seems caught in a perpetual night.

#15 – Against All Odds – Phil Collins (Against All Odds, 1984)

The film's director, Taylor Hackford, approached Collins following a Genesis concert in Chicago. Collins watched a rough cut of the film on VHS in his hotel room, and agreed to contribute a song. Originally written for his 1981 album *Face Value*, and was written following his first divorce. "My first wife and the kids had gone and I was left there. The song was written out of experience as opposed to a 'what if' song."

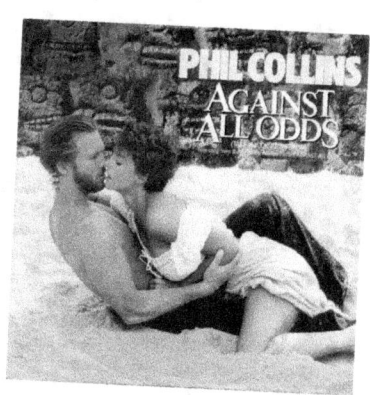

Winning a Grammy for Best Pop Vocal Performance (Male) in 1985, the song is one of Collins greatest ballads, arguably one of his greatest songs, and possibly one of the greatest movie love songs of the 1980s. It was nominated for an Oscar for Best Original Song, but singer Collins was not invited to perform it at the ceremony (and lost out to the much shallower song "I Just Called to Say I Love You" by Stevie Wonder).

#14 – Nothing's Gonna Stop Us Now – Starship (Mannequin, 1987)

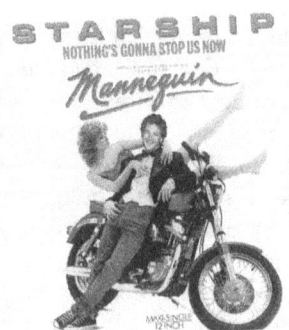

Also written by Diane Warren (along with Rhythm of the Night by DeBarge), this was commissioned by the film's director Michael Gottlieb. Even though Starship had been psychedelic pioneers Jefferson Airplane (and later Jefferson Starship), this would be their biggest hit in any iteration of the band, with two weeks at #1. Nominated for Best Original Song Oscar.

#13 – Take My Breath Away – Berlin (Top Gun, 1986)

At once heartfelt and entirely synthetic, "Take My Breath Away" quickly became a prom slow dance standby. And many a sneaky teenage grope was had.

#12 – (TIE) Crazy for You – Madonna (Vision Quest, 1985) AND Live to Tell – Madonna (At Close Range, 1986)

No 80s countdown would be complete without a mention of Miss Ciccone. None of the films here were blockbuster hits, but the songs enjoyed plenty of attention at a time when radio stations were lapping up any new Madonna they could get.

"Crazy for You"

Vision Quest producers Jon Peters and Peter Guber, along with the film's music supervisor Phil Ramone, were aware of Madonna early on – just as she was being signed with Sire Records (a label owned by Warner Brothers Records). There was little sign that she could carry a ballad, and the songs writers (John Bettis and Jon Lind) were unsure of the choice. Further arrangement of the song was done by composer Rob Mounsey and producer John "Jellybean" Benitez, transforming it into the hit song it became.

Warner Brothers didn't want the single from *Vision Quest*, which was coming out on Geffen Records, to take

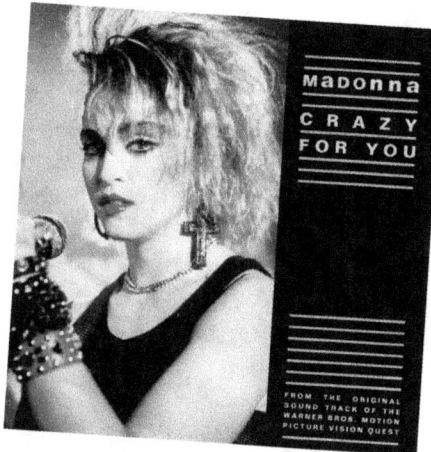

#11 - I've Had the Time of My Life - Bill Medley & Jennifer Warnes (Dirty Dancing, 1987)

Ubiquitous and overplayed, like the film in which it was featured. Probably felt like old fogey music to a lot of younger listeners due to the casting (Medley was almost 50) and the attempts to fit the period setting of the film. But huge, very very huge. Ranked #86 on AFI's 100 Years, 100 Songs countdown.

away from the then-current release of their full-length album *Like A Virgin*. It became her second Number One Billboard Hit, and deservedly so; it is certainly one of the definitive 80s music songs and nothing short of a slow dance masterpiece.

"Live to Tell"

Originally written by Patrick Leonard as an instrumental for the 1986 film *Fire With Fire*, Madonna wrote the lyrics and co-wrote the melody. Released with her studio album True Blue, the song was included in then-husband Sean Penn's film *At Close Range*. It was her third Number One hit, and is proof of her vocal and emotional range on what might be a throwaway song from this period. Along with "Crazy For You," "Live to Tell" allowed Madonna entry into the Adult Contemporary charts and established her as a force to reckon with.

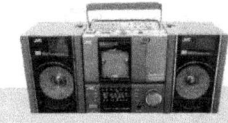

MIKE'S PICKS: ROCKIN' CUTS

Dream Warriors
Dokken
from Nightmare on Elm Street 3

The Hero
Queen
from Flash Gordon

We Fight for Love
Powerstation
from Commando

Takin' a Ride
Don Felder
from Heavy Metal

One Dream
Lou Gramm
from Highlander 2

Lost in the Shadows
Lou Gramm
from Lost Boys

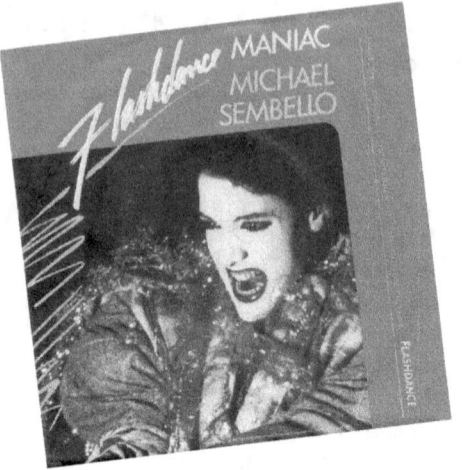

8 - Maniac - Michael Sembello (Flashdance, 1983)

Sembello's wife accidentally included this song on a demo tape sent to executives at Paramount. Worked out good for him, in the end.

#7 (TIE) - Purple Rain / When Doves Cry / I Would Die 4U - Prince (Purple Rain, 1984)

It's nearly impossible to put a value on specific tracks from *Purple Rain*, but these three were the biggest radio hits.

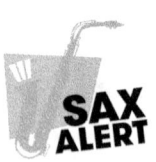

#10 - If You Leave - Orchestral Maneuvers in the Dark (Pretty in Pink, 1986)

Whether you agree with the ending of the film or not, it's hard to ignore the lilting, high-school-romantic feeling of the tune, written quickly to fit the strict 120 bps of the scene's guide track.

9 - (TIE) Call Me - Blondie/ Moroder (American Gigolo, 1980) AND Flashdance... What a Feeling Irene Cara/ Moroder (Flashdance, 1983)

It's hard to say which Moroder hit was more important - both parked at the Number One spot for six weeks. And both contributed to the rise of the pop music soundtrack of the 1980s.

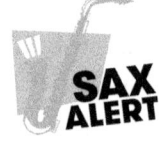

#6-Ghostbusters - Ray Parker Jr (Ghostbusters, 1984)

Ray Parker Jr had more or less retired from music after a few hits (including the great 1982 tune "The Other Woman"), but while in Los Angeles working on a cover of his song "Mr. Telephone Man" for the band New Edition he was approached by a friend at Columbia Pictures. They were getting desperate for a songwriter to deliver a song for the upcoming film, having auditioned almost sixty disappointing songs at that point. Lindsey Buckingham, who had composed "Holiday Road" for *National Lampoon's Vacation* (directed by Ghostbuster Harold Ramis), was tapped but turned it down fearing soundtrack oversaturation. Parker Jr's tasks: it had to include the movie title, it had to have a fun, uptempo "bar band" feel, and include saxophone.

"It sounds easy now because you've heard the song," says Parker Jr, "but if somebody told you to write a song with the word 'Ghostbusters' in it, it's pretty difficult. That was the hard part - getting the title in the song." If you say Ghostbusters, the accent lands naturally on the first syllable, but in the film the characters appear in a television ad for their service, with the accent and pacing similar to the song. He was further inspired by the tagline of a local television ad imploring the viewer to "call now!"

Parker Jr. only had two and a half days to deliver the minute and a half song, which was only meant to last the 20-25 seconds it took to fill the opening library scene. The song was extended after the fact to accompany the montage sequence as the Ghostbusters gain media prominence with the rise of spectral activity in the city.

Parker Jr describes the foundation of the song as a military type march, with the guitar providing more of a Detroit funk sound. The production was rapid fire, with the crew settling immediately on the first sounds they patched in on his Roland Jupiter-6 and drum machine.

The call and response in the song is performed by Parker Jr's girlfriend and her friends, shouting the title so he didn't have to figure out a way to sing those words. They were still in high school and had to make it to an 8am class. The courier was due to pick up the song at 9am, they locked him out long enough for Parker Jr to improvise

HIT MOVIE SINGLES: 1980-82

These are the first big movie-based music hits from the early 80s, but they still feel and sound like leftovers from the 1970s...

#1 **Magic** (1980)
Xanadu Olivia Newton John

#1 **9 to 5** (1981)
Dolly Parton

#1 **Arthur's Theme (The Best That You Can Do)** (1981)
Arthur, Christopher Cross

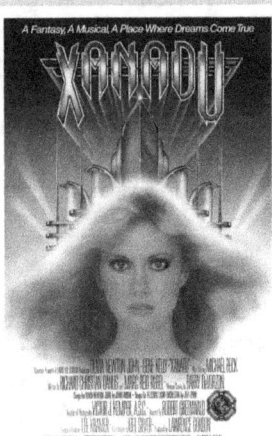

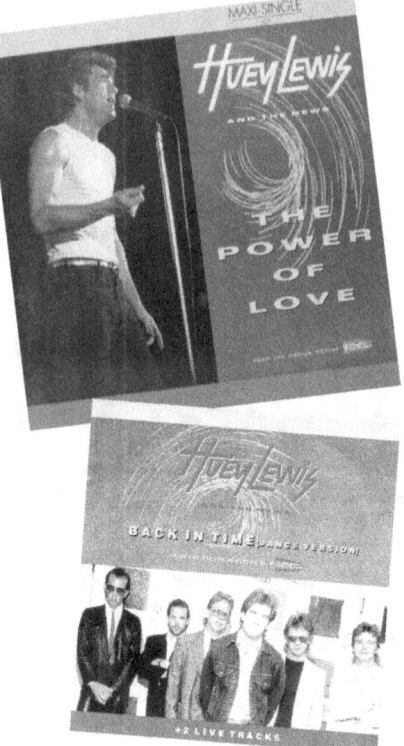

his hit "I Want a New Drug." They settled out of court. Oscar nominated, the song lost out to Stevie Wonder's "I Just Called to Say I Love You," – which perhaps answers the question, what would you say to the Ghostbusters after you called them?

#5 – Power of Love – Huey Lewis and The News (Back to the Future, 1985)

By the time Back to the Future rolled around, Huey Lewis and the News had already experienced a rise and fall – their 1982 album Picture This and its hit "Do You Believe in Love" had done well but due to record label delays they were soon back to touring small clubs. The album Sports in 1983 was supported by a series of successful music videos in 1984, including chartbusters "Heart and Soul," "I Want a New Drug," "The Heart of Rock & Roll," and "If This is It." Lewis popularity nabbed him a featured spot on the charity single "We Are The World," further cementing their pop credentials, and the same year director Robert Zemeckis called upon the band to provide an anchor for the soundtrack. This wouldn't be just another spot placement or contribution to a compilation-style soundtrack, but the emotional anchor for the movie.

Understandably, Lewis didn't want to write a song about time travel but instead opted for the more universal subject of teenage love. They purchased the name of the song from Lewis's former bandmate Alex Call (who also wrote the 80s staple "Jenny (867-5309)") and paid him with 10%

one verse, and two members of the British band Q-Feel (Martin Page, himself a hit songwriter for other acts, and Brian Fairweather) provided additional keyboards and guitar work. The phrase "I ain't 'fraid of no ghost" was a spoken placeholder, which Parker Jr intended to be sung by some female backup singers, but director Ivan Reitman wanted it left just the way it was (even if he couldn't wrap his head around the urban phrasing).

After three weeks at #1, and decades of saturation, Parker Jr says he's not sick of the song. "It's like, am I tired of holding the best lotto ticket of the best thing ever to happen? No." In one of the most famous music industry lawsuits, Huey Lewis sued Parker, claiming that the theme plagiarized

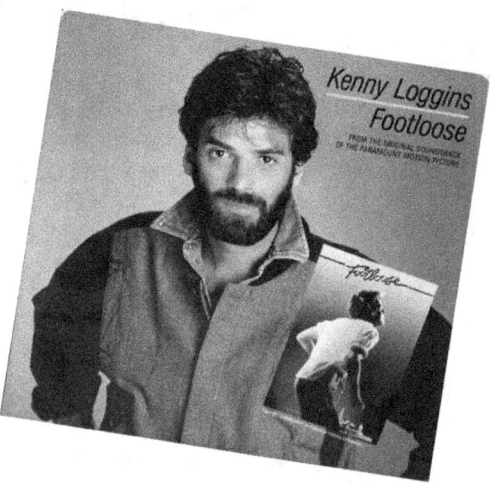

was working on with Ry Cooder called "In the Nick of Time." That song ended up in the movie *Brewster's Millions* and sung by Patti LaBelle. A more on-the-nose composition "Back in Time," was also written by Lewis and company for the film.

#4 – Footloose – Kenny Loggins (Footloose, 1984)

A hard-to-hate earworm of a song – try not to picture an ebullient Kevin Bacon in a tight tux, and when you fail, we challenge you to avoid smiling.

#3 – Danger Zone – Kenny Loggins (Top Gun, 1986)

How 80s can you get? How about lyrics inspired by the kind expensive Italian sports cars only a movie producer could afford? Lyricist Tom Whitlock was working at a friend's LA studio when composer Giorgio Moroder stomped down the hallway, complaining about his Ferrari's brakes. One trip to Pep Boys later, Whitlock had solved the problem and moved into Moroder's good graces, becoming his assistant. "If the Lamborghini broke down in Venice Beach, I would go sit there all night until the right kind of tow truck was available," Whitlock said. "If I needed to sleep on the floor to get up and let carpenters in at 5 a.m., I did that. If Brian De Palma wanted bagels, I got bagels. If Giorgio's mother wanted groceries from Gelson's, I went to Gelson's. It was a blast!" And in his

of the publishing in exchange for the title. Call's contributions – three words – netted him a great paycheck, even though he didn't write a note. "It's a lot like a song I would write," says Call. "Huey and I go back a ways together, and we used to room together... That song really could be one of my songs, which sounds crazy because they wrote it, and I think they're brilliant - Johnny Colla and Chris Hayes are the guys who really did that music. That modulation and all that kind of stuff, that's the same kind of stuff I do – going to the odd key for the bridge."

Released before the movie, the song entered the charts at #46 and quickly shot to the top (as Huey Lewis is quick to point out, about 9 to 12 weeks was considered a fast rise) in conjunction with the movie's arrival. It was the band's first number one hit, and was nominated for an Academy Award for Best Original Song (losing to Lionel Richie's "Say You Say Me"). At Zemeckis' request for an end credits song, Lewis first suggested a tune he down time, he was able to observe a daily songwriting masterclass. He'd be in the right place at the right time again, as all of Moroder's usual lyricists were unavailable when it came time to put words to this 80s movie classic.

#2 – Eye of the Tiger – Survivor (Rocky III, 1982)

Instantly recognizable, and capable of an instant 2× power boost upon consumption.

#1 – Don't You Forget About Me – Simple Minds (The Breakfast Club, 1984)

I'm going to go out on a limb and say that there are few movies, or songs, or movie songs, more unabashedly, unapologetically 1980s than this. Both indicative of the period and transcending it, inseparable from each other yet fully capable of standing on their own, the Hughes film and the Forsey-written track are a match made in heaven.

Even though they were having trouble cracking the American market, the band's inclination was to turn down the offer to perform the featured song for John Hughes' The Breakfast Club, since they didn't write it. Their manager convinced them to look at the movie, just so as to not appear rude. A screening of the film put the piece into context; the lyrics tied in neatly with Brian's (Anthony Michael Hall) sentiment about what will happen come Monday: "Will you recognize me? Call my name or walk on by?" In an interview with The Guardian, singer Jim Kerr recalls "we couldn't give a toss about teenage American schoolkids. But my wife at the time, Chrissie [Hynde], who was older and wiser, kept badgering me. "I like the song," she said. "What's the problem?" Finally, the song's writer, Keith Forsey, phoned me and rather cleverly said: "I'm a huge fan of the band. How about I just spend a couple of days with you? Maybe we'll do something in the future."

"At that stage, the song was just a demo on a battered cassette, with Keith singing over some keyboards. It didn't sound like something we would do, but in the bonding session with our new best mate we had a go. I added the big "la, la-la-la-la" ending because I didn't have any lyrics. I said I'd write some, but Keith said: "Over my dead body. We're keeping that." By the end, we were sneaking off to our rooms to listen to it." Guitarist Charlie Burchill says that his opening guitar salvo is an intentional caricature of American AOR powerchords.

The album version is a sonic improvement over the film version. Used twice in the film, the song loses some of its power, but it breaks down nicely into an instrumental reprise during the first five minutes of the opening which is reportedly writer Keith Forsey's demo version. If it holds up great as a song on its own, it should: it's a song that was equally at home on pop, rock, and alternative stations and benefited as much from radioplay as from the prominent placement in the successful film.

AMERICAN FILM INSTITUTES "100 YEARS, 100 SONGS"

In 2004, AFI compiled a list of songs from "American films [that] set a tone or mood, define character, advance plot and/or express the film's themes in a manner that elevates the moving image art form." Not surprisingly, only a few were from the decade discussed in this book. What, no "Rockula?" It all skews a little old fogey to me, and two of the songs are from the 60s anyway.

According to the accompanying literature, "these songs also capture the nation's heart and resonate across the century, enriching America's film heritage and captivating artists and audiences today." For a much lower-brow approach, the rest of this book should hold you over!

40 **Fight the Power** / Public Enemy / Do The Right Thing (1989)

44 **Wind Beneath My Wings** / Bette Midler / Beaches (1988)

51 **Fame** / Irene Cara / Fame (1980)

55 **Flashdance... What a Feeling** / Irene Cara / Flashdance (1983)

60 **It Had To Be You** / Frank Sinatra-Harry Connick Jr / When Harry Met Sally... (1989)

75 **Up Where We Belong** / Joe Cocker - Jennifer Warnes / An Officer and a Gentleman (1982)

78 **9 to 5** / Dolly Parton / Nine to Five (1980)

79 **Arthur's Theme (Best That You Can Do)** / Christopher Cross / Arthur (1981)

86 **I've Had the Time of My Life** / Bill Medley – Jennifer Warnes / Dirty Dancing (1987)

91 **Let the River Run** / Carly Simon / Working Girl (1988)

94 **Ain't Too Proud to Beg** / The Temptations / The Big Chill (1983)

96 **Footloose** / Kenny Loggins / Footloose (1984)

100 **Old Time Rock and Roll** / Bob Seger / Risky Business (1983)

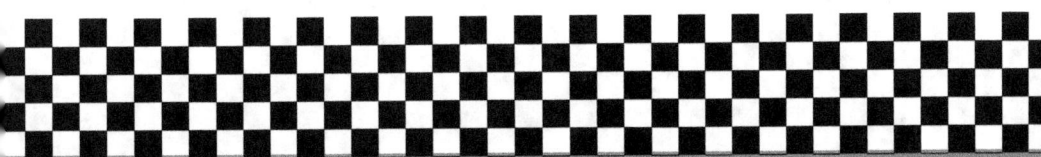

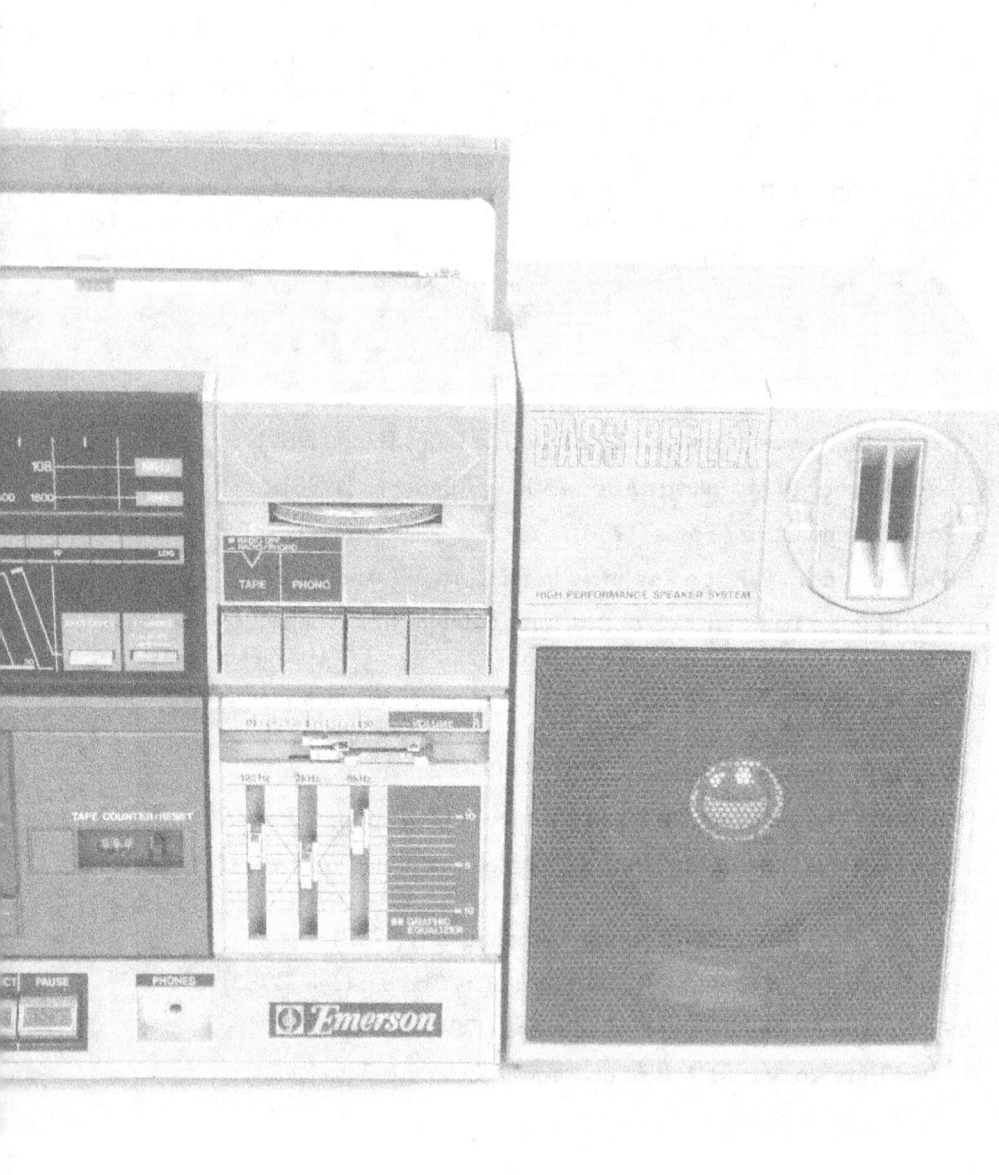

ABOUT THE AUTHOR

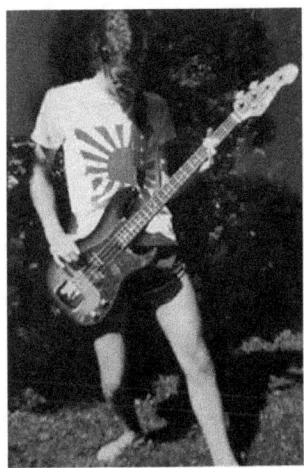

The Author at 15, with $79 bass guitar and no pants

Michael Heagle has been making movies since he was in the fifth grade, starting with Super8 he processed at K-Mart and projected on a bedsheet. He grew up in the small town of Mukwonago, Wisconsin; growing up in the 80s, Michael's creative endeavors circled around theater, role playing games, playing bass (Left, at age 15) and guitar, and making and consuming movies. He survived high school despite being a proud fan of Duran Duran.

While in college, he shot a film with his classmate Mark Borchardt (AMERICAN MOVIE) called TOGA PARTY MASSACRE. Upon graduating, Michael tried his hand at a number of self-funded, independent projects, in which he filled the roles of screenwriter, director, production designer, editor, and visual effects supervisor. Michael's film work includes writing and directing the 16mm cult-movie feature GO TO HELL (released by Troma in 2003), and the zero-budget sci fi western PLANETFALL. He is the co-creator of the puppet comedy series TRANSYLVANIA TELEVISION, writing, directing, and performing the character of Dwayne Frankenstein.

He holds a Masters Degree in Animation and Visual Effects from Academy of Art University in San Francisco and has taught in higher education since 2000. The first cassette he owned was Queen's soundtrack to Flash Gordon, he now proudly owns it in all formats including 8-Track.

FOLLOW MICHAEL AT:

michaelheagle.com   youtube.com/carschool   facebook.com/michael.heagle

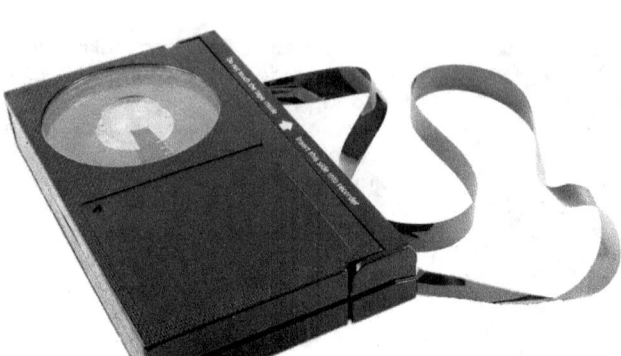

TAPE-ERA TRAVESTIES: COMING SOON

1988 FRIGHTTIME ANNUAL – 1988 was a banner year for the horror movie boom; this book brings all of those sequels (Phantasm 2, Nightmare on Elm Street 4, Hellbound: Hellraiser II) under one roof, together with remakes like The Blob and original visions like Night of the Demons and Pumpkinhead! With reviews, rankings, behind the scenes tidbits and more.

NINJAS & NUNCHUCKS – What Synthesizers & Saxophones was to musicals, Ninjas & Nunchucks does to select 80s martial arts trash movies! Ninja movies and Chuck Norris collide, with a special section on the best Hong Kong action from the period.

WARRIORS & WASTELANDS – No one had a better handle on the Road-Warrior-esque apocalyptic future than 1980s filmmakers, with Italian directors churning trashy Mad Max knock offs as fast as they could. This book reviews and ranks them, with more spiked leather and diesel fumes than you can handle!